Nietzsche On Instinct and Language

Nietzsche Today

De Gruyter

Nietzsche on Instinct and Language

Edited by
João Constâncio
and
Maria João Mayer Branco

De Gruyter

ISBN 978-3-11-048176-1
e-ISBN 978-3-11-024657-5
ISSN 2191-5741

Library of Congress Cataloging-in-Publication Data

International Conference "Nietzsche on Instinct and Language" (2009 : Universidade Nova de Lisboa)
    Nietzsche on instinct and language / edited by João Constâncio and Maria João Mayer Branco.
    p. cm. —(Nietzsche today, ISSN 2191-5741)
    Includes bibliographical references (p.   ) and indexes.
    ISBN 978-3-11-024656-8 (hardcover : alk. paper) 1. Nietzsche, Friedrich Wilhelm, 1844–1900—Congresses. 2. Language and languages—Philosophy—Congresses. 3. Instinct (Philosophy)—Congresses. I. Constâncio, João. II. Mayer Branco, Maria João. III. Title.
    B3318.L25I58 2009
    193—dc22
                                                                2011010093

Bibliographic information published by the Deutsche Nationalbibliothek

The Deutsche Nationalbibliothek lists this publication in the Deutsche Nationalbibliografie; detailed bibliographic data are available in the Internet at http://dnb.d-nb.de.

Typesetting: RefineCatch Ltd, Bungay, Suffolk
Printing: Hubert & Co. GmbH & Co. KG, Göttingen

♾ Printed on acid-free paper

Printed in Germany

www.degruyter.com

Contents

I. Nietzschean Beginnings and Developments

II. Dissolving an Opposition

III. Instinct, Language, and Philosophy

IV. The Critique of Morality and the Affirmation of Life

References, Citations and Abbreviations

All German quotations of Nietzsche's writings are from the following editions:

KSA   Nietzsche, Friedrich (1980), *Sämtliche Werke. Kritische Studienausgabe in 15 Bänden*, Giorgio Colli/Mazzino Montinari (eds.), München/Berlin (DTV/Walter de Gruyter).

KGW   Nietzsche, Friedrich (1967ff), *Werke. Kritische Gesamtausgabe*, established by Giorgio Colli und Mazzino Montinari, continued by Wolfgang Müller-Lauter und Karl Pestalozzi (eds.), Berlin/New York (Walter de Gruyter).

KSB   Nietzsche, Friedrich (1986), *Sämtliche Briefe. Kritische Studienausgabe in 8 Bänden*, Giorgio Colli/Mazzino Montinari (eds.), München/Berlin (DTV/Walter de Gruyter).

BAW   Nietzsche, Friedrich (1994), *Frühe Schriften. Schriften von 1854 bis 1869: 5 Bände*, Mette, Hans J. (ed.), München (DTV/C.H. Beck).

References to published or titled texts by Nietzsche follow the standard abbreviations, which are given below. The German abbreviations are used when a text is quoted in German; the English abbreviations, when a text is quoted in English translation.

Unless otherwise stated, the cited translations are the following:

Works By Nietzsche

Nietzsche, Friedrich (1966), *The Birth of Tragedy*, ed./transl. Kaufmann, W., New York (Random House).

Nietzsche, Friedrich (1967), *On the Genealogy of Morals*, ed./transl. Kaufmann, W., New York (Random House).

Nietzsche, Friedrich (1983), *Untimely Meditations*, transl. Hollingdale, R. J., Cambridge/London/New York/New Rochelle/Melbourne/Sydney (Cambridge University Press).

Nietzsche, Friedrich (1986), *Human, All Too Human*, ed. and tranls. Hollingdale, R. J., Cambridge (Cambridge University Press).

Nietzsche, Friedrich (1997), *Daybreak*, ed. Clark, M./Leiter, B., transl. Hollingdale, R. J., Cambridge (Cambridge University Press).
Nietzsche, Friedrich (1998), *Philosophy in the Tragic Age of the Greeks*, ed. and transl. Cowan, M., Washington (A Gateway Edition).
Nietzsche, Friedrich (1999), *On Truth and Lying in a Non-Moral Sense*, in: Nietzsche, F., *The Birth of Tragedy and Other Writings*, ed. Guess, R./ Speirs, R., transl. Speirs, R., Cambridge (Cambridge University Press).
Nietzsche, Friedrich (2001), *The Gay Science*, ed. Williams, B., transl. Nauckhoff, J., Cambridge (Cambridge University Press).
Nietzsche, Friedrich (2002), *Beyond Good and Evil*, ed. Horstmann, R-F./ Norman, J., transl. Norman, J., Cambridge (Cambridge University Press).
Nietzsche, Friedrich (2005), *The Anti-christ, Ecce Homo, Twilight of the Idols and Other Writings*, ed. Ridley, A./Norman, J., transl. Norman, J., Cambridge (Cambridge University Press).
Nietzsche, Friedrich (2005), *The Case of Wagner*, in Nietzsche, F., *The Anti-christ, Ecce Homo, Twilight of the Idols and Other Writings*, ed. Ridley, A./ Norman, J., transl. Norman, J., Cambridge (Cambridge University Press).
Nietzsche, Friedrich (2005), *Nietzsche contra Wagner*, in Nietzsche, F., *The Anti-christ, Ecce Homo, Twilight of the Idols and Other Writings*, ed. Ridley, A./Norman, J., transl. Norman, J., Cambridge (Cambridge University Press).
Nietzsche, Friedrich (2006), *Thus Spoke Zarathustra*, ed. Del Caro, A./ Pippin, R., transl. Del Caro, A., Cambridge (Cambridge University Press).

Occasionally, some of the authors have chosen to quote from the following translations:

Nietzsche, Friedrich (1966), *Beyond Good and Evil*, ed./transl. Kaufmann, W., New York (Random House).
Nietzsche, Friedrich (1984), *Human All Too Human*, transl. Faber, M./ Lehmann, S., Lincoln (University of Nebraska Press).
Nietzsche, Friedrich (1994), *On the Genealogy of Morality*, ed. Ansell-Pearson, K., transl. Diethe, C., Cambridge (Cambridge University Press).
Nietzsche, Friedrich, *The Birth of Tragedy and Other Writings*, ed. Guess, R./Speirs, R., transl. Speirs, R., Cambridge (Cambridge University Press).
Nietzsche, Friedrich (2005), *Thus Spoke Zarathustra*, transl. Parkes, G., Oxford (Oxford University Press).

Translations from the *Nachlass* follow the two most recent editions in English:

WEN Nietzsche, Friedrich (2009), *Writings from the Early Notebooks*, ed. Geuss, R./Nehamas, A., transl. Löb, L., Cambridge (Cambridge University Press).

WLN Nietzsche, Friedrich (2003), *Writings from the Late Note-books*, ed. Bittner, R., transl. Sturge, K., Cambridge (Cambridge University Press).

A few notes from the *Nachlass* not available in WEN or WLN have been quoted from:

WP Nietzsche, Friedrich (1967), *The Will to Power*, ed. Kaufmann, W., transl. Kaufmann, W./Hollingdale, R. J., New York (Random House).

Notes from the *Nachlass* not available in WEN, WLN, or WP have been translated by either the editors or the authors. Some of the authors have chosen not to have these notes translated.

As a rule, references to the *Nachlass* are given as follows: NL note KSA volume.page; e.g., NL 31[131] KSA 11.464. References to a translation are added after the references to the KSA, e.g. NL 31[131] KSA 11.464 = WLN 10; Some notes have been translated by either the editors or the authors, e.g. NL 11[164] KSA 9.505, my translation. Reference to the date of a note is added when deemed important by an author, e.g. NL 1881, 11[211] KSA 9.525. Sections or chapters that are not numbered but named in Nietzsche's text are given either in complete form (e.g. EH Why I am so Clever 9), or in the abbreviated form usually adopted in English or American books on Nietzsche (e.g. TI Errors 3). Some of the authors have added the KSA page references to the abbreviated references to English translations, e.g. KSA 5.60, BGE 43.

Abbreviations Of Nietzsche's Works In German:

AC	*Der Antichrist. Fluch auf das Christenthum*
EH	*Ecce Homo. Wie man wird, was man ist*
FW	*Die fröhliche Wissenschaft*
GD	*Götzen-Dämmerung oder Wie man mit dem Hammer philosophirt*
GM	*Zur Genealogie der Moral. Eine Streitschrift*
GT	*Die Geburt der Tragödie*
GT/VS	*Die Geburt der Tragödie, Versuch einer Selbstkritik*
JGB	*Jenseits von Gut und Böse. Vorspiel einer Philosophie der Zukunft*

M	*Morgenröthe. Gedanken über die moralischen Vorurtheile*
MA	*Menschliches, Allzumenschliches. Ein Buch für freie Geister*
NW	*Nietzsche contra Wagner. Aktenstücke eines Psychologen*
UB	*Unzeitgemässe Betrachtungen*
VM	(MA II) *Vermischte Meinungen und Sprüche*
WA	*Der Fall Wagner. Ein Musikanten-Problem*
WL	*Wahrheit und Lüge im aussermoralischen Sinne*
WS	*Der Wanderer und sein Schatten*
Z	*Also Sprach Zarathustra.* *Ein Buch für Alle und Keinen*

Abbreviations Of Nietzsche's Works In English

A	*The Antichrist*
AOM	(HH II) *Assorted Opinions and Maxims*
BGE	*Beyond Good and Evil. Prelude to a Philosophy of the Future*
BT	*The Birth of Tragedy*
BT/AS	*The Birth of Tragedy, Attempt At a Self-Criticism.*
CW	*The Case of Wagner*
D	*Daybreak*
DD	*Dithyrambs of Dionysus*
EH	*Ecce Homo. How One Becomes What One Is*
GM	*On the Genealogy of Morals. A Polemic*
GS	*The Gay Science*
HH	*Human, All Too Human*
NW	*Nietzsche contra Wagner. Out of the Files of a Psychologist*
PTAG	*Philosophy in the Tragic Age of the Greeks*
TI	*Twilight of the Idols. How To Philosophize with a Hammer*
TL	*On Truth and Lying in a Non-Moral Sense*
UM	*Untimely Meditations*
WS	(HH II) *The Wanderer and His Shadow*
ZA	*Thus Spoke Zarathustra*

Abbreviations Of Works By Other Authors

DA   Stendhal (1956), *De l'amour*, Paris (Garnier-Flammarion).

Ideen   Herder, J.G., *Ideen zur Philosophie der Geschichte der Menschheit*, in: Arnold, G. (ed.) (1985–2000), *Johann Gottfried Herder. Werke 10 in 11 Bänden*, vol. 6 Frankfurt am Main (Deutscher Klassiker Verlag).

KpV   Kant, I., *Kritik der praktischen Vernunft*, in: Kant, I. (1955–1966), *Gesammelte Schriften, ed. Königliche Preussische Akademie der Wissenschaften/Deutsche Akademie der Wissenschaften*, vol. V, Berlin (Walter De Gruyter).

KrV   Kant, I., *Kritik der reinen Vernunft*, in: Kant, I. (1955–1966), *Gesammelte Schriften, ed. Königliche Preussische Akademie der Wissenschaften/Deutsche Akademie der Wissenschaften*, vol. 3/4, Berlin (Walter De Gruyter). translations quoted from: Kant, I. (1998), *Critique of Pure Reason*, ed./transl. Guyer, P./Wood, A.W., Cambridge (Cambridge University Press).

FRGL   Herder, J.G., *Fragments on Recent German Literature*, in Herder (2002), *Philosophical Writings*, ed./transl. Forster, M.N., (Cambridge: Cambridge University Press).

TOL   Herder, J.G., *Abhandlung über den Ursprung der Sprache*, translation quoted from: Herder, *Treatise on the Origin of Language*, in Herder (2002), *Philosophical Writings*, ed./ transl. Forster, M.N., Cambridge (Cambridge University Press).

WWV I   Schopenhauer, A. (1949), *Die Welt als Wille und Vorstellung. Erster Band*, in Schopenhauer, A. (1946–1950), *Sämtliche Werke, Zweiter Band*, ed. Hübscher, A., 7 vols., Wiesbaden (Brockhaus).

WWV II Schopenhauer, A. (1949), *Die Welt als Wille und Vorstellung. Zweiter Band*, in Schopenhauer, A. (1946–1950), *Sämtliche Werke, Dritter Band*, ed. Hübscher, A., 7 vols., Wiesbaden (Brockhaus).

Acknowledgements

This volume consists of the revised and expanded versions of the papers presented at the International Conference "Nietzsche On Instinct and Language", held at the Nietzsche International Lab/ Faculdade de Ciências Sociais e Humanas/ Universidade Nova de Lisboa (Portugal), in December 2009. The editors wish to express their gratitude to the following institutions that made the Conference possible: Instituto de Filosofia da Linguagem (IFL), especially its Director, Prof. António Marques; Fundação para a Ciência e Tecnologia (FCT); Faculdade de Ciências Sociais e Humanas (FCSH), especially its Director, Prof. João Sáàgua; Philosophy Department of FCSH.

The editors also wish to express their gratitude to the following persons that worked at translating and proof-reading the papers: Richard Bates, Sara Eckerson, Marta Faustino, Katia Hay, Margarida Martins, Pedro Moura, Bartholomew Ryan, Luís Sousa. A special thank you to Marta Faustino for her work at organizing the Conference with the editors.

Editors' Introduction

All of the papers included in this volume either presuppose or explicitly emphasize the fact that Nietzsche tried to dissolve the traditional opposition between instinct and language, as well as between instinct and consciousness and instinct and reason. Given that Nietzsche interprets the instincts as affective dispositions, this also means that he tried to dissolve the traditional oppositions between affectivity and language, affectivity and consciousness, affectivity and reason. According to him, what almost all previous philosophers conceived as opposed is in fact fundamentally connected. Thus one may say that this volume as a whole aims at being a fresh look at Nietzsche's attempt to connect language to the instinctive and affective activity of the human body. The different papers consider such Nietzschean themes as morality, value, the concept of philosophy, dogmatism, naturalization, metaphor, health, sickness, tragedy, and laughter – but always from the viewpoint of Nietzsche's dissolution of those oppositions, especially of the one between instinct and language.

Perhaps the simplest way to start understanding the meaning of this dissolution is to see it as a part of a larger task Nietzsche set to himself, namely the task of dissolving all oppositions and opposite valuations created by metaphysics (or "dogmatic philosophy"), as indicated in BGE 2. According to Nietzsche, these oppositions have made us believe in the substantiality and separate existence of the terms opposed (e.g. on the supra-sensible existence of the soul as opposed to the sensible existence of the body), thereby allowing for a negative valuing of the very presuppositions of life – i.e., precisely of such presuppositions as instinct and affectivity. Accordingly, his project of "revaluing all values" and "affirming life" depends, in part, on his showing that language, consciousness, and reason do not belong to a substantially different realm from that of the instincts. Instead, Nietzsche believes, the former can and should be described as natural phenomena that develop or evolve from the instincts, so that there is no ontological ground for us to value them above the instincts.

In fact, language, consciousness, and reason can never become really detached from, even less opposed to the instincts, no matter how far they develop. In countless passages, Nietzsche expresses this idea by speaking of "drives and affects" and describing the human organism as constructed out of a multiplicity of "drives and affects". Thus, in *The Gay Science*, he declares that every conscious mental state is "*only a certain behavior of the drives towards one another*" (GS 333), and in *Beyond Good and Evil*, that "thinking is only a relation between these drives" (BGE 36). In the *Nachlass*, he adds, for example, that "behind consciousness work the drives" (NL 39[6] KSA 11.621), or "below every thought lies an affect" (NL 1[61] KSA 12.26 = WLN 60). By "drives" Nietzsche means the "forces", "under-wills", or "wills to power" that direct our behavior towards the satisfaction of organic needs. An "affect" is simply what it feels like to be driven by a drive. Another way to put this is to say that drives are valuations. In directing our behavior towards the satisfaction of a need, the drive makes us value the satisfaction of this need not only when it occurs, but also *before* it occurs, i.e. as an aim. A drive, as it were, posits an aim as valuable (or as a "value"), thereby making us *will* such a aim and *feel for* it[1]. If the drive remains unconscious, so does the affect that accompanies it. This is what leads not only to the idea that our conscious desires, inclinations, and feelings evolve from drives and affects, but also that those conscious states, once developed, are no more than "surfaces" of relations among unconscious drives and affects.

Nietzsche's use of the word "instinct" (*Instinkt*), as well as "instinctive" etc., seems often interchangeable with his use of the expression "drives and affects" (e.g. in Part 1 of BGE). But the word "instinct" has different connotations than the word "drive" (*Trieb*). Like the drives, instincts have goals that are not set by conscious mental states,

---

1   Cf., for example, HH I 32, translation modified: "A drive to something or away of something divorced from a feeling one is desiring the beneficial or avoiding the harmful, a drive without some kind of knowing evaluation of the worth of its aim (*Ziel*), does not exist in man". Note that this kind of description of the drives in terms of "aims", "goals", "ends", etc. is, for Nietzsche, wholly unteleological: such "aims" are not set by conscious mental states (they are unintentional), and thus they do not function as "final causes" (i.e. their activity creates their goal and it is not their goal that "causes" their activity).

but, unlike the drives, they seem to be akin to learned behavior, or to skills. Nietzsche sometimes calls them "automatisms" (organic habits, so to speak). However, he often designates the sum total of processes that constitute the human organism either as an alliance of instincts or as a multiplicity of drives and affects.

In any case, the essential point is that Nietzsche certainly thinks of the relation between instinct and language, as well as between instinct and consciousness and instinct and reason, in terms of continuity. Conscious thoughts have the nature of drives and affects, for they *are* drives and affects that have become partially, i.e. superficially, conscious. This is an idea that Nietzsche tries to make plausible by describing the drives and affects as perceptual, perspectival, interpretative processes, and thus by describing instinct as "the most intelligent type of intelligence discovered so far" (BGE 218). The rationality of our conscious mental life is only derivative of the unconscious rationality of the body as a whole – a continuation and always still a part of the instinctive life of the drives (*Triebleben*, BGE 36). In other words, drives and instincts are processes of unconscious "thinking, feeling, willing", and conscious mental states are only certain developments of these same processes.

As developments and "surfaces" continuous with the drives, affects and instincts, our conscious thoughts are in fact *signs* of unconscious processes. As Nietzsche writes in the *Nachlass*: "A thought, no less than a word, is only a sign: one cannot speak of a congruity between the thought and the real. The real is some sort of movement of the drives (*Trieb-bewegung*)" (NL 6[253] KSA 9.263, our translation). Given the traditional meaning of "sign" (e.g. in Leibniz, Kant, or Schopenhauer), this means that conscious thoughts are abbreviations that give expression to unconscious processes.

This is a key point for understanding Nietzsche's views on language and the relation between instinct and language. Consciousness depends on the formation of concepts, and concepts are "more or less determinate pictorial signs for sensations that occur together and recur frequently, for groups of sensations" (BGE 268). Words, in turn, are "acoustic signs for concepts" (BGE 268). Words are signs of concepts, and concepts are signs of sensations. However, these sensations and their inner experiences (*Erlebnisse*) are always already the result of the unconscious, and yet perceptive and intelligent, activity of the drives and affects. Consequently, conscious thoughts are signs that express this activity of the drives and affects, and words are signs that express part of our conscious thoughts. Put differently, language in the ordinary sense of the term is only part of the "sign language" of the instincts – it presupposes other signs (sc. conscious thoughts) and, above all, it presupposes the unconscious "language" of the instincts.

This "language" consists of power relations among the drives and affects. It enables the issuing and receiving of orders, i.e. the very struggle among drives from which those relations of command and obedience arise that make the functioning of the organism possible. Thus the idea that conscious thoughts express relations of drives and affects in abbreviated, conceptual form means that they express the power relations that occur among "a multiplicity of wills to power" (NL 1[58] KSA 12.25 = WLN 59–60). Conscious thoughts "are *signs* of a play and struggle of the affects" (NL 1[75] KSA 12.29 = WLN 60), and words are signs of these signs. No matter how neutral and descriptive a particular use of language may seem, it is always an expression of power relations and (ultimately unconscious) power strategies.

This way of describing the drives, the affects, the instincts, consciousness, reason, and language is wholly naturalistic, and it is an important part of Nietzsche's critique of metaphysics. But its status is not unproblematic. If all conscious thoughts and words are signs that express relations among the drives and affects, Nietzsche's naturalistic descriptions are no exception to this. They, too, are only a "sign language" of *his* instincts, they, too, express unconscious strivings for power or growth, and their key words – "drive", "affect", "instinct", "power", "sign", etc. – are no more than signs of the real, all too real life of the drives. And "real" is, of course, only one more sign.

Nietzsche is well aware of this, and this is one of the main reasons why he does not present his philosophy as a pure, disinterested description of reality, but rather as the result of a particular *stance* – a critical and evaluative, as well as creative, stance. Given that all descriptions express relations of drives and affects, all descriptions express instinctive evaluations. Thus, every philosophy is either naive, i.e. blind to its instinctive evaluations, or critical, i.e. purposefully evaluative. Nietzsche's *genealogy* is obviously of the latter type. His aim of "creating new values" cannot be separated from his critical task of "revaluing all values".

It is his genealogical approach that leads him to ask *why*, i.e. in response to what needs, humanity has interpreted everything sensitive, temporal or historical, and particularly the instincts, drives and affects, as something that should be fundamentally opposed to a more valuable and supra-sensible realm of intelligibility and rationality. In other words, Nietzsche's conception of philosophy makes the question about the relation between instinct and language inseparable from the question on why some valuations of instinct and language emerge rather than others.

But although this genealogical approach is part of a purposeful, conscious effort to revaluate all values and create new values, it is very far from being a product of conscious thoughts separated from the instinctive activity of the body. Nietzsche himself is not an exception to the fact that "most of a philosopher's conscious thought is secretly directed and forced into determinate channels by the instincts" (BGE 3). Put differently, no matter how critical and purposefully evaluative a particular philosophy may be, it always emerges from the instincts and is determined by the life of the drives and affects: "When we criticize, we are not doing something arbitrary and impersonal; it is, at least very often, proof that there are living, active forces within us shedding skin. We negate and have to negate because something in us *wants* to live and affirm itself, something we might not yet know or see! – This in favour of criticism" (GS 307). It is, therefore, not surprising that in *Ecce Homo* Nietzsche explicitly presents his task of revaluing all values as having emerged from "the lengthy, secret work and artistry of my instinct" (EH Why I Am So Clever 9).

This not only raises the question on the relation between conscious-ness and instinct, but also on the relation between the *language* of philosophy and the instinctual processes that lead to a philosopher's thoughts and written words. As signs of instinctual processes, philo-sophical texts are always a struggle with the limits of language, and perhaps their limitedness and inadequacy is even greater when a phi-losopher's instincts strive to a radically new affirmation of life.

Thus we see also that the question about instinct and language leads very naturally to a discussion about the concept of philosophy and philosophical language, and in fact, almost all of the papers in the volume deal with this issue at more or less length.

In the first chapter of the volume – I. Nietzschean Beginnings and Developments — we have assembled the two papers that focus the most on Nietzsche's early writings and trace his mature views on instinct and language back to his early views. **Andrea Christian Bertino** analyzes the roots of Nietzsche's project of dehumanizing nature and naturalizing man by comparing it to Johann Gottfried Herder's similar intentions in his philosophy of language and philosophical anthropology. Both Nietzsche and Herder present language as originating in natural drives or instincts and strive to overcome the metaphysical separation between nature and culture. Most importantly, according to Bertino, they both understand all human discourse about nature and culture as metaphorical and anthropomorphic. This implies that Nietzsche's naturalism does not purport to be an adequate description of the real, but only another anthropomorphic metaphor.

Maria João Mayer Branco starts by showing how Nietzsche's early views on music, metaphor, conceptualization and communication imply an intrinsic connection between language and the body, i.e. language and the affects, the drives, and the instincts. Those views are never truly abandoned, only transformed and developed in Nietzsche's mature writings. The crucial notions of "will to power" and "perspectivism" imply precisely the kind of intrinsic connection between instinct and language that Nietzsche had already adumbrated in those early writings. This becomes particularly clear when one considers his mature views on style, especially on the style of philosophical writing.

The second chapter – II. Dissolving an Opposition – assembles the three papers most concerned with the idea that in dissolving the opposition between instinct and language Nietzsche rethinks this relation in terms of continuity. **Patrick Wotling**'s paper aims at describing the radical change that Nietzsche imposes on the traditional approach to language. It shows that ordinary, conscious language is to be understood as deriving from a more fundamental form of communication, namely from the particular type of logic that rules over relations of drives. There is an originary, infra-conscious "language of the drives". The drives' ability to perceive and interpret their power relative to each other, i.e. their ability to assess relations of supremacy, and thus to struggle with each other, is the form of communication that makes their hierarchy – their relations of command and obedience – possible. Ordinary language is never neutral because it emerges from these relations and always remains dependent upon them.

João Constâncio's paper is an overview of Nietzsche's dissolution of the opposition between instinct and language in *Beyond Good* *and Evil*. First, the paper focuses on the critique of language, and particularly of grammar, implied in Nietzsche's critique of the subject, and it shows how this critique of language leads to the concept of instinct. The crucial point here is that, according to Nietzsche, the grammatical functions of our language and our conscious thought emerge from reason – but from reason as an "instinctive reason". This is one of the bases for Nietzsche's hypothesis that the relations between instinct, reason, consciousness, and language are relations of continuity. The second half of the paper deals with the consequences of this hypothesis to the problem of identity. By redefining our identity in terms of affects, drives and instincts, and particularly by looking at the philosophers' use of language as dependent upon the subterranean paths of their instinctual life, Nietzsche is able to highlight the complex and contradictory nature of human subjectivity – which is perhaps the ultimate implication of his critique of the (atomic) subject, and a crucial aspect of his new conception of philosophy.

Chiara Piazzesi's paper proposes a discussion of aphorism 14 of *The Gay Science*, generally quite neglected by the commentators. This aphorism aims at dissolving a linguistic unity ("love") by showing how its linguistic uses conceal instincts, drives, needs, power struggles and power strategies that influence the acts of nomination as well as the processes of their articulation and affirmation. The paper begins by analyzing the text of the aphorism and discussing how, according to Nietzsche, everything we call "love" is intrinsically entangled with what we call *Habsucht* ("greed"); it then focuses on the influence of Stendhal's *De l'Amour* over Nietzsche's understanding of love, and it ends by revealing the genealogical and critical purpose which inspires and informs Nietzsche's discussion of the use of the word "love" and of the corresponding moral evaluations.

The third chapter – III. Instinct, Language, and Philosophy – consists of two papers that also analyze the complex meaning of Nietzsche's dissolution of the opposition between instinct and language, but so that their main focus is ultimately on the consequences of this idea to Nietzsche's concept of philosophy. **Scarlett Marton** considers the dissolution of the opposition between instinct and language from the viewpoint of Nietzsche's critique of "dogmatic philosophy" in *Beyond Good and Evil*, especially in the Preface and in the last aphorism of this book (BGE 296). In this last aphorism, Nietzsche casts suspicion over the written form of his philosophy. Written language tends to transform living, temporary experimentations in univocal, monolithic, inflexible truths – in dogmatic doctrines. In calling attention to this tendency Nietzsche underscores the thoroughly experimental, non-dogmatic status of his philosophy, as well as its intrinsic integration in an instinctive form of life.

Werner Stegmaier's paper shows how Nietzsche intertwines instinct and language in Book V of *The Gay Science*. This intertwinement entails that they have reciprocal effects on each other. Language, consciousness, and reason depend on the instincts, but the instincts are not something "simply *given*". As Stegmaier writes, "they involuntarily conduct behavior and manifest themselves as natural because they gradually become obvious through routine or prolonged discipline or even through rational insight". Consequently, Nietzsche's philosophical experimentation, as well as its communication to his readers, may be seen as meant to enable "fearless findings" that unsettle the instincts. Through this unsettling of the instincts, new needs and thus new, subtler, perhaps healthier instincts, as well as better leeways of reciprocal understanding (e.g. between Nietzsche and his readers), become possible.

The fourth and last chapter – IV. The Critique of Morality and the Affirmation of Life – assembles the four papers that are not so much concerned with the meanders of Nietzsche's dissolution of the opposition between instinct and language as with its consequences for his critique of morality and the affirmation of life.

Marta Faustino's paper, like Marton's and Stegmaier's, deals with Nietzsche's new conception of philosophy, but it does not focus at all on how Nietzsche tries to dissolve the opposition between instinct and language. Instead, it aims at showing that *only if this dissolution is assumed* will it make sense to redefine the goals of philosophy in terms of the promotion of health rather than in terms of (absolute) truth. Her main focus is on Nietzsche's concept of "great health" (GS 382) and its connection to the claim that all philosophers so far have been "sick" due to "a misunderstanding of the body" (GS Preface 2). In accordance to these key ideas, Nietzsche's "philosophers of the future" will have to be "physicians of culture" rather than mere theoreticians. Their critique of dominant morality shall have to be capable of actually changing a culture, as well as the moral character and virtues of men (i.e. their instincts), and so the "great health" will be not only their aim, but also a *pre-condition* of their very existence as philosophers capable of achieving their task.

André Muniz Garcia begins by focusing on how, according to Nietzsche's *Beyond Good and Evil*, the language used by philosophers, and especially the grammar of this language, involuntarily expresses their instincts and promotes a particular type of life. Garcia's main concern, however, is with Nietzsche's critique of morality. According to Nietzsche, philosophers create philosophical propositions because they are compelled by their instincts to overcome certain needs, and thus philosophical propositions are always inseparable from a particular morality that a philosopher's instincts strive to make believable in order to overcome those needs. As Nietzsche writes in BGE 6: "to explain how the strangest metaphysical claims of a philosopher really come about, it is always good (and wise) to begin by asking: what morality is it (is *he* —) getting at?" Garcia's paper aims at analyzing how Nietzsche develops this idea in BGE 186 and BGE 187.

Katia Hay argues that Nietzsche's analysis of tragedy, both in *The Birth of Tragedy* and in his mature works, cannot be understood as pessimistic because it emerges from a Dionysian experience of the comic. Although her main focus is on the "Attempt at a Self-criticism" (1886), and particularly on its reference to Zarathustra's laughter, her paper aims at showing how since *The Birth of Tragedy* Nietzsche's thought on tragedy and comedy is inseparable from his concern with the possibility of an instinctive affirmation of life.

The volume closes with **Maria Filomena Molder**'s meditation on Nietzsche's "Attempt At a Self-Criticism". She presents this important text as evidence of Nietzsche's concern with the limits of language. The fact that in writing *The Birth of Tragedy* the young Nietzsche had to "stammer in a strange tongue" (BT/AS 3) was not exclusively due to his youth and his enthusiasm with Schopenhauer, Kant, and Wagner. One can never express the Dionysian intoxication of the instincts without having to "stammer in a strange tongue" – or, in other words, the Dionysian affirmation of life as a result of an experience of the tragic can never be adequately expressed within the limits of language. Thus the "tremendous hope" that speaks from out of Nietzsche's *Birth of Tragedy* depends on much more than simply words and consciousness: "tragedy, the highest art of saying yes to life, will be reborn when humanity has moved beyond consciousness of the harshest though most necessary wars without suffering from it…" (EH Why I Write Such Good Books BT 4).

The Editors,
João Constâncio,
Maria João Mayer Branco

I. Nietzschean Beginnings and Developments

"As with Bees"? Notes on Instinct and Language in Nietzsche and Herder

Andrea Christian Bertino

> *Thus the only option that remains is to consider language as a production of instinct, as with bees and anthills, etc.*
> (Nietzsche, KGW II/2.188)

> *The essential feature of our life is never enjoyment but always progression, and we have never been human beings until we – have lived our lives to the end. By contrast, the bee was already a bee when it built its first cell*
> (Herder, TOL, 131)

1. Origin of Language and Origin of Man

Any discourse regarding the origin of language is relevant not only to philosophy of language, but also to philosophical anthropology, for when one determines the nature and origin of language one is also determining the nature and origin of man as the ζῷον λόγον ἔχον. If the discourse about the origin posits a process, then man will necessarily be conceived as the outcome of a process of becoming. If human language is portrayed as the development from a natural, animal language, then the *differentia specifica* of man in relation to animals must be interpreted as something that has become and not as something timelessly given. Thus, the question regarding the relation between instinct and language constitutes an essential part of the classical problem of the origin of language: whether or not instincts are involved in the development of language in human beings is hence crucial for their self-assessment as rational beings. If the instincts play a strong role, the image of an entirely autonomous, self-determining subject will shake, for reason and reflection are commonly presumed to be possible only through language.

Although Nietzsche's critique of language is a central aspect of his critique of metaphysics, it seems, nevertheless, that he has worked only marginally on the problem of the origin of language. The only text in which he deals directly with the classical debate about the origin of language – namely the first chapter of his notes for a cycle of lectures on Latin grammar (*Vom Ursprung der Sprache*, KGW II/2.185–188, Winter Semester 1869/ 70) – is not very original. However, Nietzsche questions some well-known views, and favours the hypothesis of an instinctual origin of language:

> Therefore, the only option that remains is to consider language as a product of instinct, as with bees and anthills, etc. However, instinct is *not* conscious deliberation, nor mere consequence of the bodily organization, nor the result of a mechanism that lies in the brain, nor the effect of a mechanism that comes to the spirit from the outside and is foreign to its essence, but rather the most distinctive accomplishment that springs from an individual's or a group's character (KGW II/2.188)[2].

After concisely rejecting Maupertuis', Plato's, Rousseau's, De Bosset's and Monboddo's theories on the origin of language, Nietzsche refutes, on the basis of a teleological conception of instinct, Johann Gottfried Herder's position as presented in the *Treatise On the Origin of Language*:

> In Germany, the Academy of Berlin placed – a hundred years ago – a prize question 'regarding the origin of language'[3]. In 1770, Herder's work received the distinction. He states that language is inborn in man: 'Therefore, the genesis of language is *as much an inner imperative* as is the impulse of the embryo to be born at the moment when it reaches its maturity'[4]. However, he shares with his

---

2 KGW II/2.188: "Es bleibt also nur übrig, die Sprache als Erzeugniß des Instinktes zu betrachten, wie bei den Bienen - den Ameisenhaufen usw. Instinkt ist aber nicht bewußte Überlegung, nicht bloße Folge der körperlichen Organisation, nicht Resultat eines Mechanismus, der in das Gehirn gelegt ist, Nicht Wirkung eines dem Geiste von außen kommenden, seinem Wesen fremden Mechanismus, sondern eigenste Leistung des Individuums oder eine Masse, dem Charakter entspringend". [*Editors' translation*].
3 Neis (2003) gives a detailed reconstruction of the intellectual and institutional context of the prize question. About Herder's prize-essay cf. Ch. IV 550–604.
4 *Editors' note:* TOL, 129.

predecessors the view that language internalizes itself out of spoken sounds. Interjection [is] the mother of language: whereas it is rather its negation.

The correct insight has become current only since Kant, who in the *Critique of Judgement* accepted the teleology of nature as a matter of fact, but on the other hand stressed the marvellous antinomy that something can be purposive and yet without consciousness. This [is] the essence of instinct (KGW II/2.188)[5].

Nietzsche does not attack Herder in the context of a philosophical investigation. One cannot expect an earnest problematization of this subject in an introduction lecture to Latin grammar. Later, however, by the time Nietzsche deals with the problem of language in a deeper and more critical manner, he clearly moves closer to Herder. Between 1872 and 1873, his conception of language develops under the influence of Gustav Gerber, who, in turn, was strongly influenced by Herder[6]. Thus, as Ernst Behler has argued, while in *The Birth of Tragedy* Nietzsche still sees language in the light of a metaphysical, absolute theory of representation, in *On Truth and Lying in a*

---

5   KGW II/2.188: "In Deutschland hatte die Berliner Akademie – vor hundert Jahren – eine Preisfrage „über den Ursprung der Sprache" gestellt. 1770 erhielt Herders Schrift den Vorzug. Der Mensch sei zur Sprache geboren. 'So ist die Genesis der Sprache ein so inneres Drängniss, wie der Drang des Embryos zur Geburt beim Moment seiner Reife'. Aber mit seinen Vorgängern theilt er die Anschauung, wie die Sprache aus sich äussernden Lauten sich verinnerlicht. Die Interjektion die Mutter der Sprache: während sie doch eigentlich die Negation ist. Die richtige Erkenntniß ist erst seit Kant geläufig, der in der Kritik der Urtheilskraft die Teleologie in der Natur zugleich als etwas Thatsächliches erkannte, andrerseits die wunderbare Antinomie hervorhob, dass etwas zweckmassig sei ohne ein Bewusstsein. Dies das Wesen des Instinktes". [*Editors' translation*].

6   According to Gustav Gerber it is only with Humboldt that one can escape an inconsequent conception of the emergence of language, that is, a conception that already presupposes human consciousness (Gerber 1871, vol. 1, 119). In this connection, Herder's Prize-essay is, for him, especially important. He takes up Herder's description of man as sensorium commune, as well as his semiotics of the *differentiae* or marks (*Merkmale*) on which human reflection or awareness (*Besinnung*) depends (cf. Gerber 1871, Vol. 1, 164). He argues that it is necessary to undertake an empirical critique of language, which should replace the critique of reason, by quoting Herder (cf. Gerber 1871, Vol. 1, 245): "A people have no idea for which they do not have a word" (Ideen, 6.347). Gerber also shares with Herder the concept of a natural reason that is tied to the surrounding world. Thus, Gerber may have conveyed some of Herder's important ideas to Nietzsche. [*Gerber's and Herder's quotations translated by the editors.*]

Non-Moral Sense he clearly moves towards an anthromorphic, non-representative conception of language, which is not based in the idea of "reality" as reference[7]. He consciously abandons Schopenhauer's metaphysical image of language[8], and thus his distance to Herder diminishes, for an unconditional theory of representation is also foreign to Herder's philosophy of language. Both Herder and Nietzsche want to show that language is not absolute and, thus, that it is representative. Language, according to Herder, is invented along with the first "characteristic mark (*Merkmal*) of taking-awareness (*Besinnung*)", i.e. with the first "word of the soul" (TOL, 88). For him, reason and language are inseparable; Herder realized that "the simplest judgement of human awareness is [not] possible without a characteristic mark (*Merkmal*)" (TOL, 91). Our reason cannot express "things",

---

7   Cf. Behler (1994). According to Behler there is no break between Nietzsche's first and second theoretical positions on language, as Philippe Lacoue-Labarthe still thought (1979, 31–74), but a gradual development. Behler documents this with numerous notes from Nietzsche's *Nachlass*, especially with one "about the relationship between language and music" (NL 12[1] KSA 7.360–369 = WEN 83–91). For the significance of this note to this topic, see also Hödl (1997, 31–35). Hödl reconstructs the different stages of the note NL 2[10] KSA 7.42f and of the lectures "Das Griechieche Musikdrama" and "Die dionysische Weltanschauung". Behler (1996, 68) divides Nietzsche's early theory of language further in four moments: "Die erste Phase besteht in den *Vorlesungen über lateinische Grammatik* aus dem WS 1869/79; die zweite in der Schrift Die *Geburt der Tragödie aus dem Geist der Musik* von 1872; die dritte in den *Vorlesungen über Rhetorik* aus dem WS 1872/1873; und die vierte schließlich in der Schrift *Über Wahrheit und Lüge im außermoralischen Sinne* von 1873". In view of Nietzsche's aesthetization of science, Aldo Venturelli (2003) states that there is a continuity between the *Birth of Tragedy* and *On Truth and Lying*. According to him, the latter is the most coherent presentation of the aesthetical character of every form of knowledge and at the same time the perfect attempt to carry out the transformation of science into art – an attempt which is conveyed by the image of Socrates practising music (Venturelli 2003, 63 ff). At the same time, Venturelli remarks that in the unpublished text art does not express itself "im Rahmen einer der rationalen Wahrnehmung entzogenen reinen Sprache des Instinkts und des Unbewussten" Venturelli (2003, 65). Paul de Man (1987, 124 ff) had already identified remains of a logo-centred tradition in BT, which Nietzsche here starts to deconstruct.

8   This is indicative of the enigmatic, special place of TL in Nietzsche's intellectual development. In the Preface to volume II of HH, Nietzsche remarks that he once wrote an essay, "On Truth and Lying in a Non-Moral Sense", he "refrained from publishing", at a time when he "already 'believed in nothing any more', as the people puts it, not even in Schopenhauer" (HH II Preface 1).

only "marks of things", – as Herder will later write in his *Ideas for the Philosophy of History of Humanity* (Ideen, 6.349, editors' translation). For Herder, human reason develops along with language, i.e. by the use of acoustic signs as marks of sensations. And this relation between marks and sensations is not arbitrary. The laws of sensibility, the structure of the senses, determine the coupling of signs and representations. The further articulation of language then presupposes human freedom, which, however, cannot be understood as a complete negation of natural drives but only as their weakening. The concepts by means of which we form the representation of the world are, according to Herder, the result of abstractions developed over time from images linked with affects; therefore, they are not essentially related to the objects they refer to. The fact that we use determinate sounds as words and make concepts out of these words is also for Nietzsche the result of a process, as is shown by the famous text *On Truth and Lying in a Non-Moral Sense* – heavily influenced by Gustav Gerber[9].

To put it briefly: Herder and Nietzsche reflect on the interweavement of language, anthropology and history. They both proceed in a similar way: from the problem of language in their earlier works – Herder's *Treatise on the Origin of Language* (1770, published 1772), on the one hand, and Nietzsche's *On Truth and Lying in a Non-Moral Sense* (1873) on the other) – towards a reflection on history; Herder writes *This Too a Philosophy of History for the Formation of Humanity* (1774) and Nietzsche, his *Second Untimely Meditation On the Uses and Disadvantages of History for* (1874). Later, though, the philosophy of history remains, for Herder, at the centre, as is shown by the *Ideas for the Philosophy of History of Humanity* (1774–1791), which, as Rudolph Haym has argued, is perhaps his most important work[10]. Nietzsche, on the other hand, makes his early critique of language and his insistence on a critical use of historical knowledge fertile for a genealogical questioning of morality, religion, philosophy, and the myths of Modernity. This questioning determines his work

---

9 TL has been strongly researched in recent times. Regarding the state of the art, cf. among others Hödl (1997 and 2003), Josef Simon (1999), Emden (2005), Reuter (2009), Andresen (2010).

10 Cf. Haym (1954 [1880], 221).

from the late seventies onwards. At the beginning, however, they both reflect on man's ability to verbalize the world.

Nietzsche's premature rejection of Herder's ideas on the origin of language seems, therefore, rather hasty[11]. He, as well as Herder, seeks to naturalize language without dogmatically reducing it to mere "nature". Both take the rhetorical nature of language as their starting-point and criticise from that perspective the traditional forms of philosophy, the historiography and civilization in general. Taken as a theory, no narrative regarding the origin of language and concepts can be demonstrated; either empirically or historically. One can detect in Herder's *Treatise on the Origin of Language* a continual oscillation between different argumentative strategies, and in 1772 he seems to disown this work by calling it, in a letter to Hamann, "the writing of a joking fool (*Witztölpel)"[12]. If a discussion regarding the origin of language no longer presupposes that language represents an exterior reality, it is consistent to consider it as a philosophical myth. Although Nietzsche in TL, according to Borsche, narrates his "history of origin" with a stronger scientific tone than Herder or his contemporaries did, we cannot take it as a scientific theory, especially since Nietzsche himself acknowledges the rhetorical status of the truth of natural science: the origin of language, as Borsche has remarked, is a myth in the platonic sense of the word[13]. We may find evidence for this, according to Borsche, in the beginning of TL – for the text begins with a *fable* which seems designed either for those who already know

---

11 In his writings, Nietzsche barely mentions Herder and, when he does, it is with polemical intent: cf. HH II WS 118, 125. Almost all of the works that deal with Nietzsche's confrontation with Herder focus only on particular aspects of their thought: the critique of language, the concept of human being, the concept of history, or the critique of culture. Cf. Brodersen/Jablonsky (1935); Harth (1986, 407–456); Borsche (1994, 112–130); von Rahden (2004, 459–477); Zusi (2006, 505–525).

12 To Hamann 1.8.1772, in Johann G. Hamann (1957, Vol. III, 11). Cf. Gaier (1990, 158–159): "Den Begriff des Witztölpels kann man als Formulierung der docta ignorantia im Kontext des von Hamann und Herder bewusst geübten Sokratismus sehen wie auch im Kontext von Sternes Narrenbegriff in dem von Hamann und Herder intensiv studierten *Tristram Shandy*. Herder übernimmt Hamanns Begriff, weil er mit seiner Abhandlung vor einer Akademie auftrat, die beweisende Argumentation erwartete, während er der Überzeugung war, daß ein solcher Selbstbeweis der Vernunft a priori unmöglich ist".

13 Cf. Borsche (1994, 126).

what is truth, lying, knowledge, language, etc., or for those who can no longer understand it[14].

The myths about the origin of language function as sensible images. They operate as non-conceptual and pre-argumentative settings that offer philosophical thought a heuristic function and a fundamental orientation. On the one hand, they represent an attempt to destroy the traditional conceptual discourse of philosophy, and on the other hand, they stimulate new powers of mythopoetical activity. By tracing language back to nature, Herder and Nietzsche want to create conditions under which man will be able to carry out new individual anthropomorphizations of the world, thus launching new developments in culture and society. Both proceed from plausibility, and not from logically demonstrable necessity[15].

Both discourses on verbalization are *naturalistic*; both seek to explain how language emerges from a "state of nature" (TL, 143). The natural needs of life determine the development of language from the first uttered sound up to the conceptual fixation of inter-individual truths. This development runs through the formation of metaphors, the "unspeakable" complexity of which is reduced to comprehensible concepts that then can work as "laws" of nature and culture. The stimulation of nerves and drives however (which,

---

14 Borsche (1994, 127 ff): "Die mythische Qualität des Textes wird schon in den ersten Zeilen offen kundgetan. Denn hier wird eine 'Fabel' erzählt, die 'Jemand erfinden könnte', jemand, der erklären will, was Sprache und Erkenntnis, was Wahrheit, Irrtum und Lüge sei, und zwar für solche, die das alles schon wissen, aber noch nicht oder, genauer gesagt, nicht mehr begreifen können. […]. In diesem Sinn erscheint es durchaus sinnvoll, Nietzsches Sprachtheorie in die Tradition Herders und Humboldts zu stellen und alle drei gegenüber früheren und gleichzeitigen (auch späteren) stoisch inspirierten Sprachauffassungen abzugrenzen, die eher zeichentheoretisch argumentieren; sinnvoll bleibt das, auch wenn die textphilologische Suche nach 'Einflüssen' von Herder und Humboldt auf Nietzsche weiterhin nur negative Befunde ergeben sollte". Cf. also Kaiser (1994, 70): "die Geschichte der Sprache ist selbst eine Narration. Indem Nietzsche über Wahrheit und Lüge schreibt, schafft sich die Illusion eines philosophischen Diskurses ihren Raum, die als Begehren der Rezeption ein semantisches Korrelat im Text erzeugt".
15 On the concept of "plausibility", cf. Stegmaier (2009, 19): "Von Plausibilitäten, soweit sie artikuliert, aber nicht mehr begründet und definiert werden, Begründungen und Definitionen bei ihnen enden, kann man wohl, wie man sagt, ‚einen Begriff haben' im Sinn von ‚sich mit ihnen auskennen', ‚mit ihnen hinreichend sicher umgehen können', aber eben keine logisch definierten Begriffe".

according to Nietzsche and Herder, play such great a role in the origin of language) should only be considered as a naturalistic and scientific cover: their function is primarily rhetorical. The reflection on language is for both authors the beginning of a longer attempt to erase the fictive distance between nature and culture; a distance, which precisely came up through language. Neither of their attempts can be understood in the sense of biological reductionism. The reflection on language enables Nietzsche to understand "that man misunderstood nature thoroughly and denominated it falsely" and that "we are the heirs of these denominations of things, [that] the human spirit [is] brought up in these errors, by means of which it is nurtured and has become powerful" (NL 23[24] KSA 8.412)[16]. However, in as much as language *distinguishes* spirit and matter, or culture and nature, it is not accurate to reduce language to nature. Moreover, in *bringing the history of civilisation closer to natural history* Herder is even opening a space for religious faith on the exceptional position of man within the cosmos. Even if their conception of nature is different, they both agree on an approach to nature in general and to human nature in particular that is not ontological, but rather *heuristic* and *guided by practical perspectives*. They do not say that man *is* nature, but regard him *as if* he were nature. With their naturalization of man and language, they intend to disclose a new perspective on history and culture. Herder distinguishes a sensible-poetical language, which is able to express "sensations", from an abstract-theoretical language, in which "laws" can be formulated. Nietzsche personalizes the distinction – even more than Herder – as a distinction between the "rational" or "theoretical" man and the "intuitive man".

2. Nietzsche's Naturalization of Man

The discourse on the origin of language becomes, thus, part of a broader philosophical approach, which we can interpret as a form of methodical and self-critical naturalism. What is at stake here is a procedure[17] that is (a) heuristic-analogical, (b) functionalistic and

---

16 NL 23[24] KSA 8.412: dass „wir die Erben dieser Benennungen der Dinge [sind], der menschliche Geist in diesen Irrthümern aufgewachsen [ist], durch sie genährt und mächtig geworden". [*Editors' translation*].

17 Cf. Bertino (2011).

(c) genealogical. Following Nietzsche, we will call it "naturalization" (*Vernatürlichung*) in order to distinguish it from naturalistic reductionism. The concept "naturalization of man" (*Vernatürlichung des Menschen*) appears five times in Nietzsche's writings, always in posthumous notes. The first occurrence is in 1880/81. Here, Nietzsche makes the "naturalization of man" his "task":

> My task: the dehumanization of nature and then the naturalization of man, after he has attained the pure concept "nature" (NL 11[211] KSA 9.525)[18].

Naturalization represents a process, a transition from one conception of man to another, thus presupposing that man is not definitely determined[19]. Considered as a "task", naturalization also has a practical interest, i.e. an ethical purpose. We shall discuss this purpose in connection with our analysis of the structure of naturalization.

The task of naturalizing man arises as soon as one understands "the belief in the universe as an organism" (NL 11[201] KSA 9.522) and the belief "that the universe has a tendency" (NL 11[205] KSA 9.524) as a form of "humanization of nature" (NL 11[201] KSA 9.522)[20]. In GS 109, Nietzsche develops these thoughts and seeks to regard all traditional anthropomorphic conceptions of the world as "humanizations":

> Let us beware of thinking that the world is a living being. Where would it stretch? What would it feed on? How could it grow and procreate? After all, we know roughly what the organic is; are we then to reinterpret what is inexpressibly derivative, late, rare, accidental, which we perceive on the crust of the earth, as something essential, common, eternal, as those people do who call the universe an organism? This nauseates me. Let us beware even of believing that the universe is a machine; it is certainly not constructed to one end, and the word 'machine' pays it far too high an honour. Let us beware of assuming in general and everywhere anything as elegant

---

18 NL 11[211] KSA 9.525: "Meine Aufgabe: Entmenschung der Natur und dann die Vernatürlichung des Menschen, nachdem er den reinen Begriff „Natur" gewonnen hat". [*Editors' translation*].

19 Cf. NL 25[428] KSA 11.125; NL 2[13] KSA 12.71–74; BGE 62.

20 Cf. NL 11[201] KSA 9.522: „de[n] Glaube[n] an das All als Organismus"; NL 11[205] KSA 9.524: den Glauben, „daß das All eine Tendenz habe"; NL 11[201] KSA 9.522: eine Art von „Vermenschung der Natur". [*Editors' translation*]

as the cyclical movements of our neighbouring stars; even a glance at
the Milky Way raises doubts whether there are not much coarser and
more contradictory movements there, as well as stars with eternally
linear paths, etc. The astral order in which we live is an exception;
this order and the considerable duration that is conditioned by it have
again made possible the exception of all exceptions: the development
of the organic. The total character of the world, by contrast, is
for all eternity chaos, not in the sense of lack of necessity but of
a lack of order, organization, form, beauty, wisdom, and whatever
else our aesthetic anthropomorphisms [*Vermenschlichungen*] are
called. Judged from the vantage point of our reason, the unsuccessful
attempts are by far the rule; the exceptions are not the secret aim,
and the whole musical mechanism repeats eternally its tune, which
must never be called a melody – and ultimately even the phrase
'unsuccessful attempt' is already humanisation bearing a reproach.
But how could we reproach or praise the universe! Let us beware
of attributing to it heartlessness or unreason or their opposites: it is
neither perfect, nor beautiful, nor noble, nor does it want to become
any of these things; in no way does it strive to imitate man! In
no way do our aesthetic and moral judgements apply to it! It also has
no drive to self-preservation or any other drives; nor does it observe
any laws. Let us beware of saying that there are laws in nature
(GS 109).

Unlike the word *Vermenschung* employed in the note from the
Nachlass, the word *Vermenschlichung* used in this aphorism encloses
a moral, humanitarian component. Accordingly, the (supposed)
natural order is not only anthropomorphic but also morally good.
Later, "anthropomorphization" (*Vermenschlichung*) also becomes for
Nietzsche a synonym for "civilization" (BGE 242), and for the difference between man and animal life, which is a difference that emerges
within morality (GM II 4). With this word, Nietzsche seeks to express
a typical European process, the progress of which leads modern man
to achieve "a more mature sort of constitution, one that is weaker,
more sensitive and more vulnerable, and that will necessarily give rise
to a *considerate* morality" (TI Skirmishes 37). Anthropomorphization
is also *Verschönerung*, "beautification" (D 427, GS 24 and elsewhere)
insofar as the interpretation of nature is associated with aesthetic
pleasure. As a result of this, man, humanity itself, is also supposed
to be beautiful and, for this reason, Nietzsche asks sceptically in TI:
"does the world really become beautiful just because it is seen that

way by human beings, of all creatures? People have *anthropomor-phized* it: that is all. But nothing, absolutely nothing guarantees that a *human being* is the standard of beauty" (TI Skirmishes 19, modified).

Nietzsche does not comprehend the naturalization of man as a "theory", but rather as an *anti-belief*, by means of which he wants to unmask all traditional anthropomorphisms as beliefs. He does not present positive arguments for a realistic, non-anthropomorphic account of the world. The exposition of a true natural order, or even of a lack thereof, would only be possible with aid of a new metaphysical theory. Thus, with the *motto* "Let us beware" (which he repeats seven times), Nietzsche wants, rather, to arouse critical alertness and scepticism in the reader. He wants to warn us against a danger that has not been noticed so far. Anthropomorphisms, as shadows of God, lead to metaphysical delusions; they harbour nihilistic dangers. However, precisely because they are like shadows, we cannot address them directly, but only indirectly through their source of light. As forms of self-deception, they cannot be refuted by arguments either. Therefore, one can only warn against them. Contrarily to man's tendency of abbreviating[21] the complexity of nature through images, schemata and concepts of every kind, Nietzsche negates all allegedly pre-given natural orders, be it the order of a mechanism or that of an organism, and assesses the fundamental character of the world as lacking-of-order, as chaos. Given Nietzsche's exclusively critical stance, this should not be understood as a positive statement, as a new ontological thesis about nature. Nietzsche understands that the concept of "chaos" is also morally charged, insofar as a mere exception to a supposedly naturally given order is regarded as an "unsuccessful attempt" – which is, of course, a new anthropomorphism. Every morality is reluctant to accept a total arbitrariness, and yet, this arbitrariness is precisely what Nietzsche wants us to face. This demand is rendered even more difficult by the fact that the arbitrariness itself cannot be ascertained, but only alleged. Nietzsche even warns against the concept of "law", whether one accepts it or denies it, for laws immediately suggest a law*giver* with his good and moral ends. In *Human, All Too Human*, Nietzsche had already written:

---

21 On the "abbreviation of the means of expression" cf. BGE 12, 186; GM III 24; NL 38[2] KSA 11.597; NL 38[13] KSA 11.611–612; NL 5[16] KSA 12.190, and elsewhere, and also Stegmaier (1994).

'Law of nature' a superstition. – When you speak so rapturously of a conformity to law in nature you must either assume that all natural things freely obey laws they themselves have imposed upon themselves – in which case you are admiring the morality of nature – or you are entranced by the idea of a creative mechanic who has made the most ingenious clock, with living creatures upon it as decorations. – Necessity in nature becomes more human and a last refuge of mythological dreaming through the expression 'conformity to law' (HH II 9).

However, as he says in GS 109, there is "no one who commands, no one who obeys, no one who transgresses". Since the concept of "conformity to law" is a way of "humanizing" the fact that in nature "every power draws its final consequences at every moment" (BGE 22), Nietzsche substitutes it with the concept of "necessity" (GS 109). This concept of necessity as negation of every finality (ends) and morality (values) and even of causality in nature (cf. BGE 21) is more radical than that of Democritus, who still believed in causality as a universal law of being.

Nietzsche's discourse on necessity or on an indefinite amount of necessities is directed against *human, all too human* metaphysics; even if it is clear that human beings can hardly evade them. This discourse is only tantamount to the demand to resist all metaphysical temptations. Nietzsche knows very well that "we behold all things through the human head and cannot cut off this head" (HH I 9). Despite the fact that the attempt to "dehumanise" the "humanisation" of any interpretation of the world may be "without prospect of success" and would degenerate into a "humanization raised to a higher power"[22] as Heidegger wrote, Nietzsche urges us to try[23]. Of course, a question

---

22 Heidegger (1991, I, 100).
23 Spiekermann (1992, 46) distinguishes two "tendencies of deanthropomorphization", one which is positivistic-reductionist and another which is reflective-critical. Spiekermann says that the physicist Max Planck, like Nietzsche before him, had attempted to develop a new reflective-critical tendency very far removed from positivistic and reductionistic attempts at an objective knowledge of nature formed only on the basis of facts instead of interpretations – for he agreed with Nietzsche in that the overcoming of anthropomorphism is only partially possible. Thus, according to Spiekermann, the only thing left is to conjure up the anthropomorphic character of all knowledge concerning man and yet, to keep nature strongly in mind.

does remain, namely "what would remain of the world if one had cut it [sc. the human head] off"? (HH I 9). But this is "a purely scientific problem and one not very well calculated to bother people overmuch", not a problem from whose solution one "might let happiness, salvation and life [...] depend":

> For one cannot assert nothing at all of the metaphysical world except that it was a being-other, an inaccessible, incomprehensible being-other; it would be a thing with negative qualities. – Even if the existence of such a world were never so well demonstrated, it is certain that knowledge of it would be the most useless of all knowledge: more useless even than knowledge of the chemical composition of water must be to the sailor in danger of shipwreck (HAH I 9)[24].

However, Nietzsche knows that nature, "from which we abstract the subject", is something "very indifferent, uninteresting and not a mysterious ultimate ground (*Urgrund*), not the riddle of the world solved", for "the more we dehumanize nature, all the more it becomes meaningless for us" (NL 23[150] KSA 8.458)[25]. That is the reason why the "dehumanization" of nature should be understood only as a strategic preparation for man's return to nature, so that, in the end, man's creative forces, now understood as natural forces, may gain a new impetus[26]. Finally, the "dehumanization" of nature does not lead to a non-anthropomorphic, pure ontological determination of reality –

---

24 Cf. NL 10[D82] KSA 9.431, where Nietzsche challenges the conceivability of a "world without subject".

25 NL 23[150] KSA 8.458: "die Natur, von welcher man unser Subjekt abzieht, ist etwas sehr Gleichgültiges, Uninteressantes, kein geheimnißvoller Urgrund, kein enthülltes Welträthsel; (...) je mehr wir die Natur entmenschlichen, um so leerer bedeutungsloser wird sie für uns". [*Editors' translation*].

26 Arguably, Friedrich Kaulbach (1981/82, 448) was the first to notice Nietzsche's scepticism towards a purely dehumanised picture of nature.: "[N]icht die Principia mathematica philosophiae naturalis Newtons geben von hier aus gesehen das Stichwort für das gültige Denken der Natur, sondern die Prinzipien der frei bildenden und gestaltenden Naturkräfte, zu denen auch die Einbildungskraft des Menschen gerechnet werden muß.". The productive character of deanthropomorphization must be stressed, in so far as it creates room for new anthropomorphizations. Kaulbauch sees in Nietzsche's doctrine of the eternal return of the same precisely such a case of creation of meaning. After the meaninglessness of the whole has been recognized, we transform meaninglessness into meaning: "[wir verwandeln] die Sinn-losigkeit in Sinn dadurch, daß wir in Freiheit die Welt des ewigen Wiederkehrens zu der unserigen machen und im Sinne des Amor fati Stellung zu ihr nehmen" Kaulbach (1981/82, 462).

unless this ontology could be non-human. Every positivistic naturalism would be, also for Nietzsche, a new "-ism" (organism, materi-
alism, mechanism), which would not be in principle distinguishable
from the former shadows of the good, old God. Therefore, nature "in
itself" does not exist at all for us. Nietzsche wrote down for himself:

> Our task is to implant the correct sensation, that is, the one that
> corresponds to true things and correct judgements. Not to restore
> the natural ones: for they have never existed. Let us not be deceived
> by the word 'natural' or 'real'! This means 'folk-like', 'ancient',
> 'general" – it has nothing to do with truth (NL 5[25] KSA 9.186)[27].

The task of "dehumanizing nature" and "naturalizing man" has, for
Nietzsche, both a regulative and a methodical character. Its methodical
guiding principle is the "economy of principles", Ockham's principle
of economy[28]. However, both aspects of the process should not be
separated; they represent for Nietzsche one and the same task. Yet, at
the same time, he distinguishes them as phases ("dehumanizing nature
and *then* naturalising man", my emphasis). One should understand
their particular type of unity as conceptual and temporal, or dialectical
and processual, or else as the unity of two counter-movements[29].
Accordingly, "dehumanizing nature" implies that everything human
and anthropomorphic is removed from nature, so that nature is
uncovered as chaos, i.e. as a necessity of wills to power, each of which
draws its final consequences at every moment[30]. The "naturalization
of man" implies that man is placed in a free and, in this sense, natural
relation to nature as chaos – i.e., in a relation, in which he is not
under the prejudice of any particular morality or metaphysics and,
thus, is able to face nature under natural conditions and according to
natural needs. Free from morality and metaphysics, man can become,

---

27 NL 5[25] KSA 9.186: "Unsere Aufgabe ist, die richtige Empfindung d.h. die
   welche wahren Dingen und richtigen Urtheilen entspricht zu Pflanzen. Nicht die
   natürlichen wiederherstellen: denn sie haben nie existirt. Man lasse sich durch das
   Wort „natürlich" oder „wirklich" nicht täuschen! Das bedeutet „volksthümlich"
   „uralt, „allgemein" – mit der Wahrheit hat es nichts zu thun". [*Editors' translation*].
28 Cf. BGE 13. On this aphorism, see Abel (1985, 47).
29 On the sense of dialectics in Nietzsche (in contrast with Hegel) cf. Stegmaier
   (2001).
30 Cf. NL 11[197] KSA 9.519: "Chaos sive natura: 'on deanthropomorphizing
   nature'". [*Editors' translation*].

so to speak, "natural nature" (BGE 257). According to Nietzsche, this naturalization of man is only possible "after he has attained the pure concept of 'nature'" (NL 11[211] KSA 9.525)[31]. The naturalization happens, therefore, in a span of *time* ("then"), but its *concept* is also indissolubly bound up with nature: the "dehumanization of nature" takes place *in the process* of "naturalizing man". Man's ability to understand nature less anthropomorphically depends on his ability to develop a morally- and metaphysically-unbiased, natural, necessary, and chaotic relation to nature[32].

Insofar as human beings, in their "surface- and sign-world" (GS 354), can only envision this "natural nature" anthropomorphically, i.e. as "text", Nietzsche speaks of a de-moralised and de-metaphysicized unity of man and nature as a "basic text of *homo natura*" (BGE 230). This text is "terrible" for all those who rely on a particular morality or metaphysics (JGB 230). In his notes, Nietzsche introduces the formula "*homo natura*" directly in the context of his critique of morality. According to a draft for the book he planned to write in 1885/86 (but never carried out), *The Will to Power*[33], the first part should have dealt, among other things, with the "Return to Nature". In the draft for the second part, we can see the formula "*homo natura*" along with the formula "the 'will to power'" – as the conclusion of an "*origin and critique* of moral valuations" (NL 2[131] KSA 12.13 = WLN 86). Spinoza is also mentioned here, in particular his critique of morality ("the attempt to *rid oneself* of the moral order of the world, *so as* to have 'God' remain, *a world that holds its ground in the face of reason...*") and his formula "'*deus sive natura*'" (NL 2[131] KSA 12.13 = WLN 86). Nietzsche's analogy "*homo natura*" clearly suggests that nature does not correspond to God anymore, but to man, i.e. that man has taken God's place. Nietzsche's new insight is "the fundamental fact, which has been *overlooked*: contradiction between 'becoming more moral' and the heightening and strengthening of the human type" (NL 2[131] KSA

---

31 NL 11[211] KSA 9.525: „nachdem er den reinen Begriff „Natur" gewonnen hat". [*Editors' translation*].

32 Cox (1999, 241–242) sees in the will to power an anti-epistemological and anti-ontological point of view.

33 Cf. Montinari "Kommentar" in: KSA 14.735, with reference to NL 2[100] KSA 12.109f.

12.13 = WLN 86) – human heightening and strengthening precisely
by means of naturalization, which depends on the critique of morality and metaphysics. The affirmative character of this naturalization
stands out more clearly in the sketches for the third part of the book,
the one that should have contained its kernel. It should have determined "how men undertaking this revaluation of themselves would
have to be constituted" (NL 2[131] KSA 12.13 = WLN 87): "The
grandiose prototype: man in nature; the weakest, cleverest being making itself master, subjugating the more stupid forces" (NL 2[131] KSA
12.13 = WLN 87). Man, in as much as he is *in* nature, will only rule
over nature if he achieves an unbiased and natural relation to nature.

However, whenever it is a matter of positive definitions, one must
recall that "*homo*" and "*natura*" are only signs, clues for orientation
in the context of new moral valuations. To hypostasise them would
mean to give in to the "seduction of words" (BGE 16)[34]. If nature is
nothing but chaos and necessity, then any particular morality that
believes to be grounded on nature can be criticized from the point
of view of nature, but it is not possible to ground a morality, an
"ought", on nature. Nietzsche shows that no moral naturalism is
possible – he insists in rejecting what is known since David Hume as
the false deduction of any "ought" from what "is". Instead, Ethics
must begin with the "dehumanization of nature" and the correlative
"naturalization of man", which do not presuppose an order in nature,
upon which ethics could be grounded. Ethics must give a new meaning
to the concepts of man and nature. This is (in this context) the meaning
of Nietzsche's concept of "overman", of whom his Zarathustra says
that he is "the meaning of the earth" (ZA Prologue 3). The "earth"
is here understood as the chaotic "natural nature". Since chaos is
continual becoming, man as overman stands in the face of something
which is always changing and undetermined, something that can only
be determined anew over and over again. Man is beyond definitions
and determinations when he does not find them *involuntarily*, i.e.,
when he does not anthropomorphize nature *spontaneously*. Man and
overman are, in this respect, not different persons, but conceptual
distinctions concerning the power of man to stand in the face of

---

34 Cf. also GS 354, BGE Preface 1; BGE 20, 21, 24, 34, 54, and TI Reason 9 ("I am
   afraid we still have not got rid of God because we still have faith in grammar").

nature. The anthropomorphization or humanization of nature is the human activity *par excellence*. Thus, man is overman precisely insofar as he can stop anthropomorphizing, or at least suspend this activity for a time, in order to reflect on it. For he recognizes nature as absurd and chaotic only insofar, as he avoids any positive interpretation of it and places himself in a purely contemplative relation to it. Thus, he does not experience his anthropomorphizations as what determines him, nor as his meaning, but only as a sign of his finitude.

Once again, this leads us back to GS 109, this time to the conclusion of the aphorism. The first practical consequence brought about by these reflections on the way in which these intruding anthropomorphisms are but a result of man's own needs, is the uncertainty implanted in the man of knowledge, who spontaneously grabs hold of positive definitions and determinations. This requires from him "caution and care" and a steady critique of those particular conceptions that, simultaneously, develop into particular conceptions of nature. At the end of the aphorism, Nietzsche formulates four questions that begin with "when". At least three of these questions do not seem to be proper questions at all – Nietzsche concludes them with exclamation marks, instead of question marks. They are not so-called rhetorical questions, to which the answers are already known, but exhortations, imperatives that remain doubtful. They are – even before the concept was introduced in *Thus Spoke Zarathustra* – imperatives for man to understand himself as overman, i.e. to free himself from his involuntary anthropomorphisms, thereby redeeming himself and nature, to which he belongs:

> But when will we be done with our caution and care! When will all these shadows of god no longer darken us! When will we have completely de-deified nature! When may we begin to *naturalize* humanity with a pure, newly discovered, newly redeemed nature!" (GS 109, modified).

3. Herder's God-Nature and the Limits of Knowledge

Nietzsche's "economy of principles" requirement seems to contrast with Herder's religion-inspired naturalism. According to Herder, God has "ordered everything in nature according to proportion, number and weight" and "contrived the essence of things, their shape and connection, their course and conservation" (*Ideen*, 6.14, editors' translation). It is obvious that Herder presupposes without questioning that nature, being "rich in understanding", does not pursue a meaningless game. This justifies his teleological argumentation and the introduction of supra-empirical entities such as the "kingdom of invisible forces" (*Ideen*, 6.14). However, he wants his discourse on the origin of language to develop "not from voluntary or societal forces, but from the general economy of animal life" (TOL, 82). Herder's religiously inspired speech on nature also has a philosophical dynamic, which in the end leads to its self-overcoming. For precisely his religious-inspired thought is, as was already mentioned, constantly aware of its bounds: being critical of itself, it must lead beyond itself. Herder also considers the use of the word "nature" metaphorically: "Hence let no one be deceived by the fact that I sometimes use the name nature personified. Nature is no autonomous being, instead *God is everything in His works*" (*Ideen*, 6.17, editors' translation). Nature becomes a sign of something invisible and ineffable: "Let he, for whom the word nature through many writings of our epoch has become meaningless and base, imagine instead that almighty force, goodness and wisdom and name in his soul the invisible being that no earthly language is able to name" (*Ideen*, 6.17, editors' translation). Thus, nature, no less than God, cannot be understood as a totality *objectively* determined as good and meaningful. For Herder, as for Nietzsche, such concepts can only be anthropomorphic. And he also introduces the idea that the anthropomorphic nature of human knowledge is unavoidable and can only be overcome provisionally: Herder begins what Nietzsche called the "naturalization of man". This is already visible in Herder's investigations of the origin of language, in which he assumes the existence of God as Creator, and yet does not want to employ the concept of God as an explanatory principle. Unlike the theologian Johann Peter Süßmilch and his *Attempt to Prove that the First Language Did not Originate in Man, but Instead in His Creator* (1766), Herder firmly refuses the idea of a divine origin of language:

> One cannot judge at all about divine productions, and all philoso-
> phizing about them *kat' anthrôpon* becomes awkward and useless;
> for of course we always have to consider them as human produc-
> tions, to presuppose secretly a human originator all the time, only a
> human originator who stands out on a higher level and operates with
> higher powers (FRGL, 58).

Even when he undertakes a "general consideration of human cognition" (FRGL, 49), he only considers turning to a "negative philosophy."[35] Such a "negative world wisdom" should draw man's attention to the limits of knowledge. It should be a kind of Socratic ignorance, which should only contribute to a purification of metaphysics and rational theology:

> In that case ideas would creep away out of our whole metaphysics, from ontology to natural theology, to which merely the words have given admission and a false citizenship – and they are precisely the ideas about which there has been most conflict (FRGL, 49).

According to Herder, as long as one posits God as a mere a sign of an overmanly productive principle, no objective judgment is possible, for God creates everything. However, one can interpret this in a twofold manner. On the one hand, it could be the expression of a radical scepticism about human knowledge. The theory of the origin of language would then be, as mentioned, only a game, the "writing of a joking fool (*Witztölpel)*". In this case, one can ask why should someone want to play this game. The answer could be: what is now at stake is only a new performative conception of truth and not a purely theoretical one. On the other hand, we could make a distinction between those things directly created by God and those that He indirectly creates. For the latter we could claim a human co-creation, thereby confirming Vico's (whom Herder could have read) principle of *verum ipsum factum*[36]. This would mean that man is indeed in a position to reach the truth, but only in relation to what he himself has created, only in relation to his own culture. This too corresponds, in part, to Herder's position, insofar as he deduces specific laws from the principle of human productivity. In this case, however, in as much as the origin of language is founded in nature, the discourse

---

35 For an interpretation of Herder's negative philosophy as a "point of discursive rupture between classical knowledge and modernity" and the conditions for the emergence of modern "human sciences", cf. Levanthal (1990, 187 ff).

36 About the question whether and to what extent Vico influenced Herder, cf. Albus (2001, chap. 1.8). Although Herder certainly studied Vico, according to Albus we can barely assume an influence of Vico on Herder. First because Herder learned more about Vico's doctrines by reading about them than by reading Vico's works; and second, because this happened when Herder's lifework was almost finished, and he had already written all the theses which bring Vico to mind (cf. Albus 2001, 128).

on the origin of language could not claim any truth, for nature is not produced by man. Therefore, the necessity of "dehumanizing nature" and "naturalizing man" could have been in Herder's mind too.

In a similar way, Herder does not consider anthropomorphism to provide an absolute falsification of nature, because such a falsification would only be recognizable through the comparison with a true and objective presentation of the world, which is not given to human beings. Later, in his *Kalligone*, Herder seems to speak of chaos in this way:

> No one saw the chaos of nature; taken absolutely it is a non-concept: for chaos and nature cancel each other out. The poets describe it, therefore, only as a transition to order. Our soul does not think it differently. In chaos all essential features and properties of things were already present; each one of them expressed its drive disorderly and strove to take its place; thus arose order (*Kalligone* 8.866, editors' translation).

For Herder chaos can never be given as an object of experience. We always experience nature as a realm of regular order, which we call, not without certain moral pathos, "laws". Even "chaos" qua counter-concept to order is still, as such, an anthropomorphism. Herder would have had no problem in conceiving of his organismic metaphysics simultaneously as "shadows of god" and shadows of humanity. For he is aware that we are not capable of anything but the production of shadows, that all cognitive activity of man is only a primordial production of shadows, by which man emulates the primordial production of God, namely creation.

If, however, the only possibility of overcoming anthropomorphism is again a form of anthropomorphism, then the only way we can explain the natural origin of language and culture is by recurring to principles that are cultural, and hence, linguistically conceived, i.e. by recurring to principles that are already a result of that origin. Thus, we can definitely regard Herder in this respect as a precursor of the concept of "naturalization" in Nietzsche's sense. Naturalization in Herder combines a scepticism motivated by religion with a scepticism motivated by the critique of language. In any case, religious scepticism has its motivation and, at the same time, its limitations in religious faith. Along with his naturalization of anthropology and culture, the theologian has a religious confidence in the truth of his own perspectives. Although Nietzsche, for his part, might have seen this as a limit of thought, it is no less true that Herder addressed, before him, the project of 'de-humanizing nature', and that he did attempt to reflect on nature bearing in mind its subjective and bodily determinants. Herder views the shadows of God, which Nietzsche wants to reject precisely by naturalising man, as a possibility of throwing light upon the truth of faith. This also entails the conception, rejected by Nietzsche, of nature as an organism. Nevertheless, if there is no definitive naturalization (because such a naturalization never attains nature such as it is created by God), then God becomes a sign of the limits of naturalization. A further question to Nietzsche could then be whether the naturalization of man could not also continue under the conditions of a religious faith – provided that God is understood as nothing but the sign for the fallibility of human knowledge and, thus, of its infinite incompleteness, which Herder had already discovered. In that case, Nietzsche's answer to this question could be: Yes, although only if religious faith does not preclude us from interpreting the individual as creator[37]. For Nietzsche knows very well that the mere negation of anthropomorphisms is not enough to "destroy the world that counts as 'real', so-called 'reality' (…) Only as creators can we destroy" (GS 58). However, this means for Nietzsche what it meant for Herder: "to create new names and valuations and probabilities" (GS 58, modified); it means, in other words, a work of language on language that does not seek an ultimate assurance in an outside reality, nor does it need one. According to Josef Simon, the fact that both Nietzsche and Herder hold on to the temporal and context-bound character of all human knowledge reflects their common "acquaintance with Old-Testament's consciousness of time"[38].

4. The Sign "Drive" and the Metaphorical Origin of Language

Both Nietzsche and Herder set up a scenery, in which human language is presented as originating in nature, and this is what lends

---

37 If one accepts as valid the inversion of Zarathustra's famous saying: "*if* there were Gods, how could I stand not to be a God! *Therefore* there are no Gods." (ZA II On the Blessed Isles). If, like God, I can create, then I can endure the existence of Gods.

38 Simon (1987, 13).

persuasiveness to their aim, which is namely, to overcome the metaphysical separation of nature and culture. "Origin of language" (cf.
Herder's *Treatise*) or "genesis of language" and "emergence of language" (cf. TL) are names used for describing an original condition
in which "nature" and "culture", as well as "natural history" and
"human history", may find their original unity *and* the conditions of
their first differentiation. However, in order to conceive this original
condition, the use of more or less explicit assumptions about man
as the bearer of language becomes unavoidable, and this creates a
vicious circle between the conception of language and anthropology.
For Herder and Nietzsche, who ultimately do not believe man to be
conceivable before the development of language, this circle takes on
a critical form, which also enables cultural claims. Despite the fact
that they both turn to "nature" in the context of the pragmatically
oriented "naturalization" discourse, their conceptions of man present
some differences, which indicate the strategic character of their return
to nature: different paths are explored when different practical aims
are sought.

Herder's and Nietzsche's critiques of language display a common
metaphor-logical concern. Nietzsche's formulae: "before something
being 'thought', it must have already been fabulated" and "the form-
giving sense is more original than the 'thinking' sense"[39], fit into the
tradition to which Herder also belongs. This tradition claims a logical
and temporal primacy of the metaphor over the concept. It distinguishes between a poetical and a prosaic phase in the development
of human language and turns metaphor into the decisive mark of the
first phase, thus suggesting a dependence of the "proper" forms of
expression on the first, improper, figurative formulas. Both Herder
and Nietzsche use the emphasis they give to the original metaphorical
nature of language as a device for challenging philosophy's claim to
absolute validity in the form of a conceptual science. The naturalization of conceptual discourse uses metaphors as *focus imaginarius* of
a genetic reconstruction of the formation of concepts, which is then
conceived of as an achievement of sensible and organic living beings.

---

39 NL 40[17] KSA 11.636: "bevor also „gedacht" wurde, muß schon gedichtet
   worden sein, der formende Sinn ist ursprünglicher als der „denkende"". [*Editors'
   translation*].

In as much as concepts emerge under the strain of life, they cannot provide a firm starting point for thought. They are no more than particular signs, which only count as concepts insofar as their abstraction from the sensible elements of language is useful for communication. Abstraction is something characteristically human, but it also points out to a transcendent realm beyond language, a realm that presents the limits of human conceptualization. What Josef Simon remarks about Nietzsche can also be applied to Herder, namely that Nietzsche does not have a theory of metaphor and his talk of metaphors is itself metaphorical[40].

The origin of concepts from metaphors is described as an increasingly vivid and active origin. This vividness is regularly restrained by the use of concepts, which are supposed to neutralize the ambiguity of metaphors for good practical reasons. Herder and Nietzsche propose an inquiry on the meaning and co-effects of neutralizing the metaphorical origin of concepts in favour of a linguistic stabilisation of becoming. So, for both, the understanding of language as a bodily, natural process "refreshes the intellect", which, according to Wittgenstein, is the function of every "good simile"[41]. As part of a renovation of culture, the critique of language seeks to reassert, by means of a particular naturalistic genealogy of language, individual creativity in the face of standardized and technical forms of thought.

For this reason, Nietzsche and Herder try out a procedure that also uses metaphors, but without laying claim to an absolute and timeless mirroring of becoming. If concepts are metaphors, it is also plausible to assert that becoming can be described by means of metaphors. Thus, knowledge as a whole is conceived of as a linguistic achievement

---

40 Simon (1999, 90): "[Nietzsche] spricht auch 'über' Metaphern nicht 'theoretisch' im Sinne einer Metapherntheorie. *Sein Sprechen über Metaphern ist 'notgedrungen' selbst metaphorisch.* Es drückt ein 'Urerlebnis' aus, das nicht notwendig allen mitteilbar ist".

41 Wittgenstein (1998, 3e). Blumenberg (1979, 78) quotes this sentence and formulates, with the outmost incisiveness, the relation between the theoretical use of language and metaphor: "Die in der rigorosen Selbstverschärfung der theoretischen Sprache verächtlich gewordene Ungenauigkeit der Metapher entspricht auf andere Weise der oft so eindrucksvollen höchsten Abstraktionsstufe von Begriffen wie ,Sein', ,Geschichte', ,Welt', die uns zu imponieren nicht nachgelassen haben. Die Metapher jedoch konserviert den Reichtum ihrer Herkunft, den die Abstraktion verleugnen muß".

and, for this reason, as a metaphorical movement. This is, in turn, a metaphor, insofar as the original metaphorical character of language is distinct from the metaphorical character of a rhetorical figure built on purpose[42]. Only insofar as this discourse regarding the metaphorical character of concepts conceives of itself as a strategic game and not as ultimately true, does it avoid self-contradiction. Nietzsche is more aware of this than Herder is, since he, unlike Herder, does not link his genealogy of conceptual language to a meaningful natural order and, thus, does not posit a realm of being which we could refer to non-metaphorically. Strategic metaphorization avoids a self-contradictory theory of metaphor, or a "metaphorical theory" of language, and sticks to critical deconstruction. Whereas Herder seems to have slowed down this critical deconstruction; Nietzsche speeds it up.

Both Herder's and Nietzsche's effort to trace concepts back to metaphors posits an *unconscious principle* in human spirit; this is how they make it anthropologically plausible. Herder, for whom "the initial metaphor" was already "a desire to speak", talks of a "drive in us for drawing analogies" (Herder, *Werke* 4.673, editors translation); Nietzsche speaks of a "drive to form metaphors" as a "fundamental human drive" (TL, 150). For Nietzsche, this drive is an essential feature of man, so that "it cannot be left out of consideration for even a second without also leaving out human beings themselves" (TL, 150–151). As with other drives in the context of the discussion of naturalization, Herder and Nietzsche cannot claim a scientific demonstrability of these drives towards the formation of metaphors and analogies; they can only construct them heuristically. That such concepts are not biological or physiological becomes clear when one sees that the drives for analogy and metaphor are mainly mentioned in texts that deal with themes related to poetology and the critique of language, and not to biological or scientific themes. Herder discusses them in the work *On Image, Poetry and Fable*, Nietzsche in an essay such as *Truth and Lying in a Non-Moral Sense*, which begins with a fable. The reason for them to place the drives at the onset of the

---

42 Tietz (2000, 219) argues for the convincing view that Nietzsche's "metaphor" should be read as an "absolute metaphor" in Blumenberg's sense. Cf. Blumenberg (1998 and 2007).

process of metaphorization, is that this enables them to portray the fact that the onset of conceptualization is not at the disposal of an autonomous and self-conscious reflection of the subject. We are always already immersed in this process, and any conceptualisation of it belongs to it too.

In addition, the particular way in which both Herder and Nietzsche talk about the drives, i.e. the vagueness, weakness and the uncertainty they associate with instincts and drives, turns them into the appropriate candidates for describing the metaphorical game. In the same way that the drives place man in the difficult position of having to satisfy his needs in ways that are uncertain and undetermined, metaphors too are equivocal and movable forms of expression, and this, precisely because they have their origin in man's drives. The drives' fragility is also genetically comprehensible: involuntarily, the weakness of the drive for metaphors demands a concept, some kind of structuring in a net of stable relations, in order to relief human action from the uncertainty of the life of the drives.

As the starting point of the activity of *metaphérein*, i.e. of transferring, the sign "drive" is very persuasive: even though it is a concept, at the same time it points out to the limits of conceptualization. Due to its relational nature, a "drive" does not seem to be thoroughly graspable by means of a concept and, precisely for this reason, it is fit to plausibly portray the mobility of language, that is, its oscillation between metaphors and concepts. The concept "drive" points immediately to the necessity and uncontrollability of the metaphorical transfer by means of signs, for a drive is always "a drive for something" and without this "something", which is always something different from the drive itself, it cannot be grasped. The non-autarchic concept "drive" cancels out the metaphysical dualism between *potentia* and *actus*, thus confirming that there is no ontological ground for the critique of language.

The meaning of a "drive" cannot be grasped through the concepts of "cause" and "effect" either; and thus, the seemingly absolute and objective validity of this explanatory model is shaken by the concept of "drive" itself. Inasmuch as our reason, according to Herder, cannot express "things", but only their common *differentiae* or "marks", we do not see directly "any connection between cause and effect", "for we do not see inwardly neither what acts nor what is affected, and we do not have any concept from the being of a thing" (*Ideen*, 6.349, editors' translation). Nietzsche's scepticism regarding the concepts of cause and effect is also motivated by the critique of language:

> A perceived stimulus and a glimpse of a movement, combined, result in causality, at first as an empirical statement: two things, i.e. a certain sensation and a certain visual image, always appear together: that one is the cause of the other is a *metaphor, borrowed from the will and the deed*: a conclusion by analogy" (NL 19 [209] KSA 7.483 = WEN 148–149).

A drive is recognized by its expression. No distance between the physiological condition that prepares the action and the action itself can be ascertained by means of the sign "drive". Thus, a deterministic explanation of our behaviour becomes problematic by means of the concept "drive", although no human "free will" is posited here either.

Since we cannot know where individual drives begin or end, we cannot distinguish them from one another. The use of the word "drive" weakens the tendency to distinguish several faculties of *metaphérein*. These are no longer hypostasised and reified as substantial entities. "Drive" is a sign for a fluid plurality of powers in us, the differentiation of which is merely functional. Herder links the drive for analogy with an "inner pleasure in recognizing it [the analogy] and thus expanding, exercising and strengthening its concepts each time" (Herder, *Werke* 4.673, editors' translation), so that the drive becomes part of a complex sensation of pleasure in knowledge. This corresponds to Herder's anthropological model of the *sensorium commune*, according to which no sense perception belongs to a single sense organ, because, although its inception may lie in one of the senses, it affects the others afterwards. The fact that we attach a perception to a particular sense organ is due to human thought, which discriminates by means of language and is more than a *sensorium commune*. The isolation of "sensibility" is a theoretical construction that occurs in the course of linguistic self-reflection. Herder seems to be even more radical than Gerber and Nietzsche's TL, because, according to him, not only the transfers from stimuli to images are possible, but also synaesthetic transfers from particular forms of sensation to other forms of sensation[43].

---

43 Cf. Fürst (1988, 289–291).

In any case, Nietzsche does not atomize the drive for metaphor either. He does not separate it from the "drive for truth", the origin of which he also enquires in TL. He does not transform the drive for metaphor into a timeless part of a natural pre-disposition, which would then lead to a second drive, the drive for truth, but rather sees the first in constant interaction with the second: the drive for metaphor is held back and disciplined by the drive towards truth. Being instinctive, the origin of verbalization is closely connected with a drive for imitation, which Nietzsche describes as a basic anthropological phenomenon: "A translation of one sense perception into another takes place: some people see or taste something when they hear certain tones. This is quite a common phenomenon" (NL 19[227] KSA 7.489 = WEN 154). The drive for imitation is even more important; it is even closer to Herder's idea that there is a tendency to draw analogies. Although it is also true that, for Nietzsche, imitation does not presuppose, as it does for Herder, a "great analogy of creation" (Herder, Werke 4.360, editors' translation), in accordance with which "everything" senses "itself and its kind" (*Werke* 4.360, editors' translation). However, what is at stake for both is "to sense everywhere resemblance to us" and "to enliven everything with our sentiment" (Herder, *Werke* 4.329, editors' translation). Even if for Nietzsche "our senses imitate nature by mimicking it more and more" (NL 19[226] KSA 7.490 = WEN 153), he is aware that "imitation presupposes reception, followed by the continuous transfer of the received image into thousand metaphors, all active" (NL 19[226] KSA 7.490 = WEN 153). On this basis, the use of concepts becomes problematic and knowledge as a mirror of reality becomes uncertain: "*imitation* is the opposite of knowledge", because "knowledge does not want to accept any transference, but wants to grasp the impression without a metaphor and without any consequences" (NL 19[228] KSA 7.491 = WEN 154). At the same time, Nietzsche knows that "there are no 'literal' expressions and *no knowing the literal sense without metaphor*" (NL 19[226] KSA 7.490 = WEN 154). Knowing is, in particular, "working with the most popular metaphors, i.e., an imitation that is no longer perceived as imitation" (NL 19[226] KSA 7.490 = WEN 154), and a concept is "an imitation of the relations of time, space, and number on the foundations of metaphors" (TL, 150). The relations grasped by means of the categories of time, space, and causality are not concepts in themselves, but only "*metaphors* of knowledge by which we interpret things for ourselves" (NL 19[210] KSA 7.487 = WEN 149). For the anthropological presuppositions of *metaphérein*, it is decisive that imitation has a retroactive effect on instinct, and can therefore modify even the effect of instincts. Imitation is in fact for Nietzsche the "medium of all culture; it gradually produces instinct" (NL 19[226] KSA 7.489 = WEN 153). Consciousness may influence imitation, but imitation originates under the influence of a hidden impulse. When Nietzsche asks, "what is the power that enforces imitation", he comes up with the following answer: "the appropriation of an alien impression through metaphors" (NL 19[227] KSA 7.490 = WEN 154). It seems, therefore, that Nietzsche thinks, as early as this, that there is a prototypal will to power that offers a heuristic guideline for the interpretation of phenomena ranging from the organic to the cultural dimension.

5. Conclusion

The classical metaphysical model: consciousness → language → communication is radically shaken by the concepts of "drive" and "instinct". "Drives" and "instincts" describe a dimension of man that pre-determines consciousness; a dimension, however, that must remain inaccessible to consciousness, i.e., instincts and drives become signs of consciousness' conditioned nature and incomplete self-referenciality. However, Herder and Nietzsche do not intend to present the drives and instincts as the essence of man. Instead, drives and instincts are, first of all, working hypotheses, in accordance with the heuristic procedure of naturalization. Since instincts are signs of an inscrutable dimension of man, one must use brackets to speak of them: (instincts) → consciousness → language → communication. With respect to this latter model, Herder goes a step further and effaces the temporal distance between instincts and consciousness, since, for him, awareness, reflection (*Besonnenheit*) must unfold between the empty spaces of the constellations of instincts. This being the case, the scheme may be reformulated as follows: (instincts)/consciousness → language → communication. Nietzsche's more consequent and methodical naturalization radicalizes the functionalist perspective of anthropological and linguistic-philosophical discourse, thus questioning even the last remains regarding the substantiality of consciousness. The substantiality of consciousness becomes a semiotic outcome of a dynamical interaction between individuals, i.e. an outcome of communication. Therefore, Nietzsche's model can be schematised in this way: (instincts) → language/communication → consciousness (cf. GS 354). Consciousness, as an outcome and no longer as the original dimension of humanity, loses not only all originality and centrality in spiritual life[44], but also all normative meaning. Nietzsche unmasks consciousness as the beginning of a levelling of the individual under the pressure of a community of language-users.

Bibliography

Abel, Günter (2001), „Bewusstsein – Sprache – Natur. Nietzsches Philosophie des Geistes", in: *Nietzsche-Studien* 30 (2001), 1–43.

Abel, Günter (1985), „Nominalismus und Interpretation. Die Überwindung der Metaphysik im Denken Nietzsches", in: Simon, J. (ed.) (1985) *Nietzsche und die philosophische Tradition*, vol. 2., Würzburg (Königshausen & Neumann), 35–90.

Albus, Vanessa (2001), *Weltbild und Metapher. Untersuchungen zur Philosophie im 18. Jahrhundert*, Würzburg (Königshausen & Neumann).

Andresen, Joshua (2010), "Truth and Illusion Beyond Falsification: Re-reading 'Truth and Lie'", in: *Nietzsche-Studien* 39 (2010), 255–281.

Behler, Ernst (1994), "Die Sprachtheorie des frühen Nietzsche", in: Borsche, T./Gerratana, F./Venturelli, A. (ed.) *"Centauren-Geburten"*. *Wissenschaft, Kunst und Philosophie beim jungen Nietzsche*, Berlin/New York (Walter de Gruyter), 99–111.

Behler, Ernst (1996), "Nietzsches Sprachtheorie und der Aussagecharakter seiner Schriften", in: *Nietzsche-Studien* 25 (1996), 64–86.

Bertino, Andrea (2011), *"Vernatürlichung". Ursprünge von Friedrich Nietzsches Entidealisierung des Menschen, seiner Sprache und seiner Geschichte bei Johann Gottfried Herder*, Berlin/New York (Walter de Gruyter).

---

44 The polemical aim of Nietzsche's reflections regarding language and spirit is exemplarily summarised by Günter Abel (2001). Abel points out that Nietzsche's model of consciousness and self-consciousness is above all a critique of the Cartesian-model, of which the following positions are typical: (a) one should start with a "pure inner experience"; (b) by means of introspection, the I of consciousness has direct and transparent access to its inner world and experience, i.e. to itself and the contents of consciousness; (c) consciousness has a central and localizable place in the brain; (d) the subject of consciousness is able to reflect on itself from an ultimate and fix standpoint; (e) the "I" is a substance; (f) consciousness should assert and possess itself in self-consciousness.

Blumenberg, Hans (1998), *Paradigmen zu einer Metaphorologie*, Frankfurt am Main (Suhrkamp).

Blumenberg, Hans (1979), *Schiffbruch mit Zuschauer*, Frankfurt am Main (Suhrkamp).

Blumenberg, Hans (2007), *Theorie der Unbegrifflichkeit*, Frankfurt am Main (Suhrkamp).

Borsche, Tilman (1994), "Natur-Sprache. Herder – Humboldt – Nietzsche", in: Borsche, T./Gerratana, F./Venturelli, A. (ed.), *"Centauren-Geburten". Wissenschaft, Kunst und Philosophie beim jungen Nietzsche* Berlin/New York (Walter de Gruyter), 112–130.

Brodersen, Arvid/Jablonsky, Walter (1935), *Herder und Nietzsche oder die philosophische Einheit des Goethejahrhunderts*, Trondheim (Det Kongelige Norske Videwnskabers Sleskabs Skrifter 10).

Cox, Christoph (1999), *Nietzsche. Naturalism and Interpretation*, Berkeley/Los Angeles (University of California Press).

Emden, Christian J. (2005), *Nietzsche on Language, Consciousness and the Body*, Illinois (University of Illinois Press).

Fürst, Gebhard (1988), *Sprache als metaphorischer Prozess. Johann Gottfried Herders hermeneutische Theorie der Sprache*, Mainz (Matthias-Grünewald-Verlag).

Gaier, Ulrich (1990), "Herders Abhandlung über den Ursprung der Sprache als „Schrift eines Witztölpels", in: Gabriel, G./Schildknecht, C. (ed.) *Literarische Formen der Philosophie*, Stuttgart (Metzler), 155–165.

Gerber, Gustav (1871), *Die Sprache als Kunst*, vol. 1, Bromberg (Mittler).

Hamann, Johann G. (1957), *Briefwechsel*, ed. Ziesemer, W./Henkel, A., vol. III, Wiesbaden (Insel Verlag).

Harth, Dietrich (1986), "Kritik der Geschichte im Namen des Lebens. Zur Aktualität von Herders und Nietzsches geschichtstheoretischen Schriften", in: *Archiv für Kulturgeschichte* (68), 407–456.

Haym, Rudolph (1954 [1880]), *Herder nach seinem Leben und seinen Werken*, vol. 2, Berlin (Rudolf Gaertner).

Heidegger, Martin (1991), *Nietzsche I and II, The Will to Power as Art. The Eternal Recurrence of the Same*, transl. David Farrell Krell, New York (Harper Collins).

Herder, Johann Gottfried (1985–2000), "Ideen zur Philosophie der Geschichte der Menschheit", in: Bollacher, M. (ed.), *Johann Gottfried Herder. Werke. 10 in 11 Bänden*, vol. 6, Frankfurt am Main (Deutscher Klassiker Verlag).

Herder, Johann Gottfried (2002), "Treatise on the Origin of Language", in: *Herder's Philosophical Writings"*, transl. Michael N. Forster., Cambridge (Cambridge University Press).

Hödl, Hans Gerald (1997), *Nietzsches frühe Sprachkritik. Lektüren zu Ueber Wahrheit und Lüge im aussermoralischen Sinne*, Wien (WUV).

Hödl, Hans Gerald (2003), "Metaphern ohne Referenten. Anmerkungen zur neueren Diskussion um Nietzsches Sprachphilosophie", in: *Allgemeine Zeitschrift für Philosophie* (28), 183–199.

Kaiser, Stefan (1994), "Über Wahrheit und Klarheit. Aspekte des Rhetorischen in ,Ueber Wahrheit und Lüge im außermoralischen Sinne'", in: *Nietzsche-Studien* 23 (1994), 65–78.

Kaulbach, Friedrich (1981/1982), "Nietzsches Interpretation der Natur", in: *Nietzsche-Studien* 10/11 (1981/1982), 462–464.

Lacoue-Labarthe, Philippe (1979), *Le sujet de la philosophie. Typographies I*, Paris (Aubier-Flammarion).

Levanthal, Robert S. (1990), "Herder's Foundation of the Human Sciences", in: Mueller-Vollmer (ed.) *Herder Toda*, Berlin/New York (Walter de Gruyter), 173–189.

Man, Paul de (1987), *Allegorien des Lesens*, transl. Werner Hamacher and Peter Krumme, Frankfurt am Main (Suhrkamp).

Neis, Cordula (2003), *Anthropologie im Sprachdenken des 18. Jahrhunderts. Die Berliner Preisfrage nach dem Ursprung der Sprache*, Berlin/New York (Walter de Gruyter).

Rahden, Wolfert von (2004), „'Nie wirklich satt und froh…' Nietzsches Herder", in: Groß, S./Sauder, G. (ed.), *Der frühe und der späte Herder: Kontinuität und/oder Korrektur*, Saarbrücken (Synchron Wissenschaftsverlag der Autoren), 459–477.

Reuter, Sören (2009), *An der "Begräbnisstätte der Anschauung". Nietzsches Bild- und Wahrnehmungstheorie in ,Ueber Wahrheit und Lüge im aussermoralischen Sinne'*, Basel (Schwabe Verlag).

Simon, Josef (1999), "Der Name "Wahrheit". Zu Nietzsches früher Schrift "Über Wahrheit und Lüge im außermoralischen Sinne", in: Riedel, M. (ed.) *"Jedes Wort ist ein Vorurteil", Philologie und Philosophie in Nietzsches Denken*, Köln/Weimar/Wien (Böhlau), 77–93.

Simon, Josef (1987), "Herder und Kant. Sprache und 'historischer Sinn'", in: Sauder, G. (ed.) *Johann Gottfried Herder 1744–1803*, Hamburg (Felix Meiner), 1–13.

Stegmaier, Werner (2001), „Die Substanz muss Fluktuanz werden. Nietzsches Aufhebung der Hegelschen Dialektik", in: *Berliner Debatte Initial* 12.4 (2001) Themenheft "Unaufhörliche Dialektik", 3–12.

Stegmaier, Werner (2009), *Philosophie der Orientierung*, Berlin/New York (Walter de Gruyter).

Stegmaier, Werner (1994), "Weltabkürzungskunst. Orientierung durch Zeichen", in: Simon, J. (ed.) (1994), *Zeichen und Interpretation*, Frankfurt am Main (Suhrkamp), 119–141.

Spiekermann, Klaus (1992), *Naturwissenschaft als subjektlose Macht? Nietzsches Kritik physikalischer Grundkonzepte*, Berlin/New York (Walter de Gruyter).

Tietz, Udo (2000), "Phänomenologie des Schein. Nietzsches sprachkritischer Perspektivismus", in: *Nietzscheforschung* 7, 215–241.

Venturelli, Aldo (2003), *Kunst, Wissenschaft und Geschichte bei Nietzsche. Quellenkritishe Untersuchungen*, transl. from Italian by Leonie Schröder, editorial collaboration of Silke Richter, Berlin/New York (Walter de Gruyter).

Wittgenstein, Ludwig (1998), *Vermischte Bemerkungen/Culture and Value. A Selection from the Posthumous Remains*, ed. von Wright, G.H., revised by Pichler, A., transl. Peter Winch Oxford (Blackwell).

Zusi, Peter (2006), "Toward a Genealogy of Modernism, Herder, Nietzsche, History", in: *Modern Language Quarterly* 67.4, 505–525.

Nietzsche on Metaphor, Musicality, and Style. From Language to the Life of the Drives

Maria João Mayer Branco

> *"(...) the whole world as linked to humankind, as the infinitely refracted echo of an original sound, that of humanity, and as the multiple copy of a single, original image, that of humanity."*
> On Truth and Lying in a Non-Moral Sense

1.

In the celebrated definition from the *Poetics*, Aristotle defines metaphor saying it "is the application of a word that belongs to another thing: either from genus to species, species to genus, species to species, or by analogy"[1]. According to Aristotle, the word, and therefore also the concept, is first in relation to metaphor; and metaphor is the transfer of a concept to another object, a passing from one logical place to another, from its proper place to a figurative place. Nietzsche, however, did not share the Aristotelian division of the world into genera and species that correspond to essences. Instead, he understands those genera and species as human metaphors, as he claims in his text *On Truth and Lying in a Non-Moral Sense.*[2] As he defends in this text, "(...) the opposition we make between individual and species is also anthropomorphic and does not stem from the essence of things" (TL, 145); and "if I create the definition of a mammal and then, having inspected a camel, I declare, 'Behold, a mammal!', then a truth has certainly been brought to light, but it is of limited value, by which I mean that it is anthropomorphic through and through and contains not a single point which could be said to be 'true in itself', really

---

1 Cf. *Poetics* 1457b6–9.
2 "We divide things up by gender, describing a tree as masculine and a plant as feminine – how arbitrary these translations are!" (TL, 144).

and in a generally valid sense, regardless of mankind" (TL, 147).
Therefore, a metaphor is not an adequate picture of the world, and
metaphorization is in fact a "metamorphosis of the world in human
beings" (TL, 148).

Nevertheless, and despite the "limited value" of metaphorical
truth, Nietzsche expresses his preference for metaphorical language
already since *The Birth of Tragedy*, where the basis for his diagnosis
of the decadence of modern culture is precisely his preference for
metaphor and his critique of concepts. The reciprocal action between
the Dionysian musical sonority and the Apollinian, imagetic nature of
words makes new linguistic creations possible, as well as new modes
of expression. This idea is developed in *The Birth of Tragedy* in the
paragraphs on lyric poetry: as a Dionysian artist, the poet unites
himself with the primordial One and is able to reproduce it in the
form of music; afterwards, under the influence of the Apollinian,
music makes itself "visible" (*sichtbar*, GT 5). In lyrical expression,
music reaches an unprecedented relation with words, and this relation
intensifies it and gives it something which it would otherwise never
have, namely visibility. Thus, lyric poetry is described in §5 and §6
as a metaphorical transference of Dionysian music because "for a
genuine poet, metaphor is not a rhetorical figure but a vicarious image
that he actually beholds in place of a concept" (BT 8).

Transposing something into a metaphor enhances its expressive
possibilities and enriches its meaning. Nietzsche calls this a process
of "transfiguration" (BT 4)[3] in which the reciprocal action between
the Dionysian and the Apollinian creates "new births ever following and mutually augmenting one another" (BT 4). Apollo makes
music "emit image sparks" (BT 5), lyric poems born from the relation between words and music, and the same goes for tragedy, which
consists of lyric poems "in their highest development" (BT 5). On the
other hand, Dionysus brings to the Apollinian world "something new
and unheard-of", "something never before experienced" for whose
expression "we need a new world of symbols" (BT 2).

The relation between these two tendencies, which Nietzsche calls
"drives of nature" (*Triebe*, BT 1), is the starting point of aesthetics

---

3   On the importance of the notion of "transfiguration" in Nietzsche's aesthetics and
    his preference for an expressive, instead of a representative model, see Schacht
    (1985, 476–529).

(BT 16) and it explains the possibility of new artistic and linguistic creations. These creations expand the limits of common, established intelligibility in a given culture and open up space for new forms of experience and feeling, as well as for their expression. When one of the two drives is suppressed, the other weakens (BT 10). This is what Nietzsche has in mind when he claims that Socrates' "logical drive" (*logischer Trieb*, BT 13) expelled out the Dionysian and forced the Apollinian to "withdraw into the cocoon of logical schematism" (BT 14). Nietzsche associates Socrates' "instinct-disintegrating influence" (*Instinkte auflösender Einfluss*, BT 13)[4] with the primacy given to concepts over metaphors. This association culminates in his criticism of the culture of the opera, which favors the conceptual and semantic content of words and transforms music into a convention at odds both with the Apollinian and the Dionysian artistic drives, indeed with "*aller Künstlerischer Instincte*" (BT 19). In *The Birth of Tragedy*, the culture of the opera is another name for Socratic culture, whose basic instinct is no longer an artistic one, but rather the logical and theoretical "instinct of science" (*Instinct der Wissenschaft*, BT 15) – an instinct that aims at rendering the world universally intelligible by determining the meaning of things through the abstract concepts of dialectic. With Socrates, the musical-Dionsyian is expelled and replaced with the syllogisms of the "optimistic dialectic" (BT 14).

This implies a loss because creative and linguistic abundance depends on the interweaving and reciprocal stimulation of both drives. This is why the "tremendous opposition" (BT 1) between the Apollinian and the Dionysian drives is a fertile opposition. The two drives can relate to each other without canceling each other out, for given that the dynamic of their opposition is aesthetic and not logical, it does not violate the principle of contradiction. In fact, transferences from one drive to the other make words go beyond their semantic meaning, and they make music give birth to images. The limits of both drives can thus shift and expand because the Apollinian and the Dionysian are no fixed entities with completely determined borders. On the contrary, they effect one another and the limits of their expressive powers are always contracting or expanding. Moreover, the lyrical-

---

4   Throughout *The Birth of Tragedy* Nietzsche seems to use the words *Trieb* ("drive", "impulse") and *Instinkt* ("instinct") interchangeably; on this theme, see the Introduction to this volume and Stegmaier's and Constâncio's papers.

Dionysian state intensifies all expressive powers without privileging
one particular drive (like the logical or rational drive) – instead, it
enhances a multiplicity of instincts and "symbolic drives" acting in
the "entire body" (BT 2). In such a state, the meaning being communicated is neither abstract nor purely logical, but rather a concrete and affective meaning that, in addition to words, includes facial
expression, gesturing, and bodily movements (BT 2). In contrast to
this, modern opera gave primacy to words over music and created a
musical culture in which intelligibility was reduced to conceptual and
semantic meaningfulness, so that text dominated music. Within this
culture concepts gained ground on metaphor, in an analogous way to
what happened to philosophical discourse since Socrates, the "despotic logician" (BT 14).

For Nietzsche, this process whereby one single drive becomes
dominant is a symptom of the decadence of the instincts. The logical instinct reduces all multiplicity to conceptual abstraction and
immobilizes, in linguistic unities, every dynamic relation between
non-identicals. Thus, the decadence of the instincts entails linguistic
impoverishment, for conceptual language is rigid and totalizing, i.e.
it aims at encompassing and making equivalent all singularities in a
given multiplicity of singularities, thereby stabilizing and delimitating
their meaning. It dispenses with Dionysian musicality, that is to say,
with the expressive, non-conceptual and non-semantic element that
gives birth to metaphoric images. Nietzsche understood the conceptual and demonstrative discourse as a sign of a lack, because it aims
at making abstract notions absolute and gives primacy to the kind
of logical reasoning in accordance to which all non-logical detours
and transferences are illegitimate. In contrast, metaphorical discourse
conveys an abundance of possibilities and yet it does not assume the
universal validity of its creations; it constantly renews the creative
force which gives birth to language instead of imposing the particular linguistic forms it creates. The force or drive to metaphor, as
Nietzsche calls it in *On Truth and Lying in a Non-Moral Sense*, is
thus symptomatic of a fecundity and vitality more powerful than its
particular creations. No metaphor exhausts the meaning that can be
given to something. All metaphors evoke more than they say, and
the fact that something remains, as it were, unsaid makes possible
the co-existing of each metaphorical image with other metaphors,
as well as the birth of new metaphors, which are not as despotic as

concepts are. Metaphorical language does not claim to demonstrate, it is not apt for of logical argumentation, it even breaks with logical principles like the principle of contradiction. Its relation to things is not one of *adequatio*, but of transference, and it preserves a sensible, concrete, non-abstract element.

Commentators like Sarah Kofman[5] and Lacoue-Labarthe[6] have negleted the fact that in *The Birth of Tragedy* Nietzsche conceives of a relation between music and words that is not disjunctive, but rather expressive of an affinity – a relation in which "Dionysus speaks the language of Apollo; and Apollo, finally, the language of Dionysus" (BT 21). In fact, Nietzsche also evokes the possibility of a relation between music and philosophy, expressed in the image of Socrates practising music (BT 14)[7].

---

5   In *Nietzsche et la métaphore* (1972), Sarah Kofman has argued that metaphorical transference is, within *The Birth of Tragedy*, a transposition of the truth of being to symbolic languages (Apollinian and Dionysian); since these languages refer to the primordial One, Kofman claims, Nietzsche, in this work, does not call the traditional relation between original and copy into question. However, it should be stressed that on several notes from the *Nachlass* from 1871–1872 Nietzsche already doubted we could have access to the essence of the world, and called the Schopenhauerian concept of Will an appearance (e.g. NL 1871, 7[167] KSA 7.203 = WEN 55: "the will is already a form of appearance" and NL 1871, 7[170] KSA 7.205 = WEN 56: "There is no road of the primal One for man. He is all appearance"). On Nietzsche's criticisms of the schopenhauerian concept of Will as thing in itself already in this period, cf. Barbera (1994, 217–233) and Dufour (2005, especially chapter III, "Le schopenhauerisme de Nietzsche en 1871", 51–71).

6   Cf. Lacoue-Labarthe (1979, 31–74). According to Lacoue-Labarthe, both TL as well as the posthumous note NL 1871, 12[1] KSA 7.205 = WEN 83–91 seem to invert the order of transference presented in BT, which progressed from the primitive One to music and then to image/word, and break the distinction between the Apollinian and the Dionysian or, at least, what that distinction had of an opposition or contradiction. Thus Lacoue-Labarthe concluded that it is only in those texts that the border separating philosophy from its "other" – namely, music considered as philosophy's "outside" – starts vanishing. Behler's analysis of these same texts (TL and NL 1871, 12[1] KSA 7.359) has shown that, contrary to what Lacoue-Labarthe claimed, they do not represent a radical break with Nietzsche's views in BT, but rather a gradual development of those views. It should, however, be stressed that, for Behler, BT's model is still one of an absolute theory of representation, i.e. a metaphysical model where music – not language – expresses the primordial unity of all things. Cf. Behler (1994, 99–111).

7   This image is the basis of Venturelli's defense of a continuity between BT and TL. Cf. Venturelli (2003).

However, Lacoue-Labarthe admitted that Nietzsche raised the possibility of this relationship in the posthumous fragment 12[1] of 1871. In this text, Nietzsche valorizes vocal music as a guide for a theory of language, declaring that "we must regard the duality in the essence of language which is prefigured by nature as the original model of that combination of music and poetry" (NL 12[1] KSA 7.360 = WEN 84). Language and music are not separable spheres, for they always include the duality of the "tone of the speaker" and "the gestural symbolism of the speaker" (NL 12[1] KSA 7.361 = WEN 85). The concrete, vocal and bodily element, which is not determined in any abstract or definite way, manifests the affective and affecting nature of both spheres. Here Nietzsche associates the origin of music with the lyric impulse, the "vocal music, the combination of sound with image and concept" (NL 12[1] KSA 7.360 = WEN 84), showing that its source is not metaphysical, but human – i.e. linguistic. "Absolute", i.e. purely instrumental music, is, therefore, an abstraction that forgets the original connection between music and the use of the human voice in lyric poetry[8]. There is always an impure, non-absolute, human element in music understood as "vocal music". Its origin is song: sung words, intoned by someone's voice.

Thus, music is only recognizable in the medium of language. That is why Nietzsche highlights, in the same text, that in spite of the original active power that pertains to musicality in the production of lyric songs, "a musical impulse" (*Musikerregung*) chooses a text "as a metaphorical expression of itself" (NL 12[1] KSA 7.366 = WEN 88). And this obviously means that such impulse does not exist as an irreducible and auto-sufficient unit. Only when transferred into words – when affected and transfigured by words – does music acquire a fuller expressivity. Its metaphorization is an increase, an intensification of musicality itself. But the inverse is also valid: words gain expressivity

---

8   "The music of every people begins in a close alliance with lyric poetry, and long before there can be any thought of an absolute music it undergoes the most important stages of development in that combination." (NL 12[1] KSA 7.360 = WEN 84). With these words in mind, it is difficult to accept Pascal David's view (2002), for whom, throughout all of his writings, Nietzsche understood music as absolute music, i.e. as a "metaphysician". On "absolute" or "pure" music, cf. Dahlhaus (1994) and on a critique of this concept (understood as "music from mars"), cf. Ridley (2004).

in their interweaving with music. This interaction intensifies or enhances the sensitive element, the sonority, thereby preventing the words from being reduced to abstract and conceptual meanings, as Nietzsche shows with the example of the 4th movement of Beethoven's Ninth Symphony. If the text is a metaphor — an expression of the "musical impulse" that intensifies the human, vocal side of music —, words, when affected by sonority, become more than the pure vehicles of semantic meaning: music forces the text (which is its metaphor) to show its sonority (which is also linguistic).

To sum up, the relation between music and language, like the relation between the Dionysian and Apollinian drives, brings about a comprehensive and expressive gain that is not purely logical, but aesthetic or sensitive, and a heightened intelligibility to both spheres. Music prevents its textual metaphor from reducing itself to a fixed or determinate meaning, and text allows music to show itself in its most concrete, sensitive dimension and not as abstract or "absolute" music.

2.

"Words are like a keyboard of drives"

NL 1880, 6[264] KSA 9.266
(my translation)

The interactions between drives and language, sensibility and rationality, metaphor and concept are the explicit theme of *On Truth and Lying in the Non-Moral Sense*. In this essay, Nietzsche shows that the relation between both spheres is a struggle by pointing out that linguistic restitution of particulars is highly problematic. When we name a particular, we abstract from that which is intuitive and sensitive in it, i.e. we can only name a particular through a concept, and a concept is a *general* content suitable for a multiplicity. This problem is at the base of Nietzsche's general suspicion regarding conceptual language[9], and is already at stake in *The Birth of Tragedy*.

---

9   According to Patrick Wotling (1999, 40), "le soupçon à l'égard du langage aboutit
    à la contestation du concept, et à la substitution de la métaphore à ce dernier
    comme outil philosophique fondamental".

But this work does not really present a thesis on metaphor[10], which is the object of TL. Here, Nietzsche distinguishes between a "drive to truth" (*Trieb zur Wahrheit*, TL, 143) and a "drive to form metaphors" (*Trieb zur Metapherbildung*, TL, 150), and tackles, from the viewpoint of these drives, the problems of the inadequacy between words and things, of the conventional and arbitrary foundation of languages, as well as of the emergence of concepts from a "making equivalent that which is non-equivalent" and "overlooking what is individual" (TL, 145). Thus the essay analyzes the conflictual relation between two instinctive movements which affect one another.

This is what is at stake in the idea that, on the one hand, metaphor is the ancestor of concept, but on the other, metaphorization is opposed to conceptualization as life is opposed to death[11]. Each intuitive metaphor (TL, 146) is simultaneously the origin of concepts and opposed to concepts because conceptualization is the immediate dissolution of metaphors in a conceptual schema. Each metaphor, as well as each word, "immediately becomes a concept, not by virtue of the fact that it is intended to serve as memory (say) of the unique, utterly individualized, primary experience to which it owes it existence, but because at the same time it must fit countless other, more or less similar cases (...) [which] are never equivalent" (TL, 145). Any concept implies, thus, the death of the intuition of a singularity, which means that knowledge of particulars depends on a self-created illusion regarding its independence from its origin in transference or metaphorization. In other words, every concept is a metaphor, and the "proper", the "adequate" is always already an improper or inadequate discourse that forgets itself as such[12], inasmuch as "even the relation of a nervous stimulus to the image produced thereby is

---

10 As shown by Detlef Otto (1988), the notions of *Metapher* e *Übertragung* are rare in BT, where Nietzsche uses more often words such as *Spiegelung, Symbolisierung, Abbildung, Bild, Gleichnis, Projektion, Ausdruck, Nachahmung* to define the relations between Apollo and Dionysus.

11 As stated by Otto's interpretation of TL (1994).

12 "Only by forgetting this primitive world of metaphor, only by virtue of the fact that a mass of images, which originally flowed in a hot, liquid stream from the primal power of the human imagination, has become hard and rigid (...) – in short only because man forgets himself as a subject, and indeed as an artistically creative subject, does he live with some degree of peace, security, and consistency" (TL, 148).

inherently not a necessary relationship" (TL, 149). On the other hand, the instinct for the formation of metaphors works not only at the creation but also at the destruction or disarticulation of conceptual and abstract structures: if man does not wish to fall silent before these structures, "he will speak only in forbidden metaphors and unheard-of combinations of concepts so that, by at least demolishing and deriding the old conceptual barriers, he may do creative justice to the impression made on him by the mighty, present intuition" (TL, 152). The destruction of concepts comes about by way of a non-regulated and boundary-free game undertaken by man's metaphorical powers, whose simultaneously disorderly and creative force shatters the limits of concepts.

To this definition of the double and conflictual nature of the linguistic movement correspond two definitions of man: man is the being that reduces intuitive metaphors to conceptual schemas[13], and man is the being whose fundamental drive to form metaphors constantly undermines conceptual schemas[14]. In presenting two definitions of man, Nietzsche suggests that man's nature is not uniform, substantial and permanent, but plural, relational, dynamic. In fact, man is a "dissonance" (BT 25) or, as Nietzsche would say later, man is "the *as yet undetermined animal*" (BGE 62, Kaufmann's translation)[15]. The human being is constructed out of more than one fundamental drive, and what defines it is the reciprocal action of its drives – the way they affect each other, conflict with each other, continuously relate to each other. This dynamic also defines the drive for metaphor and its tendency either to petrify itself in conceptual structures or to undermine its conceptual constructions. Concepts are metaphors whose metaphorical origin we forget, i.e., "residues of metaphors" (TL, 147), "cooler, less colourful" (TL, 146) metaphors

---

13 "Everything which distinguishes human beings from animals depends on this ability to sublimate sensuous metaphors into a schema, in other words, to dissolve an image into a concept." (TL, 146)

14 "That drive to form metaphors, that fundamental human drive which cannot be left out of consideration for even a second without also leaving human beings themselves, is in truth not defeated, indeed hardly even tamed, by the process whereby a regular and rigid new world is built from its own sublimated products – concepts" (TL, 151).

15 On Nietzsche's philosophical anthropology and its relation to the human ability for language, see Bertino's paper in this volume.

that have lost their "intuitive" content. At their origin, metaphors are the opposite of abstractions and conceptual fixations: they are movement, transference, transport of nervous stimulations into images and sounds, – and therefore, they open up new possibilities of understanding, multiple interpretations. They have within them the power to "liberate" the intellect from its servitude to the rigid limits, the "boundary stones", of conceptual abstractions (TL, 152). Nietzsche associates metaphor with freedom, creativity, abundance, splendor and joy while connecting concepts to the images of a "burial site of perceptions" (TL, 150) and a "fortress" (TL, 151) that protects against the current of intuitive forces and impressions, as well as with "neediness", fear, and the mere aspiration to the absence of pain (TL, 152–153).

Whereas *The Birth of Tragedy* described the relation between the Apollinian and the Dionysian drives and the posthumous note from 1871 the interaction between language and music, in *On Truth and Lying in the Non-Moral Sense* the relation is between three steps in the formation of words, namely nervous stimulation, image, and sound. Transference is understood as "an aesthetic way of relating" (TL, 148) where the metaphor acts as a "substitution of one sphere for another" (TL, 149). Through the example of a painter who had no hands and expressed in song the image hovering before him, Nietzsche suggests that this song, although akin to a "stammering translation into a quite different language" (TL, 148–149), would always be more meaningful than ordinary, conceptual language[16]. The example combines a positive aspect with a negative one. The gain in expressivity and the creation of something new arises from a move from one sphere into another – in fact, from a move to a sphere that is different from the one we dominate (or different from the dominant sphere) —, and this results from a lack, an impotence to use a familiar language (the painter cannot paint). It is that lack or state of

---

16 It should be noticed that in BGE 274 Nietzsche returns to this image and associates "Raphael without hands" to genius. In the posthumous note from 1871 considered above, Nietzsche speaks of Raphael's painting of St Cecilia – an image that expresses music – and in BT 4 Raphael's *Transfiguration* is the pictoric example chosen to analyze the conflict and expressive interaction between the Apollinian and Dionysian drives. On the importance of Raphael's paintings for Nietzsche, cf. Wotling (1999, 165–173) and Buddensieg (2006, 97–98). On Nietzsche's interest for specific painters and for visual art, cf. Stegmaier (2005).

need that forces us to open up space for new means of expression, for widening conceptual limits, and for creating new, "unheard-of" (TL, 152) names. It is an expressive, linguistic need that compels the creation of new forms of expression, that is to say, such creations result from no rational demand, but from the need to satisfy a drive, i.e. from an instinct. Such new creations or metaphorical transferences are illogical – "things do not proceed logically when language comes to being" (TL, 145) —, and they challenge reason and its categories, threaten and destabilize conceptual comprehension. Thus, although the drive for metaphor is the genealogical origin of concepts ("if not the mother, at least the grandmother of each and every concept", TL, 147), the relation between metaphor and concept is a relation of permanent conflict, and only this conflict between instinct and intellect, between instinct and contra-instinct or movement and contra-movement, allows for the creation of new words, that Nietzsche defines as "copies of a nervous stimulation in sounds" (TL, 144).

According to *On Truth and Lying in a Non-Moral Sense*, language is born from the "desire to rule over life" which is common to the "man of reason" and to the "man of intuition" (TL, 152), and Nietzsche identifies the first with the scientist and the second with the artist. But inasmuch as the instinct for truth and the instinct for metaphor co-exist in human beings, i.e. considering that man is constituted by more than one fundamental drive and that his drives find themselves in constant interaction, Nietzsche's description of linguistic creation dissolves the rigid dichotomy between science and art, reason and instinct, truth and lying. Linguistic "legislations" (TL, 143) are in fact human inventions that human beings never cease to remodel, and they presuppose a non-dichotomic, dynamic relation between the drives for destruction and construction, between sensitive impressions and reason.

Moreover, while instinct and rationality are not irreducible domains, the senses of hearing and sight are also not confined, nor clearly delimited, respectively, to the perception of sound and of figures and colors. This means that it is an abstraction to conceive them in this way, when, in fact, there are synesthetic transferences between the senses[17]. Since the senses interact with each other, they

---

17 In a posthumous note from 1872/1873, Nietzsche refers to synesthetic phenomena, stating that the "translation of one sense perception into another" is "quite a

are capable of expanding beyond the limits to which our abstract concepts might tend to confine them, and so they are capable of offering "something never before experienced" (BT 2), "unheard-of" sensations. Furthermore, Nietzsche believes that the interaction between the senses, as well as between instinct and rationality, is a symptom of health, and therefore philosophy should promote the intensification of their interaction as well as the instinctive vitality of metaphor instead of the (allegedly) univocal and despotic domination of a conceptual language that abstracts from concrete experiences. For, as he writes in 1881, if one of the instincts "dominates absolutely", "man perishes" (NL 11[162] KSA 9.504, my translation).

3.

> "We never communicate thoughts, we only communicate movements, mimic signs that we *read backwards* as thoughts…"
>
> NL Frühjar 1888, 14 [119] KSA 13.296–299, my translation.

In his mature writings, Nietzsche remains critical of conceptual language and its relation to knowledge and philosophy. Conceptualization as a process of abstracting from singularity and fixating the meaning of particulars through general contents still seems to him to be symptomatic of the decadence of modern culture and the general decline of the vital instincts. The reflections on metaphor, concept, music, and communication developed in his first texts are developed further in later writings and never truly abandoned.

In aphorism 354 of *The Gay Science*, language is the expression of a herd instinct or need that developed in man along side consciousness. Contrary to what philosophers have always claimed in our Western tradition, Nietzsche asserts that consciousness "actually belongs not to man's existence as an individual but rather to the community- and herd-aspects of his nature" (GS 354). In this aphorism, Nietzsche returns to the question of the inadequacy of words to express individual, singular experiences, and claims that the development of

---

common phenomenon" and that "some people see or taste something when they hear certain tones" (NL 19[227] KSA 7.489 = WEN 154). On Nietzsche's views on the transferences between the metaphors of vision and audition and their extension to the other senses, cf. Babich (2006, chapters 3, 4 and 7).

consciousness and the capacity to fix our sensitive impressions and our understanding of ourselves in common, gregarious, linguistic signs is the modern disease *par excellence*: "each of us", Nietzsche writes, "even with the best will in the world to *understand* ourselves as individually as possible, 'to know ourselves', will always bring to consciousness precisely that in ourselves which is 'non-individual', that is 'average'" (GS 354). Faithful to the dissolution of the abstract and dogmatic dichotomy between rationality and instinct, Nietzsche shows that conscious activity is merely the surface of the organism's instinctive and physiological activity, and very often uses bodily functions as metaphors for describing the activity of our intellectual states of consciousness[18]. This marks a contrast to the traditional conceptual opposition between body and soul and shows that there is an original and reciprocal relation of expressivity[19], indeed a continuity between them[20]. Thus the conceptual model that the philosophical tradition had rigidly constructed in order to understand the specificity of the human being is not only shattered but also widened by Nietzsche's philosophical strategy: the fixed boundaries of what was traditionally understood as "consciousness" and "instinct" are no longer clear, and now each one of these false, atomic unities contaminates the other.

With this, not only the definition of what man is, but even the concept of knowledge is subject to boundary shifts and transpositions, namely via the notion of perspectivism and its resistance "against the dangerous old conceptual fiction that posited a 'pure, will-les, painless, timeless knowing subject'", i.e. "an eye turned in no particular direction" (GM III 12). According to Nietzsche, there is only a "perspective seeing" and "the *more* affects we allow to speak about one thing, the *more* eyes, different eyes, we can use to observe one thing, the more completely will our 'concept' of this thing, our 'objectivity', be" (GM III 12). Just like metaphor, perspectivism implies digression, transposition, transference of the point of view through a movement that is not purely logical, but affective and instinctive. Perspectivism implies that it makes no sense to believe in the construction of a

---

18 Cf. Blondel (2006) and Lupo (2006, 159–174).
19 As had been claimed by Kofman (1972, 45).
20 Cf. Abel (2001).

totalizing, universal perspective, and presents this effort as a failure to explore the multiplicity of drives out of which we are made[21].

In opposition to the tendency to totalization inherent to conceptual abstractions, perspectivism entails the idea that the world interprets itself in metaphorical perspectives, that the world *is* an irreducible conflict of perspectives, correspondences and relations, and not a permanently fixed totality susceptible to being understood in terms of concepts[22]. Metaphor interprets and is meant to be interpreted, it consists in a detour, it is always dislocated in relation to that which it says while it overflows into something else in a movement of transference. As discourse, it is movement: a movement of interpretation, that movement which defines the will to power[23], Nietzsche's philosophical formula to express life[24].

This interpretation or philosophical formula, as presented in aphorism 36 of *Beyond Good and Evil*, belongs to the context of the revaluation of the value of the affects and the senses for philosophical thought[25]. With it Nietzsche wishes to broaden a particular scientific explanation of the world, namely the mechanistic interpretation. If, as this text affirms, we do not have access to any kind of reality except "our world of desires and passions", and if "thinking is only a relation between drives", we can thus raise the hypothesis that this "world of affects" will also allow us to develop a better interpretation of "the mechanistic world", one that does not assume that such a world consists in outer causal relations. In other words, the

---

21 Richard Schacht (1996) has argued that perspectivism can be understood as knowledge if knowledge is itself a drive for knowledge, i.e., if we think of knowledge, as Nietzsche did, from the prism of life. According to Schacht, interpretative and metaphoric vitality is what distinguishes true philosophers from dogmatists and scholars, i.e. from the theoretical-Socratic modern men whose instinctive decline led to the impoverishment of philosophical interpretations. If everything is interpretation, if knowledge is always metaphorical, it is possible to understand at least something about what is created by humans – although only in human terms, i.e. anthropomorphically. And even if we cannot do much more than to understand ourselves and our creations, that is already something valuable.

22 Cf. Blondel (2006, 257 ff).

23 NL 2[148] KSA 12.140 = WLN 90.

24 NL 2[190] KSA 12.161 = WLN 96: "But what is life? Here a new, more definite version of the concept 'life' is needed. My formula for it is: life is will to power."

25 On this revaluation, cf. Stegmaier (2004).

hypothesis of the will to power is an interpretation of the world in accordance to which every "effect" is in fact continuous with its "cause", so that a sequence of events is not composed of an outer relation of exteriority between parts, but rather by the continuity of a movement of affection. For Nietzsche, the mechanistic interpretation of the world is based on a defective interpretation of the senses: "the mechanistic notion of pressing and pushing is merely a hypothesis based on sight and touch"[26]. In focusing on the type of relations that can be apprehended by the visual and tactile senses, and in understanding these senses as irreducible, non-permeable, non-contaminated by the other senses, the mechanistic interpretation is unable to explain that which for Nietzsche is the "fundamental fact", namely "action at a distance"[27]. Physics is unable to exclude action at a distance (e.g. attraction and repulsion) from its principles, and this is why Nietzsche finds it necessary to add a "supplement" to the concept of force in Physics – an "inner world", which he calls "will to power"[28]. The will to power shifts the limits of the mechanistic interpretation of reality, it allows for an expansion of the visual and tactile senses' boundaries, so that the world can now be seen also "from inside" (BGE 36). Put differently, the will to power is a way of widening the mechanistic way of thinking and feeling. Conceived of as a force endowed with interiority, the will to power allows for an explanation of the "action at a distance" and how it connects what, seen from the outside, seem to be separate units. This is not to deny the visible, exterior aspect of things, but rather to make things understandable as essentially constituted by an affect or force, so that their existence is a relational existence. In the final analysis, what is at stake is the rejection of the idea that reality consists of simple, atomic, discontinuous or isolated units, and that their articulation depends on a force that is external to them and pressures them one against one another, as if their relations depended on "causes" separable from their "effects".

Nietzsche's philosophical interpretation of the world implies not merely a relation between the senses, but also the end of the dichotomy

---

26 NL 34[247] KSA 11.504 = WLN 15.
27 NL 34[247] KSA 11.504 = WLN 15.
28 NL 36[31] KSA 11.610f = WLN 26.

between rationality and instinct and the inseparability of thought and feelings (*Gefühle*), as stated in *Human, All Too Human* and *Beyond Good and Evil*. Just as "true" and "false" are not "intrisically opposed" and there are only "levels of appearance" (BGE 34), sensations, dispositions and feelings cannot be separated from "certain complex groups of thoughts" (HH I 15) to which they are connected. Thus there is no "inner and outer" (HH I 15), for depth, i.e. interiority, is porous and interacts with the exterior, with the surface. We only have access to surfaces, appearances, because sensations and thoughts, or the sensible and the intelligible, are a plural and continuous plane of relations through which we access the world. This is also the reason why Nietzsche concludes that sensations and feelings are not fixed or closed units, but complex connections of feelings and thoughts, "rivers with a hundred tributaries and sources", where "the unity of the word is no guarantee of the unity of the thing" (HH I 14). There are no "pure" feelings, just as there are no "pure" thoughts; sensations and thoughts affect each other, they are always already interwoven with one another and connected to other sensations and thoughts, subject to incessant exchanges and transferences, constant boundary shifts and reciprocal transformations.

Now if, according to the logic of the will to power, the world is a plurality of perspectives that relate to each other and continuously create more perspectives, more world, then in the absence of the human perspective – in the absence of the drive for metaphor and interpretation, that "fundamental will of the spirit" which is a "binding (...) will" (BGE 230) – what obtains is an absence of relations, i.e. "chaos" (GS 109). Nietzsche's hypothesis questions, thus, the very notion of anthropomorphization implied in the concept of metaphorical interpretation. If metaphor is interpretation and interpretation is will to power, then it cannot be exclusively human, for the will to power is the name for the totality of the real, of which man is only a part[29]. As "an attempt at a new interpretation of all that happens" (NL 39[1] KSA 11.619, my translation), the will to power cannot be limited to human life[30]. The will to power allows for the interpretation of all events as moments of life itself, that is,

29 Cf. Müller-Lauter (1999, 122–160).
30 Cf. Figal (2001, 251–254).

for the thought that nothing is foreign to life. In this sense, there is no gap between the human and non-human spheres. Moreover, an adequate and definitive representation of the whole is inconceivable, because any representation will always be part of this whole, i.e. a form that will not be able to stabilize the world's interpretative force, only one more contribution to the world's general interpretative tendency – to the multiplication of interpretations. Everything that is alive is a force, and no form of life abides, for it will always want to overcome itself by integrating and interpretating something else.

As anthropomorphization, metaphor necessarily leaves out what does not concern man, everything that is not "world", but chaos. However, it is exactly the totality of forces that affect each other in a constant expansive and auto-reproductive movement that philosophy's dominant drive will want to reach – particularly Nietzsche's philosophy —, via a strategy of metaphorization that pressuposes the creation of a "new language" (BGE 4).

If the insufficiency of the mechanistic interpretation was grounded on a reductionist interpretation of the senses, i.e. on scientific "prejudice" and "crudity" (GS 373), Nietzsche's "new language" intends to overcome this crude interpretation by offering a subtler one. Thus, it will not be grounded on logical principles, like the principle of contradiction – which, as mentioned, will always be violated by metaphorical transferences. That is a principle in which "the crude, sensualist prejudice reigns", for it implies that "I cannot have two opposite sensations at the same time" (NL 9[97] KSA 12.389–391 = WLN 158). The language that Nietzsche proposes – a language that runs the risk of being incomprehensible[31] because it is impervious to a conceptual and demonstrative logic —, tries to overcome the alleged irreducibility of the senses and express their continuous interaction through what Nietzsche calls "style".

This concept of style aims at underlining the importance of not separating rationality and language from the body and physiology, and it is a means to the end of rehabilitating the affects for philosophy. Most importantly, it points towards a new way of reading and writing philosophy, and it is an essential aspect of Nietzsche's alternative to

---

31 On this question, cf. Stegmaier's paper in this volume.

the argumentative strategies of systematic modern philosophy and the aim of universal validation of propositions[32].

The idea of a personal, non-universal and non-demonstrative – and yet irrefutable – style of communicating and philosophizing makes its first appearance in Nietzsche's early essay, *Philosophy in the Tragic Age of the Greeks*. In this text, Nietzsche shows how the un-demonstrability of philosophical theses constrasts with the demonstrability of scientific doctrines, and he presents the only "completely irrefutable point" (*ein Punkt, der ganz unwiderleglich ist*) of every philosophical thought as a "personal disposition" (*eine persönliche Stimmung*), a "colour" (*Farbe*), a "fragment of personality" (*ein Stück Persönlichkeit*, PTAG Preface, translation modified). These words clarify Nietzsche's critique of the modern ideals of objectivity and disinterested knowledge, the so-called impersonality and neutrality that, according to Nietzsche, are in fact symptoms of instinctual and affective decadence.

Moreover, those words help to make sense of how Nietzsche associates the idea of a new philosophical language with the concept of style. In aphorism 246 of *Beyond Good and Evil*, the demands of style are depicted via the image of a "third ear". This aphorism, like the one that follows, is dedicated to style in writing, showing that this is inseparable from the art of reading[33]. The "third ear" is a "subtle and patient ear", sensitive to the "rhythmically decisive syllables" and to "every *staccato* and every *rubato*" (BGE 246). For one to be able to guess the "meaning of the order of vowels and diphthongs, and how tenderly and richly they can change color and change it again when put next to each other", it is necessary to have "the most subtle artistry" (BGE 246). In aphorism 247, Nietzsche criticizes German style for having very little to do "with tones and with ears" (BGE 247). Contrary to the ancients, who read aloud, Germans "do not read for the ear but only with the eye, keeping their ears in a drawer in the meantime" (BGE 247). Reading aloud means reading "with all

---

32 Cf. GM Preface 4: "what have I to do with refutations?"; TI Germans 6: "[my type] is affirmative and only reluctantly and parenthetically has anything to do with dispute or criticism". Wotling (2008) has shown how the rejection of argument and demonstration is part of Nietzsche's task of revaluating all values (including the value of truth) and creating new values.

33 On these two aphorisms, cf. Renzi (1997).

the swells, inflections, sudden changes in tone, and shifts in tempo" that pleased the Ancient world, a world where "the rules for written style were the same as those for spoken style" (BGE 247). Among the Ancients, writing therefore obeyed physiological criteria, depending both on the ear and larynx and on "the strength, endurance, and power of the ancient lung" (BGE 247).

Nietzsche demands these kinds of criteria for his new philosophical language. Style should be intimately connected to physiology, to the body. In style there should be a "breath", that is, a life that breathes so that it is felt rather than understood conceptually or deduced logically. Thus the notion of style implies a broadening of the concepts of thinking and feeling, an expansion that is presented with great detail in these texts: to see colors in sounds, to make words breathe, to feel the *staccatos and rubatos* of the phrases with the ear, to read with the ears, to hear with the eyes, so that all of this arouses a profusion of thoughts in the reader and infuses his body with the life of the text. In other words, the function of style is to arouse an "aesthetic state" that Nietzsche considers "the source of languages", since that state is the "hearth from where the languages come to being: the language of sounds, as well as the language of gestures and looks. The most complete phenomenon is always the beginning: our capacities (*Vermögen*) as civilized men are reductions of more complete capacities. But still today we hear with our muscles, and we even read with our muscles" (NL 14[119] KSA 13.296–299, my translation). To read a text with the muscles recalls the Dionysian model of communication described in *Twilight of the Idols* (TI Skirmishes 10). What is affected by reading is always the *life* of the reader, i.e. his physiology as a plurality of drives and affects in constant interaction with each other.

On the other hand, as Nietzsche says regarding his own experience as a reader, reading instills life and blood into dead texts and, so to speak, even into the dead themselves[34]. Since, among the ancients, the written style had orality and spoken discourse as its model, it was directed at the listeners' physiology, body, and breath. In other words, the text summoned the participation of the listeners, not allowing them to remain sterilely passive; it made the listeners go through an

---

34 Cf. the "Descent to Hades", AOM 408.

experience of sharing, of being affected by a connecting force and
relating to something sensuous and concrete instead of merely having
access to a semantic content. Thus the very life of the text was able to
expand beyond itself and overcome itself in the listeners.

These considerations regarding style clarify Nietzsche's critique
of language as vulgarization, petrification, and falsification, for
they suggest a positive reverse of this critique[35]. Nietzsche's frequent
pronoucements against language, particularly against written language[36], belong to his philosophical style and, as such, they express
the creativity, singularity, and vitality of a thinker,— even if the non-
universality of this style means risking unintelligibility and misunderstanding. Conceived as an "instinctive activity" (BGE 3), written
philosophical thought exercises an action at a distance and an action
by contagion[37]. Since gesturing, sonority and coloration are always
involved in writing, thoughts are not disconnected from the sensitive
elements of the body, nor from its expressivity and the contagion it
arouses. Just as bodies are affected by other bodies and communicate with other bodies, also written thoughts may engage in reciprocal relations of affection – at a distance and by contagion. This
type of relation between text and listener/reader depends, according
to Nietzsche, on the use of the same words for "the same species
of inner experiences" (BGE 268). Thus, as he writes in *Ecce Homo*:
"Ultimately, nobody can get more out of things – including books –
than they already know. You will not have an ear for something
untill experience has given you some headway into it" (EH Books
1). Nietzsche's demand that we "read with the ears" is connected to
the creation of a new language that "sounds most foreign" (BGE 4)
because it dismisses the dualism between thought and instinct and
between texts and life, thereby creating concepts that are "unheard-
of". Philosophical texts contain "thoughts of the kind that produces thoughts" (WS 214, translation modified), for they are never
disconnected from the body and its affectivity. Only thus can they
express reality as the intensification of itself, i.e. as "self-overcoming"
(*Selbstüberwindung*).

---

35 On Nietzsche's style as the art of using de-individualizing signs in an individualizing
    manner, cf. Stegmaier (2006).
36 Cf., for example, TI Skirmishes 26 and BGE 296.
37 On the latter, cf. Wotling (2008, 421–445).

In doing this, philosophical texts enhance the senses and thoughts of the reader – the thoughts expressed produce more thoughts, in fact they produce more of a reality that never ceases, that is neither static, nor rigid, but rather a dynamic, infinite and creative process. This implies a relation between philosophy and the body that Nietzsche presents as an innovation. Dance is Nietzsche's metaphor for expressing this coincidence between body and thought, the intensification of a movement that, in the "ease of metamorphosis", shows a "much fuller world of expressive affects" (TI Skirmishes 10). If there is nothing that a philosopher would love more to be than a dancer, if dance is the philosopher's ideal, as Nietzsche says in aphorism 381 of *The Gay Science*, this requires the learning of "a technique", for "thinking wants to be learned like dancing, as a *type* of dancing" (TI Germans 7): "A *noble education* has to include *dancing* in every form, being able to dance with your feet, with concepts, with words; do I still have to say that you need to be able to do it with a pen too – that you need to learn to write?" (TI Germans 7). Since *The Birth of Tragedy*, Nietzsche associates dance to a Dionysian state and an "epidemic" phenomenon (BT 8). As a form of philosophical communication dance should have this same kind of effect. The new philosophical language is the communication of a Dionysian state that gives rise to metamorphoses. The philosopher communicates creative states that incite creation and linguistic expression, and to understand what is thus expressed requires, so to speak, more of a physiological affinity than just a purely intellectual ability. This means that the body and its movement are the "law" of style, but it also means that style is like Procrustes's bed: not all bodies fit to the same style and not all bodies move in the same way, for style has always something of a personal and, as mentioned, "irrefutable" colour. At least this is how Nietzsche describes his "art of style" in *Ecce Homo*:

> To *communicate* a state, an inward tension of pathos, with signs, including the tempo of these signs – that is the meaning of every style; (…) Every style that really communicates an inner state is *good*, every style that is not wrong about the signs, about the tempo of the signs, about *gestures* – all laws concerning periods involve the art of gestures. (…) Always supposing that there are ears – that there are people capable and worthy of a similar pathos, that there people you *can* communicate with" (EH Books 4).

The metaphorical images of ear and of music indicate that style has to be able to say what no word "in itself" can say – what no word isolated from a specific life, i.e. from the tonality, rhythm, voice and gestures of a body, can say. Style must be able to neutralize the limitations of common, herd language and communicate what conceptual abstractions prevent from being communicated.

In fact, thought is communicated by variations in rhythm, gesture, sound, no less than through concepts: "One should listen to how a spirit sounds when it speaks: every spirit has its own sound and loves its own sound" (GM III 8). We should read the philosophers with ears and eyes, and thus it is clear that the musical model of Nietzsche's writings is not at all "absolute music", but rather a sonority intertwined with thoughts and words. This is why reading his texts requires a "venerable art", a philology that "teaches to read well, that is to say, to read slowly, deeply, looking cautiously before and aft, with reservations, with doors left open, with delicate eyes and fingers" (D Preface 5). This way of reading makes one discover that there is life in words, that a text infused with style is anything but a corpse – that style reveals a sensible and affective reality to which the readers should relate[38].

Accordingly, the connection between affect and thought can also be seen in written language, namely as an expression of mobility, an instinctive expression that reveals a concrete life, a personality that directs itself to others, that affects others through its words. This type of writing awaits dialogue, it is not closed within itself, and gives birth to the "dancing star" mentioned by Zarathustra (ZA Prologue 5), – it gives birth to luminous images that slide and are not fixed, images where the tension between metaphorization and conceptualization creates a movement that can be described as a *pathos*, as a will to power, an affect that "can only act on something of the same nature" (NL 40[37] KSA 11.646f, my translation)[39]. If, as Nietzsche claims,

---

38 Cf. NL 1[45] KSA 10.22, my translation: "The first thing that is necessary is *life*: style *should live.*/Style should always suit *you* in relation to a definite person to whom you want to communicate what you are./(...) Style should prove that one *believes* in one's thoughts, and that one does not simply think these thoughts, but feels them".

39 On Nietzsche's notion of *pathos* and its relation to the notion of will to power, cf. Wotling's paper in this volume.

"there is absolutely nothing impersonal" in philosophers (BGE 6), and if what they communicate through their style always expresses a "this is I" (BGE 231, Kaufmann's translation), philosophy will have to combat the false aspiration to desinterested objectivity and intellectual purity. It will have to recover the "polyphony" that Nietzsche mentioned in the essay on *Philosophy in the Tragic Age of the Greeks*, for philosophy lives of its relentless intensification, of the way philosophers act upon each other, thereby creating new thoughts, new movements. Just as music moves its listeners, philosophical writings should make us "sing their melodies":

> "Just as the Italians appropriate a piece of music by involving it in their passion — and this music awaits for being interpreted in such a personal fashion, and receives more from this than from all art of harmony — in the same way I read the writings of thinkers and begin to sing their melodies: I know that behind all those cold words, a desiring soul is moving, I hear it singing, because my own soul sings when it is moved" (NL 7[18] KSA 9.320, my translation).

Bibliography

Abel, Günter (2001), "Bewusstsein- Sprache- Natur: Nietzsches Philosophie des Geistes", in: *Nietzsche-Studien* 30 (2001), 1–43.

Aristotle (1995), *Poetics*, transl. by Stephen Halliwell, Harvard (Harvard University Press).

Babich, Babette (2006), *Words in blood, like flowers. Philosophy and Poetry, Music and Eros in Hölderlin, Nietzsche and Heidegger*, Albany (State University of New York Press).

Barbera, Sandro (1994), "Ein Sinn und unzählige Hieroglyphen. Einige Motive von Nietzsches Auseinandersetzung mit Schopenhauer in der Basler Zeit", in: Borsche, T./Gerratana, F./Venturelli, A. (ed.), *"Centauren-Geburten". Wissenschaft, Kunst und Philosophie beim jungen Nietzsche*, Berlin/New York (Walter de Gruyter), 217–233.

Behler, Ernst (1994), "Die Sprachtheorie des frühen Nietzsche", in: Borsche, T./ Gerratana, F./ Venturelli, A. (ed.), *"Centauren-Geburten". Wissenschaft, Kunst und Philosophie beim jungen Nietzsche*, Berlin/ New York (Walter de Gruyter), 99–111.

Blondel, Éric (2006), *Nietzsche, le corps et la culture. La philosophie comme généalogie philologique*, Paris (L'Harmattan).

Buddensieg, Tilmann (2006), *L'Italia di Nietzsche*, traduzione di Laura Novati, Milano (Libri Scheiwiller).

Dahlhaus, Carl (1994), *Die Idee der Absoluten Musik*, Kassel (Bärenreiter Verlag).

David, Pascal (2002), "Hören und lieben lernen – Nietzsche und das Wesen der Musik", in: Seubert, H. (ed.), *Natur und Kunst in Nietzsches Denken*, Köln (Böhlau Verlag GmbH & Cie), 137–151.

Dufour, Éric (2005), *L'esthétique musicale de Nietzsche*, Villeneuve d'Ascq (Presses Universitaires du Septentrion).

Figal, Günter (2001), *Nietzsche. Eine philosophische Einführung*, Stuttgart (Reclam).

Kofman, Sarah (1972), *Nietzsche et la métaphore*, Payot (Paris).

Lacoue-Labarthe, Philippe (1979), *Le sujet de la philosophie. Typographies I*, Paris (Aubier-Flammarion).

Lupo, Luca (2006), *Le colombe dello scettico. Riflessioni sulla coscienza negli anni 1880–1888*, Pisa (Edizioni ETS).

Müller-Lauter, Wolfgang (1999), *Nietzsche. His Philosophy of Contradictions and the Contradictions of His Philosophy*, Urbana and Chicago (Illinois Press).

Otto, Detlef (1994), "Die Version der Metapher zwischen Musik und Begriff", in: Borsche, T./Gerratana, F./Venturelli, A. (ed.), *"Centauren-Geburten". Wissenschaft, Kunst und Philosophie beim jungen Nietzsche*, Berlin/New York (Walter de Gruyter), 169–190.

Otto, Detlef (1998), "(Kon-)Figurationen der Philosophie. Eine metaphorologische Lektüre von Nietzsches Darstellungen der vorplatonischen Philosophen", in: *Nietzsche-Studien* 27 (1998), 119–152.

Renzi, Luca (1997), "Das Ohr-Motiv als Metapher des Stils und der «Zugänglichkeit». Eine Lektüre der Aphorismen 246 und 247 von Nietzsches «Jenseits von Gut und Böse»", in: *Nietzsche-Studien* 26 (1997), 331–349.

Ridley, Aaron (2004), *The philosophy of music. Theme and Variations*, Edinburgh (Edinburgh University Press).

Schacht, Richard (1985), *Nietzsche*, London/Boston/Melbourne/Henley (Routledge & Kegan Paul).

Schacht, Richard (1996), "Nietzsche's kind of philosophy", in: Magnus, B./Higgins, K. M. (ed.), *The Cambridge Companion to Nietzsche*, Cambridge/New York (Cambridge University Press), 151–179.

Stegmaier, Werner (2006), "Nietzsche's doctrines, Nietzsche's signs", in: *Journal of Nietzsche Studies* 31, 20–41.

Stegmaier, Werner (2005), "Nietzsches Philosophie der Kunst und seine Kunst der Philosophie. Zur aktuellen Forschung und Forschungsmethodik", in: *Nietzsche-Studien* 34 (2005), 348–374.

Stegmaier, Werner (2004), "'Philosophischer Idealismus' und die 'Musik des Lebens': zu Nietzsches Umgang mit Paradoxien. Eine kontextuelle Interpretation des Aphorismus Nr. 372 der Fröhlichen Wissenschaft", in: *Nietzsche-Studien* 33 (2004), 90–128.

Venturelli, Aldo (2003), *Kunst, Wissenschaft und Geschichte bei Nietzsche. Quellenkritische Untersuchungen*, transl. from Italian by Leonie Schröder, editorial collaboration of Silke Richter, Berlin/New York (Walter de Gruyter).

Wotling, Patrick (2008), "La culture comme problème. La redetermination nietzschéenne du questionement philosophique", in: *Nietzsche-Studien* 37 (2008), 1–50.

Wotling, Patrick (2008), *La philosophie de l'esprit libre. Introduction à Nietzsche*, Paris (Flammarion).

Wotling, Patrick (1995), *Nietzsche et le problème de la civilisation*, Paris (PUF).

II. Dissolving an Opposition

What Language Do Drives Speak?

Patrick Wotling

The purpose of this study will be to show the radical movement that Nietzsche's reflection on drives imposes on our approach to language. The following remarks intend to pursue and reveal the logic that takes the author of *Thus spoke Zarathustra* to acknowledge the existence of an elemental or originary mode of communication underlying all interpretative acts, whichever the content of the interpretation may be. In comparison to this originary mode of communication, ordinary language (understood merely as the vehicle of meaning through words) always appears as being a derived form, and never the original or the presupposed mode of communication.

In order to locate the problem, and bearing in mind the fact that Nietzsche's critique of language is probably as well known as his critique of morals, we shall begin by recalling only certain crucial elements. To be brief, we would like to emphasize that Nietzsche's criticism is a result of a twofold line of approach.

The first approach is based on the poverty of language. This is a thesis that Nietzsche defends particularly early, from the very first years of his philosophical activity and which is especially tangible in his thoughts on the nature of music. "Word and music in opera. The words are intended to interpret the music for us, but the music expresses the soul of the action. *Words are of course the most deficient of all signs*" (NL 2[11] KSA 7.48 = WEN 15, our italics). This topic plays an important role within his reflections on music and tragedy, where Nietzsche questions the effects of words on the one side, and of music on the other. In this sense, Nietzsche insists on the inaptitude of language to express and more precisely to share the uniqueness of feelings: "Language explains only through concepts, so that the shared sensation is created through the medium of thought. This sets a limit for it" (NL 2[10] KSA 7.47 = WEN 14). And some lines later he specifies: "The largest amount of feeling does not express itself through words. And the word itself barely hints: it is the surface of the choppy sea, while the storm rages in the depths. This is the limit of spoken drama. The inability to represent things that exist side by side" (NL 2[10] KSA 7.47 = WEN 14–15).

Nietzsche's second angle of approach concerns the lack of neutrality in language which, as he shows, is always steered by values – by unconscious, and hence, unperceived choices – that determine, most notably, the grammatical structures through which meaning is conveyed. To put an example, we will refer to a central passage from *Twilight of the Idols*; it is the passage where Nietzsche shows how dualism also affects grammar, suggesting the idea that reality is torn between the acting subjects on the one hand, and the actions caused by them on the other:

> Language began at a time when psychology was in its most rudimentary form: we enter into a crudely fetishistic mindset when we call into consciousness the basic presuppositions of the metaphysics of language – in the vernacular: the presuppositions of *reason*. It sees doers and deeds all over: it believes that will has causal efficacy: it believes in the 'I', in the I as being, in the I as substance, and it *projects* this belief in the I-substance onto all things – this is how it *creates* the concept of 'thing' in the first place... Being is imagined into everything – *pushed under everything* – as a cause; the concept of 'being' is only derived from the concept of 'I'... In the beginning there was the great disaster of an error, the belief that the will is a thing with *causal efficacy*, – that will is a *faculty*... These days we know that it is just a word (TI Errors 5).

On the one hand, as this text suggests, language constantly and somehow misleadingly insinuates the existence of imaginary things, which do not correspond to anything in reality (such as the existence of an entity called "will", or the existence of "subjects" considered as autonomous beings). But, on the other hand, Nietzsche equally stresses the limitations of the expressive possibilities of language. In opposition to what could be a common assumption: language cannot express everything. Moreover, in our Platonic-inspired culture, ordinary language is utterly incapable of translating certain interpretations, especially those that conflict with the existence of (ideal) values preceding grammatical structures. This is why an interpretation of reality in terms of pure processuality, i.e. an interpretation which rejects any idea of a permanent "being", such as the interpretation conveyed by the thought of a will to power is inexpressible within the ordinary structures of natural language.

It is in this context that we understand Nietzsche's critique of language, a critique which clearly exceeds the traditional reproach philosophers, ever since Plato's *Cratylus*, have made against language and which tends to focus on the gap between language and things. In other words: the traditional critique of language as formulated by former philosophers is in this sense superficial, for it does not take into consideration that the mere notion of a "thing" is already a prejudice derived or inherited from language.

Yet, however brilliant and original this critical perspective may be, it does by no means exhaust Nietzsche's reflection on language. On the contrary, there still remains an essential point that must be considered and which concerns the significant extension that the *notion* of language acquires throughout Nietzsche's thought: "There are many more languages than one might think: and man unintentionally unveils himself more than he would like. What doesn't speak!"[1]. *Was redet nicht* ! For Nietzsche, reality is in fact subsumed by the drives' interpretative activity. In this sense, the real is language. Nietzsche's rigorous analysis takes him to subsume language into the sphere of the drives, or to be more precise, to reduce language to a certain manifestation derived from the drives. We find one of the sharpest expressions for this idea, an idea which Nietzsche very often reiterates, in a posthumous text from the time period of his *Daybreak*: "Words are like a keyboard of drives, and thoughts (in words) are the chords that are played"[2]. Words, in as much as they are expression of thoughts, are the more or less distant result of a combinatory of particular instincts attempting to satisfy their own needs. Through his metaphor drawn from music, Nietzsche also seems to be suggesting that in actual fact language, or rather the use of language follows an artistic and creative logic, much more than a theoretical one. A thought we will come back to later on.

Language is thus always already figurative: that is to say that the code of signification is encrypted. This is why, from this perspective, language is always a *symptom* and never the transparent expression of a meaning. And this is precisely what persistently forces the

---

1 NL 7[62] KSA 10.262: "Es giebt viel mehr Sprachen als man denkt: und der Mensch verräth sich viel öfter als er wünscht. Was redet nicht!" [*Editors' translation*].

2 NL 6[264] KSA 9.266: "Die Worte sind gleichsam eine Claviatur der Triebe, und Gedanken (in Worten) sind Akkorde darauf" [*Editors' translation*].

philosopher to look for the profound and hidden meaning of each and every one of the texts he reads and of each and every one of the formulations he hears.

All discourse, such as all human activity, is always the encoded and deformed expression of a much more fundamental discourse uttered by the constituent instincts of the individual or of the type of man who speaks. To be sure, Nietzsche will always consider moralities as if they were languages, the particularity of which would be: never to express themselves in a truthful manner. "In short, moralities are also merely a *sign language of the affects*" (BGE 187, Kaufmann's translation). This idea is clearly present in the following posthumous passage, where Nietzsche advances a decoding hypothesis which he develops in line with the analysis of the instincts, as an expression of practical needs of a particular type of life: "My attempt to understand moral judgments as symptoms and sign languages in which appear processes of physiological thriving or failure as well as consciousness of the conditions of preservation and growth: as a way of interpreting that has the same value as astrology – prejudices prompted by the whispers of instincts (of races, communities, of different phases such as youth, withering, etc.)

Applied to the specific Christian-European morality: our moral judgments are signs of decay, of a disbelief in *life*, a preparation for pessimism" (NL 2[165] KSA 12.149 = WLN 93–94).

To put an example, the discourse proper to Christian ascetic morality is issued by the dominant instincts of the Christian type of man as a virulent protest and even a condemnation of real life and its conditions, which he (or she) perceives as unfair and intrinsically immoral.

All these elements are certainly well known, and we have only mentioned them briefly in order to sketch out the general lines and method followed by Nietzsche. And yet Nietzsche's reflection on language still operates from a third perspective or angle of investigation; a perspective which has hardly been taken into consideration until now by Nietzsche scholars and which should be investigated, namely the one which refers to the mysterious and intricate, but absolutely determinant question about the communication among the drives. If everything which is produced, the whole of reality, is to be described as a permanent confrontation among the drives struggling for an intensification of the feeling of power; and if this struggle takes place in the form of a regrouping and a coalition of the drives, then how is the "agreement", *Verständigung* (a word which Nietzsche uses quite often), how can the agreement or understanding among the drives be possible? How is it carried out? For we must not forget that the activity of the drives always presupposes multiplicity. Nietzsche stresses the fact that the basis of all interpretation is the collaboration of the drives; or what he calls a "supremacy formation" (*Herrschaftsgebilde*). As we can read in a text from 1885–1886:

> Everything which enters consciousness is the last link in a chain, a closure. It is just an illusion that one thought is the immediate cause of another thought. The events which are actually connected are played out below our consciousness: the series and sequences of feelings, thoughts, etc., that appear are symptoms of what actually happens! – Below every thought lies an affect. *Every thought*, every feeling, every will is *not* born of one particular drive but is a *total state*, a whole surface of the whole consciousness, and results from how the power of *all* the drives that constitute us is fixed at that moment – thus, the power of the drive that dominates just now as well as of the drives obeying or resisting. The next thought is a sign of how the total power situation has now shifted again (NL 1[61] KSA 12.26 = WLN 60).

The problem concerning the specific nature of the language of the drives draws Nietzsche's attention especially during the period between 1884 and 1886. We can see this in a large number of posthumous texts, but also and most strikingly in *Beyond Good and Evil*, which provides material of extreme value for this matter. In what follows, we will refer mostly to these texts in order to approach and study the way in which Nietzsche poses the problem and seeks for a solution.

As we have already suggested, this problem, which appears to be essentially a technical problem, is of a great complexity. Indeed, at first glance, it seems that Nietzsche's analysis is confronted here with a principial difficulty: the explication of the nature of language (i.e. of interpretations as results of the drives' activity) seems to presuppose from the very start the existence of language (which would enable the drives to communicate). One could be tempted to think that ultimately everything is always already language; from the most elementary level, the level of instincts, drives and affections, to the most derivative level, formed by the results of the drives' activity. In this case we would be dealing with a sort of monism or a universal substantialism of language, which would be something like the secret principle underlying Nietzsche's philosophy. Indeed, one could interpret the sentence commented above "*Was redet nicht!*" in this particular way.

But this is precisely not the case: Nietzsche does not claim in such an undifferentiated manner that everything is language. On the contrary, Nietzsche's analysis shows that there is a fundamental difference between interpretative modes of expression and signification on the one side, and the nature of communication by which the drives attempt to establish a basis which will then enable the construction of an interpretation of reality or a part of reality, on the other. Nietzsche is not detecting language – with all its structures, its creative suggestions and deficiencies – in the profound level of the drives; his gesture consists much more in identifying the specific nature of the communication that takes place among the drives, in order to understand the type of displacement that takes place as we move on to the level of words, i.e. of language in its strictest sense. This is the logic we intend to pursue in the following pages.

We shall now resume our examination taking the idea of a multiplicity of drives, underlying all situations, as our starting point, for this seems to be Nietzsche's most fundamental assumption. The concert between multiple forces is only possible through a special form of collaboration and communication; but, of what nature is this communication? Nietzsche's first step towards finding a solution to this difficult problem consists in the exclusion of the false explanation based on psychological causality. If thoughts are the result of the drives, this does not necessarily mean that they should be considered to emerge from causal processes. Thoughts do not cause other thoughts, and furthermore, the way in which thoughts are engendered from the drives cannot be explained in terms of causality. Nietzsche maintains this position following two lines of argumentation: first, he shows the limits of introspective analysis and the impossibility of identifying with certainty any process of causal production; but in addition to this and as a result of his investigation of the nature of causality, he shows, in a more radical manner, that the mere idea of causality is not the result of an objective appreciation, but the result of an interpretation, an interpretation derived from a particular (and questionable) comprehension of the will.

We find the first line of argumentation in many posthumous texts: "Distrust of introspection. That a thought is the cause of a thought cannot be established. On the table of our consciousness there appears a succession of thoughts, as if one thought were the cause of the next. But in fact we don't see the struggle going on under the table" (NL 2[103] KSA 12.112 = WLN 78, modified). On a note from 1888 he adds: "We deny there to be a real causality among thoughts, such as logic believes there to be"[3].

To depicture Nietzsche's second argumentation, we will quote another posthumous fragment from 1885: "for we have come to build up the illusion of cause and effect following only the model of our own will considered as cause"[4]. We could also refer to *Twilight of the Idols*, where Nietzsche explores the logic inherent to this false interpretation of the will, and other posthumous texts (e.g. NL 4[8] KSA 12.181).

The relation between the drives is, thus, from a totally different type. And, as we have already advanced above, the term Nietzsche often uses to refer to this relation is "agreement". But what does Nietzsche mean to say by "agreement"? And, most importantly, in which way does this notion enable him to avoid the paradoxes attached to the idea of a causal relation? In accepting the idea of a concert or accordance, is he not yielding to an idyllic and optimistic vision of the regulation of the drives?

In order to analyze this difficult question following Nietzsche's own approach, it is important to take the body as a point of reference. As we can see in many texts, especially from the posthumous fragments, for Nietzsche, the body is constituted by an ensemble of drives organized and structured into a hierarchy, each ensemble being hence characteristic to a particular form of living being. And it is not by chance that in many of these texts Nietzsche upholds the necessity of referring to the body to solve these issues. In effect, this may be one of the most important aspects of Nietzsche's thought and must be taken into consideration, if we want to grasp the importance and originality

---

3   NL 15[13] KSA 13.414: "wir leugnen, daß zwischen den Gedanken eine reale Causalität besteht wie sie die Logik glaubt". [*Editors' translation*].

4   NL 40[37] KSA 11.647: "denn wir haben uns die Vorstellung von Ursache und Wirkung nur nach dem Vorbilde unseres Willens als Ursache gebildet!". [*Editors' translation*].

of his philosophy in all its richness and profundity. In this respect
we would like to refer to the work undertaken by Céline Denat,
certainly the best specialist on this matter. In her forthcomming study
*Histoire et interprétation du corps dans la philosophie de Nietzsche.
La recherche d'un « fil conducteur » du texte nietzschéen*, she shows
the interpretative advantage of taking the body as the guiding thread
of Nietzsche's texts, revealing a new comprehension of the inner
organization and structure of his thought.

Let us thus start from the body. We will consider fragment NL 37[4]
(KSA 11.576 = WLN 30–31), which presents both determinations
mentioned above. In his analysis of the body – which is now our guiding thread –, Nietzsche insistently stresses the "prodigious alliance of
living beings", "the magnificent binding together of the most diverse
life, the ordering and arrangement of the higher and lower activities",
"such a prodigious synthesis of living beings and intellects as is called
'man'", a "subtle system of connections and mediations" such as the
corporal regulations, or the "lightning-fast communication between all
these higher and lower beings", as well as "the cooperation" or "interaction" of all the elements which constitute us, or as Nietzsche puts
it (with an expression that will become crucial for our understanding
of the body): "those smallest living beings which constitute our body
(more correctly: for whose interaction the thing we call 'body' is the
best simile —)" (NL 37[4] KSA 11.576 = WLN 30–31). Indeed one
cannot avoid reading these lines with astonishment: quite surprisingly
and in an almost tedious way, Nietzsche incessantly stresses the idea
of an internal cooperation underlying the structure and/or functioning
of the body. And yet Nietzsche's last remarks are even more striking,
when he concludes that "this, however, is a problem of morality, not
of mechanics!" (NL 37[4] KSA 11.576 = WLN 31).

If we were to take this certainly surprising sentence literally, we
would have to conclude that (at least in its most fundamental level)
language must be analyzed from a moral perspective and must be
understood as a result of a process of moral nature. In this sense,
Nietzsche's enthusiasm in these texts from 1885 leaves us confronted
with a new difficulty. There is certainly not any form of causality
that could be mechanically applied as an external regulation to the
universe of the drives; particularly because the elements combin-
ing and communicating here are lively – and not fixed unities,
perpetually identical to themselves and which could be added, in-

serted or combined as inert things. In other words, the second part of the sentence does not pose any special difficulty: Nietzsche is merely stating that communication among the drives is not a problem that can be understood mechanically. Conversely, though, the preceding affirmation is quite obscure. Indeed, what does he mean when he says that it is a problem of *morality* – especially given his constant effort to show that moralities are nothing but particular interpretations, derived from the drives' activity and which cannot be seen as being founders of drives? Thus is the mysterious nature of the problem which certainly requires the comprehension of the nature of the language used by the drives.

In order to grasp the meaning of this posthumous text, we need to bear in mind two aspects: firstly we need to examine the exact meaning in which Nietzsche uses the word "morality", and then we need to consider the possibility given to us, philosophers, of investigating the secret functioning of the body. Where will we be able to observe the drives' activity? We must not forget that we are dealing with the so called posthumous texts which were preparatory for Nietzsche's *Beyond Good and Evil*. Our hypothesis is therefore the following: it is very probable that Nietzsche is operating with the meaning that he himself gives to "morality" in *Beyond Good and Evil*. In the conclusion to aphorism 19 of this text Nietzsche writes: "Hence a philosopher should claim the right to include willing as such within the sphere of morals – morals being understood as the doctrine of the relations of supremacy under which the phenomenon of 'life' comes to be" (BGE 19, Kaufmann's translation).

With this original definition, Nietzsche is defending both a radical and most importantly, positive characterization of morality which might surprise the reader more or less used to him adopting a much more critical approach. What Nietzsche is claiming here is the fact that life is not an aim in itself (in fact Nietzsche also defines life as a particular form of the will to power), but the result of a certain form of regulation of a moral nature. And what is more important: Nietzsche specifies that this form of regulation obeys or follows *relations of power* or *"supremacy"* (*Herrschafts-Verhältnisse*). In other words, the conclusion to aphorism 19 from *Beyond Good and Evil* seems to maintain that life takes place as soon as a certain form of relations of supremacy is established among the drives. But, what does this have to do with the analysis of the type of language characteristic of the drives?

Bearing this in mind, we now need to consider the second aspect we alluded to before: what kind of material, what kind of evidence do we dispose of in order to analyze the functioning and communication between the drives? Following Nietzsche's analyses from these years we can infer that the main focus of study is constituted by all the phenomena falling in what we ordinarily call the category of the "will". During these years Nietzsche dedicates a considerable number of texts to the analysis of the will, or to be more precise: of the "will" – the quotation marks hinting the inaccuracy or illegitimacy of ordinary interpretations, especially those which believe it having an atomic character. The culmination of these analyses, the trace of which is still appreciable in the posthumous texts, is precisely aphorism 19 of *Beyond Good and Evil*.

If we recall Nietzsche's general line of argumentation: the will, such as it is understood both from an ordinary point of view and within the philosophical tradition, that is, the will understood as the subject's faculty or the subject's power of acting (or of refraining from acting), such a will does not exist. *But*, even if this will, understood as the power of starting or launching an action is not but a pipe dream, resulting from a lack of rigor and honesty among philosophers, what we usually refer to by using this misleading word nevertheless involves a whole ensemble of processes which are quite real. What Nietzsche is trying to do in aphorism 19 of *Beyond Good and Evil* is precisely to identify these processes and the relations that arise among them. The "will" provides a favorable case, i.e. a case where the agreement among the drives is happily or efficiently accomplished, in the sense that a result – an action – has actually taken place; or in other words, a case where the drives do not neutralize themselves, as is sometimes the case. And in this precise case, we can certainly say that communication has taken place. The question is, thus, whether we can analyze this phenomenon and identify the type of language which enables the drives to communicate with one another enabling them to act in concert. To put it metaphorically: is it possible to analyse the type of language "spoken" by the drives?

We shall now consider the essential aspects that Nietzsche brings into play in the numerous texts where he analyses the nature of the drives. In fact, Nietzsche persistently recurs to certain descriptions or characterizations:

Firstly: the drives are all related to one another. This is indeed an aspect which Nietzsche strongly emphasizes and which might seem surprising at first sight; but this "common nature" should be understood as the condition of possibility for an exchange and perchance an agreement among drives. In a posthumous text from 1885 he writes: "That man is a multiplicity of forces which stand in an order of rank, so that there are those which command, but what commands, too, must provide for those which obey everything they need to preserve themselves, and is thus itself *conditioned* by their existence. *All these living beings must be related in kind, otherwise they could not serve and obey one another like this*" (NL 34[123] KSA 11.461 = WLN 8, our italics). In another text from the same period he notes: "Starting point the *body* and physiology: why? – What we gain is the right idea of the nature of our subject-unity – namely as rulers at the head of a commonwealth. (...) What's most important, however: that we understand the ruler and his subjects as being *of the same kind, all feeling, thinking, willing*" (NL 40[21] KSA 11.638 = WLN 43–44, our italics at the end). In a later text, Nietzsche insists on the same point, stressing decisive importance of this condition: "What is the nature of the coercion that a stronger soul exerts upon a weaker one? – And it would be possible that what seemed to be 'disobedience' to the higher soul actually arose from a failure to understand its will, e.g., a rock cannot be commanded. But – the differentiation of degree and rank must be gradual: *only* the closest relatives can understand each other, and consequently it's here that there can be obedience" (NL 2[69] KSA 12.92 = WLN 72). And, finally, we find the same claim in one of the most important aphorisms of Nietzsche's work, namely aphorism 36 of *Beyond Good and Evil*, where he justifies the hypothesis of the will to power as an interpretation of reality as a whole: "'will', of course, can affect only 'will' – and not 'matter' (not 'nerves,' for example)" (BGE 36, Kaufmann's translation). It is important to note that all these texts, which underline the relation between all the constitutive elements of the body, systematically take these relations as relations of obedience and command; something that now might still seem mysterious.

Is it now possible to say anything else about the nature of the relation between the drives? In this case, it is once again in *Beyond Good and Evil* where we find a decisive clue. Throughout aphorism 19, after having showed the way in which will-processes involve an ensemble of drives

and affects, just before reaching his conclusion, Nietzsche resumes his
analysis in the following way: "the person exercising volition adds the
feelings of delight of his successful executive instruments, the useful
'under-wills' or under-souls – indeed, our body is but a social structure
composed of many souls —" (BGE 19, Kaufmann's translation).
What is most striking, as we can see, is how Nietzsche, instead of
referring to the drives to talk about the body, now resorts to the word
"souls". The body, as an organized ensemble of drives, has become
a "social structure composed of many souls". But how should we
understand the meaning of this substitution? And, most importantly,
can this help us to address the question about the communication
among the drives? The answer to this is that it does, and in order to
understand how, we must recall what Nietzsche had said in aphorism
12 of *Beyond Good and Evil*. Here, what seemed to be an incidental
suggestion, now finds all its significance. This aphorism offers an
analysis of the notion of soul. It shows us what we must reject from
the classical concept of soul: namely its metaphysical substantiality,
its atomism (the obsessive necessity of unity); but Nietzsche also notes
that there is something which is still possible to hold on to: the idea of
a perceptive apparatus, but an elementary, infra-conscious apparatus.
This special characteristic is what Nietzsche will later transfer to the
drives and which justifies Nietzsche's metaphorical reference to the
drives as "souls" or "small souls".

A third element must now be noticed: Nietzsche's insistence on the
affective or emotional dimension of this perception – and hence his
insistence on the affective dimension of the drives as such —, which,
as we shall see, constitutes the basis for communication among the
drives. This is indeed the characteristic that Nietzsche means to
underline when he talks about the "affect", a term he uses as synonym
for "drive" or "instinct". He also refers to "pathos" in this same
sense, for instance in a very important fragment from 1888, where he
defines the will to power as pathos:

> "*Phenomenal*, then, is this: mixing in the concept of number, the
> concept of subject, the concept of motion: we still have our *eyes*, our
> *psychology* in the world.
>   If we eliminate these ingredients, what remains are not things
> but dynamic quanta in a relationship of tension with all other
> dynamic quanta, whose essence consists in their relation to all other
> quanta, in their 'effects' on these – the will to power not a being, not

a becoming, but a *pathos*, is the most elementary fact, and becoming, effecting, is only a result of this..." (NL 14[79] KSA 13.259 = WLN 247).

The notion of pathos, hence, designates the drives' capacity to perceive or to be affected by other drives. And in this way Nietzsche is suggesting that through this affective dimension a new possibility is opened up for the drives to relate and communicate. In effect, the presence of communication implies that the drives are indeed sensitive to one another. The conception of the will to power as a pathos makes this possible – given that the drives are nothing else than particular wills to power.

The problem now concerns the true content of this affection. To solve this, we have to come back to aphorism 19 of *Beyond Good and Evil*. Here Nietzsche introduces a specific model of intelligibility: namely the psychology of command. In aphorism 19, in effect, a particular affect is identified as playing a central role in the complex process which we globally experience or feel as "will"; namely the affect of command. With the notion of an *affect of command*, Nietzsche designates the type of affectivity attached to the issuing of an order, that is to say, the commander's immense feeling of hierarchic superiority, power and authority, as well as the conviction that s/he will be obeyed and the certitude of exerting an invincible constraint over the one to whom the order is addressed. Two aspects are decisive: on the one hand, the communication of order and obedience is a particular form of communication, a particular mode of language; on the other, there is indeed a very particular affectivity following this mode of communication which consequently does not remain a neutral one. To command is a language. And, in order to comprehend the logic of Nietzsche's analysis, it is absolutely crucial to understand the implications of this point: the command as language is not reducible to the linguistic articulation of the order. Furthermore, in this context it is central to distinguish command and order, that is, to distinguish, such as Nietzsche does, between the words through which the injunction is transmitted, by means of the use of ordinary language, and the deep process which is effectively taking place within the act of commanding. To understand this, we must refer to a particular indication given in a passage from a posthumous text of 1885:

> Will – a command: but insofar as there is an unconscious act
> underlying this conscious act, we also need to think only of the
> former as being effective. But what about the case of a command to
> one that obeys? The commanding word does *not* work as a word,
> *not* as sound, but as that which hides beneath the sound: and by
> virtue of this action something will be transmitted. But to reduce
> sound to 'vibrations' is only the expression of the same phenomenon
> but for another *sense* – it is not an 'explanation'. Behind the 'visible'
> vibration hides, once again, the real event[5].

"The real event", the essential process, hides beneath the "'visible'
vibration": but what is this "real event"? Now is when the model of
intelligibility introduced by Nietzsche is most tangible: the psychology of command; which presupposes that every drive communicates
with the other drives on the basis of an (interpretative) perception of
the distribution of power relations. In this way, the problem we indicated above – what is the true content of the affection sensed by the
drives? —, is answered by Nietzsche as follows: the relative degrees
of power of the other drives; all this in a certain context, and never
in and for itself, which would make no sense at all. But this assessment presupposes an evaluation – an evaluation which consists in
the organization of the life of the body, and establishes the role of
its different elements by means of a division of work that creates a
chain of transmission and execution of orders emanating from the
dominant group.

This, in its turn, poses a new question: how do the drives come
to evaluate these relative degrees of power? Nietzsche points out
something absolutely vital: the drives develop their interpretative
perceptions as they assess their capacity to control this or that other
drive and to incorporate it in their action. That is, in their capacity to
turn the other drives into "functions", in Nietzsche's technical sense

---

5   NL 25[389] KSA 11.113f: "Wille – ein Befehlen: insofern aber diesem bewußten
    Akte ein unbewußter zu Grunde liegt, brauchen wir uns auch nur diesen wirksam
    zu denken. Aber bei einem Befehl an einen Gehorchenden? Das Wort des Befehls
    wirkt *nicht* als Wort, *nicht* als Laut, sondern als das, was sich verbirgt hinter
    dem Laut: und vermöge dieser Aktion wird etwas fortgeleitet. Aber die Reduktion
    der Laute auf 'Schwingungen' ist doch nur der Ausdruck desselben Phänomens
    für einen anderen *Sinn* – keine 'Erklärung'. Hinter der 'sichtbaren' Schwingung
    verbirgt sich wieder der eigentliche Vorgang". [*Editors' translation*].

of the term. We find this idea also in a posthumous fragment from the period of *Beyond Good and Evil*:

> "— that it is the will to power which guides the inorganic world as well, or rather, that there *is* no inorganic world. 'Action at a distance' cannot be eliminated: *something draws something else closer, something feels drawn*. This is the fundamental fact (…).
>
> — that for this will to power to express itself, it must perceive those things which it draws closer; that it *feels* the approach of something it can assimilate" (NL 34[247] KSA 11.503 = WLN 15).

Choosing the term "feel", Nietzsche is without any doubt making reference to pathos as being equal to the will to power; and using the notion of "assimilation", he refers to the capacity of a force to control a rival force by making the latter work for the profit of the former. This is precisely what he designates with the term "function", such as he uses the term in *The Gay Science* (see, for instance, GS 11, 110 and 113, 116, 118, 119 in particular). In relation to this analysis, the crucial point is to understand that there is never an order in itself or an absolute emission of a command indifferent to the surrounding environment. To command is always a relative, conditioned action, which presupposes a preliminary consideration of the surrounding forces. As we can see in aphorism 19 of *Beyond Good and Evil*, a drive or a group of drives does not issue a command unless it can expect with a very high degree of certitude to be obeyed, that is, if it perceives its force in relation to the others as being extremely favorable. The outcome of these analyses is that the language of the drives is fundamentally fixation of superior and inferior functions within the body, within a living organism (for the question of the constitution of the organic, living being from the fixation of superior and inferior functions, the following passages are most relevant: NL 25[411] KSA 11.119; 25[426] KSA 11.124; 25[437] KSA 11.128 and NL 6[49] KSA 9.205). This sensitivity, this pathos which perceives power disparities in a primordial manner and fixates differences of rank is what Nietzsche recurrently calls "pathos of distance".

To summarize the conclusions that can be drawn from our investigation on the logic of the life of the drives such as this is explored by Nietzsche, it seems that we have to contemplate the existence of an infra-conscious language, i.e. a language which does not translate into words (which would take us to a conscious level), but ultimately renders them possible. The question we need to ask is thus, is it still possible to deepen more into this logic of communication?

In relation to the logic of the drives, Nietzsche's fundamental discovery is the existence of an intimate bond between language and struggle. The aim of the most elemental "language" of the drives is not to produce an objective picture of the world. The nature of language is not essentially cognitive; neither on the basic level of the drives, nor on a conscious level, i.e. on the level of ordinary language. All in all, one should never forget, as Nietzsche often remarks, that the drives as such are not objective realities; they are not little things, but interpretations – there is no possible objective perception. As we can read in a posthumous fragment: "Everything that happens is a struggle" (NL 1[92] KSA 12.33 = WLN 61). This sentence primarily concerns the relations between the drives: they too are in rivalry and struggle. And this struggle, which does not pursue to annihilate the adversary, but to the contrary, tries to establish its domain over the other as part of its longing to increase power; this struggle, which can and relentlessly does generate forms of collaboration and coalition between the drives, this struggle presupposes a language enabling at least the possibility of them to relate to one another, and hence their confrontation. In this respect we would like to recall those posthumous texts which explain how to obey and to command must be understood as forms of struggle and rivalry; in particular: "struggle also expresses itself in obeying and commanding" (NL 40[21] KSA 11.638 = WLN 43–44), and: "*to dominate* is to endure the counterweight of the weakest force, it is thus a form of *continuing* the struggle. *To obey* is likewise a *struggle*: as long as a force of resisting *remains*" (NL 26[276] KSA 11.222)[6]. There is no neutral language on a basic or elemental level, which means to say: there is no language which is not based on the assessment of power-disparities. In other words, language is fundamentally bound to a hierarchy, that is, to an interpretation of the relations of supremacy within a given context. In this way it is the fundamental form of the pathos of distance.

Nietzsche's analyses during the years 1884 and 1886 establish the existence of an originary form of communication which we have cho-

---

6   NL 26[276] KSA 11.222: "*Herrschen* ist das Gegengewicht der schwächeren Kraft ertragen, also eine Art *Fortsetzung* des Kampfs. *Gehorchen* ebenso ein Kampf: so viel Kraft eben zum Widerstehen *bleibt*". [*Editors' translation*].

sen to call, metaphorically, the language of the drives. Our foremost purpose in commenting and gathering Nietzsche's texts, such as we have done for the present study, is to show the general framework within which this special analysis takes place, as well as to demarcate the disconcerting logic which precedes the dialogue between interpretative processes. To cover each and every angle of the present subject there still remains, however, the task of exploring another series of analyses already advanced by Nietzsche himself, in particular that other crucial aspect of this dialogic mode: the fact that the elemental language, which constitutes the communication among the drives, follows the logic of abbreviation and selection. This logic of abbreviation can only be understood in as much as it is related to an effort of enhancing the efficiency of command. Drives talk, and they talk among themselves; but in a well regulated organism structured by a clearly hierarchical chain of commandments, the drives are everything except for chatterboxes.

Instinct and Language in Nietzsche's
Beyond Good and Evil
João Constâncio

I. Introducing the Problem

In aphorism 191 of *Beyond Good and Evil* (BGE 191), Nietzsche criticizes the traditional opposition between instinct and reason. His main concern in this aphorism is the way philosophy, since Plato, has tried to avoid facing the Socratic paradox that it is not possible to give "reasons" for one's instinctive inclinations. However, throughout the whole of BGE, one of his main tasks, perhaps his main task, is to dissolve the oppositions and the opposite valuations created by metaphysics (or "dogmatic philosophy"), and so he also handles the opposition between instinct and reason in another sense – namely in the sense of trying to show that such an opposition is in fact illusory and what we call "reason" is only something that develops out of the instincts along a *continuum*[1].

Such an opposition, as it is conceived of in the philosophical tradition, is usually identified with the opposition between instinct and *language*. Schopenhauer, for instance, defines language as "the necessary instrument of reason" (WWV I §8, my translation), and he argues that it is surely not by chance that in Greek, as in Italian, language and reason are designated by the same word: ὁ λόγος, *il discorso* (WWV I §8, 44). They cannot be separated. Reasoning presupposes the use of language – for you cannot think abstractly if

---

1   On Nietzsche's task of showing that where metaphysical thinkers see "opposites" or "oppositions" (*Gegensätze*) there is only a *continuum*, and that, therefore, all "oppositions" – and especially the ones that imply a negative value for everything sensitive, temporal or historical, and a positive value for everything intelligible, supra-sensible, eternal – are actually based on mere differences of degree, "refinements", "gradations", subtle variations of shade that develop out of each other along the same continuum (BGE 2, BGE 24), see Müller-Lauter (1999a and 1999b).

you do not have words for your abstractions. In fact, reasoning has always been seen in philosophy as the *adequate* use of language, the one that allows for language to display its magical power of naming the essence of things.

Schopenhauer no longer believed in this magical power because he thought Kant had proved that there is no rational access to any *aeternae veritates* (e.g. WWV I Anhang, 497). But, for instance, in Plato's writings, λόγος, like λογιστικόν, means "reason" as much as it means "language", and the problem the characters of the Socratic dialogues are faced with is, no doubt, their incapacity to *say* the reasons for their moral beliefs and actions. These are "instinctive" in the sense that they arise from the soul's "communion with the body" (τῆς τοῦ σώματος κοινωνίας, *Phaedo* 65a, my translation) – and not from "philosophy" as the soul's effort to turn away from the body and to find itself "as much as possible all alone by itself" (ὅτι μάλιστα αὐτὴ καθ' αὑτήν, *Phaedo* 65c, my translation). Only through "dialectics" – only through a reasoning use of language that separates the soul from the body— is the soul able to seek direct knowledge of "eternal truths" about reality as such (i.e. about justice as such, truth as such, and so on).

Since Nietzsche radically questions this type of separation of body and soul, or instinct and reason, he also questions the thesis that language arises from reason – as if reason were an entity that might be separable from the body. It may be true that language is "the instrument of reason", as Schopenhauer believes – but also "reason", Nietzsche claims in BGE 191, "is just an instrument" (BGE 191): "reason (…) works in the *service* of the organic drives", as he adds in a posthumous note (NL 11[243] KSA 9.533, my translation). Reason is primarily an activity of the instincts, and language emerges, together with consciousness, from the activity of the instincts. Thus, in sum, Nietzsche replaces the traditional oppositions of metaphysics with the hypothesis that the relations between instinct, reason, consciousness, and language are relations of *continuity*.

If, in order to understand how Nietzsche develops this hypothesis throughout BGE, we begin by looking at the Preface, we find an important clue there. Nietzsche writes that, among the conditions that made philosophical dogmatism possible, at least the following four must be named: (1) "the soul-superstition that still causes trouble as the superstition of the subject and of the I", (2) "some word-play perhaps", (3) "a seduction of grammar", (4) "an over-eager generalization from facts that are really very local, very personal, very human-all-too-human" (BGE Preface). These conditions, which Nietzsche starts naming as if at random, are deeply connected. For the time being, let us leave the fourth one aside, and focus, first, on the connection between the other three.

The "superstition of the subject and of the I" is the form the "superstition of the soul" has taken at least since Plato invented "the pure spirit and the good in itself" (BGE Preface), i.e. since the time when what Nietzsche calls "the atomism of the soul" (BGE 12) became dominant in Western civilization: the conception of the soul as "something indestructible, eternal, indivisible, (...) a monad, an *atomon*" (BGE 12) – the soul as something whose essential identity is simple, non-relational, not related to the body nor the world, and whose value is higher than that of the body and the world on account of belonging to the transcendent domain of the "in-itself".

This is why a very important part of Nietzsche's critique of the "superstition of the subject and of the I" is a critique of *language*. Such a superstition consists in interpreting the soul as an *atomon*, and this, in turn, is made possible by "some word-play" and the "seduction of grammar". Most importantly, the critique of this "word-play" and of "grammar" redirects the interpretation of the Self from the domain of consciousness to the domain of the "body", and this means that it leads to the idea that our *identity* belongs primarily to the domain of the *instincts*.

Thus, the steps of our analyses should be clear: first, try to understand the critique of language, i.e. the critique of grammar, implied in Nietzsche's critique of the subject (section II); then, make clear how the concept of instinct emerges from such a critique of language (section III); third, discuss how this analysis of instinct and language leads to a redefinition of our identity (section IV). As we shall see, this discussion must take into account Nietzsche's views on philosophy and the history of philosophy (section V), and it ultimately leads to Nietzsche's conception of a new philosophical language (section VI).

II. Nietzsche's Critique of Grammar

Perhaps the most fundamental concept of Nietzsche's critique of language is the concept of *grammar*. We find this concept, for instance, in aphorism 20 of BGE. Here, Nietzsche declares that all philosophical thinking is carried out under the unconscious domination of certain "grammatical functions" (BGE 20) so that some thoughts are in a way simply deduced from those functions, while certain other possibilities of interpreting the world are blocked out from the start (BGE 20). Philosophy, Nietzsche says, has always been "a type of atavism" (BGE 20), a "philosophy of grammar" (BGE 20) – a developing of concepts that are already implicitly contained in the structure of the language one inherits and within which one is born. The fundamental concepts of philosophy – the concepts the philosophical tradition calls "categories" (concepts such as "cause", "effect", "substance", "accident", "identity", "equal", and so on) —, these concepts are the very structure of language, the "grammar" that is common to all languages. And it is from them, Nietzsche thinks, that the "superstition of the subject and of the I" arises.

This is precisely Nietzsche's idea in BGE 17 and 54. The conception of our identity as the identity of an "I" is a "superstition of the logicians" (BGE 17), and the reason for this is that it consists in believing that "the subject 'I' is the condition of the predicate 'think'" (BGE 17). The activity of "thinking" (*cogitare*) is interpreted in the light of the grammatical structure of our language: given the judgement "I think" (*cogito*, i.e. *ego cogito*), one deduces that there must exist an *ego* or "I" that is a substance, an "I" whose identity must be simple and independent, an "I" that abides and underlies the flux of thought, and, therefore, an "I" that may be the "cause", the "condition" of the activity of thinking. The grammatical relation between a subject and a predicate is the basis for the ontological distinction between a substantial "I" (the "subject") and its accidental activity ("thinking").

Thus, the decisive idea of Descartes' philosophy, according to BGE 54, is that "the 'I' is the condition, 'thinking' is a predicate and conditioned – thinking is an activity, and a subject *must* be thought of as its cause" (BGE 54). In this way, Descartes, according to Nietzsche, is only making explicit what was already the prejudice of the "atomism of the soul" – and, for this reason, Modernity is not a radical break with pre-Modernity: it is still, at the most fundamental level, a continuation of Platonism and also of Christianity as "Platonism for the 'people'" (BGE Preface). But, on the other hand, according to BGE 54, the Cartesian *cogito* represents, against Descartes' own intentions, "a criminal assault against the old concept of the soul", "against the fundamental presupposition of the Christian doctrine" (BGE 54, my translation) – the beginning of a skeptical and *"anti-Christian"* movement against the superstition of the subject and of the I.

The moment when Descartes makes the relation between the grammatical structure of language and the "atomism of the soul" explicit is the same moment when this atomism begins to be in peril. Thus, the evolution of Modern Philosophy from Descartes onwards eventually leads to Kant raising the possibility that the actual relation between the "I" and "think" should be inverted – the possibility, as Nietzsche says, "that 'think' is the condition and 'I' is conditioned, in which case 'I' would be a synthesis that only gets *produced* through thought itself" (BGE 54). Nietzsche is obviously referring to Kant's thesis that "the I *think* should *be able* to accompany all my representations" (KrV B131/132), but that, on the other hand, it does not give any "knowledge of myself as I am" (KrV B157). The judgement "I think" is *merely* the "originally synthetic unity of apperception" and it does not contain in itself the *existence* of a thinking being, i.e. it does not entail the existence of the Cartesian *res cogitans*. In truth, the only reason why that judgement is not empty is because it gives unity, through the categories, to the multiplicity of sensible intuition. Only the *synthesis* of this multiplicity gives any meaning or content to the "I think"[2]. And that is why Nietzsche writes: "*Kant* essentially wanted to prove that the subject cannot be proven on the basis of the subject – and neither can the object. The possibility that the subject (and therefore 'the soul') has a *merely apparent existence* might not always have been foreign to him" (BGE 54).

Kant's reduction of the "I" to a "function" of judgement – or to "the synthetic concept of 'I'", according to the formula of BGE 19 – is a fundamental thought for Nietzsche's critique of the subject.

Let us now consider several of the main aspects of the critique of language implied in this critique of the subject.

(i) First, Nietzsche's idea is that one should reject the implicit presupposition of our way of thinking, and especially of philosophy, that conceives "the *word*" as if it were already, by itself, "a cognition

---

2   Cf., in the *Critique of Pure Reason*, the two versions of the "Transcendental Deduction of the Categories", but also the "Paralogisms of Pure Reason".

of something" (NL 40[27] KSA 11.643 = WLN 44)[3]. This is the belief in a magical power of language, the rashness which, unconsciously, makes one think of the "grammatical categories" as if they were "metaphysical truths" (NL 6[11] KSA 12.237 = WLN 124), i.e. which makes us "use unity, identity, permanence, substance, cause, thingness, being" (TI Reason 5) as if they were realities, as if they were properties of the things themselves, and not mere "grammatical categories". Embedded in language there is a certain metaphysics (a "metaphysics of the people", as Nietzsche calls it in GS 354). Language makes us think of reality in the terms of its (that is, language's) internal logic – in the terms of grammar. There is a *Sprach-Metaphysik*, a "metaphysics of language" (TI Reason 5): language generates a net of categories which anticipates all possible experience of reality, and which functions as if it were the structure of *reality itself*, not merely of *our* language and our phenomenal world.

(ii) The projection of the structure of language onto the structure of the world shows itself to be illegitimate when one reflects on what is in fact a "word". According to BGE 268, words are "acoustic signs for concepts" (BGE 268), and concepts are "more or less determinate pictorial signs for sensations that occur together and recur frequently, for groups of sensations" (BGE 268). By "signs" Nietzsche (like Leibniz, Kant or Schopenhauer) means abbreviations that enable us to express something. Thus words are abbreviations that signal concepts, and concepts are abbreviations that signal sensations, i.e. words enable us to refer to concepts without thinking them through, and concepts enable us to refer to sensations without reliving them[4]. The key to these sign relations, however, is the fact that each concept is a feature or property believed to be *common (gemein)* to a multiplicity of given

---

3   Cf. also NL 5[3] KSA 12.185 = WLN 106: "We place a word at the place where our ignorance begins – where we can't see further, e.g., the word 'I', the words 'do' and 'done to': these may be the horizons of our knowledge, but they are not 'truths'".

4   Note that Nietzsche understands consciousness not as simple awareness but rather as conceptualization: cf. Simon (1984), Katsafanas (2005). Thoughts, i.e. conscious thoughts, *are* conceptualizations, and thus the idea that concepts are signs entails that thoughts are signs: cf. Stegmaier (2000); cf., for example, NL 6[253] KSA 9.263, my translation: "A thought, no less than a word, is only a sign: one cannot speak of a congruity between the thought and the real. The real is some sort of movement of the drives (*Trieb-bewegung*)".

sensations, or to groups of sensations and their inner experiences (*Erlebnisse*, BGE 268). Concepts are generalizations abstracted from sensations, and this is why they function as signs for sensations. Since their formation as signs for sensations goes hand in hand with the formation of other signs which designate them, i.e. with the formation of words, Nietzsche is allowed to conclude that the men (or peoples) who create words are *Abstraktions-Künstler*, "artists of abstraction" (NL 6[11] KSA 12.237 = WLN 124). This implies that generalizations are not simply "found", but rather *creatively invented*, and often in a way that is inseparable from the creative invention of words. Words as signs that express concepts *create* a given form for the phenomena, a form that determines the way things appear to us[5].

From this it follows that the content of words, as well as the very structure of language, does not correspond at all to the inner essence of the things themselves, and it is not drawn from them. Since the content of words is creatively abstracted from given sensations and inner experiences, the formation of words and concepts is, rather, a process of *simplification* and, therefore, of *falsification* which effaces what is unique and individual in those sensations and inner experiences[6].

---

5   See, for instance, NL 24[14] KSA 10.650, my translation: "Man is a creature who constructs forms (*ein formenbildendes Geschöpf*). Man believes in "being" and things because he is a creature who constructs forms and rhythms (*ein formen- und rhythmenbildendes Geschöpf*). The shapes and forms we see and in which we believe to have things do not exist. We simplify ourselves and connect a number of "impressions" through shapes that *we* create. If someone closes his eyes, he realizes that a drive for the construction of forms (*ein formenbildender Trieb*) is constantly in exercise, and that it tries innumerable stuff to which no reality corresponds".

6   Cf. GS 354: Consciousness and language involve a "vast and thorough corruption, falsification, superficialization, and generalization" of experience, so that we live not in the realm of the things "themselves", but only in a "surface- and sign-world" (GS 354). This way of understanding language and the formation of concepts is already present in *On Truth and Lying in a Non-Moral Sense*: "Let us consider in particular how concepts are formed; each word immediately becomes a concept, not by virtue of the fact that it is intended to serve as memory (say) of the unique, utterly individualized, primary experience to which it owes its existence, but because at the same time it must fit countless other, more or less similar cases, i.e. cases which, strictly speaking, are never equivalent, and thus nothing other than non-equivalent cases. Every concept comes into being by making equivalent what is non-equivalent" (TL, 143). For the concepts of "simplification" and "falsification" in BGE, see BGE 24, 34, 230; see Nehamas (1985, 56–59); Katsafanas (2005, 18–24).

However, these processes of simplification and falsification, although creative or "artistic", are not arbitrary – not only because, to some extent, they take heed of what is actually experienced, but also because they respond to certain needs. Words and concepts, like consciousness itself, satisfy certain needs of man as a "social animal" (GS 354), for they have only developed in our species *"under the pressure of the need to communicate"* (GS 354). This need, in turn, emerges from other needs of social life, and thus, according to BGE 268, the ultimate origin of language has been the need to respond to danger and to "agree quickly and easily about necessities" (BGE 268). In brief: language emerges, is preserved and develops because it is a "process of abbreviation" (*Abkürzungs-Prozess*, BGE 268) which allows the "herd", or a "people", or any social group, to communicate more quickly the needs it has, the danger it must overcome. Such abbreviations are called "signs"[7].

Thus, the "need to communicate", in Nietzsche's sense, is not a need of *individuals* as individuals (for instance, a need individuals might have to get out of their isolation). Since it is the need to communicate the dangers and necessities of a social form of life, it should be understood as "the most violent" of the forces that have controlled man so far (BGE 268). Man's entry into the symbolic order of language forces the substitution of individual experiences with "average and *base* [or 'vulgar', or 'common', *gemein*] experiences" (BGE 268). The use of words and concepts, inasmuch as it is based on the creation of contents that are "common" (*gemein*) to pluralities of individual sensations and inner experiences, *makes people "base"*, *"vulgar", "common"* (*gemein*). The effect of language on man is an expropriation of personal or individual identity.

---

7 Note how this transforms the traditional idea that concepts are abstractions. Nietzsche agrees that concepts are abstractions, but he adds that they depend on a drive not so much to "abstract" in the sense of classifying according to "higher" concepts, but rather to "abridge" – to create *signs* that enhance our orientation in social contexts, to find the *"shortest* (most abbreviated) *description* of what happens" (NL 26[227] KSA 11.209, my translation); cf. Stegmaier (2000, 61–62). As Stegmaier points out, Nietzsche believes that even in science the dominant drive is this drive to abbreviate, i.e. to make things understandable *for us* and communicable *within particular social contexts*. Cf. BGE 24, which is quoted below.

(iii) Thus, language and its grammar are elements of a given *perspective* – namely, of our perspective as a "social animal", or even as a "function of the herd" (GS 116). The projection of the structure of language onto the structure of the world is, consequently, unfounded: it is an unwarranted claim to knowledge about reality "in-itself" made from a merely phenomenal domain – from what Nietzsche calls in *Daybreak* the "prison" of our sensations (D 117). Our concepts, and therefore also the grammatical categories of our language, have no meaning outside this domain of sensation (and then only as simplifications to the effect of communicating). They are like a "spider web" that we, "spiders", weave around us, and which we cannot tear: "there is absolutely no escape, no backway or bypath" out of this net and into the things "in themselves" (D 117). We have no "organ" that would enable us to know something beyond it, to reach into a "truth" that might transcend it (GS 354).

It is essentially this fact that leads Nietzsche to argue, in *Twilight of the Idols*, that (a) we cannot know a "true world" beyond the "apparent world", (b) the idea of a "true world", being entirely fictitious, has no normative consequences, (c) the idea of such a world has already been "refuted", and above all (d) abolishing the "true world" also entails abolishing the idea that the sensible world of appearances is an "apparent world" (TI Fable)[8]. I cannot discuss here the many difficulties attached to the development of these assertions in Nietzsche's work, but there should be no doubt that these ideas are already present in *Beyond Good and Evil*: in BGE 24, Nietzsche claims that it is *language* which makes us believe in "oppositions" where there are only "degrees and multiple, subtle shades of gradation" (BGE 24) – and it is, therefore, only language that makes us believe in the *opposition* between a "true world" and an "apparent world", preventing us from realizing that even "the best science" tries to "keep us in this *simplified*, utterly artificial, well-invented, well-falsified world" (BGE 24), i.e. in the world onto which the "grammatical categories" are projected[9]; BGE 34, in turn, starts with the assertion that "the *erroneousness* of the world we think we

---

8   See also NL 11[50] KSA 13.24, NL 14[103] KSA 13.280, NL 14[134] KSA 13.319, NL 14[153] KSA 13.336.

9   Cf. also BGE 14, where we find the assertion that "physics too is only an interpretation and arrangement of the world" (BGE 14).

live in is the most certain and solid fact that our eyes can still grab hold of", and then Nietzsche goes on to develop the idea that, instead of believing in the opposition between a "true world" and an "apparent world", we should only assume the existence of different "levels of appearance", i.e. a *continuum* of "lighter and darker shades and tones of appearance" – which implies that "the world *that is relevant to us*" is only a "fiction" (BGE 34). Only the "belief in grammar" (BGE 34) could force us to suppose that such a fiction would have to have an "author", i.e. would have to be the "predicate" of a subject, therefore of an "I" – namely of a God that created it with intrinsic properties unknown to us. And since governesses commonly taught grammar to philosophers, Nietzsche adds: "With all due respect to governesses, isn't it about time philosophy renounced governess-beliefs?" (BGE 34). This question is then echoed in one of the most famous assertions of *Twilight of the Idols*: "I am afraid that we have not got rid of God because we still have faith in grammar" (TI Reason 5).

Maudemarie Clark[10] has argued that thesis (d), i.e. that abolishing the "true world" also entails abolishing the idea that the sensible world of appearances is an "apparent world", means that in *Twilight of the Idols* Nietzsche *no longer* regards the empirical world as merely apparent or illusory, and that it is only up to *The Gay Science* that he conceives of our "simplification" of the world as "falsification". In *Beyond Good and Evil*, according to Clark, Nietzsche is already thinking in this direction, but the book "retains some formulations" from the stage of Nietzsche's development where, allegedly, he still believes that the empirical world is merely apparent or illusory[11]. I do not find Clark's argument sufficiently convincing, and I believe Nehamas[12], whom she criticizes, is right in claiming that, for Nietzsche, simplification (and especially "simplification" through grammatical functions or "logical fictions") always implies "falsification" (including in *Twilight of the Idols*). Both in *Beyond Good and Evil* and *Twilight of the Idols*, Nietzsche's idea seems to me to be that this "falsification" should not be understood as a false representation *at all* – because this would still imply the existence of something (ideally) knowable in itself, therefore also the possibility

---

10   Cf. Clark (1990).
11   See Clark (1990, 115, 175–180).
12   Cf. Nehamas (1985).

of "truth" as an adequate, presuppositions-free representation of an "in-itself" (i.e. of intrinsic properties). The kernel of Nietzsche's argument is that the very concept of an "in-itself", and thus of false or adequate representation, is created *from within* the "surface- and sign-world" (GS 354) we live in, or "believe we live in" (BGE 34). The phenomenal world is indeed a "fictitious world" (A 15) and the "true world" of the "in-itself" is a *second* fictitious world created from within the first – but this does not put these two fictions on an equal stand. Instead, it implies that the phenomenal world is *not* a copy or representation of the "true world", for it is the latter that duplicates the former and this duplication is the only reason why philosophers since Plato have come to think of the phenomenal world as an apparent world. From this it follows, according to Nietzsche, that (a) we can say that the simplification of our world through signs makes it "false" and a "fiction" without implying that it is unreal or apparent – for we need only to think of its "erroneousness" as a certain "level of appearance" in a *continuum* of different levels of appearance (i.e. of possible perspectives)[13]; (b) we can experiment with the genealogical hypothesis that the notion of an ultimate truth about intrinsic properties of the world is a response to certain nihilistic needs, and so we are free to "abolish" the "true world" in response to new, life-affirming needs[14].

(iv) However, this still does not exhaust Nietzsche's critique of language and its connection with his critique of the subject and of the I. At least two more points must be made. The first is that the

---

13   It is important to notice the crucial importance of the concept of sign and sign relations. What concepts and words simplify and falsify is the world *as represented by unconscious drives and affects* in sensations and inner experiences; and these unconscious and sensuous representations are also creative simplifications and falsifications, for the senses are already a "simplifying apparatus" (cf. NL 34[46] KSA 11.434 = WLN 2). Thus the "fictitious world" created by consciousness and language is continuous with the life of the drives, therefore with "life" itself – with the whole of "nature", with the only world there is. This means that such a world is not "fictitious" in the sense of being a false picture of the in-itself of things, but only in the sense of being a plurality of *signs* of the real, all too real life of our drives. (On unconscious representations and the simplifying activity of the senses, see more below).

14   An argument for a more unified view of Nietzsche's thought on this matter (from BGE to GS V, GM III and TI) would, however, be out of place in this paper. Cf. Poellner (2000, 22–24, 123–125) for some important insights on this matter.

fiction of the I as a substantial I has primacy over the projection of the grammatical categories onto things – better still, that the I is the fiction which generates the very idea of "thing". As Nietzsche says in *Twilight of the Idols*: " [The metaphysics of language] sees doers and deeds all over: it believes that will has causal efficacy: it believes in the 'I', in the I as being, in the I as substance, and it *projects* this belief in the I-substance onto all things – this is how it *creates* the concept of 'thing' in the first place" (TI Reason 5).

(v) The second point is that the perspective which generates the "metaphysics of language" is anything but a merely theoretical perspective. As mentioned above, according to Nietzsche, the origin of language lies in man's "need to communicate" as a "social animal", and this implies that the perspective within which and out of which language develops is the perspective of an *organic* being that lives *in society*. What this means, however, is that language, and especially the metaphysics of language, although a "fiction", although "false", satisfies the needs of an organic, social being – i.e. it is a *condition for the preservation of this particular form of life*[15].

Now, this is exactly the fundamental thought of BGE 4:

> We do not consider the falsity of a judgement as itself an objection to a judgement; this is perhaps where our new language will sound most foreign. The question is how far the judgement promotes and preserves life, how well it preserves, and perhaps even cultivates, the type. And we are fundamentally inclined to claim that the falsest judgements (which include the synthetic judgements *a priori*) are the most indispensable to us, and that without accepting the fictions of logic, without measuring reality against the wholly invented world of the unconditioned and self-identical, without a constant falsification of the world through numbers, people could not live – that a renunciation of false judgements would be a renunciation of life, a negation of life. To acknowledge untruth as a condition of life: this clearly means resisting the usual value feelings in a dangerous manner; and a philosophy that risks such a thing would by that gesture alone place itself beyond good and evil (BGE 4).

The synthetic judgements *a priori* Kant believes to be legitimate in the *Critique of Pure Reason* – especially the synthetic judgements *a*

---

15   The posthumous note 35[35] (KSA 11.526 = WLN 20–21) condenses almost all of the points made so far.

priori of the Analytic of Principles, as for example, "all intuitions are extensive magnitudes" or "everything that happens has its cause"[16] – are, according to Nietzsche, *false*. They are "errors". Insofar as they express the meaning of the categories (for instance, of the categories of quantity, or of the category of causality), they are based on "logical fictions" – they are merely, as we already know, "grammatical categories" we illegitimately project onto the world, thereby simplifying and *falsifying* our previous apprehension of it in our sensations and inner experiences. The crucial point for Nietzsche, however, is that these judgements are the judgements of a given *form of life* – judgements that develop and are preserved in a given form of life (i.e. that are selected in its evolution) only insofar as they help preserve this form of life (i.e. help its being selected): only insofar as they are "conditions" for this form of life.

It must be underscored here that what is thereby selected is the form of life "man" (the "type 'man'") *as a social animal*. This has two immediate consequences: first, what is preserved (or "bred", as Nietzsche likes to say) is not only a biological species, but also a given form of *social* existence, a given "group" or "society"; secondly, the judgements at stake here belong to an organic being, to a given natural organization, so that they themselves are organic realities. If it is true, as Kant argues, that they are "transcendental" – that they are conditions for the possibility of the *objects* of experience, i.e. that they make it possible for objects to appear to us and become known by us according to such concepts as "unity" or "causality" —, on the other hand their "transcendental" nature cannot imply that they belong to a "pure reason" one might understand as independent of

---

16 On the Principles of the "Axioms of Intuition", the "Anticipations of Perception", the "Analogies of Experience" and the "Postulates of Empirical Thought in General" as synthetic judgements *a priori*, see especially the section of the Analytic of Principles named "On the supreme principle of all synthetic judgements" (KrV, B193/A154-B198/A158). Note that the Principle "all intuitions are extensive magnitudes" is "the transcendental principle of the mathematics of appearances", which "makes pure mathematics in its complete precision applicable to the objects of experience" (i.e. it justifies the use of *number* as a means to know the phenomena: KrV B206/A165); the Principle that "everything that happens has its cause" (or "all changes are effects of causes", "all alterations occur in accordance with the law of the connection of cause and effect") is, obviously, the Principle of Causality.

our body, of our organic existence, of the evolution of our species and of our social life (i.e. of history). They are, instead, *instincts* of man as a social, historical animal.

And so we arrive at the concept of "instinct" through the critique of language. Our next step is to analyze this concept as it emerges from Nietzsche's critique of language.

III. Language and the Instincts

In a posthumous fragment from 1881, Nietzsche defines instinct as follows: "I speak of *instinct* when some *judgement* (or *taste* at its lowest level) is incorporated, so that it now excites itself spontaneously and it does not need to wait for stimuli anymore" (NL 11[164] KSA 9.505, my translation). An instinct, in this sense, is a way of judging that belongs to the spontaneous and habitual behavior of a given organism, or that is "incorporated" in it, so that it functions without mediation, especially without the mediation of consciousness[17]. It is thus virtually identical to "taste (*Geschmack*) at its lowest level" – if "taste" means, as it does for Nietzsche, a perspectival and instinctual relation with the world which has "its Yes and No *before* the intellect has had a chance to speak" (NL 10[167] KSA 12.555 = WLN 202).

On the basis of such passages as these, Luca Lupo[18] has tried to distinguish "instinct" (*Instinkt*) from "drive" (*Trieb*) by arguing that instincts are built on the drives. Judgement and memory consolidate successful responses of the drives to events in the external world, thereby giving rise to *habits*, i.e. well-practised automatisms, more or less permanent forms of organization and connected activity of the drives. Such (organic) habits are the "instincts".

We can add to this that, in some contexts, Nietzsche seems to follow Schopenhauer in understanding the instincts as *skills*. Instincts are

---

17 See GS 11, A 14, 39, 57 for the idea that nothing works perfectly if it is still conscious, i.e. not instinctive. On "incorporation" (*Einverleibung*), cf. Müller-Lauter (1999, 54–62), Richardson (2004, 101–103, 174, 209); cf. GS 11, 110, 111 (also GS 21, 135); BGE 213, 230, 259; GM II 1; NL 11[41] KSA 9.494, NL 11[162] KSA 9.503, NL 11[268] KSA 9.543, NL 12[40] KSA 9.583, NL 20[10] KSA 9.583, NL 24[14] KSA 11.650, NL 26[448] KSA 11.269, NL 38[10] KSA 11.608, NL 9[151] 12.424.

18 Lupo (2006, 75–79, 55, 59).

akin to learned behavior but have goals that are not set by conscious mental states. As skills or "automatisms", they are more permanent and complex processes than the drives. *One* drive is not a skill; only a consolidated relation of drives can be understood as a skill. Unlike basic drives, the instincts have precise (although unintentional) goals and give rise to routined behavior; they can be described as responses to needs, but, unlike basic drives, they cannot be described as intermittent and quasi-innate urges or pressures to satisfy basic organic needs (like an objectless need of food or sexual satisfaction). This is why Nietzsche sees a close affinity not only between instinct and taste, but also between instinct and character[19]. The instincts are a person's most ingrained valuations, i.e. those that define a person's taste and character – a person's identity.

Nevertheless, Nietzsche does not try to fixate a clear technical distinction between "instinct" and "drive". In some contexts, he uses the words "instinct" and "drive" interchangeably. For example, in BGE 3 he claims that consciousness is not opposed to instinct and in BGE 12 he makes the same point by describing the soul as constructed out of "drives and affects". Moreover, he very often uses the word "drive" to describe complex and habitual urges (like the "drive for knowledge") and never explicitly opposes basic drives to (complex) instincts.

In any case, if we are to approach the concept of instinct from the viewpoint of Nietzsche's critique of language, we have, above all, to focus on the notion of an instinctive reason. In the passages of *Twilight of the Idols* we quoted above the invention or creation of the grammatical categories as logical fictions is attributed to "reason"

---

19 In EH Why I Am So Clever 9, for instance, "my instinct" (and not "my instinct*s*") means virtually the same as "my character", i.e. "what I am". But to think of a person's character in terms of drives, one has to conceive a *multiplicity* of drives relating to each other in a particular "order of rank" (cf. BGE 6). Vinzens (1999, 225ff) argues that in *Ecce Homo* "instinct" no longer refers to something universal in man, but rather to something personal, actually to what is most personal. However, he himself quotes the very first of Nietzsche's texts on instinct (a lecture called *Vom Ursprung der Sprache*, which deals precisely with the instinctive origin of language), where the term is already defined as referring either to the *character* of a group (e.g. a species or a social group), *or* to the character of an individual: "instinct is (...) the most distinctive accomplishment that springs from an individual's or a group's character" (*eigenste Leistung des Individuums oder einer Masse, dem Charakter entspringend*, KGW II/2, 188).

(*Vernunft*, TI Reason 4, 5). But already in *Daybreak* Nietzsche speaks of an *erdichtende Vernunft*, an "inventive" or "fabulating" reason which does its specific work of inventing or fabulating causes (i.e. "reasons") even in dreams and, therefore, does not depend on consciousness (D 119). The inventive force of our organism precedes and lays the ground for our conscious thoughts: "before something being 'thought', it must have already been *invented* [or *fabulated, erdichtet*]; the form-giving sense is more original than the 'thinking' sense" (NL 40[17] KSA 11.636, my translation).

Consciousness is only a "surface" (D 125, GS 354, EH Why I Am So Clever 9), which means that concepts are only *signs* of instinctive processes, abbreviated (and therefore, "superficial") expressions of the activities that go on among the "drives and affects": "behind consciousness work the *drives*" (NL 39[6] KSA 11.621, my translation); "below every thought lies an affect" (NL 1[61] KSA 12.26 = WLN 60). The "sensations" and "inner experiences" that, as we saw, become conceptualized and named in conscious mental states result from the instinctive activity of the drives. They do *not* offer pure "sense data", for they are always elaborated by inventive, "artistic" forces. The senses themselves simplify what they sense (cf. NL 34[46] KSA 11.434 = WLN 2) and, moreover, their activity is not independent of the *perceptive, perspectival, representing* activity of the drives. The drives *are* perceptions, or elementary perspectives, and as such they generate unconscious representations that already simplify and falsify our experience[20]. Thus conscious mental states are simplifications and falsifications *of* previous processes of simplification and falsification that take place at the unconscious level of the senses, the stimuli, the affects, the drives, and the instincts. As surfaces and signs, they are "outcomes" (*Endphänomene*) of unconscious processes of perception and representation (cf. NL 34[46] KSA 11.434).

This is why Nietzsche can say that "the entire organism thinks" (NL 27[19] KSA 11.279, my translation) and that my identity lies

---

20   Cf., for instance, Patrick Wotling's paper in this volume and Wotling (2008b, 226 ff, 235 ff, 373 ff). See GS 354, 357, where Nietzsche makes the eulogy of Leibniz for having discovered that perception can take place with or without consciousness ("consciousness is merely an *accidens* of the power of representation", GS 357). This is the basis for Nietzsche's quite frequent assertion that the drives "see", "perceive", "interpret", "feel", "will", etc.

"in the intelligence of my whole organism", not in my "conscious I" (NL 34[46] KSA 11.434 = WLN 2). The organism is intelligent, smart – and in fact, "'instinct' is the most intelligent type of intelligence discovered so far" (BGE 218). The interactions among the organic, unconscious perceptions achieved by the drives enable the organism to relate and adapt to its environment by *reasoning*, and this organic reasoning is the basis for all conscious reasoning. As Nietzsche writes in the *Nachlass*: "The organic, which 'judges', acts like an *artist*: from excitations, stimuli, it creates a whole, it sets aside many particular things and creates a *simplificatio*, it makes equal and affirms its creation as something that is (*als seiend*). *The logical is in the drive itself, which makes the world happen in a logical way, in accordance with our judgement*" (NL 25[333] KSA 11.97, my translation)[21]. Reason, the capacity that generates "logic" (or the "logical"), the capacity that creates the rationality of the "logical fictions", is, therefore, primarily *an activity of the drives*, an *instinctive capacity* – an instinctive reason.

Accordingly, in *The Gay Science* Nietzsche distinguishes reason from "the becoming conscious of reason" (GS 354), i.e. he distinguishes the pre-conscious, instinctive activity of reasoning from the conscious surface of that *same* activity. This is also how one should understand Nietzsche's distinction, in *Thus Spoke Zarathustra*, between the body as "a big reason" and the soul as "your small reason" (ZA I On the Despisers of the Body). This well-known distinction implies the *continuity* between reasoning as it takes place in conscious mental states and reasoning as an activity of the body. In fact, it also clarifies the thesis of *Beyond Good and Evil* that "reason is only an instrument" (BGE 191). The "small reason" (or "reason" in the usual sense implied in BGE 191) is an "I" that should be understood as a mere "instrument" or "tool" (*Werkzeug*) of the "big reason" – i.e. of the body as our true "Self" (*Selbst*, Za I On the Despisers of the Body). This idea goes well beyond Schopenhauer's doctrine of the primacy of the "will" over the intellect, i.e. of the doctrine according to which conscious reasoning tends to follow and serve the "will" and, consequently, it tends not to be an autonomous theoretical drive (e.g. WWV II §19). In addition to this, Nietzsche thinks that all organic

---

21   See also BGE 230 and e.g. NL 34[49] KSA 12.435.

drives and instincts have an element of "reason": all of them are "smart" and "inventive" or "artistic" – all of them struggle to impose "a Yes and a No" and coordinate with other drives in an instinctive but also intelligent relation with the world. Thus all contents one may call "reasonable" can be traced back to (although not reduced to) organic drives and instincts because conscious reasoning follows and serves unconscious reasoning, i.e. develops it further along a *continuum*.

This idea of a *continuum* is of crucial importance. First, it implies that consciousness and language are not ontologically distinct from the organic affects, drives and instincts. Conscious reasoning is an activity of the organism – a surface *of* organic processes[22]. Second, Nietzsche's *continuum* model implies that, being continuous, conscious and unconscious states interpenetrate and communicate with each other. Consciousness and language are based on pre-conceptual fictions weaved by organic affects, drives and instincts – but the organic domain is also always already contaminated and co-determined by consciousness and language. If we had to think of the relations between conscious and unconscious mental states and processes in terms of causality, we would have to conceive of a bi-directional path of causality, for although conscious mental states are always "caused" and sustained by unconscious mental processes, they also influence and change the life of the unconscious drives[23]. Strictly speaking, however, Nietzsche conceives of such relations in terms of sign- and power-relations instead of causal relations[24]. As signs, conscious mental states create abbreviations for power relations among the drives – but in doing this, they make new power claims: "reason (opinion and knowledge) fights with the drives as a new independent drive – and later, much later it fights to *overweight* them" (NL 11[243] KSA 9.533, my translation). Conscious reason struggles to impose the signs it generates, which is to say that it struggles for

---

22 See Günter Abel (2001) for an analyzis of Nietzsche's "continuum model". Abel tries to show that this model entails both a rejection of the dualism mind/body (i.e. mind/brain) and a rejection of reductive monism (i.e. eliminism, the reduction of the mind to events in the brain). Abel calls Nietzsche's non-reductive monism "adualistic".

23 For Nietzsche's questioning of the dualistic opposition between "cause" and "effect", see Wotling (2008a, 5–27); see also Katsafanas (2005) for the idea of bi-directional causality.

24 Cf. Constâncio (2011).

the *incorporation* of their meanings into the organism – i.e. for their becoming *instinctive*[25].

This is perhaps the key to understanding Nietzsche's claim in *Beyond Good and Evil* that consciousness is not "*opposed* to instinct in any decisive way" and "the greatest part of conscious thought must still be attributed to instinctive activity" (BGE 3). Conscious thought is never discontinuous with instinctive activity, but it cannot be *reduced* to instinctive activity. While working in the service of the instincts, conscious thoughts create something new (sc. signs) – something that actually changes the organism's relation to its surrounding world[26]. The power of conscious thoughts may be of "fifth rate importance" (A 39) and the role of consciousness, a "subsidiary role, almost indifferent, superfluous, perhaps destined to vanish and give way to a perfect automatism" (NL 14[144] KSA 13.328f = WP 523) – but this is different from not having any role at all[27].

Of course, this idea of a *continuum* has implications for the concept of language as well. Words create "forms", they create a certain vision

---

25 See the whole posthumous note 11[243] in KSA 9.533, on "die Selbstregulirung durch die Vernunft" ("Self-regulation through reason").

26 This is emphasized by Nietzsche's metaphorical images for consciousness. For the metaphorical image of consciousness as a "tool", see NL 34[46] KSA 11.434 = WLN 2 ("... the sustaining, appropriating, expelling, watchful intelligence [*Klugheit*] of my whole organism, of which my conscious self is only a tool"; note that Nietzsche states very clearly in this fragment that "the intellect and the senses are, above all, a *simplifying* apparatus. Yet our *erroneous*, miniaturised, *logicised* world of causes is the one we can live in. We are 'knowers' to the extent that we are able to satisfy our needs"). For the metaphorical image of consciousness as an "organ", see for instance NL 11[145] KSA 13.67 = WLN 228 ("consciousness is not the management but an *organ of the management*"). This latter fragment also introduces the idea that consciousness is "only a means for communication" (i.e. that the "sign-world" is the world of man as a "social animal"), which is developed in GS 354 and BGE 268. For the metaphorical image of consciousness as a "hand" ("consciousness is the hand with which the organism reaches out furthest: it must be a firm hand"), see NL 34[131] KSA 13.67 = WLN 9. This "firm hand" creates concepts and transforms our world into a "sign-world" – which is essential for our orientation and survival. For the metaphorical image of consciousness as a "mirror", as "just a net connecting one person to another" and as "genius of the species", see GS 354. For the metaphorical image of consciousness as "a commentary on an unknown text", see D 119. For the image of consciousness as "a certain behaviour of the drives towards one another", see GS 333 (BGE 36 also defines "thinking" (*Denken*) as "a relation between these drives").

27 On the question of epiphenomenalism, see again Constâncio (2011).

of the world and a certain self-interpretation of the ones who use them. These acts of creation, as we saw, are grounded in the "logical fictions" that are the very structure of language. Their origin is the primary fiction of the "grammatical functions". What we are now given to understand is that these categories are, on the one hand, developments or "outcomes" of pre-linguistic perspectives and, on the other, that the contents they originate tend to be "incorporated", transformed into instincts. In other words, Kant's categories are in fact grammatical functions, but these functions are signs of pre-linguistic processes: they abbreviate, but also consolidate and fixate unconscious representations achieved by drives and affects. Given the *continuum* model and the fact that transferences from conscious mental states to unconscious mental processes are possible, the vital importance of the categories for a successful relation of the organism with the world necessarily leads to their "incorporation", i.e. their mutation into instincts that ensure a functioning orientation of the organism in its environment. They easily become permanently active as instinctive judgements.

Note that Nietzsche's conception of all organic activities as continuous does not only entail that consciousness and language are continuous with each other, but also that they are mutually dependent: "*We cease thinking when we no longer want to think within the constraints of language*", he writes in the notebooks (NL 5[22] KSA 12.193 = WLN 110)[28]. Some conscious thoughts may consist of conceptualizations for which we do not find or do not need words; some of them arise through such forms of sign-communication as gestural language (cf. GS 354) – but they are not truly independent of the whole symbolic order of spoken and written language. All conscious thoughts occur either within language or, as it were, at the margins of language, and their level of clarity depends on their verbalization.

But what, then, is the exact relation between instinct and language? And what is the exact relation between reason and language? Obviously, it follows from the preceding points that both relations are relations of continuity – or (even more precisely) of development along the same *continuum*. Language develops, or originates, or

---

28   Cf. Abel (2001).

emerges from pre-linguistic drives – from organic instincts. Since these organic instincts use reason as a tool or instrument, one may conclude that language emerges from reason – but from reason as an "instinctive reason". Another way of putting this is to say that language emerges from a pre-"language" of the organic drives[29]. This process is the same as the development of consciousness (GS 11, 33, 354, A 14), and the *milieu* where it arises is the social *milieu* of communication: consciousness is "just a net connecting one person to another" (GS 354), and "the history of language is the history of a process of abbreviation" (BGE 268) which facilitates understanding in a community and satisfies its members' need to communicate.

It is, however, very important to underscore again that this process (or long "development", or "history") cannot be reduced to a one-way process with a simple "origin" or "cause"[30]. From the beginning of this process, many contents created by consciousness and language become "incorporated" – not so much because they prove to be "true", but rather because they serve life or become conditions for the preservation of a given form of life: "It will hardly be a history of 'truth', but rather of an organic structure of errors which merges into the body and soul and dominates the *sensations* and *instincts*" (NL 11[262] KSA 9.541, my translation). This is, of course, especially true for all generations which come after the very first stages of the process, i.e. for all generations which, since time immemorial, are born into a language – into a net of signs one inherits and does not create from scratch: into a given tradition and its concepts, judgements, and moral prescriptions or customs.

From this it follows that the individual identity of a human organism is always already contaminated and co-determined by its identity as a "social animal". Language, as an open-system of acoustic signs that serve the necessities of the "social animal", is, as we have seen, a violent force (*Gewalt*) which expropriates the individual from its individual identity. It "vulgarizes" the individual, and it leads the

---

29 See Patrick Wotling's paper in this volume. Wotling emphasizes the fact that "communication" among the drives consists of power relations, for the drives are "wills to power" and the functioning of the organism depends on a "order of rank" among the drives, i.e. of relations of command and obedience.

30 That, for Nietzsche, no process or development has a simple "origin" is one of the most obvious conclusions one can draw from GM II 12–13.

individual to interpret his or her own identity as that of a "subject" or of a "conscious I" whose essence is supposed to be the same in everyone. Nietzsche's effort to trace consciousness and language back to the organic and instinctive domain – his "naturalism", his intention of "translating man back into nature" (BGE 230, Kaufmann's translation) – does not lead to an ultimate causal ground of activity or reality one might still understand in the light of the traditional concepts of "essence" or atomic, monadic identity (or to an "intelligible character" as an "inner nature" or "inner mechanism" of the organism, to use the language of Schopenhauer). Nietzsche's "naturalism" is, at the same time, a translation of man back into *history* (or into "culture", "civilization", and "socialization"), and this implies that it is an affirmation of the plastic, dynamic, relational nature of the organism's identity[31].

Put differently, Nietzsche's critique of the "atomism of the soul" leads to the idea that our identity – the "Self" (*Selbst*) – is the body, but this should not deceive us into believing that he is satisfied with a facile reduction of our identity to a strictly biological, individual organism. First, because the organism's "identity" is through and through *relational*: its unity "is *only* unity as *organization* and *connected activity*" (NL 2[87] KSA 12.104 = WLN 76), i.e. as a complex and dynamic relation among a multiplicity of affects, drives and instincts, as well as among conscious and unconscious mental states. Second, the continuity of the organism's activity *with the world* – and thus with "history" – entails that its character (its "organization and connected activity") is constantly being transformed by its social *milieu*.

However, it would be a mistake to think that, by saying this, we have already drawn up all the consequences for the problem of identity. This problem has been, in fact, barely touched upon.

IV. The Problem of Identity

At the start, we saw that Nietzsche's Preface to BGE lists four conditions that made philosophical dogmatism possible. We still have

---

31   For the idea that Nietzsche's naturalism does not intend to lead to an ultimate causal ground of activity or reality, see Wotling (2008a, 27; 2008b, 228–229; 1995), *passim*; see also Andrea Bertino's paper in this volume. On Nietzsche's naturalism, see also Janaway (2007, 21, 44–50, 114–115, 148–149), *contra* Leiter (2002).

to consider the fourth one: "an over-eager generalization from facts that are really very local, very personal, very human-all-too-human" (BGE Preface).

At first sight, this assertion seems to contradict the point we made at the end of the last section. Now, Nietzsche's idea seems to be that the reason why certain metaphysical beliefs emerge and are preserved is not, after all, because the "need to communicate" and language create a "herd-perspective" through which the needs of the "social animal" come to be (partly) satisfied – but rather because *individual needs*, "very personal" needs of given individuals, are at the origin of those metaphysical beliefs and come to be satisfied by them.

Several of the first aphorisms of BGE seem to confirm this interpretation. In BGE 3, Nietzsche states that, behind the development of philosophical beliefs, there must be "physiological requirements for the preservation of a particular type of life" (BGE 3). These "physiological requirements" seem to be the needs of individual organisms. Thus in BGE 5 we find the assertion that all philosophers are "advocates" – that each philosopher creates the philosophical theses and arguments that justify their "prejudices" (BGE 5) —, and this assertion is reinforced, in BGE 6, by the further assertion that all philosophy so far has been "a confession on the part of its author, and a type of involuntary and unself-conscious memoir" (BGE 6)[32]. A philosophy is always a "rationalization", a justification of certain prejudices, but, involuntarily, such a rationalization reveals *"who is"* its author – "which means, in what order of rank the innermost drives of his nature stand with respect to each other" (BGE 6). These drives are what is more personal in someone, and therefore Nietzsche seems to be saying in all these passages that there is always a certain *individual* physiology which is unconscious, instinctive and affective, and which has precedence over philosophical rationalizations insofar as it *causes* them. BGE 7 gives an example of this: Epicureanism was caused by Epicurus' "anger and ambition against Plato" (BGE 7).

In fact, there is no doubt that these passages imply a primacy of the organic, the physiological, the instinctive, the unconscious and also of

---

32   See also BGE 289: "Every philosophy *conceals* a philosophy too; every opinion is also a hiding place, every word is also a mask".

the affects over conscious rationality. However, if we go deeper into their interpretation, we may perhaps come to see that such primacy does not imply that the identity of the organic, of the "body", should be conceived of as a simply individual identity.

And we may go deeper into their interpretation if we now consider BGE 187, which deals with the Kantian categorical imperative. For Nietzsche, Kantian morality is, of course, "an involuntary confession on the part of its author" (BGE 6) – a "sign language of the affects", as he now says in BGE 187. The affective predisposition one should read in its author's involuntary confession is, however, the following: "the worthy thing about me is that I can obey – and it *should* be the same for you as it is for me!" (BGE 187). This is what Kant involuntarily reveals of himself in his moral philosophy – but this, for Nietzsche, is nothing but the most radical "herd-perspective": a perspective whose affectivity is dominated by the interest of the "group" or "society", and whose individuality is, so to say, canceled and transformed into a mere "function of the herd". In such an affectivity, what is most personal and individual is, at the same time, non-personal and non-individual. And it is precisely this kind of affectivity, this kind of "herd perspective" (or, simply, of "herd morality") which, according to Nietzsche, leads to ("causes") every particular form of metaphysics or dogmatic philosophy. The metaphysical beliefs of dogmatic philosophy are effects of the unconscious domination of "herd morality" over man, and they are, at the same time, rationalizations or justifications of this domination. The need that has driven every philosopher in the history of Western thought since Plato (or Socrates) has been the need to justify or ground morality: "[Philosophers] wanted morality to be *grounded*, —and every philosopher so far has thought he has provided a ground for morality. Morality itself, however, was thought to be 'given'" (BGE 186). Kant's case is very far from being unique. All philosophers so far have been "sly spokesman for prejudices that they christen as 'truths'" (BGE 5), and their "rationalizations after the fact" (BGE 5) have reinforced the unconscious domination of herd morality. Such rationalizations are effects of this domination, but they also stand in a causal relation to its further development. Each philosopher is just a link in the long chain of this development.

As Nietzsche says in BGE 202, the novelty of his "new vision", of *his* philosophy, is precisely the idea that "morality in Europe these days is the morality of herd animals" (BGE 202), and the history of the West since Plato is the history of how "the instinct of the herd animal man (...) came to the fore, gaining and continuing to gain predominance and supremacy over the other instincts" (BGE 202).

Thus, if, as Nietzsche sustains in BGE 9, philosophy is a "tyrannic drive", "the most spiritual will to power", a will to the "creation of the world", to be "*causa prima*" (BGE 9) – if, in other words, all philosophy emerges from the will to project a certain vision of the world and to make it dominant —, it should be added that, according to Nietzsche's "new vision" (BGE 202), such a "will", at least since Plato, has never been a merely individual will. Instead, every single philosophical will has been a new form that the herd instinct and the herd perspective have taken in a given individual.

Of course, for Nietzsche, this development is not a pure spiritual development in the realm of abstraction or rationality. Every single link of the chain is rooted in the instincts, and the evolution of instinctual life depends on *custom* – on "culture" (*Kultur*) as a mechanism of "discipline and breeding" (*Zucht und Züchtung*): on the social, cultural, historical "domestication" (*Zähmung*) of man[33]. Morality (if it is effective) is "a long compulsion" (BGE 188), and the domestication of man means that *obedience* is slowly inculcated in man. According to BGE 188, willingness to obey is more "natural" than the "*laisser aller*" generally supposed to be "natural": "'You should obey someone, anyone, and for a long time: *or else* you will deteriorate and lose all respect for yourself' – this seems to me to be the moral imperative of nature, which is clearly neither 'categorical', as

---

33 For morality as "custom" (as *Sittlichkeit der Sitte*), cf. especially D 9 (where it is implied that also modern moralities are still moralities of custom: "morality is nothing other (therefore *no more!*) than obedience to customs"); for the idea that no morality is effective if it is not embodied in "juridical institutions and customs", see e.g. NL 34[176] KSA 11.478, A 57; for the concept of "discipline and breeding" (*Zucht und Züchtung*) in BGE, cf. BGE 61, 203, 213, 219, 225, 251, 252, 262, 263, 264, 242 (obviously, the concept is also implied in BGE 188); for the explicit statement that every morality is connected to the process of breeding a certain "type" or "form of life" or "species", see e.g NL 35[20] KSA 11.515; for morality as "domestication" (*Zähmung*), see GM I 11, II 22, III 13, III 21, TI Humanity 2, TI Humanity 5, A 22, NL 25[236] KSA 11.74 ("so far, the *domestication* of man has been misunderstood as 'morality'"), NL 27[56] KSA 11.288, NL 27[79] KSA 11.294 and Wotling (1995, 232–235); on *Züchtung* as a "technique of selection", cf. Wotling (1995, 218–242); on *Zucht und Züchtung* as "social selection", cf. Richardson (2004, 38, 146, 190–200, 209, 259–260, 268).

the old Kant demanded it to be (hence the 'or else'—), nor directed to the individual (what does nature care about the individual!), but rather to peoples, races, ages, classes, and above all to the whole 'human' animal, to *the* human" (BGE 188).

In accordance with what we saw above about language, it is obvious that Nietzsche thinks language has an important role in the processes of "domesticating" man and breeding the "social animal" and its many "types". Inasmuch as language makes one "common" or "base" (BGE 268), those men who are "more exceptional, refined, rare, and difficult to understand" are endangered by language (BGE 268). They tend to become too isolated, or to debase themselves. Language gives an edge to those who, by nature, are already "more alike and ordinary" (BGE 268), and it contributes to what Nietzsche calls "this natural, all-too-natural *progressus in simile*" whereby people are becoming "increasingly similar, average, herd-like – increasingly *base (gemein)*!" (BGE 268).

Thus, by looking at the philosophers' use of language as dependent upon the subterranean paths of their instinctual life, we reach a paradox. On the one hand, it seems that the dominant instinct in a philosopher is "the herd instinct of obedience" (BGE 199), the "instinct of submissiveness" (BGE 261). Given that no philosopher is ever able to rise himself above his "belief in grammar" (BGE 34) and only uses language as an "advocate" of morality, every philosopher must be labeled as "base" (*gemein*). But, on the other hand, philosophy, as mentioned, is a "tyrannic drive", "the most spiritual will to power", a will for the "creation of the world", to be "*causa prima*" (BGE 9). It aims at command, not obedience[34].

We must now look a little bit closer at this paradox – which will force us to consider Nietzsche's concept of philosophy and, especially, its relation to the concepts of instinct and language.

V. Philosophers and Their Contradictory Identity

For Nietzsche, the opposite of "base" (*gemein*) is "noble" (*vornehm*), and the opposite instinct to the "instinct of submissiveness" (BGE

---

34 In BGE 6, Nietzsche even argues that every single drive is a philosopher (or like a philosopher), because every drive craves mastery: "every drive craves mastery (*ist herrschsüchtig*), and as *such* it tries to philosophize" (BGE 6, modified).

261) is the "instinct for rank" (BGE 263) – which Nietzsche also calls the "instinct for reverence" (*Instinkt der Ehrfurcht*, BGE 263, my translation). If one asks oneself "what is noble?" (as Nietzsche does in Part 9 of BGE), one must take the concept of "reverence" into account – and especially of reverence (or respect) for oneself and for one's own value. "*The noble soul has reverence for itself*", writes Nietzsche (BGE 287). Reverence for oneself is what is lacking in a soul dominated by the "instinct of submissiveness" (BGE 261). In its highest forms (the ones Nietzsche is really interested in), such reverence is *not* the mere "pathos of distance" understood as a *social* feeling typical of the nobles in an aristocratic society – it is, rather, an *inner* "pathos of distance": "that *other*, more mysterious pathos", which is a "demand for new expansions of distance within the soul itself, the development of states that are increasingly high, rare, distant, tautly drawn and comprehensive, and in short, the enhancement of the type 'man', the constant 'self-overcoming of man' (to use a moral formula in a supra-moral sense)" (BGE 257). *This* pathos – or "high spirituality" (*hohe Geistigkeit*) – is described in several ways throughout BGE, and is, of course, the pathos proper to *philosophy*[35]. It is from the viewpoint of this pathos that all true philosophers "*create values*" (BGE 211) – as every type of noble man creates his own values (BGE 260). And from the fact that they are creators of values follows that "(...) *true philosophers are commanders and legislators*: they say: 'That is how it *should* be!' they are the ones who first determine the 'where to?' and 'what for?' of people" (BGE 211). To repeat: command, and not obedience, is their *proprium*.

It might be that Nietzsche's idea was simply that some of the great philosophers are not "true philosophers" after all. On Kant, for instance, he writes that "the great Chinaman of Königsberg was only

---

35   Cf. BGE 219, 40, 44, 61, 201, 213, 252, 257 and Stegmaier (1997, 309–311) on *Geist*, spirit, and "high spirituality". BGE 252, for instance, defines a "lack in philosophy" as a lack in "real *power* of spirituality, real *profundity* of spiritual vision" (BGE 252, my translation) – which implies, first, the idea that philosophy has always been "the most spiritual will to power" (BGE 9), and second, the idea that philosophy is where the greater "expansions of distance within the soul itself" (BGE 257) take place. Nietzsche's insistence on the philosopher's need for "masks" and for "solitude" is intrinsically connected with this concept of philosophy as "high spirituality".

a great critic" (BGE 210) – and not a true philosopher. But Nietzsche is well known for his ambivalent valuations, and if we set the rhetoric aside (or if we are able to see *through* it), it is clear that he describes all his great predecessors both as "base" *and* "noble". As paradoxical as this may sound, it is, however, an important statement about philosophy – and also about instinct and language.

Throughout BGE, Nietzsche emphasizes the *complex and contradictory* nature of human subjectivity. This is perhaps the ultimate implication of Nietzsche's critique of the (atomic) subject and its replacement with the hypothesis of "the soul as subject-multiplicity" (BGE 12), or "the soul as a society constructed out of drives and affects" (BGE 12) – the soul as a "body". Thus, for instance, when Nietzsche introduces the famous distinction between "master morality" and "slave morality" (BGE 260), he immediately declares that "you sometimes find them sharply juxtaposed – inside the same person even, within a single soul" (BGE 260). In the same vein, BGE 215 expresses the idea that modern man is "determined by a *diversity* of moralities" (BGE 215, my translation), and that our actions are "rarely unambiguous, – and it happens often enough that we perform *multi-colored* actions" (BGE 215). In BGE 244, in turn, he deals with "the contradictory nature at the base of the German soul" (*die Widerspruchs-Natur im Grunde der deutschen Seele*, BGE 244), and he points out that in the German soul "the noblest stands right next to the most base" (*Wie steht da das Edelste und Gemeinste neben einander!*, JGB 244). According to Nietzsche, it is *hereditariness* (in a broad sense which includes genes and memes) which necessarily determines the complexity and contradictoriness of the human soul, for "what a man's forefathers liked doing the most, and most often, cannot be wiped from his soul" (BGE 264), and "it is utterly impossible that a person might *fail* to have the qualities and propensities of his elders and ancestors in his body" (BGE 264). In the modern age, the mixture of classes and races and the development of the historical sense have even determined that "the past of every form and way of life, of cultures that used to lie side by side or on top of each other, radiates into us" (BGE 224), so that "at this point, our instincts are running back everywhere and we ourselves are a type of chaos" (BGE 224). The human being – and especially the modern man – is "a complex (*vielfaches*), hypocritical, artificial, and opaque animal" (BGE 291, my translation), and only the invention of "good conscience" and the "lengthy falsification" we call "morality" have made possible for him to "enjoy his soul as something *simple*" (*einfach*, BGE 291).

In the case of a philosopher that broad type of hereditariness is, of course, decisive: "You need to have been born for any higher world; to say it more clearly, you need to have been *bred* for it: only your descent, your ancestry can give you a right to philosophy – taking the word in the highest sense. Even here, 'bloodline' is decisive. The preparatory labor of many generations is needed for a philosopher to come about; each of his virtues needs to have been individually acquired, passed down, and incorporated" (BGE 213). And these virtues are the *noble* virtues *par excellence*: "(...) the eagerness for great responsibilities, the sovereignty of his ruling gazes and downward gazes, the feeling of separation from the crowd (...)" (BGE 213) – and, in the end, "the art of command, the expanse of the will" (BGE 213).

Naturally, Nietzsche thinks that only his "philosophers of the future" (BGE 42–44, 210) will be able to achieve perfection in the exercise of these virtues. But he also thinks that *all philosophers in every age* have partaken of them, for "their task, their harsh, unwanted, undeniable task (though in the end, the *greatness* of their task) lay in being the bad conscience of their age. In applying a vivisecting knife directly to the chest of the *virtues of the age*, they gave away their own secret: to know a new *greatness* in humanity, a new, untravelled path to human greatness" (BGE 212). An aspiration for *greatness* – a new form of greatness, beyond the common, *base* aspirations of the age – is the mark of a philosophical soul, and such an aspiration is of course an effect of the "instinct for reverence", or of the "instinct for rank" – which "more than anything else, is itself the sign of a *high* rank" (BGE 263). To some extent, all philosophers "so far" have *also* been "base"· – for they have been "complex, hypocritical, artificial, and opaque" animals. They have willed and have *not* willed their task – their "harsh, *unwanted*, undeniable task" (BGE 212, my emphasis).

Precisely for this reason the nobility of Nietzsche's "philosophers of the future" cannot be a *simple* quality or virtue. They will have to look for the greatness of man "precisely in his range and multiplicity, in his wholeness in manifoldness" (BGE 212, Kaufmann's translation). The "enhancement of the type "man"", which they are meant to accomplish, shall have to be a *development* and a new *synthesis* of the qualities or virtues philosophers have had so far.

BGE 219 is a very clear statement of this – of the idea that "a high spirituality is itself only the final, monstrous product of moral qualities; that it is a synthesis of all the states attributed to the 'merely moral' men after they had been acquired individually, through long discipline and practice, perhaps through whole series of generations (...)" (BGE 219). What shall be at stake for the "philosophers of the future" will not be the mere suppression or canceling out of morality, but rather a *"self-sublimation of morality"* (*die Selbstaufhebung der Moral*, D Preface 4). If we understand "morality" as "a doctrine of the power relations under which the phenomenon of 'life' arises" (BGE 19), i.e. as the expression of a certain type of instinctual life or of the order of rank in which the innermost drives of one's nature stand with respect to each other (BGE 6), then it should be clear that what is at stake for the "philosophers of the future" is a new arrangement of their instincts – a new, and higher, *spiritualization* (*Vergeistigung*) of the pre-existing "moral qualities" and valuations embedded in their instinctual life[36].

---

36 On Nietzsche's concepts of "self-sublimation" (*Selbstaufhebung*), "self-overcoming" (*Selbstüberwindung*) and "spiritualization" (*Vergeistigung*), cf. Kaufmann (1974, 235–238) and Wotling (1995, 205–210, 231–242). Such concepts express the idea of *internal development* (*Entwicklung*) and *synthesis*, not the idea of a break or a leap into something entirely new. This is what is implied, for instance, in the thesis that "almost everything we call 'higher culture' is based on the spiritualization and deepening of cruelty" (BGE 229, see also M 18, 30, 53, 77, 23, 113; GM II 6, II 7). What has already been achieved is a result of such "spiritualization of cruelty" – and what can still be achieved depends on further processes of spiritualization of cruelty and other instincts. Note also, in this context, the relation between aphorisms 211, 212, 224 and 225. In the modern age, the development of the historical sense has determined that men now have "a sense and instinct for everything, a taste and tongue for everything: by which it immediately shows itself to be an *ignoble* (*unvornehmer*) sense" (BGE 224). Man itself has become a "type of chaos" (BGE 224). However, "in human beings, *creature and creator* are combined" (BGE 225): our "chaos" can be molded, transformed, *spiritualized* by ourselves as creators. The means for that is "the discipline of suffering, of *great* suffering" (BGE 225), which has been "the sole cause of every enhancement in humanity so far" (BGE 225). Therefore, Nietzsche understands the values which the philosophers of the future are expected to create (BGE 211) as the ones needed for the painful spiritualization of the extreme complexity and contradictoriness of the modern soul – i.e. for a new "greatness" which might be able to take into account and sublimate as many aspects of the chaotic modern soul as possible (cf. BGE 212).

From the point of view of language, this is equivalent to the task of creating new developments and syntheses of the concepts and valuations we know of, or are conscious of, in our modern age. Let us conclude by briefly examining this last point.

VI. Nietzsche's "New Language"

Nietzsche claims he has a "new language" (BGE 4) – one that perhaps prepares the way for the language the "philosophers of the future" will create. But his "new language" is not *entirely new*, nor does it purport to be. The words and rules of common language remain Nietzsche's tools (in spite of their "baseness"). The "new language" identifies "unity", "substance", (monadic) "identity" as "lies" or "fictions", and it tries to be "nobler" than the common language and to think beyond such simplifications and falsifications. But it is certainly not meant to be a language of sheer logical contradiction or nonsense. Likewise, it debunks the grammar of "being" (*Sein, Seiendes*) as fictional, but this does not lead to an alternative grammar of "becoming" (*Werden*): "the means of expression that language offers are of no use to express becoming: it's part of our *inescapable need for preservation* that we constantly posit a cruder world of the permanent, of 'things', etc. In relative terms, we may speak of atoms and monads" (NL 11[73] KSA 13.36 = WLN 213). Nietzsche does not aim at creating a "new language" in the sense of a new set of rules and propositions that might adequately *name* or *denote* reality as such. Actually, his "new language" does not aim at truth *at all* – not, that is, if "truth" is understood as *adequatio intellectus et rei*:

> "The demand for an *adequate mode of expression* is *nonsensical*: it's of the essence of a language, of a means of expression, to express only a relation… The concept of 'truth' is absurd… the whole realm of 'true', 'false' refers only to relations between entities, not to the 'in-itself'" (NL 14[122] KSA 13.303 = WLN 258).

It is our belief in "being" (*an' s Seinde*, TI Reason 1), it is the grammar of "being" which creates the belief that there are "things" one may represent truly or falsely – but this is only an illusion created by reason: "Heraclitus will always be right in thinking that being is an empty fiction" (*dass das Sein eine leere Fiktion ist*, TI Reason 2). All knowledge is relational and perspectival, all reference is reference to relations, and there is no way we can untangle the whole net of relations in which we are entangled. *We* fabricate both the concept of a non-relational reality and the concept of a non-relational "subject" that might free himself from all prejudices, presuppositions, and affects and be able to adequately represent and give expression to an independent reality (e.g. TI Fable, GM III 12). Put differently, what is "given" and constitutes the only possible starting point for philosophy is always already a field of perspectives and interpretations: both the "things" we find out there in the world and the "faculties" we find within us (e.g. the "I", the "will", etc.) are always already our "artistic", interpretative simplifications and falsifications, and the thoughts and words through which we refer to such "things" and "faculties" are always already signs (i.e. creative abbreviations) of previous unconscious perspectives and interpretations carried out by our drives and affects. Not only are all these "signs", both old and new, inseparably related to a whole constellation of other signs – i.e. to *language* —, but they are also inseparably related to our instinctual interpretations of ourselves and the world – i.e. to the *instinctual* "language" of our drives and affects[37].

But what, then, is "new" in Nietzsche's language? First, it is precisely the fact that it is *his* language: it does not purport to be a language spoken by a "subject" free from every entanglement in history and in the world. Second, it is meant to be a language which does not purport to tell *the* "truth". Nietzsche's "theses" are, in fact, his *hypotheses* – not as hypotheses that might one day be definitively confirmed, but as true "experiments" (BGE 36, 42, 205, 210), i.e. means for his philosophical "attempt" (*Versuch*, JGB 36, 42, 205, 210)[38]. They are *his* truths (*meine Wahrheiten*, BGE 231), his "hard"

---

37   On interpretation and Nietzsche's critique of truth as *adequatio* or correspondence, cf. Stegmaier (1985), Stegmaier (1992, 314–330), Abel (1998, 142–157); on thoughts and words as signs and the relation of this idea to the critique of truth, cf. Stegmaier (2000, 51, 60–64); on the instinctual "language of our drives", cf., again, Patrick Wotling's paper in this volume. For the idea that the starting point of philosophy is always already a constellation of interpretations, and there are no "immediate certainties" that could allow philosophy to posit a particular entity as its starting point, cf. BGE 16, 19.

38   Note Nietzsche's use of the terms "hypothesis", "hypotheses" and "hypothetical" in BGE 12, 15, 23, 36 and 208. For the idea that his "attempt" or "experimentation" (*Versuch*) is also a *temptation* (*Versuchung*), cf. BGE 42, 205, 295. See also Scarlett's Marton paper in this volume.

truths – but this means that they are his way of questioning *the* "truth", his way of exposing the lies that have so far counted as truths[39]. Far from being arbitrary, they have their own "objectivity" (GM III 12) – an "objectivity" which is due to the fact that they stem from someone who is, as far as possible, *true to himself*. Being true to oneself implies not pretending to be an universal "subject", but rather recognizing one's prejudices, values, conscious and unconscious beliefs, conscious and unconscious affects. If one conjures up one's affects and questions, from as many perspectives as possible, the valuations that are embedded in them, one reaches a perspective which can be called more "objective" than previous ones: "(...) the *more* affects we allow to speak about one thing, the *more* eyes, different eyes, we can use to observe one thing, the more complete will our 'concept' of this thing, our 'objectivity', be" (GM III 12). Being "objective" in this sense is to be *honest (redlich)*, *truthful (wahrhaftig)* – and honesty (*Redlichkeit*), truthfulness (*Wahrhaftigkeit*) is, Nietzsche believes, precisely his *virtue*. His "truths" are what he must believe if he is truthful. His "truths" are not "theses" —they are his truthfulness[40].

Thus, it is out of truthfulness that Nietzsche questions the traditional meaning and value of truth. It is out of truthfulness that he is led to believe that (1) "the character of existence is not 'true', is *false*... one simply no longer has any reason to talk oneself into there being a *true* world" (NL 11[99] KSA 13.48 = WLN 219), "we don't have the truth" (NL 3[19] KSA 9.52, my translation), "(...) the *erroneousness* of the world we think we live in is the most certain and solid fact that our eyes can still grab hold of" (BGE 34); (2) the existence of the concept of truth depends on the existence of a certain kind of *will* – there is a concept of truth only insofar as there is a "will to truth" (cf. BGE 1, 10, GM III 23–28); (3) this "will to truth" is not the opposite of the will not to know, of the will to what is uncertain, to what is

---

39   See BGE 39, 59, 257, EH Why I am a Destiny 1 ("(...) my truth is *terrible*: because *lies* have been called truth so far"), and Stegmaier (2008, 94–96) on this particular passage of EH; on Nietzsche's new concept of truth, cf. Stegmaier (1985). On the hardness of truth, cf. BGE 257, 39, 59; GM I 1, GM III 19.

40   On honesty (*Redlichkeit*) and truthfulness (*Wahrhaftigkeit*), cf. BGE 227, EH Preface 3, EH Why I am a Destiny 1–3; see also BGE 5 (philosophers so far have not been "honest enough"), 43, 205, 211, 230, 295. On truth as truthfulness, cf., again, Stegmaier (1985 and 2008), Richardson (1996, 260–276).

false, illusory, the "will to lie", but rather its "refinement" (BGE 24), i.e. a given development from this other, moral fundamental will of our organism[41]; (4) untruth is "a condition of life" (BGE 4) and the traditional concept of truth is just a lie which is necessary for "the preservation of a particular type of life" (BGE 3, cf. BGE 34, GM I 13, III 12); and, finally, (5) "it is no more than a moral prejudice that the truth is worth more than appearance" (BGE 34) – i.e. the unconditional value that has been attributed to truth so far can and even must be questioned (cf. BGE Preface, 1, 2, GM III 24–27).

This questioning and the new type of "truths" that result from it are, in fact, nothing other than Nietzsche's *genealogical insights*. Nietzschean genealogy does not inquire on what "is", neither does it focus on the arguments for or against theses that purport to be adequate representations of an independent reality, nor does it ask for the "conditions of possibility" of certain judgements. Instead, it probes the *history* of our beliefs – and this means that it probes the history of our *instinctual life*, the history of the organic *needs* out of which such beliefs have *developed*. Thus, for instance, the Kantian question "How are synthetic judgements *a priori* possible?" should be replaced by the genealogical question "Why is the belief in such judgements *necessary*?" (BGE 11), i.e. why do certain forms of life *need to believe* in such judgements? How did they emerge and why have they been preserved? What is the history of their development? For whom have they had value so far? And what is their present day meaning and their value for us?[42]

Raising these kinds of questions – raising genealogical questions – is Nietzsche's "new language". This is his way of thinking beyond the grammar of being and beyond the oppositions that have dominated Western thought for millennia (cf., again, BGE 2). It is his way of *overcoming* such oppositions – of allowing more affects to speak

---

41   Cf. also BGE 2:"How *could* anything originate out of its opposite? Truth from error, for instance?", BGE 229, 230 and e.g. NL 14[18] KSA 13.226, NL 14[24] KSA 13.229, NL 17[3] KSA 13.520.

42   In BGE, Nietzsche does not yet use the term "genealogy". Instead, he speaks of "psychology" as a "morphology and *doctrine of the development of the will to power*" (*Morphologie und Entwicklungslehre des Willens zur Macht*, BGE 23, my translation). This is, however, an excellent definition of what he later calls "genealogy" in GM.

about one thing, of using more "eyes" to observe one thing, of building a more complete concept of this thing. This "more complete concept" comes from insight into the history of mankind's *beliefs* and *valuations* of such a thing. What is questioned and investigated is not the thing "itself", but rather the "needs" that have led to opposite beliefs concerning that same thing (and to a general belief in opposite values). It is by overcoming this type of oppositions that Nietzsche reaches "new expansions of distance within the soul itself" (BGE 257). Practicing genealogy in order to ascend from opposite perspectives and valuations to more comprehensive perspectives and revaluations – this is Nietzsche's particular type of "high spirituality" (BGE 219), or of philosophy as a "real *power* of spirituality, of real *profundity* of spiritual vision" (BGE 252)[43].

One such opposition is the traditional opposition between instinct and reason, or instinct and language. Its intrinsic connection with the several problems we have analyzed implies that its overcoming must be a part of the larger project of "revaluation of all values". As in all other cases, overcoming such an important opposition inherited from metaphysics leads to the "enormous, practically untouched realm of dangerous knowledge" (BGE 23)[44].

It leads – or Nietzsche believes it leads – "beyond good and evil" (BGE 4, 212, 260).

Bibliography

Abel, Günter (1998), *Nietzsche. Die Dynamik der Willen Zur Macht und die ewige Wiederkehr*, Berlin/New York (Walter de Gruyter).

Abel, Günter (2001), "Bewußtsein- Sprache- Natur. Nietzsches Philosophie des Geistes", in: *Nietzsche-Studien* 30 (2000), 1–43.

---

43 Cf., for example, NL 2[108] KSA 12.114 = WLN 80: "that every *heightening of man* brings with it an overcoming of narrower interpretations; that every increase in strength and expansion of power opens up new perspectives and demands a belief in new horizons – this runs through my writings". And Nietzsche adds: "The world *which matters to us* is false, i.e., is not a fact but a fictional elaboration and filling out of a meagre store of observations; it is 'in flux', as something becoming, as a constantly shifting falsity that never gets any nearer to truth, for – there is no 'truth'".

44 Cf. Werner Stegmaier's paper in this volume.

Clark, Maudemarie (1990), *Nietzsche On Truth and Philosophy*, Cambridge/ New York/Port Chester/Melbourne/Sydney (Cambridge University Press).

Constâncio, João (2011), *On Consciousness: Nietzsche's Departure From Schopenhauer* forthcoming in *Nietzsche-Studien* 40.

Janaway, Christopher (2007), *Beyond Selflessness, Reading Nietzsche's Genealogy*, Oxford/New York (Oxford University Press).

Katsafanas, Paul (2005), "Nietzsche's Theory of Mind: Consciousness and Conceptualization", in: *European Journal of Philosophy* 13, 1–31.

Kaufmann, Walter (1974), *Nietzsche: Philosopher, Psychologist, Antichrist*, Princeton (Princeton University Press).

Leiter, Brian (2002), *Nietzsche on Morality*, London: (Routledge).

Lupo, Luca, (2006), *Le Colombe dello Scettico, Riflessioni di Nietzsche sulla Coscienza negli anni 1880–1888*, Pisa (Edizioni ETS).

Müller-Lauter, Wolfgang (1999a), *Nietzsche. His Philosophy of Contradictions and the Contradictions of his Philosophy*, transl. David J. Parent, Urbana and Chicago (University of Illinois Press).

Müller-Lauter, Wolfgang (1999b), *Über Werden und Wille zur Macht, Nietzsche- Interpretationen I*, Berlin/New York (Walter de Gruyter).

Nehamas, Alexander (1985), *Nietzsche. Life as Literature*, Cambridge MA/ London England (Harvard University Press).

Plato (1900, repr. 1991), "Phaedo", in: *Platonis Opera Tomus*, ed. I. Burnet, Oxford (Clarendon Press).

Poellner, Peter (2000), *Nietzsche and Metaphysics*, Oxford (Oxford University Press).

Richardson, John (1996), *Nietzsche's System*, Oxford/New York (Oxford University Press).

Richardson, John (2004), *Nietzsche's New Darwinism*, Oxford/New York (Oxford University Press).

Simon, Josef (1984), "Das Problem des Bewusstseins bei Nietzsche und der traditionelle Bewusstseinsbegriff", in: Djuric, M./ Simon, J., *Nietzsche in der Diskussion, Zur Aktualität Nietzsches*, vol. II, Würzburg (Königshausen und Neumann), 17–33.

Stegmaier, Werner (1985), "Nietzsches Neubestimmung der Wahrheit", in: *Nietsche-Studien* 14 (1985), 69–95.

Stegmaier, Werner (1992), *Philosophie der Fluktuanz. Dilthey und Nietzsche*, Göttingen (Vandenhoeck & Ruprecht).

Stegmaier, Werner (2000), "Nietzsches Zeichen", in: *Nietzsche-Studien* 29 (2000), 41–69.

Stegmaier, Werner (2008), "Schicksal Nietzsche? Zu Nietzsches Selbsteinschätzung als Schicksal der Philosophie und der Menschheit (Ecce Homo, Warum Ich Ein Schicksal Bin 1)", in: *Nietzsche-Studien* 37 (2008), 1–53.

Vinzens, Albert (1999), *Friedrich Nietzsches Instinktverwandlung*, Basel (Schwabe).

João Constâncio

Wotling, Patrick (1995), *Nietzsche et le problème de la civilisation*, Paris (PUF).
Wotling, Patrick (2008a), "La culture comme problème. La redetermination
    nietzscheenne du questionnement philosophique", in: *Nietzsche-Studien*
    37 (2008), 1–50.
Wotling, Patrick (2008b), *La philosophie de l'esprit libre, Introduction à
    Nietzsche*, Flammarion (Paris).

Greed and *Love*:
Genealogy, Dissolution and Therapeutic
Effects of a Linguistic Difference in FW 14*

Chiara Piazzesi

> *Was wir lieben, das ist unser:*
> *aber durch das Verlangen darnach*
> *berauben wir uns desselben.*
> (F. Nietzsche, NL 1882, 17[36])

My aim in this paper is to analyse the little-commented aphorism 14 of *Die Fröhliche Wissenschaft*[1], to bring out its characteristics as a "pre-genealogical exercise", in line with the task of philosophical research that Nietzsche presented as his aim at the outset of his work, in section FW 7.

All kinds of passions have to be thought through separately, pursued separately through ages, peoples, great and small individuals; their entire reason and all their evaluations and modes of illuminating things must be revealed! So far, all that has given colour to existence still lacks a history: where could you find a history of love, of avarice, of envy, of conscience, of piety, of cruelty? (GS 7)[2].

---

* This work is part of a wider research project, which I have been able to carry out thanks to the support of the Fritz-Thyssen Stiftung. A previous version was delivered at the International Conference of the GIRN *Lectures du Gai Savoir* (Reims, 12–13 March 2009) and is included in the *Atti* of the conference – *Letture della* Gaia scienza – *Lectures du* Gai savoir (2010), ed. Campioni, G./Piazzesi, C./Wotling, P., Pisa (ETS). A Portuguese translation of a previous version has been published in the *Cadernos Nietzsche*, vol. 27 (2010), 73–115. I am grateful to Giuliano Campioni, Marco Brusotti, Patrick Wotling, Scarlett Marton, Maria João Branco, Maria Filomena Molder, Luca Lupo, Blaise Benoit, Silvio Pfeuffer and Andrea Bertino for their constructive suggestions.

1   A survey of the register of *Nietzsche-Studien* shows as clearly as one could wish, that the little-quoted aphorism is usually remembered mainly for its final remark on friendship, and not for its examination of the phenomeon of love.

2   FW 7, KSA 3.378: "Alle Arten Passionen müssen einzeln durchdacht, einzeln durch Zeiten, Völker, grosse und kleine Einzelne verfolgt werden; ihre ganze Vernunft und alle ihre Werthschätzungen und Beleuchtungen der Dinge sollen an's Licht hinaus! Bisher hat alles Das, was dem Dasein Farbe gegeben hat, noch

Chiara Piazzesi

I use the expression "pre-genealogical exercise" as, in the spirit of the title *"The things people call love"* (*Was Alles Liebe genannt wird*), FW 14 dissolves an apparently unproblematic linguistic unit (love, *Liebe*), showing that linguistic usage does not denote the essence of things, but actually responds to needs and strategies that transcend it. Pointing out these strategies of power underlying language dissolves not only the solidity of language, but also that of the experience that it circumscribes and denotes: as the framework of self-understanding (*Selbstverständnis*) is subjected to criticism and relativization, what is called into question is psychology itself and the individual, "psychology-carrying" subject.

Nietzsche himself, in the Preface to GM, accepted that his genealogical aim could be extended to his earlier works from MA I on, although he noted their relative immaturity in defining aim and methodology[3]. The main issues remain basically the same: recognizing our extraneousness from ourselves in those very judgments and categories that are most familiar to us, analysing the conditions in which the values that structure our (moral) perception of the world developed, and questioning their value (the value of values), their effect on life itself, and their nature as signs or symptoms of a certain form of life etc. (GM *Vorrede* 1–3).

We can therefore adopt here M. Saar's definition of genealogy as a program of relativization and critique of present-day self-understanding and self-relations via the analysis of historical power relations[4], which, he claims, also transcends the specific context of GM and may refer to a more general aim in Nietzsche's critical procedure.

To bring out these general aims from the example of FW 14, I intend in this paper to provide: 1) an analysis of the text of the aphorism and its characteristics, which will make use of a two-fold

---

keine Geschichte: oder wo gäbe es eine Geschichte der Liebe, der Habsucht, des Neides, des Gewissens, der Pietät, der Grausamkeit?"

3   Cf. GM *Vorrede* 4, KSA 5.251: "Damals brachte ich, wie gesagt, zum ersten Male jene Herkunfts-Hypothesen an's Tageslicht, denen diese Abhandlungen gewidmet sind, mit Ungeschick, wie ich mir selbst am letzten verbergen möchte, noch unfrei, noch ohne eine eigne Sprache für diese eignen Dinge und mit mancherlei Rückfälligkeit und Schwankung".

4   Cf. Saar (2007, 293). Saar defines genealogy as "das Programm der historisierenden und machtanalytischen Relativierung und Kritik gegenwärtiger Selbstverständnisse und Selbstverhältnisse".

digression on other contexts in Nietzsche, but above all on points of contact between the analysis of love in FW 14 and Stendhal's theory of *cristallisation*; 2) an analysis of the genealogical-critical intentions in the aphorism, which it carries out *performatively* (with additional reference to present-day sociological research, in order to better contextualize Nietzsche's undertaking); 3) a survey of the results of this critical *action* and of the new horizons of experience that it opens.

1. FW 14: Analysis and Interpretation of the Text.

> *Gefahr der Sprache für die geistige Freiheit. –*
> *Jedes Wort ist ein Vorurtheil.*

(WS 55)

Let us analyse the main stages of the text of FW 14.

The title introduces the task[5]: Love is not assumed as denoting something for which we have a univocal definition, but as a linguistic container ("genannt wird") for many, presumably heterogeneous, things ("was Alles"). Nietzsche then immediately defines the question:

> Greed and love; such different feelings these terms evoke! And yet it could be the same instinct, named twice: once disparaged by those who already *have*, in whom the instinct has somewhat calmed down and who now fear for what they 'have'; the other time seen from the standpoint of the unsatisfied, the thirsty, and therefore glorified as 'good' (GS 14)[6].

Not only might what language induces us to regard as unitary (*Liebe*) actually be a multiplicity of things; but also what language induces us to regard as different/dual (*Habsucht* "against" *Liebe*, greed "against"

---

5   In a note of 1880 Nietzsche set himself this precise task: "Wie ein Trieb, je nachdem man ihn lobt und tadelt, als gut oder böse empfunden wird, an der *Liebe* zu zeigen (bei Griechen, bei asketischen Christen, in der christlichen Ehe usw.) Alle *Idealisierung eines Triebes* beginnt damit, daß man ihn unter die lobenswerthen Dinge rechnet" (NL1880, 7[75] KSA 9.332).

6   FW 14, KSA 3.386, 7–14: "Habsucht und Liebe: wie verschieden empfinden wir bei jedem dieser Worte! - und doch könnte es der selbe Trieb sein, zweimal benannt, das eine Mal verunglimpft vom Standpuncte der bereits Habenden aus, in denen der Trieb etwas zur Ruhe gekommen ist und die nun für ihre «Habe» fürchten; das andere Mal vorn Standpuncte der Unbefriedigten, Durstigen aus, und daher verherrlicht als «gut»".

love) might actually denote the same thing, more precisely the same drive or instinct (*Trieb*), but given different names and so *made* into different things. The **first point**, then: a double linguistic demysti- fication, which brings out the performative character of language.

The phenomenon also has another characteristic: naming is deter- mined by the different viewpoints from which we name a thing, a feeling, or an action. So, the **second point**: naming depends on intentionality, more precisely on a *strategy*[7] on the part of the namer. Put differently: the relation between word and object denoted can be modified starting from different strategic pressures at different times. Not only that: Nietzsche writes that "we feel" ("*wir empfinden*") differently in relation to *words*. And so the **third point**: on the one hand, moral attributions, attributions of value, are hidden in the apparent neutrality of language, and these can vary over time, in different ages and places and in the relations between people and between groups[8]; but, on the other, these valuations are set off again in our psycho-linguistic experience, which means they structure not only language, but our psychology and so our experience[9] – and all this is concentrated in different ways of "understanding" (*verstehen*, as, for

---

7   The term "strategy" here does not only indicate rational and reflexive calculation, so much as what we might call a broader, characteristic "intentionality" of the relations of power. According to Foucault (1994, 241 ff) a "stratégie de pouvoir" is "l'ensemble des moyens mis en œuvre pour faire fonctionner ou pour maintenir un dispositif de pouvoir", and power relations are always strategic as they "constituent des modes d'action sur l'action possible, éventuelle, supposée des autres", and, if it is true that there is no power relation without "résistance", "toute relation de pouvoir implique donc, du moins de façon virtuelle, une stratégie de lutte".

8   "Die moralischen Worte sind in den verschiedensten Zeiten eines Volkes dieselben: dagegen ist das Gefühl, welches sie begleitet, wenn sie ausgesprochen werden, immer im Wandel. Jede Zeit färbt dieselben alten Worte neu: jede Zeit stellt einige dieser Worte in den Vordergrund und andere zurück" (NL 1882, 20[3] KSA 9.680).

9   The reference to *Empfinden* in relation to experiences connected with words and the valuations, that words involve, is fundamental. Our reaction to a word or an expression is not immediately conceptual, but happens first on the level of emotions, sensations and impressions. To put it better: concepts conceal valuations, images of the world and the self that human beings crystallize in language; they are not 'arbitrary' signs, but the fruit and constant re-production of an activity, and so of a way of being human. The alternative between a purely arbitrary concept that becomes a convention, and a concept that has an ontologically necessary internal relation with the thing denoted is misleading:

example, in FW 88 in relation to "truth"). This last point seems to me
central: it is the basis of the therapeutic intention, characteristic of the
genealogical procedure, which the aphorism seems to me to be trying
to achieve. More generally, Nietzsche seems to me to have expounded
the theoretical premises of his argument in FW 14 here, justifying the
aphorism being characterized as a pre-genealogical exercise – we shall
come back to this (§ 2).

Nietzsche later offers a questioning reading of the most different
types of love as articulations of *Habsucht* or the *Drang nach
Eigenthum*:

> Our love of our neighbours – is it not a craving for new *property*?
> And likewise our love of knowledge, of truth, and altogether any
> craving for what is new? (GS 14)[10].

I say he *offers* it, because this questioning formulation is followed by
an explanation that indirectly turns it into an affirmation:

> We slowly grow tired of the old, of what we safely possess, and we
> strech out our hands again; even the most beautiful landscape is no
> longer sure of our love after we have lived in it for three months,
> and some more distant coast excites our greed: possession usually
> diminishes the possession. The pleasure we take in ourselves tries
> to preserve itself by time and again changing something new *into
> ourselves* – that is simply what possession means (GS 14)[11].

All the forms of love cited thus come down to a desire for possession

---

there is also the possibility of a concept being the precipitate of judgments,
practices and activities (in short, a Wittgensteinian "use") that are reactivated
as the concept is used, and *so* arouse impressions, feelings, sensations, and
emotional and imaginative experiences of various kinds in those who come
into contact with the specific occurrences of this use. On the other hand, for
Nietzsche, creative, emotional activity is already enough to give rise to linguistic
conceptions and give them their "nuance", which then functions in directing
how the concept is used. Take the description of the "linguistic-constitutive"
work – in a sense that is by no means purely conceptual: it is a "Dichtung" –
carried out by the "Denken-Empfindenden" in FW 301.

10   FW 14, KSA 3.386, 14–17: "Unsere Nächstenliebe - ist sie nicht ein Drang nach
     neuem Eigenthum? Und ebenso unsere Liebe zum Wissen, zur Wahrheit und
     überhaupt all jener Drang nach Neuigkeiten?"

11   FW 14, KSA 3.386, 17–25: "Wir werden des Alten, sicher Besessenen allmählich
     überdrüssig und strecken die Hände wieder aus; selbst die schönste Landschaft,
     in der wir drei Monate leben, ist unserer Liebe nicht mehr gewiss, und irgend eine
     fernere Küste reizt unsere Habsucht an: der Besitz wird durch das Besitzen

that is inexhaustible because it coincides with straining towards a reflexive pleasure (*Lust an uns selber*) that seems in the end unsatisfiable and so constantly goes beyond satisfaction in the possession that has been acquired. The desire for a new possession of something (or possession of something new) is a desire for change, for modifying and going beyond oneself, and so for a new form of pleasure that is drawn from oneself. To clarify what Nietzsche is referring to, let us move away from the text of FW 14 and seek elsewhere the key to this phenomenology of *Habsucht* ("greed"): first in other passages of Nietzsche, and then in a famous source of his inspiration and thought – Stendhal.

Habsucht and the Idealizing Process

The word *Habsucht* (usually translated as "greed") appears for the first time in the printed works in FW 7, in which Nietzsche contemplates a future history of "all that has given colour to existence" (*was dem Dasein Farbe gegeben hat*) – not only *Habsucht*, but love, envy, conscience, piety and cruelty (*Liebe, Neid, Gewissen, Pietät* and *Grausamkeit*) too; and for the second time in FW 14 itself, which clarifies with an example how we should see this history: not as the search for "original" moral valuations, so to speak, which fixed the definition (the essence) of this or that feeling, but, it seems to me, as the history of the development of the subsequent systems of moral valuation, and, with them, the subjective experience that can occur in their framework. It is not so much a question of defining greed or love, as seeing the reciprocities, legitimacies and spaces of meaning that moral language in various periods ("through ages, peoples, great and small individuals", GS 7) has assigned to a certain feeling or disposition *in a polar relation* – in "tension" – with all the others, which at the same time it specifies in the given moral framework (for example: greed "against" love).

In the posthumous texts of 1881, Nietzsche frees *Habsucht* of its negative moral definition, and characterizes it as a natural drive *par excellence*, a vital tendency of self-affirmation[12]: once he has

---

zumeist geringer. Unsere Lust an uns selber will sich so aufrecht erhalten, dass sie immer wieder etwas Neues *in uns selber* verwandelt, - das eben heisst Besitzen. Eines Besitzes überdrüssig werden, das ist: unserer selber überdrüssig werden".

recognized the fundamentally physiological character of this drive having its "end" in itself, in enlarging itself, Nietzsche challenges the possibility of there being intrinsically moral drives in human beings. The appearance of moral dispositions is the result of upbringing, which establishes priorities in the satisfaction of this elemental drive and in this way determines how it will be articulated[13]. We shall return to this.

In JGB 23 too Nietzsche was to speak (hypothetically) of a "Lehre von der Ableitbarkeit aller guten Triebe aus den schlimmen", ("a doctrine of the derivation of all good drives from the bad", BGE 23), which he regarded as "the affects of hatred, envy, greed, and power-lust as the conditioning affects of life, as elements that fundamentally and essentially need to be present in the total economy of life, and consequently need to be enhanced where life is enhanced" (BGE 23)[14]. (i) *Habsucht*, like *Grausamkeit*, is thus also the basis of experiences we perceive and describe as impersonal, detached, and far from the passions and the personality of desire: Nietzsche's description of knowledge as passion and the resulting direct relation between *Habsucht* and *Erkenntnis* is also part of the context of the dissolution of these moralistic illusions[15]. In FW 14 too the linguistic demystification of the moralization of language (and, with it, of thought, feelings and experience) is carried out through reference to our drives, which are in turn moulded by linguistic articulation.

But how does this articulation of *Habsucht* occur in all the moral

---

12 Cf. the critique of Spencer's moral Darwinism, which leaves "das Böse" outside the conditions favourable to human evolution: "was wäre denn ohne Furcht Neid Habsucht aus dem Menschen geworden! Er existierte nicht mehr: und wenn man sich den reichsten edelsten und fruchtbarsten Menschen denkt, *ohne Böses* – so denkt man einen Widerspruch" (NL 1881, 11[43] KSA 9.457). 'Altruistic' dispositions too are only hierarchies of drives, and so anything but 'selbstlos' (NL 1881, 11[56] KSA 9.461 f). In this conception of the struggle between drives the influence of his reading of W. Roux also plays a role in this period, cf. the comment on the corresponding fragments in KSA 14.645; see also Müller-Lauter (1978).

13 See, for example, the metaphor of the man who treats himself as a *dividuum* in morality, sacrificing one drive for another (HH I 57).

14 JGB 23, KSA 5.38: "(...) die Affekte Hass, Neid, Habsucht, Herrschsucht als lebenbedingende Affekte, als Etwas, das im Gesammt-Haushalte des Lebens grundsätzlich und grundwesentlich vorhanden sein muss, folglich noch gesteigert werden muss, falls das Leben noch gesteigert werden soll"

15 Cf. FW 242 and 249 (with the respective *Vorstufe* 13[7] of 1881, KSA 9.619).

forms, of which *Habsucht* itself is the "basic" drive?

(ii) In knowledge too *Habsucht* acts as a creative and imaginative force, as an idealizing power. In an interesting 1881 note on the subject Nietzsche conjectures that all moral feelings may be traced back to a thirst for having and keeping ("Haben-wollen und Halten-wollen", NL 11[19] KSA 9.449), and he thus offers a key for imagining both the moralization of the desire for possession and the idealization it generates. As regards the first aspect, the real difficulty of the longed-for total possession of something or someone leads to the rarefaction of desire and a "long-distance" affirmation of it, so to speak, so that we shift the investment of our drive from real to imaginary possession. It is in the context of this process that knowledge develops, starting from the recognition of possession as difficult and unattainable: in that it is a self-limiting deviation from "Haben" to "völlige[s] Erkennen", which is considered a satisfactory form of possession, knowledge would then be "die letzte Stufe der Moralität", "the last stage of morality"[16]. As for the second aspect, the idealization of the desired object, which takes place at the intermediary *Stufen* of the process described, is in turn functional to an active adjustment to the difficulty of possession: the enrichment of the desired object increases the pleasure of the representation of possession and so the pleasure that is received from the effort to obtain it[17]. Thus, "wir denken uns die Dinge, *die wir erreichen können*, so, daß ihr Besitz

---

16   Cf. NL Frühjahr - Herbst 1881, 11[19] KSA 9.466. In fragment 11[10] of spring-autumn 1881 Nietzsche underlines that it is not love for another, so much as the capacity to change many points of view (to see with other eyes) in knowledge, that is the opposite of *Selbstsucht* (KSA 9.444). Cf. also NL 11[65] KSA 9.466.

17   This convergence of *Distanzierung* and *Idealisierung* might explain why aristocratic morality regards *amour-passion* as a form of *freiwillige Selbstunterwerfung*, a disposition to *Selbststeigerung* and to self-strengthening through the tie with freedom, which increases the stimulus towards the desired object and leads constantly to *Selbstüberwindung* (JGB 260); by contrast, in Christian morality (JGB 189) it is seen as a sublimation and rarefaction of *Geschlechtstrieb*, thus both partly defusing its violence, but also simply redirecting it towards another investment of the drive – in moral restraint and self-discipline. In both cases mechanism and effects are the same – the power of the drive itself when deviated becomes a power for the drive's self-limitation – but the procedure is part of a different moral system of valuations. On the basic procedure of self-moulding as a fundamental anthropological activity, which Nietzsche analyses in other contexts too, see the interesting reflections of Sloterdijk (2009, particularly 52ff and 521ff).

uns höchst werthvoll erscheint". This is what the lover does with the loved one, the father with his son, what we do with the enemy we hope to overcome, etc.: "wir suchen die Philosophie, die zu unserem Besitz paßt d.h. ihn vergoldet" (NL Frühjahr - Herbst 1881, 11[19] KSA 9.449). It is in this sense, by virtue of this process of rarefaction, idealization and moralization that, *before* any moral valuation, *Liebe* and *Wohlwollen* are in a relation of continuity with *Habsucht* and *Besitzen-wollen*: love as "Schätzung und Überschätzung von etwas, dessen Besitz man begehrt", *Wohlwollen* as "Schätzung von etwas, dessen Besitz man hat, das man sich erhalten will" (NL Frühjahr - Herbst 1881, 11[105] KSA 9.478).

Nietzsche claims that the moral feelings (and corresponding actions) defined as altruistic are not qualitatively different, as regards their root in the drives, from those feelings (and corresponding actions) that are contrasted with them in the given system of moral valuations, and defined as egoistic and discouraged as immoral[18]. But he also reflects on the origin of the idealization[19] and transfiguration that is the basis of these oppositions of value, which distinguish and contrast impulses and feelings that are fundamentally related: how does it happen, he wonders in FW 14, that the fundamental characteristic of strongly self-affirming drives and feelings is denied and they are defined as non-egoistic/altruistic? (iii)

In the same way, in the text of FW 14:

(i) Benefactors and those who have compassion (*Wohltätige und Mitleidige*) are unmasked as "interested", moved by drives that are absolutely not "moral"[20] (= not altruistic):

When we see someone suffering, we like to use this opportunity to

---

18 Nietzsche mentions in note 11[56] of 1881 (KSA 9.461f) "die Habsucht der Geschlechtssinn, Grausamkeit Eroberungslust usw." and refers to the "Bann" concerning them.

19 *Ibid.*, Nietzsche uses the verb *idealisieren*.

20 Salaquarda (1997,175), who sees this critical form as characteristic of FW and explicitly cites the example of FW 14, points out that Nietzsche really began systematically subjecting the virtues to this analytic procedure in MA I 1: "Als er die traditionelle Moral mit ihren grundlegenden Werten und Tugenden zum zentralen Gegenstand seiner Analyse machte, bemühte er sich, die Triebe aufzudecken, die in ihnen zum Ausdruck kommen. Tugenden [...] sind nichts Ursprüngliches und schon gar nichts Einheitliches. Sie haben eine Triebbasis, die vielfältig und mitunter auch disparat sein kann".

take possession of him; that is for example what those who become his benefactors and those who have compassion for him do, and they call the lust for new possessions that is awakened in them 'love'; and this delight is like that aroused by the prospect of a new conquest (GS 14)[21].

As we shall see, FW 13 had already clarified how *Wohltun*, just like *Wehtun*, is no more than an exercise of power (*Macht*) over the other. In FW 14, however, also unlike some preparatory fragments (e.g. NL Herbst 1880, 6[446] KSA 9.314), the reference to the linguistic problem, with which the aphorism opens, also modifies the polemical nature of this unmasking, giving it a strongly proto-genealogical nuance. This shifting of the polemical plane also applies to the following point, and becomes still clearer, as we shall see, in relation to point (iii).

(ii) As was hinted in M 145 too[22], we are offered a phenomenology of love between the sexes as thirst for possession, violence and "egoism", in contrast with its positive moral characterization[23] (FW 14, KSA 3.386, 32; 387, 15);

(iii) this poses the central question, which reveals the genealogical interest at stake, taking the argument to the *Arbeit für Arbeitsame* in FW 7 ("Alle Arten Passionen müssen einzeln durchdacht, einzeln durch Zeiten, Völker, grosse und kleine Einzelne verfolgt werden; ihre ganze Vernunft und alle ihre Werthschätzungen und Beleuchtungen der Dinge sollen an's Licht hinaus!", KSA 3.378):

then one is indeed amazed that this wild greed and injustice of sexual love has been as glorified and deified as it has in all ages – yes, that this love has furnished the concept of love as the opposite of

---

21   FW 14, KSA 3.386, 27–32: "Wenn wir jemanden leiden sehen, so benutzen wir gerne die jetzt gebotene Gelegenheit, Besitz von ihm zu ergreifen; diess thut zum Beispiel der Wohlthätige und Mitleidige, auch er nennt die in ihm erweckte Begierde nach neuem Besitz 'Liebe', und hat seine Lust dabei wie bei einer neuen ihm winkenden Eroberung".

22   "'Unegoistisch!' – Jener ist hohl und will voll werden, Dieser ist überfüllt und will sich ausleeren, – Beide treibt es, sich ein Individuum zu suchen, das ihnen dazu dient. Und diesen Vorgang, im höchsten Sinne verstanden, nennt man beidemal mit Einem Worte: Liebe, – wie? die Liebe sollte etwas Unegoistisches sein?" (M 145, KSA 3.137).

23   On the egoism of love cf. also NL Herbst 1881, KSA 9: 6[54] (which recalls Stendhal), 6[164], 6[446], 6[454] Herbst 1880, and 12[20].

egoism when it may in fact be the most candid expression of egoism (GS 14)[24].

The example of love, because of the extensive spectrum of moral actions that are denoted with its name (*Was Alles Liebe genannt wird*), is probably the best for examining the significance of these phenomena of idealization and moralization. We should bear in mind that they do not have a hierarchical or causal relation with each other, in the sense that one can be traced back to the other, but are two aspects of the process of articulating desire in discourse, which in our civilization seems to have taken place, so far, only in relation to moral distinctions[25].

As we have already suggested, the process of idealization is inherent to the self-referential and reflexive structure of desire itself in that it is thirst for possession and conquest so as to increase "the pleasure we take in ourselves" (*die Lust an sich selbst*). Desire itself increases as the image of the desired object is enriched and beautified: it stimulates itself at once, through the effect of its imaginative creativity, whether possession is not yet achieved[26], or whether it is. In the lattter case Nietzsche sees in the difficulty of completely possessing another individual the very possibility of love enduring[27]: the prospect of new

---

24 FW 14, KSA 3.387, 15–2: "so wundert man sich in der That, dass diese wilde Habsucht und Ungerechtigkeit der Geschlechtsliebe dermaassen verherrlicht und vergöttlicht worden ist, wie zu allen Zeiten geschehen, ja, dass man aus dieser Liebe den Begriff Liebe als den Gegensatz des Egoismus hergenommen hat, während sie vielleicht gerade der unbefangenste Ausdruck des Egoismus ist".

25 As Sloterdijk suggests (2009, 194 and 520), Nietzsche was very probably thinking precisely of the separation of the human being's self-shaping ascetic potential (and so of idealization processes too) from the moral values on which it has so far drawn for its own value, when he claims he wants to make ascesis natural again, putting it at the service of an increase in strength and power (cf. NL 1887, 9[93] KSA 12.387). See on this Abel (1984, 70ff) and Piazzesi, *"Pour une nouvelle conception du rapport entre théorie et pratique: la philologie comme éthique et méthodologie"* (forthcoming).

26 "Wir denken die Dinge, *die wir erreichen können*, so, daß ihr Besitz uns höchst werthvoll erscheint [...]. Wir haben zuerst eine ungefähre Berechnung was wir überhaupt *erbeuten können* – und nun ist unsere Phantasie thätig, diese zukünftigen Besitzthümer uns äußerst *werth*voll zu machen (auch Ämter Ehren Verkehr usw.)" (NL1881, 11[19] KSA 9.449). Nietzsche closes the note quoted with a reference to the reflexiveness of the desire for possession in the form of "Selbstbeherrschung".

lands to conquer stimulates desire, as this is what it aspires to (in FW 14: desire for new transformations of itself through possession, or perhaps just *the idea*, of the new). In the process of idealization and rarefaction or deviation of immediate satisfaction, when – as we saw in note 11[19] of 1881 – direct possession is in itself difficult, the solution of doing one's utmost for the good of the desired object also falls away. In FW 13, where he sketches a phenomenology of *Machtgefühl* as pleasure in control or possession, which is achieved in the possibility of doing good or ill to those over whom power is exercised (*Wohlthun, Wehethun*), Nietzsche writes:

> Benefiting and hurting others are ways of exercising one's power over them (…). We *benefit* and show benevolence toward those who already depend on us in some way (that is, who are used to thinking of us as their causes); we want to increase their power because we thus increase our own, or we want to show them the advantage of being in our power (GS 13)[28].

Idealization no longer concerns only the object, which in a sense remains unaware of it, but the very elation of dependence or mutual belonging, which nevertheless still aims at increasing the desire for possession and the pleasure deriving from it[29]. At this point, I think, idealization and moralization become confused, and the possible mechanisms of the moralization process come to light more clearly. In the case of *Wohlthun*, we can speak of idealization, as it does not imply only an advantage for the one who receives its benefits, but also a fundamental negation, a concealing of the real motives for the effort that the desirer or lover makes to do the loved one good. This

---

27 Cf. NL 1881, 12[194] KSA 9.609: the possibility of "lange Liebe" depends on the fact that "es thun sich immer neue, noch unentdeckte Gründe und Hinterräume der Seele auf, und auch nach diesen streckt sich die unendliche Habsucht der Liebe aus".

28 FW 13, KSA 3.384: "Mit Wohlthun und Wehethun übt man seine Macht an Andern aus […]. Mit *Wohlthun* und Wohlwollen an Solchen, die irgendwie schon von uns abhängen (das heisst gewohnt sind, an uns als ihre Ursachen zu denken); wir wollen ihre Macht mehren, weil wir so die unsere mehren, oder wir wollen ihnen den Vortheil zeigen, den es hat, in unserer Macht zu stehen".

29 FW 118 even distinguishes between "Aneignungstrieb" and "Unterwerfungstrieb" in the relation of *Wohlwollen*, "je nachdem der Stärkere oder der Schwächere Wohlwollen empfindet", and FW 119 clarifies how this desire to assimilate the other as a function or become the function of another has basically nothing to do with altruism.

strategic negation performs an important function of mediation, of articulating the violence and blindness of desire, which significantly advances, in Luhmann's words[30], the probability that (loving) communication is accepted by the other. It is also accompanied, one may imagine, by a subjective negation: the delusion that one is *really* doing the other good out of love for him or her – for love of the object of desire, which is enriched and adorned with every possible perfection by desire itself[31] (which forgets it was the first to attribute those perfections to it)[32].

There is good reason for thinking that the fundamental source for Nietzsche's conception of idealization of the passions here is the theory of *cristallisation*, which Stendhal expounds particularly in chapters XI and XII of *De l'Amour* (1822). In my view, this is the second place in which to seek clarification of Nietzsche's phenomenology of *Habsucht* in FW 14.

The Link between Passion, Idealization and Language and Stendhal's Theory of Cristallisation

Stendhal, and particularly *De l'amour*[33] [DA], are constantly referred to by Nietzsche in the period when he was preparing and writing *Die Fröhliche Wissenschaft*. Montinari's critical apparatus had already

---

30 Cf. particularly Luhmann (1982).
31 That may be why "Die Liebe vergiebt dem Geliebten sogar die Begierde" (FW 62).
32 A similar forgetfulness may also be the cause of the disappointments women receive from love, though they are themselves at the origin of the centuries-old idealization to which love has been subjected: "Die Abgötterei, welche die Frauen mit der Liebe treiben, ist im Grunde und ursprünglich eine Erfindung der Klugheit, insofern sie ihre Macht durch alle jene Idealisirungen der Liebe erhöhen und sich in den Augen der Männer als immer begehrenswerther darstellen. Aber durch die Jahrhundertelange Gewöhnung an diese übertriebene Schätzung der Liebe ist es geschehen, dass sie in ihr eigenes Netz gelaufen sind und jenen Ursprung vergessen haben. Sie selber sind jetzt noch mehr die Getäuschten, als die Männer, und leiden desshalb auch mehr an der Enttäuschung, welche fast nothwendig im Leben jeder Frau eintreten wird —sofern sie überhaupt Phantasie und Verstand genug hat, um getäuscht und enttäuscht werden zu können"(MA I 415, KSA 2.274).
33 Brusotti (1997, 290) conjectures that the edition owned by Nietzsche, which is not to be found in his library, was probably that of the *Œuvres completes*, cf. Stendahl (1854), *De l'amour. Seule Édition complète. Augmentée de Préfaces et de Fragments entièrement inédits*, Paris (Michel Lévy).

referred to traces of his reading of Stendhal's text in FW 84 and 123, where there are explicit refereces to the types of love Stendhal classifies (*amour plaisir, amour vanité*)[34]. But there are others in the posthumous notes too, above all, as we shall see, in the case of 8[40] of winter 1882 (KSA 9.391)[35]. Marco Brusotti has found other references to Stendhal's work in the context of *Morgenröthe*, and in particular aphorism 327, in which the description of the cognitive attitude of the Don Juan of knowledge is modelled, he claims, on Stendhal's classification of the forms of love, which reappears in FW 123[36]. Brusotti's main interest in this context is, more specifically, reconstructing the role Stendhal's idea of *amour-passion* plays in Nietzsche's development of the concept of *Leidenschaft der Erkenntnis* – knowledge seen as a passion[37].

The comparison I offer in what follows is not based on explicit textual references in FW 14 and is not specifically connected with the question of the passion of knowledge, although it shares some philosophical points of reference with it. Nietzsche briefly considers the idea of *cristallisation* in the above-mentioned posthumous piece 8[40] of 1882, where he extends the creative, and partly distorting, effect of love to the passions in general[38]. There are no direct references or similar terminology to the text of FW 14[39]. That said, I think we

---

34 Cf. the *Kommentar* in KSA 14.249 and 256. Brusotti (1997, 427) points out that the reference to Stendhal's classification is even clearer in the *Vorstufe* of FW 123 (cited in KSA 14.256).

35 The *Kommentar* (KSA 14.630 and 636) refers again to 4[81] of summer 1880 (KSA 9.120) and 6[301] of autumn 1880 (KSA 9.275f).

36 Cf. Brusotti (1997, 296, note 166). Brusotti's text also contains much information on the general influence of the reading of Stendhal's writings on Nietzsche's thought in the period of *Morgenröthe* and *Fröhliche Wissenschaft*. See also Brusotti (1993, 392 ff), which indicates further *excerpta* by Nietzsche from Stendhal, particularly in fragments 7[232] and 7[238] of late 1880 (KSA 9.365 and 367), in aphorism 135 of *Morgenröthe* and in section 3 of the *Vorrede* to *Fröhliche Wissenschaft*. In another *Beitrag* (2001, 432 ff), Brusotti indicates a source from *De l'amour* in M 162 and in a *Vorstufe* of the passage, 8[17] of winter 1880/81 (KSA 9.387).

37 Brusotti (1997, 113, 209 ff and notes 156, 636 ff in particular). On this subject see also Chaves (2005).

38 "Aber wenn wir unsere Leidenschaften wachsen lassen, so damit auch, wie wir wissen, die "Cristallisation": ich meine, wir werden *unredlich* und begeben uns freiwillig in den Irrthum?" NL 1882, 8[40] KSA 9.391.

can find interesting resemblances with the theory of *cristallisation* in the way that Nietzsche treats the relation between drive (*Trieb*), idealization and language. They are "simple" resemblances, both because there is no obvious textual evidence and because Nietzsche's argument is actually much more critically-deconstructively elaborate than Stendhal's, by virtue of the genealogical intention underlying the analysis in FW 14, as I am trying to show.

The phenomenon of *cristallisation* is "l'opération de l'esprit, qui tire de tout ce qui se présente la découverte que l'objet aimé a de nouvelles perfections" (DA, 35). The first *cristallisation* begins immediately after a love is born and consists in a form of idealization of the loved object, which magnifies a possession of which one is, for the moment, certain[40]. The phenomeon has its roots in the physiological structure of pleasure, according to Stendhal: it "vient de la nature qui nous commande d'avoir du plaisir et qui nous envoie le sang au cerveau, du sentiment que les plaisirs augmentent avec les perfections de l'objet aimé, et de l'idée: elle est à moi" (DA, 36). It is the first stage in that partial self-referentiality of the idealization of the passions, which modifies in return how and if we can find and feel pleasure: the immediacy with which a need is satisfied, as in the case, for example, of "le sauvage", is replaced as civilization develops by an ever more sophisticated expression of the relation between drive and object, by virtue of which the emotional-imaginative activity that makes up this expression to a certain extent subverts physiology and becomes the condition for satisfying the desire that it fuels[41]. Stendhal writes: "À l'autre extrême de la civilisation, je ne doute pas qu'une femme tendre n'arrive à ce point, de ne trouver le plaisir physique qu'aupres de l'homme qu'elle aime" (DA, 35). However, the psychology of pleasure

---

39 One of the texts for which the *Kommentar* of KSA refers to FW 14, e.g. 6[54] of autumn 1880 (KSA 9.207), does, however, contain an important echo of Stendhal. It begins: "*Liebe* als Passion ist *Verlangen nach absoluter Macht* über eine Person", etc. See later for a discussion of the passage.

40 "On se plaît à orner de mille perfections une femme de l'amour de laquelle on est sûr; on se détaille tout son bonheur avec une complaisance infinie. Cela se réduit à s'exagérer une propriété superbe, qui vient de nous tomber du ciel, que l'on ne connaît pas, et de la possession de laquelle on est assuré" (DA, chap. 2, 34).

41 For Stendhal this is a reason for seeing love as a "miracle de la civilisation. On ne trouve qu'un amour physique et des plus grossiers chez les peuples sauvages ou trop barbares" (DA, chap. 26, 86).

quickly leads to saturation, even with the most perfect happiness
("l'âme se rassaisie de tout ce qui est uniforme", *ibidem*). Attention
for the object weakens, one tries to revive the pleasure, or find new
pleasure, and with it confirmation, more intense forms of possession.
Doubt, which intervenes to reawaken the attention, is the psychological
state that accompanies the difficulty of finding confirmation: the
psychological condition deriving from the irremediable disproportion
between desire for the confirmation of possession and real signs from
the loved object. And so every reason for uncertainty serves in turn as
a stimulus to desire, in the tension of the search for intenser happiness.
If (or since) confirmation does not arrive as hoped or expected, and so
as to placate the desire once and for all, "l'amant arrive à douter du
bonheur qu'il se promettait; il devient sévère sur les raisons d'espérer
qu'il a cru voir". Here begins the *seconde cristallisation*, which this
time – and this is most interesting – does not embellish the loved
object in itself so much as the representation of possession that is
hoped for or despaired of[42]:

> Alors commence la seconde cristallisation produisant pour diamants
> des confirmations à cette idée:
> Elle m'aime.
> À chaque quart d'heure de la nuit qui suit la naissance des doutes,
> après un moment de malheur affreux, l'amant se dit: Oui, elle m'aime;
> et la cristallisation se tourne à découvrir de nouveaux charmes; puis
> le doute à l'œil hagard s'empare de lui, et l'arrête en sursaut. Sa
> poitrine oublie de respirer; il se dit: Mais est-ce qu'elle m'aime? Au
> milieu de ces alternatives déchirantes et délicieuses, le pauvre amant
> sent vivement: Elle me donnerait des plaisirs qu'elle seule au monde
> peut me donner.
> C'est l'évidence de cette vérité, c'est ce chemin sur l'extrême bord d'un
> précipice affreux, et touchant de l'autre main le bonheur parfait, qui
> donne tant de supériorité à la seconde cristallisation sur la première"
> (DA, chap. 2, 36 f)

The perfections attributed to the loved object have first of all *created*
or aroused the object of desire for how it is represented in desire, for
how it is desired. In addition, according to Stendhal, the constant

---

42   On the specific dynamics of *plaisir* and *crainte*, cf. DA, chap. 59, 242; chap. 33,
     118; chap. 36, 127.

wavering between hope and despair, between faith and doubt, is part
of the structure of the passion, and stimulates it and keeps it alive
by constantly upping the stakes – where the value of the longed-for
possession in this second phase is self-referential, and is not intrinsic
to the object itself[43]. The second *cristallisation* ensures the duration
of love, rooting a habit of living in the tension of this alternative
between "être aimé ou [...] mourir" (DA, chap. 3, 38).

There seem to be numerous points of contact between Nietzsche's
account and Stendhal's, which takes up several chapters of *De
l'amour*. In the first place (1) – our starting point – there is the central
role played by idealization in the development of our drives and in
the relation with the object of desire. Stendhal seems to some extent
to be part of the materials Nietzsche uses to advance his critique of
the *Wertschätzungen* and their influence on *Empfindungen* and on the
Triebe, which the fragments of 1880 and *Morgenröthe* bear ample
witness to. In a fragment of summer 1880 we find linked, as later in
FW 14, the themes of the critique of language and the idealization of
the drives (including that of love) and an interesting echo of Stendhal,
which Nietzsche uses to outline a critical discourse that to some extent
underlies the argument of FW 14.

> Die Sprache trägt große Vorurtheile in sich und unterhält sie z. B. daß,
> was mit Einem Wort bezeichnet wird, auch Ein Vorgang sei: Wollen,
> Begehren, Trieb – complicirte Dinge! Der Schmerz bei allen Dreien
> (in Folge eines Druckes Nothstand\<es\>) wird in den Prozeß 'wohin?'
> verlegt: damit hat er gar nichts zu thun, es ist ein gewohnter Irrthum
> aus Association. 'Ich habe solches Bedürfniß nach dir' Nein! Ich
> habe eine Noth, und ich meine, du kannst sie stillen (ein **Glauben** ist
> eingeschoben) 'ich liebe dich' nein! es ist in mir ein verliebter Zustand
> und ich **meine**, du werdest ihn lindern. Diese Objektaccusative!
> ein Glauben ist bei all diesen Empfindungsworten enthalten z.B.
> wollen hassen usw. Ein **Schmerz** und eine **Meinung** in Betreff seiner
> Linderung – das ist die Thatsache. Ebenso wo von Zwecken geredet
> wird. – Eine heftige Liebe ist die **fanatische** hartnäckige **Meinung**,
> daß nur die und die Person meine Noth lindern kann, es ist Glaube

---

43 DA, chap. 3, 39: "Dès que les cristallisations ont opéré, surtout la seconde, qui de
   beaucoup est la plus forte, les yeux indifférents ne reconnaissent plus la branche
   d'arbre; Car, I° elle est ornée de perfections ou de diamants qu'ils ne voient pas;
   2° elle est ornée de perfections qui n'en sont pas pour eux".

der selig und unselig macht, mitunter selbst im Besitze noch stark
genug gegen jede Enttäuschung d. h. Wahrheit[44] (NL Sommer 1880,
5[45] KSA 9.191 f).

The concentration of the drive, the desire and the will on an object
happens through linguistic mediation, particularly the use of the
Objektakkusative, which convey a *Meinung* as to the possibility of
satisfying the desire or drive, and create a binding relation between
desire and object – so much so that, as the following fragment claims,
"Veränderung der Wertschätzung ist Veränderung des Willens" (NL
5[46] KSA 9.192). Interpretation, transmitted by prejudices rooted
in linguistic use, modifies the direction and concentration of the physiological states, which in themselves are independent of the intrinsic
qualities of the object to which they are linked in this process. The last
lines, in which Nietzsche describes a *heftige Liebe*, recall Stendhal's
observations, to the effect that in the alternation of hope and despair
in the second *cristallisation* ("alternatives déchirantes et délicieuses",
Stendhal claims), "le pauvre amant sent vivement: Elle me donnerait
des plaisirs qu'elle seule au monde peut me donner" (DA, chap. 2,
37). Characterizing love as the fanatical power of a *Meinung* immediately suggests *cristallisation* and the transformation it works on the
perception of reality (see, for example, chapter 3 of Stendhal's work).
Nietzsche's generalization of Stendhal's suggested connection between
the physiology of the drives, idealization, fixation on an object and
the transformation that is the result of the drive *and* the object itself,
is, as I argue below, actually prepared by Stendhal in his treatise.
Nietzsche's originality can be seen in the addition of the critique of
linguistic usage, which had already appeared in this first note and is
the backbone of the analysis in FW 14. A declaration of intent dating
from late 1880 began to make clear precisely this union of materials
collected in the notes of the period and the genealogical intention ani-
mating Nietzsche's thinking as early as *Morgenröthe*: "wie ein Trieb,
je nachdem man ihn lobt und tadelt, als gut oder böse empfunden
wird, an der **Liebe** zu zeigen (bei Griechen, bei asketischen Christen,
in der christlichen Ehe usw.) Alle **Idealisirung eines Triebes** beginnt
damit, daß man ihn unter die lobenswerthen Dinge rechnet. Wink für
die Zukunft??" (NL 1880, 7[75] KSA 9.333). In other words, what

---

44   Cf. on this also NL Sommer 1880, 5[14] KSA 9.184.

was to be accomplished in FW 14. The aphorism's debt to Stendhal begins to emerge, but along with it, the importance of Nietzsche's emphasis on linguistic usage as a vehicle for moral valuations, and on its retroactive effect on the *Triebe* and the relative *Empfindungen* (FW 14, KSA 9.386, 8 ff).

This analytical vanishing point also gives a particular colouring to another aspect (2) of the analogy between Stendhal's account and Nietzsche's ideas on the passion of love: the characterization of passion as able to reorganize perception, imagination, significance, and above all the structural relevance of this process of interpretation of the real to the physiology of pleasure, which, as we have seen, increases and is stimulated by representations and attributions that renew its satisfaction and resolve the saturation that naturally supervenes. In this sense, in the third place (3), for both writers it is not reality that is important so much as the fantasy/illusion/conviction of possessing the desired object. Imagining or being convinced we possess an object, even if the imagined possession is also real, means the object is never completely possessed (*or rather* it may be possessed in ever changing ways, so many are the ways in which, as Nietzsche writes, the pleasure we take in ourselves is always changing something new *"into ourselves"*: "die Lust [...] immer wieder etwas Neues *in uns selber* verwandelt", FW 14, KSA 386, 22–24), and this makes the self-intensification of passion potentially infinite[45]. In this sense Stendhal can claim, criticizing the figure of Don Giovanni (as Nietzsche too was to do in M 327), that "les plaisirs de l'amour sont toujours en proportion de la crainte" (DA, chap. 59, 242).

Nietzsche also seems to draw on Stendhal in his reflections on the influence that the desirer seeks to have on the object desired (4). Stendhal insists on the passionate lover's fundamental need for constant confirmation of his conviction of being loved, of possessing the loved object. If the first *cristallisation* enriches the object that is desired and possessed, the second, as we have seen, is mainly a matter of seeking and interpreting signs that encourage hope and, more precisely, that certify the first of the two fundamental ideas that lacerate the lover: *elle est à moi* – while the signs will also always give

---

45   This aspect seems to me essential in the economy of Marco Brusotti's convincing interpretation, which considers the *Leidenschaft der Erkenntnis* as modelled on Stendhal's idea of passion.

the lover reason to doubt *as well*. This confirmation may be in turn
imaginary, or, "après l'intimité", may be "des solutions plus réelles",
as Stendhal writes (DA, chap. 6, 43). Already in the posthumous note
6[54] of autumn 1880, cited above, Nietzsche effects an interesting
transition: he at once translates, it seems to me, this process that is
inherent to passion into the terminology of one of the problems that
he reflected on most assiduously in the period in question (as we can
see from *Morgenröthe*) – that of *Macht*, *Machtgefühl* and the related
Steigerung.

> **Liebe** als Passion ist **Verlangen nach absoluter Macht** über eine
> Person: (z.B. wollen, daß man der einzige Gegenstand von Gedanken
> und Empfindungen sei) Der Liebende sieht die übrige Welt kaum
> und opfert alle anderen Interessen in diesem Machtdurste. An das
> Geliebtwerden glauben bringt eine tiefe Sättigung mit sich: 'wir
> werden als absolute Macht empfunden'! (NL Herbst 1880, 6[54]
> KSA 9.207).

This extension and interpretation of Stendhal's doctrine can be found
in Nietzsceh's description of love between the sexes in FW 14 and,
extending his idea of tracing moral attitudes to the *Besitzen-wollen*,
in his account of *Wohlthun* too in FW 13. Nietzsche insists on the
contrast between the strong moral overtone of the idea of love, which
is adored and glorified even in its passionate form, and the processes
described, which bring together the passion of love and the more
rarefied forms of love and the thirst for possession, lust, and desire for
appropriation. Still greater is the emphasis on the power of linguistic
use, whose distinctions Nietzsche traces to different combinations of
drives and intentions in this framework.

As the characterization of *cristallisation* already suggests, Stendhal
is quite open to the idea that, to paraphrase Wittgenstein, the world
of the lover is different from that of the non-lover, or of the person
who is *no longer* a lover[46]. In the long note to chapter 3 of his treatise,
in which he justifies the use of the term *cristallisation* and its "coldly"
analytical procedure, Stendhal clarifies that his description of the

---

[46] At the end of chapter 36 on jealousy, Stendhal cites a delightful anecdote of Mlle
de Sommery: "surprise en flagrant délit par son amant, lui nie le fait hardiment,
et comme l'autre se récrie 'Ah! Je vois bien, lui dit-elle, que vous ne m'aimez plus;
vous croyez plus ce que vous voyez que ce que je vous dis'" (DA, chap. 36, 129).

phenomenon of love is also functional to understanding its dissolution and, above all, the possibility of its being "cured" (DA, chap. 3, 39). Thus, in the two chapters on *Remèdes à l'amour*, Stendhal illustrates a strategy that consists in gradually leading the lover to re-interpret – developing a different emotional attachment to the signs he is constantly seeking and reading. The friend who "cures" him will then suggest a reading that reduces the passionate attachment and arouses doubt and indifference. "Les plus petites choses suffisent, car tout est *signe* en amour", writes Stendhal[47] (DA, chap. 39 *ter*, 147). The difference between the lover's world and that of one who does not love or no longer loves, consists in a different emotional framework, articulated in different perception, representation, imagination and communication – an emotional framework that is related to the physiology of pleasure and its dynamics of satisfaction, saturation, etc.[48]

Nietzsche concentrates on the dividing line of achieving possession, which acts as a watershed in the economy of the lust for pleasure. For those who already possess, the economy of drives, and so of imagination, idealization, etc., is quite different from that of those who aspire to possess. This different economy accounts for the difference in linguistic usage. In the *bereits Habende* the drive is "etwas zur Ruhe gekommen" and with it also all the idealization, enrichment of the world, of the desired object and of the relation with it: and so in this stage it is now still only a question of maintaining possession ("Habe") and acting in the interests of maintaining the

---

47 As Roland Barthes notes (1995, 788ff), the lover is "le sémiologue sauvage à l'état pur": "il passe son temps à lire des signes [...] des signes de bonheur, des signes de malheur. Sur le visage de l'autre, dans ses conduites. Il est véritablement en proie aux signes". Yet he cannot check his incredible "puissance de déchiffrement": "il ne sait pas où ni comment arrêter les signes".

48 See too in this connection the extremely interesting fragment 140 of the section *Fragments divers* in *De l'amour*, in which Stendhal organizes his conception of pleasure and its physiology: "Lorsque le plaisir a entièrement parcouru sa carrière, il est clair que nous retombons dans l'indifférence; mais cette indifférence n'est pas la même que celle d'auparavant. Ce second état diffère du premier, en ce que nous ne serions plus capables de goûter, avec autant de délices, le plaisir que nous venons d'avoir. Les organes qui servent à le cueillir sont fatigués, et l'imagination n'a plus autant de propensions à présenter les images qui seraient agréables aux désirs qui se trouvent satisfaits" (DA, 291f).

status quo (FW 14). In this case, as Stendhal writes, one seeks *plus réelles* solutions for one's fears of losing possession. Conversely, the idealizing and glorifying linguistic usage originates in the economy of drives and desires of those who do not yet possess, who "love" in the sense that is attributed to this term in Stendhal's, and then Nietzsche's, framework.

This is how we can explain Nietzsche's claim that the *Nichtbesitzenden* and *Begehrenden* have literally "made" the *Sprachgebrauch* that opposes love to egoism and injustice, when love "may in fact be the most candid expression of egoism" ("während sie [die Liebe] vielleicht gerade der unbefangenste Ausdruck des Egoismus ist", FW 14, KSA 3.387, 20–21). This *Sprachgebrauch* has been gradually colonized from a moral point of view, and so it conveys a value judgment in defining *Liebe* and *Habsucht* as opposites.

I have already said that I think Nietzsche's intention in FW 14 should be read against the background of what he proposed in FW 7: to trace the connections between the *Triebe* that developed in human beings in different places and times in relation to the *moralisches Klima*, then the causes and reasons for this moral climate, and finally to show their erroneousness and the essence of moral judgment down to our day. This means a fundamental enquiry on the plane of language and communication, with special attention to the value of moral judgment in linguistic attribution and its retroactive effect on the drives. The idea of FW 7 is that the *Passionen* are specified and articulated by all the practices for disciplining them (organization of work time and holidays, food, communal life and, for example, monastic life, the dialectic of marriage and love etc). Not that they are simply sedated or repressed, but that, as Foucault teaches[49], they are *developed* in relation to the practices, contexts and social structures that control and channel them. These practices are mediated linguistically: they assume their very form through linguistic attributions that define different states, moments, processes, attributions of the practices themselves and of those who perform them, involving a value judgment on what the definition designates. In turn, this valuation influences the drives, guiding their further articulation in the individual. As I shall show in section 2, one might read the analytical sketch on love in FW 14

---

49   Cf. in particular Foucault (1976).

as the prototype of an enquiry that is applicable to all the *Passionen* (FW 7) and aimed at bringing to light the connections between drives, language, moral valuations and human psychological development. *Passion*, in this sense, already indicates a stabilization of the *Trieb*, based on a stable connection between drive and object, context and value towards which the drive is directed.

Stendhal aims mainly at offering a descriptive theory of the phenomenon of love[50], in which the physiological level stands in a positive relation with that of the imagination, the resulting emotional articulation and nomination. Yet he explicitly indicates the possibility of generalizing his theory: not only in the case of love is passion a form of constancy in emotional-imaginative investment, articulated in a linguistic-representational sense. In the important chapter 6 of *De l'amour*, Stendhal extends the process of *cristallisation* to gambling too, in which he traces a similar dynamic to that of love: attachment to the object, to what is at stake, is given by the *rêverie* that is woven around it and that makes it more and more desirable. The same goes for hatred: "dès qu'on peut espérer de se venger, on recommence de haïr" (DA, 44); for every belief in which there is "de l'*absurde* ou du *non-demontré*", which "tend toujours à mettre à la tête du parti les gens les plus absurdes"; finally, there is a *cristallisation* in mathematics too, "dans les têtes qui ne peuvent pas à tout moment se rendre présentes toutes les parties de la démonstration de ce qu'elles croient" (DA, 44). One the one hand, this confirms Brusotti's reading, by which Nietzsche's *Leidenschaft der Erkenntnis* is modelled on the form of Stendhal's *passion*. But in this sense it is Stendhal himself who extends his phenomenology of passion to the realm of knowledge too, and precisely in relation to those contexts in which the object sought is uncertain in all sorts of different ways. On the other hand, the introduction of the pole of *Habsucht* in Nietzsche's analysis[51] seems in turn to be prepared by Stendhal: *amour passion* is an example of a general process that characterizes our way of seeking pleasure, desiring and developing a passionate interest in something real and/

---

50 Stendhal's third preface, written in 1842 and reprinted in the 1854 edition, which, Brusotti claims, Nietzsche had to hand, begins: "Je viens solliciter l'indulgence du lecteur pour la forme singulière de cette *Physiologie de l'Amour*".

51 In relation to the central role of *Habsucht* in knowledge and with reference to *Leidenschaft der Erkenntnis*, see specifically FW 242 and 249.

or imaginary, which we try to possess – and precisely in aspiring to possess, the 'soul', to paraphrase Nietzsche, develops. I should like to examine this aspect a little more closely.

In a study of sections 57–75 of *Fröhliche Wissenschaft* Scarlett Marton[52] links Nietzsche's deconstruction of the idea of woman in those aphorisms with the metaphor of truth as a woman, which closes the *Vorrede* to FW and opens the *Vorrede* to JGB. In all these cases, says Marton, the issue is the critique of dogmatism and the idea of truth or anything else being wholly and finally available to us. As regards woman, Nietzsche shows her indefinability and unfathomability as being the result of projections and idealizations (FW 60, 67, 75) or special kinds of upbringing and socialization (FW 68). As Marton rightly notes, sections 59 and 60 of FW are very important in this sense: in the first the idealization that accompanies every feeling and every *Empfinden* is illustrated and problematized by the example of male repulsion at the thought of female physiology, which sits ill with the idealized image of woman (FW 59); in the second, it is again a question of idealization and distance: what attracts and stimulates is not reality so much as the representation of women as mediums for transfiguring life into dream, as a refuge, a place of calm where one can feel happily reconciled with the immanence of being. Actually things are very different, and so Nietzsche claims that "der Zauber und die mächstigste Wirkung der Frauen" is, philosophically speaking, "eine Wirkung in die Ferne, eine *actio in distans*", and recommends this *Distanz* (FW 60, KSA 3.425).

Marton's reflections can be developed and linked to the present analysis of the influence of Stendhal's conception of the idealization of love. Nietzsche's critique of the dogmatic philosophers, particularly in JGB, seems to me complementary to his polemic against the realists, which opens the second book of FW, in section 57. In this sense sections 57–60 can be read as stages of a single argument. Nietzsche questions the opposition of *Wirklichkeit* with *Leidenschaft* or *Phantasterei*, which the realist uses to claim access to the reality of things against the distortions of passion and *Verliebtheit*. The "Liebe zur 'Wirklichkeit'" too is a form of falling in love, "eine uralte Liebe", and in every *Empfindung* and *Sinneseindruck* is hidden "eine

---

52   Marton (2010).

Phantasterei, ein Vorurtheil, eine Unvernunft, eine Unwissheit, eine Furcht und was sonst alles!" (FW 57, KSA 3.421). In the following section he makes clear that the name, appearance, valuation or value attributed to things count much more for us than what things "actually are". If FW 57 might tempt one to think that a demystification of "Wirklichkeit" as appearance and *Phantasterei* might be enough to eliminate the "Wirklichkeit" itself, FW 58 makes clear that this is not so, and ends up sweeping away the contrast between reality and *Phantasterei* (as creation, imagination, daydreaming of passion) from a diametrically opposed point of view to that of FW 57: we cannot have access to truth by revealing that "Wirklichkeit" is wrapped up in the "Nebelhülle des Wahnes". The only way we can "vernichten" is as *Schaffende* – creating new names and new judgments of things (FW 58, KSA 3.422).

Neither in one sense nor the other, then, can illusion be unmasked and the one, true and eternal Truth of things be brought to light: love of "Wirklichkeit" too is an ancient form of love (FW 57); anyone who thinks he can penetrate the fog of "Wahn" and so destroy "Wirklichkeit" is a "Narr", a madman (FW 58). As he makes clear in the new *Vorrede* to FW, Nietzsche rejects this form of searching for the truth as a love in bad taste that wants to strip truth of all its veils: "wir glauben nicht mehr daran, dass Wahrheit noch Wahrheit bleibt, wenn man ihr die Schleier abzieht" (FW, *Vorrede* 4, KSA 3.352). As well as being a critique of dogmatism, sections FW 57–60 (which Scarlett Marton rightly links with the *Vorrede* of JGB), and later the *Vorrede* to FW, seem to propose a positive idea of cognitive pudeur, of "tact" in the search for truth. Like woman, truth too seems to act *in die Ferne* – under the condition of always remaining at a certain *distance*. Rather than the concrete act of gaining access to truth once and for all, like achieving possession of the desired woman and wholly enjoying the revelation of her, it is the distance from the desired object that generates creativity, expansion that stimulates imagination and the artistic potential of the lover or of the man who desires. The passion of desiring and aspiring, of seeking possession of things, even in the form of knowing them, opens and expands that space of creation in which sensations, feelings, thoughts, images, representations and fantasies constitute "things" as how they are "for us".

This phenomenon is in every way similar to the idealization that Stendhal speaks of in relation to *amour passion*. Not only does

Nietzsche recognise a physiological basis to idealization similar to Stendhal's, but, more specifically, the *long-distance* relation with truth is productive precisely in the reaction to the pressure of the tension towards the loved/desired object and its unreachability. In this case the idea of *cristallisation* is reworked by Nietzsche in a positive formulation of the effect of the partial frustration of desire united with the persistence of passion: imagination, creativity and innovation are the result, but at the same time, thanks to doubt and scepticism, also self-discipline and self-formation – continual illusion and disillusion, as in the model of the *deuxième cristallisation*.

> Restless discovering and divining has such an attraction for us, and has grown as indispensable to us as is to the lover his unrequited love, which he would at no price relinquish for a state of indifference – perhaps, indeed, we too are *unrequited* lovers! Knowledge has in us been transformed into a passion which shrinks at no sacrifice and at bottom fears nothing but its own extinction (D 429)[53].

The dialectical relation, intense and unrequited, with the loved woman, which characterizes *amour passion* and which is the context, or rather the *humus*, of *cristallisation*, is also desirable with regard to the man of knowledge's relation with the truth he seeks, so much so that, in a sense, the stimulus to desire and further satisfaction always depends on doubt, the risk of despair, and fear. It is knowledge in itself that becomes the object of passionate investment – in the same way in which the passion of love is developed reflexively: "l'amour est la seule passion qui se paye d'une monnaie qu'elle fabrique elle-même" (DA, nr. 145, 293).

After these two long digressions, let us return to the analysis of FW 14 with these new tools for our enquiry. Apart from subjective idealization, whose structure and characteristics we have just examined, there seems to be an *objective* form of idealization of the phenomenon of love – connected to and complementary to the former. One

---

53 M 429, KSA 3.264: "Die Unruhe des Entdeckens und Erratens ist uns so reizvoll und unentbehrlich geworden, wie die unglückliche Liebe dem Liebenden wird: welche er um keinen Preis gegen den Zustand der Gleichgültigkeit hergeben würde; – ja vielleicht sind wir auch *unglücklich* Liebende! Die Erkenntnis hat sich in uns zur Leidenschaft verwandelt, die vor keinem Opfer erschrickt und im Grunde nichts fürchtet, als ihr eignes Erlöschen".

of the sources of the altruistic mystification of love and *Wohltun* in FW 13 might, then, be sought in a false causal inference starting from the effects they create: the reality of the advantage that the loved object draws from this exertion of the lover or desirer leads to positing an intention consistent with its effects. That is what Nietzsche conjectures in the case of the disinterest that is attributed to heroism ("der Vaterlandsliebe der Treue der 'Wahrheit', der Forschung usw."), venerated as something superior and whose passionate nature is misunderstood[54], and actually *dangerous* for others. We might assume a similar process in the case of *Habsucht*, which is articulated and denoted in a moral sense in the forms, cited in FW 14, of *Nächstenliebe, Liebe zum Wissen* or *Liebe zur Wahrheit* (we have seen how Nietzsche actually underlines the passionate character of the desire for knowledge), *Liebe der Geschlechter* – but we might also extend it to paternal/maternal love, for example[55].

However, we should reflect that beyond this more superficial and, so to speak, phenomenal, plane, this altruistic interpretation of desire and love is supported in a wider system of values and valuations, and that it is functional to that system. Also, this system of valuations and attributions, which in itself is arbitrary, like every attribution, is legitimized in a configuration of power and reciprocity – that is to say, in a social pattern. In other words, the rarefaction and objective and subjective idealization of desire moves in a direction that is in line with the discursive articulation of the passions and drives, that is necessary in a community that must maintain its internal order: in a direction, that is, of regularizing – through the incorporation of morality – the behaviour of the individual members of the community, and creating and maintaining a system of reciprocity (duties/rights, legitimacy etc). The community encourages, through each of its members, the control of itself, of impulses and desire, so as to mitigate the danger that each person's drives represents for others[56].

---

54 Cf. NL 1881, 11[56] KSA 9.461f.
55 Nietzsche refers to it in MA I 57, in NL 11[19] KSA 9.449.
56 This phenomenon of internal differentiation through the moralization of interpersonal relations – the morality of *Nächstenliebe* is the most explicit concrete form of it – supervenes, according to Nietzsche, once the community has stabilized in the face of external threats (JGB 201). We can read in this sense the morality of *Nächstenliebe* as a development of the struggles for "immunization"

The moralization of drives is therefore much more than their mere moral mystification: as indicated above, it is the energy of each individual's drives that is exploited by upbringing and socialization so as to redirect his investiment in his drives by encouraging behaviour that corresponds to the social rules. It was in this sense that I spoke above of the discursive articulation of the drives:

> What is, therefore, first really praised when virtues are praised is their instrumental nature and then the blind drive in every virtue that refuses to be held in check by the overall advantage of the individual – in short, the unreason in virtue that leads the individual to allow himself to be transformed into a mere function of the whole (GS 21).[57]

Through the encouragement of social recognition ("durch eine Reihe von Reizen und Vortheilen"), in which self-sacrifice and altruism are praised and rewarded, the individual is induced to invest in organizing the multiplicity of his drives in the direction of mediation, the deferment of satisfaction, the mitigation of desire, etc: in this way he incorporates a "Denk- und Handlungsweise" that becomes in turn "Gewohnheit, Trieb und Leidenschaft", and that leads him to disregard his own advantage and, by virtue of a process of constant self-motivation, become led by his drives, a "naive" "function of the whole ("Funktion des Ganzen")[58] – which means, however, that "the praise of the selfless, the self-sacrificing, the virtuous (…) is certainly not born out of the spirit of selflessness" ("das Lob des Selbstlosen,

---

[*Immunsystemkämpfe*], which, according to Sloterdijk (2009, 712) makes up the whole of human history. Religions have a similar value in this context: the entity and different quality of the threats, to which the practices of immunization must respond each time, also distinguish the direction and significance of the practices.

57   FW 21, KSA 3.392: "Es ist also einmal die Werkzeug-Natur in den Tugenden, die eigentlich gelobt wird, wenn die Tugenden gelobt werden, und sodann der blinde in jeder Tugend waltende Trieb, welcher durch den Gesammt-Vortheil des Individuums sich nicht in Schranken halten lässt, kurz: die Unvernunft in der Tugend, vermöge deren das Einzelwesen sich zur Function des Ganzen umwandeln lässt".

58   "Gelingt die Erziehung, so ist jede Tugend des Einzelnen eine öffentliche Nützlichkeit und ein privater Nachtheil im Sinne des höchsten privaten Zieles" (FW 21, KSA 3.393).

Aufopfernden, Tugendhaften (...) ist jedenfalls nicht aus dem Geiste der Selbstlosigkeit entsprungen!", FW 21, KSA 3.392)[59].

That this process, in its various stages and specific forms, is the basis of a real transformation of the stock of our drives, and so of our experience of ourselves and the world, is clear from, for example, FW 47, where Nietzsche writes that the effort to contain the communicative expression of the passions also ends up weakening and transforming the passions themselves[60]. In this sense – this is also important for the second part of our analysis – the social "discoursivation" of desire differs from a pure game of linguistic attributions because it involves a transformation of psychology and the categories of experience[61]. Similarly, Nietzsche later described, in the second *Abhandlung* of *Zur Genealogie der Moral*, a specific case of this process, which he called *Verinnerlichung des Menschen*: the internalization of the *Instinkte*, which are not externally released, are directed inwards and lead to the growth of what is normally called the "soul"[62] (*Seele*, GM II 16, KSA 5.322). As Norbert Elias' analyses showed too, the processes of disciplining the drives, obstructing them, deferring them, deviating them from the path of satisfaction and internalizing the ban are what articulate, deepen and extend the inner life and the complexity of the human psyche[63].

On the one hand, then, Nietzsche's wonder at the idealization to which the *Habsucht* of love between the sexes has been subject is, so to speak, strictly rhetorical: it aims to emphasize the surprising

---

59 Both in MA I 133 and, more cursorily, in FW 147, Nietzsche reduces to the absurd the idea both of a universal disposition to altruism and of its desirability: the point being that the praise of *selbstlose Liebe* or *Menschenliebe* is anything but disinterested.

60 "Wenn man sich anhaltend den Ausdruck der Leidenschaften verbietet, wie als etwas den "Gemeinen", den gröberen, bürgerlichen, bäuerlichen Naturen zu Ueberlassendes, - also nicht die Leidenschaften selber unterdrücken will, sondern nur ihre Sprache und Gebärde: so erreicht man nichtsdestoweniger eben Das mit, was man nicht will: die Unterdrückung der Leidenschaften selber, mindestens ihre Schwächung und Veränderung" (FW 47).

61 In Wittgensteinian terms, the language game has repercussions on the form of life from which it arises and on which it impresses a form. On the constitutive and dynamic character of the relation between form of life and communicative signs, see also Abel (2004), in particular chap. 4.

62 See also GM I 6, KSA 5.266.

63 Cf. Piazzesi (2010).

nature of the obvious, once it is observed from a genealogical, critical viewpoint. Overturning the valuations of drives and desires, for example, interpreting *Habsucht* as something anti-egoistic – love, in fact – takes the concrete form of structuring an experience that, oblivious of its origin, is unable to perceive itself as relative and not obvious – to which I shall return later.

On the other hand, we can see more clearly what is at stake in the question of *Sprachgebrauch*, which I have deliberately left to one side so far. These are the points in the text:

> And yet it could be the same instinct, named twice: once disparaged by those who already *have*, in whom the instinct has somewhat calmed down and who now fear for what they 'have'; the other time seen from the standpoint of the unsatisfied, the thirsty, and therefore glorified as 'good' (GS 14)[64];
>
> Here it is evidently the have-nots and the yearning ones who have formed linguistic usage – there have probably always been too many of them (GS 14)[65].

The two levels of naming are not homogeneous: one, that of those who have decided linguistic usage (*Sprachgebrauch*) contains a mystification (the egoism of the thirst for possession idealized as *love*), while the other presumably reflects a state of fact (it calls things by their "name", so to speak). This difference can be traced back to the aspects of idealization just set out: in those who already have (*die bereits Habende*) the violence of the drive is momentarily sedated and there are the conditions for a distance that encourages reflection and even the devaluation of the drive[66].

---

64 FW 14, KSA 3.386, 9–14: "und doch könnte es der selbe Trieb sein, zweimal benannt, das eine Mal verunglimpft vom Standpuncte der bereits Habenden aus, in denen der Trieb etwas zur Ruhe gekommen ist und die nun für ihre 'Habe' fürchten; das andere Mal vom Standpuncte der Unbefriedigten, Durstigen aus, und daher verherrlicht als 'gut'".

65 FW 14, KSA 3.387, 21–22: "Hier haben offenbar die Nichtbesitzenden und Begehrenden den Sprachgebrauch gemacht, – es gab wohl ihrer immer zu viele".

66 This is similar to those who "am Zuviel leiden", whom Nietzsche cites in brackets in FW 14: generosity of giving and "wegwerfen", and the gratuitousness of "austheilen" might be unmasked not only as a means to an end (receiving and gaining possession), but also functionally, as pure *Entladung* of an excessive energy (KSA 3.386, 25–27).

There is nothing in itself surprising about the *Sprachgebrauch* that has been established and handed down. Surprise, which, as we have seen, Nietzsche expresses heuristically, can stir under the gaze of the genealogical aim, which wonders *how* things have become what they are/appear, historicizing them, and so dissolving their "naturalness". The historical-linguistic treatment of *gut, böse, Strafe, Gewissen* etc. in GM is still missing in FW 14, but the theoretical premises and analytical framework seem to me clearly recognizable, partly thanks to FW 7: in this sense compare the declaration of intentions in FW 7 and its exemplary treatment in FW 14 with the *Anmerkung* note at the end of the first dissertation in GM.

Before taking up this point in the next section, I offer some brief remarks on the end of the aphorism, which has often attracted the attention of interpreters. Up to this point Nietzsche has been speaking of love, which he treats as a meeting and a dialogue, as improbable as it is structured, between drives and desires for possession. He now shifts his argument to friendship, which is seen as the *Fortsetzung* of love[67] – and in turn a form of love – but at the same time as a shifting of the fire of amorous passion: both participants now concentrate their *Habsucht* and *Begierde* not directly on each other, but on a shared ideal, which becomes their aspiration, superordinate to both, following the traditional, once Aristotelian, conception of *philia*. This opposition, which indicates an alternative path to the moralization of desire so as to mitigate its violence and thirst for possession, and tend its (self)destructive blindness, recurs regularly in Nietzsche's works[68].

---

67 Giuliano Campioni (2009a, 20ff), has recently shown that the end of FW 14 draws partly on Nietzsche's reading of Claude Adrien Helvetius (1760). Although it is not a direct quotation, fragment 12[169] and especially 12[174] of autumn 1881 ("Freundschaft – verschieden von der Liebe", KSA 9.606) refer to the context of Helvetius' argument. On this see also Campioni (2009b).

68 Cf. for example NL Herbst 1880, 6[191] KSA 9.246. On the contrast between sexual love and friendship, cf. M 503. FW 60 too takes the same subject of the danger of excessive closeness to women, as does FW 363. One might see friendship as a further step in the idealization and, with it, the rarefaction of love, in the sense of self-criticism of the amorous disposition that recognises its own blindness and tries to remedy it. I am grateful to Silvio Pfeuffer for drawing my attention to this point. As Olivier Ponton has suggested, one might read the "Sternen-Freundschaft" of FW 279 in turn as overcoming the concrete condition of separation by means of another ideal.

2. The Genealogical Intention of FW 14.

> *Une sorte de pólemos concerne*
> *déjà l'appropriation de la langue.*

(J. Derrida, *Force de loi*)

I want now to try to bring out the analytical-critical aims – mainly implicit – and premises of FW 14, which will allow us to see the aphorism as a preparatory exercise for a genealogical investigation.

a. Linguistic demystification/dissolution of the linguistic usage. An attack on the strictly linguistic appearance (*how many things are called love*) shows the non-neutrality of *Sprachgebrauch* in relation to what it names:

a.1 language is *performative*, in that it influences what it expresses and denotes and *who* uses it to express and denote (saying *love* or saying *Habsucht* directs the experience of the feeling); on the one hand:

a.2 linguistic usage – and so its performativity – depends on strategic intentions underlying the linguistic determinations, i.e. it is not neutral towards the dynamics of power (intentions determine *Spachgebrauch*); on the other:

a.3 the apparent neutrality of linguistic use hides moral valuations, linked to these dynamics of power, which, by virtue of *a.1*, influence *moralistically* the subjective experience connected with the linguistic use in question (for example, that love is regarded as an altruistic feeling).

b. The linguistic dissolution or demystification also involves

b.1 the dissolution of subjective experience and its related psychology (by virtue of *a.1* and *a.2*), as well as

b.2 a critique of its moralistic premises (by virtue of *a.3*). One might define this point as a therapeutic intention of the critical-genealogical proceeding (I shall also come back to this in the conclusions, § 3).

c. A sketch of a *diagnosis* of the "modern" soul: it brings to light, not exactly the psychological and physiological contradictions generated by linguistic usage and by its related valuations, but at least some of their causes. The experience of love is linked to one of these fundamental contradictions: it contains various, different drives and opposing valuations, etc.

These three aspects are evidently closely connected and simultaneous in their effects.

As for *a.1* and *a.2*, discussion of the non-neutrality of *Sprachgebrauch* towards experience and the concurrent instances of power that define social relations does not begin with FW 14. *Der Wanderer und sein Schatten*, in which the linguistic problem weighs heavily, discusses in aphorism 5 the link between the imposition of a *Sprachgebrauch* and the determination of experiences and corresponding valuations, as well as contradictions of subjective experience caused by it (I shall come back to this in relation to *c*). In line with this, FW 58 claims:

> This has caused me the greatest trouble and still does always cause me the greatest trouble: to realize that *what things are called* is unspeakable more important than what they are. The reputation, name, and appearance, the worth, the usual measure and weigth of a thing – originally almost always something mistaken and arbitrary, thrown over things like a dress and quite foreign to their nature and even to their skin – has, through the belief in it and its growth from generation to generation, slowly grown onto and into the thing and has become its very body: what started as appearance in the end nearly always becomes essence and *effectively acts* as its essence! (GS 58)[69].

More specifically, in M 38 Nietzsche showed how the material of the drives, which in itself is inarticulate and inert compared with value differences, takes on its very first form through a value judgment about it: a drive (*Trieb*) receives a moral valuation in a specific social context (through *Loben* und *Tadeln*), i.e. it is given a character and a name, which, in conveying a value judgment, are not neutral. This social valuation is incorporated individually and articulated as the subjective experience of the good or bad conscience (*gutes/böses Gewissen*) in relation to the drive itself: the "attendant sensation of pleasure or displeasure" ("begleitende Empfindung der Lust oder Unlust", M 38), which itself does *not* belong to the *Trieb*, is

---

69 FW 58, KSA 3.422: "Diess hat mir die grösste Mühe gemacht und macht mir noch immerfort die grösste Mühe: einzusehen, dass unsäglich mehr daran liegt, *wie die Dinge heissen*, als was sie sind. Der Ruf, Name und Anschein, die Geltung, das übliche Maass und Gewicht eines Dinges - im Ursprunge zuallermeist ein Irrthum und eine Willkürlichkeit, den Dingen übergeworfen wie ein Kleid und seinem Wesen und selbst seiner Haut ganz fremd - ist durch den Glauben daran und sein Fortwachsen von Geschlecht zu Geschlecht dem Dinge allmählich gleichsam an- und eingewachsen und zu seinem Leibe selber geworden: der Schein von Anbeginn wird zuletzt fast immer zum Wesen und *wirkt* als Wesen!"

the subjective equivalent of a social sanction – a self-sanction (this is the function of the *Gewissen*). In this sense the value of a drive is not determined *absolutely*, but in the context of a system of moral valuations: thus it develops in a feeling and then in a word that is different each time (*Feigheit/Demuth*) depending on the historical value system in which it is valued or the social value of those who are its carriers[70]. The attributions, which create the moral polarities not only between concepts, but also between individuals and their actions, are connected with social positions and power strategies.

Attributing a name transforms the material of the drives, as it already contains a moral judgment (M 38) and transforms the experience of oneself associated with the manifestation of the drive. In other words, the linguistic use *does what it says*: carrying with it a value distinction, it is now a social and psychological *performance*, a stance in a context of values, and not just the bare neutrality or naive convention of linguistic convention. The convention of the sign, like discourse, is neither naive nor innocent.

As Foucault underlines, on the one hand the idea of an absolute continuity and coherence in *discourse* is in itself part of the mystification to be dissolved: "the" discourse is actually a series of "discursive events", corresponding to acts of strategic appropriation that colonize it with valuations and intentions to legitimize certain positions. On the other hand, in precisely this sense linguistic determinations delineate spaces of legitimacy and illegitimacy, of inclusion and exclusion. Not everything can be said, not every "discursive event" is equally probable or possible and can come true indiscriminately[71]. In the case of the contrast in FW 14, for example, that the experience and expression of *Habsucht* and *Liebe* are unlikely to be equally legitimate and equally possible, although they are probably articulations of the same underlying drive: moral condemnation hangs over one, while the other is socially encouraged and recognized as a moral feeling –

---

70   "An sich hat er, wie *jeder Trieb*, weder diess noch überhaupt einen moralischen Charakter und Namen, noch selbst eine bestimmte begleitende Empfindung der Lust oder Unlust: er erwirbt diess Alles erst, als seine zweite Natur, wenn er in Relation zu schon auf gut und böse getauften Trieben tritt, oder als Eigenschaft von Wesen bemerkt wird, welche vom Volke schon moralisch festgestellt und abgeschätzt sind" (M 38, KSA 3.45).
71   Foucault (1971, 53ff).

and this is because of the different names attributed to them. The battle for determining *Sprachgebrauch* is the battle for recognizing and staking a claim to an interpretation of things that is favourable to a certain form of life: and so when the religious define heresy – which Nietzsche sees as a sign of *Aufklärung* – as heresy, this is not a neutral linguistic convention, but conveys a denigration, a devaluation (FW 23), and so defines a space of exclusion, of illegitimate discourse. Because we have forgotten the original reasons, this confers a Montaigne-like or Pascalian mystic foundation on moral values (WS 40), but also mystifies the corresponding discourse as absolute, i.e. not dependent on specific conditions of possibility. The dissolution of this continuity does not aim to restore things with their original value, which has been "mystified" by unjustifed appropriations, but rather to show that this constant work of interpretation and valuation is the only thing that gives us access to things[72] (for example, to our drives).

This also brings us to point *a.3* and also a *b*. According to Nietzsche, *Sittlichkeit* "verdummt" (something like Pascal's *abêtir*), i.e. it prevents "bessere Sitten" from arising (M 19). Moral valuations – expressed in language – are no longer posed on the plane of hypothetical valuations of advantage and utility, which presumably guided early human experience of things. Value judgments intervene between us and things, blinding us to their genealogies: they are the articulation of the experience of things that is allowed us. New *Sitten* cannot arise because those we have do not have the character of functional choices, of clear strategic derivation and liable to better alternatives, so much as of self-referential absolute values. Just as Wittgenstein compared the ideal to a pair of glasses[73], the glasses of our categories of experience are so natural to us that there is no reason for us to think of removing them: we cannot see that things might be otherwise because all our experience of ourselves and our *understanding* of ourselves rest on these in-built categories. It is this undisturbed self-

---

72 *Ivi*, 55: 'Ne pas s'imaginer que le monde tourne vers nous un visage lisible que nous n'aurions plus qu'à déchiffrer; il n'est pas complice de notre connaissance; il n'y a pas de providence prédiscursive qui le dispose en notre paveur. Il faut concevoir le discours come une violence que nous faisons aux choses, en tout cas comme pratique que nous leur imposons'.

73 Wittgenstein (1967), *Philosophical Investigations*, §103.

referentiality of the obvious that a genealogical approach, like FW
14, tries to undermine[74]. And so criticism of *Sprachgebrauch* involves
criticism of a form of subjectivity, which is performed as a therapeutic
procedure.

The "naive" subjective experience, shared by author and reader
as part of the same moral community, so to speak, is weakened by
its relativization and by the demystification of its innocence: the
critical-genealogical gaze reveals the alliance between linguistic use,
the experience it structures, the blankness as to its historicity and
arbitrariness, and the mystification of the strategic function it performs
in the dynamics of power. Following the experience of demystification
in FW 14, for example, a naive experience of love is no longer possible:
Nietzsche's argument starts from mistrust: first, of words, and then of
our *Empfindungen* about words, and as a result, of our experience
of what they denote – which means, in fact, self-mistrust. Through
the transition from the dissolution of the obvious by means of its
relativization, Nietzsche's critique gives the subject a self-alienating
viewpoint and, in this sense, necessarily a self-critical one, because
its object is precisely those categories or those values on which the
subjective possibility of self-representation and understanding is
founded[75]. If the critical exercise did not have this significance, if it did
not question something crucial, it would not unleash on itself those
psychological-emotional resistances that Nietzsche discusses both in
BGE 23, a propos of the already cited "Lehre von der Ableitbarkeit
aller guten Triebe aus den schlimmen" ("a doctrine of the derivation
of all good drives from the bad")[76], and, much earlier, in HH I 107,

---

74   As Norbert Elias (2001, 144), underlines too, there is no possibility of mnemonic
     access to the previous stages of what he calls the "Wendeltreppe des Bewusstsein":
     only historical (and historical-critical) reconstruction can bring the subject face
     to face with its *own* historical character, thus problematizing the "obvious".
     Cf. too Saar (2007, chap. 3 and 7 in particular). On the link between the forms
     of Nietzsche's philosophical writing and this deferring of ordinary perception,
     rooted in ordinary language, cf. Wotling (2007).
75   Cf. Saar (2007, 106).
76   "Eine eigentliche Physio-Psychologie hat mit unbewussten Widerständen im
     Herzen des Forschers zu kämpfen, sie hat 'das Herz' gegen sich: schon eine Lehre
     von der gegenseitigen Bedingtheit der 'guten' und der 'schlimmen' Triebe, macht,
     als feinere Immoralität, einem noch kräftigen und herzhaften Gewissen Noth
     und Überdruss, - noch mehr eine Lehre von der Ableitbarkeit aller guten Triebe
     aus den schlimmen" (JGB 23, KSA 5.38).

a propos of the "Lehre von der völligen Unverantwortlichkeit des Menschen" (a doctrine of the "total unaccountability" of man)[77]: abandoning a viewpoint in this critical context means becoming aware of the conditions of possibility of one's image and experience of oneself.

This is the dual analytical and therapeutic value of the genealogical intervention, which operates in the awareness of obliviousness – to the interpretative nature of every interpretation – being complementary to the violence that is not only asserted in, but is also intrinsic to, interpretation. In *ordering* things, and also the subjective perceptions of things, in legitimizing itself in its ordering of discourse, every interpretation exercises a violence that is inherent to its being at the root of will to power, desire for possession and appropriation. This fundamental violence, which it institutes, is not then reiterated openly as a disruptive event in every circumstance, but as "invisible" violence, which it preserves, as it is repeated in the form and the order of things: the corresponding language and subjectivity reflect and reiterate this "naturalized" order, whose violent arbitrariness and whose character have now become lost in oblivion. The effectiveness of genealogy, like that of deconstruction[78], depends on the awareness of this necessary process, an awareness that, if honestly conducted, also involves genealogical criticism or deconstruction in the same destiny as the objects it is analysing. I shall return to this point at the end.

Self-estrangement consists above all, and this is the last point (*c*), in showing how many and which valuations, judgments etc, inherited and acquired, are hidden beneath the surface of our representation of

---

77 "Die völlige Unverantwortlichkeit des Menschen für sein Handeln und sein Wesen ist der bitterste Tropfen, welchen der Erkennende schlucken muss, wenn er gewohnt war, in der Verantwortlichkeit und der Pflicht den Adelsbrief seines Menschenthums zu sehen. Alle seine Schätzungen, Auszeichnungen, Abneigungen sind dadurch entwerthet und falsch geworden: sein tiefstes Gefühl, das er dem Dulder, dem Helden entgegenbrachte, hat einem Irrthume gegolten" (MA I 107, KSA 2.103).

78 Cf. in particular Derrida (1994, 32 ff): "l'opération qui revient à fonder, à inaugurer, à justifier le droit, à *faire la loi*, consisterait en un coup de force, en une violence performative et donc interprétative qui en elle-même n'est ni juste ni injuste et qu'aucune justice, aucun droit préalable et antérieurement fondateur, aucune fondation préexistante, par définition, ne pourrait ni garantir ni contredir ou invalider". See also, § 3.

our experiences and beneath the categories of our psychology[79] (one example is also FW 335), and how some of these in-built coexisting valuations contradict each other. In *Der Fall Wagner* and then in *Götzen-Dämmerung* Nietzsche defined modernity as physiological self-contradiction[80]:

> But against our knowledge and our wills, our bodies all have values, words, formulas, and morals with *contrary* derivations, – physiologically considered, we are *false*... A *diagnosis of the modern soul* – where would it begin? With a resolute incision into this contracdictoriness of instincts, by separating out its opposing values, by performing a vivisection on its most *instructive* case (CW Epilogue)[81].

The treatment in FW 14 seems to share a similar viewpoint, for all the necessary differences of context and development. Nietzsche is undertaking there a kind of *Diagnostik* of subjectivity: starting from phenomenal data (our *Empfindungen* towards this or that word, that is to say our spontaneous reactions in contexts of discourse), he shows how they are symptoms of the cohabitation and interaction in ourselves of values, in-built judgments and corresponding *words* that have different origins, histories and intentions, and that correspond to different stages in the sedimentation of western subjectivity. Nietzsche's observations, designed to clarify linguistic use, provide a greater *Übersichtlichkeit* of it (how *Liebe* indicates a series of heterogeneous experiences; how *Habsucht* and *Liebe* are arbitrarily contrasted, etc.), are aimed more deeply at showing the articulations of our psychology and physiology, which are invisible to the "natural" gaze, but immediate to introspection or subjective reflexiveness – precisely because it has no other categories available than those

---

79   On this topic see Wotling (1999).
80   "Diese Instinkte widersprechen, stören sich, zerstören sich unter einander; ich definirte das *Moderne* bereits als den physiologischen Selbst-Widerspruch" (GD Streifzüge eines Unzeitgemässen 41).
81   WA Epilog, KSA 6.53: "Aber wir Alle haben, wider Wissen, wider Willen, Werthe, Worte, Formeln, Moralen *entgegengesetzter* Abkunft im Leibe, – wir sind, physiologisch betrachtet, *falsch*... Eine *Diagnostik der modernen Seele* – womit begönne sie? Mit einem resoluten Einschnitt in diese Instinkt-Widersprüchlichkeit, mit der Herauslösung ihrer Gegensatz-Werthe, mit der Vivisektion vollzogen an ihrem *lehrreichsten* Fall".

on which it fixes its gaze[82]. The incoherence and complexity that Nietzsche brings out in linguistic usage, how they have evolved, and, especially, how they are not neutral as regards moral valuations, are above all inherent to the subjectivity and psychology of the reader he is addressing.

The procedure by which Nietzsche diagnoses the contradictions and inconsistencies of the experience of love in western society thus implies that the reader realizes that the "natural" relation with his experience is thereby interrupted, and also, presumably, that he realizes that he is resisting the realization and adopts a *self-critical* distance, a mistrust —*Misstrauen*.

Examples of similar contradictions, notably regarding love, are also known to the recent sociological literature on the subject. Analysis of amorous interactions and relations often shows the emergence in the communicative and relational practices of subjects, of diverging or opposite representations linked to words, situations, experiences, and understanding of oneself and the other. The conscious and reflexive definition that we are able to give of a situation often enters into conflict with the in-built judgments and valuation of which we are the unconscious carriers, and that emerge in contact with situations that set them off again. Thus, in an enquiry into the dynamics and construction of a couple's identity in a domestic context (division and performance of housework, particularly the laundry), J.-C. Kaufmann shows how the openly negotiated positions of symmetry and non-discrimination cohabit in most cases with a stock of in-built values,

---

82   And in this sense it perpetuates, along with those categories that it cannot help using, the relations of dominion to which they are functional. As Bourdieu (1998, 41) points out, this self-referentiality of the available categories and judgments, in the context of a relation of dominion or power, is the cognitive and emotional bond that makes a reconsideration of the relation extremely improbable, if not impossible: "la violence symbolique s'institue par l'intermédiaire de l'adhésion que le dominé ne peut pas ne pas accorder au dominant (donc à la domination) lorsqu'il ne dispose, pour le penser et pour se penser ou, mieux, pour penser sa relation avec lui, que d'instruments de connaissance qu'il a en commun avec lui et qui, n'étant que la forme incorporée de la relation de domination, font apparaître cette relation comme naturelle; ou, en d'autres termes, lorsque les schèmes qu'il met en œuvre pour se percevoir et s'apprécier, ou pour s'apercevoir et apprécier les dominants [...] sont le produit de l'incorporation des classements, ainsi naturalisés, dont son être social est le produit".

judgments, models and schemes of behaviour that interfere with them and make communication contradictory, and emotional interaction problematic[83]. Eva Illouz comes to similar conclusions in her research on the function of the consumption of goods and "romantic" contexts in the construction and development of intimate relations: the widespread commercialization of the ideal of romantic love in western societies conditions the social behaviours and consumer choices of social actors, yet, when asked about the value of that ideal, those social actors show increasing mistrust or ironical detachment towards it. Faced with different narratives of a love story, the subjects interviewed who have a greater cultural capital tend to distance themselves from the narrative that is most saturated with the romantic ideal, regarding it as an uncertain and unreliable basis for building a relation (a rival ideal is that of love as *working* at the relation); but on the other hand, the same subjects offer narratives of themselves that show the romantic ideal remains a reference point in amorous interaction and imagination[84].

These contradictory instances, the result of different contexts of socialization, learning and emotional experience, tend to remain mainly invisible or non-problematic for the reflecting consciousness, precisely because the semantic and representational unity of the linguistic term concerned, in this case *love*, tends both to unify in practice different experiences and contexts, and, as a result, to exercise a regulatory function, inducing subjects to try to adjust their experience and their understanding of that experience to the "code" that the term prescribes[85] (e.g., ideal of love as unity, accord, understanding, sincerity and openness, total communication etc.). Yet underneath the regulatory directives of behaviour and experience, conveyed mainly through language and its constructive/prescriptive significance, the

---

83 Cf. J.-C. Kaufmann (1992, 53): "Comme si nous portions en nous-mêmes un capital dormant, constitué de schémas de manières susceptibles à tout instant d'être réactivées (ou de servir de référence en vue d'"inventer' de nouvelles pratiques adaptées à une situation donnée). Cet héritage passif, secrètement sédimenté hors de la mémoire consciente, hors des interactions sociales et hors des habitudes constituées, peut ne jamais se révéler ou au contraire apparaître au grand jour, parfois brusquement, à la faveur des circonstances propices".
84 Cf. E. Illouz (1997).
85 Cf. some interesting remarks in Hahn (1983).

conflicts of representations, ideas, emotional dispositions, experiences, and projections of all kinds have repercussions on the concrete experience of relations, interactions, feelings etc.

3. Results: New Horizons of Creative Nomination

> Woran glaubst du? –
> *Daran: dass die Gewichte*
> *aller Dinge neu bestimmt*
> *werden müssen.*
>
> (FW 269)

Rather than seeking the essence and universal definition, Nietzsche aims at increasing the number of perspectives in play and their connections: FW 14 does not clarify what love is, but dissolves the surface of the linguistic unit and its related mystifications (for example, the opposition *Habsucht-Liebe*), leaving the reader in the end with a handful of critical deconstructions and possibilities but without the usual tools for classifying phenomena and valuating experience. What is being sought in FW 14 is neither an essence of love that at last tells us, after the enquiry and demystification, *what* it *really is*; nor the *reduction* of the forms of love to the drive underlying them[86]. In line with the premises of his method of enquiry, Nietzsche does not want to show the "falsity" of our forms of experience as they are conveyed by language, as if there were a "true" reality to discover beneath them. That is not the function of the appeal to physiology and

---

86 It is worth noting that in *Massenpsychologie und Ich-Analyse* Freud (1921, 42ff) offers a famous analysis of love, in which, very like Nietzsche in FW 14, he traces all forms of love (love between the sexes, *Eltern- un Kindesliebe, allgemeine Menschenliebe* etc.) to *libido*. Unlike Nietzsche, Freud does not question the linguistic unit, which he sees as justified precisely by the possibility of reducing multiplicity to a shared root in the drives, and so takes over the linguistic synthesis as the basis of his considerations on the psychoanalysis of love ("Wir meinen also, daß die Sprache mit dem Wort 'Liebe' in seinen vielfältigen Anwendungen eine durchaus berechtigte Zusammenfassung geschaffen hat, und daß wir nichts Besseres tun können, als dieselbe auch unseren wissenschaftlichen Erörterungen und Darstellungen zugrunde zu legen"). In Freud's vision the structures of deep psychology correspond in this case to those of language. Nietzsche starts from the opposite idea.

the drives in Nietzsche's argument. His critique aims at questioning the *obviousness* of these forms of experience, showing their derived and evolutionary character through reference to their genealogies; and once their obviousness seems suspect, at drawing our attention to their fundamental regulatory function, which is deeply rooted in us, so much so that it is a structural part of our understanding of ourselves and the world; and finally, at creating methodical distrust of these categories of self-understanding contained in our language, our emotions, our perceptions etc., and their (prescriptive) moral character.

Precisely by virtue of the already cited "laborious" discovery and awareness that the names of things – and the genealogies of these names – decide their essence for us, Nietzsche claims that it would be madness to believe one could eliminate this appearance ("die als wesenhaft geltende Welt"), returning to a theoretical origin (*Ursprung*), to the point at which the "true" essence of things was concealed by the convention of naming. The only possible destruction of the illusion of language is a *creative* dissolution: "Nur als Schaffende können wir vernichten!", "Only as creators can we destroy!" (GS 58) – i.e., destroy *through* language. Nietsche's constructive position, by which "it is enough to create new names and valuations and plausibilities in order to create new 'things'" (GS 58, modified: "es genügt, neue Namen und Schätzungen und Wahrscheinlichkeiten zu schaffen, um auf die Länge hin neue 'Dinge' zu schaffen", FW 58), is the upshot of the assimilation of the critical awareness of the fact that the stratifications of interpretation and naming are the only reality available, that they constitute the world and its related subjectivity. It is the upshot, in short, of the internalization not only of perspectivism, but of the certainty of its epistemological and existential primacy.

The dissolution of the mythology of language and moral valuations that it passes on thus opens an otherwise unsuspected creative horizon: it offers him the absolutely destabilizing recognition that *it is certainly possible* and *legitimate* to imagine the world otherwise, "create it" differently. Once the arbitrary and historical nature of moral judgments and the words that convey them is brought out, we can see that they *tolerate* alternatives, and that the right way to free oneself from the prison of their mytology is to overcome them through a new interpretation, impose a new *appearance* on them. This position is part of the context of the gradual aestheticization of knowledge and of life itself, which, as Marco Brusotti shows, characterizes Nietzsche's thinking from FW on[87].

Knowledge, and with it genealogical enquiry, which reveals how things have always been newly "gefärbt" and so been given a new face (FW 152), is not attacking the discovery or rediscovery of a positive, original, universal truth, but offers the awareness – which is above all a question of the *ethics* of knowledge – that the very idea of such a truth is functional to certain strategies and certain processes of social formation. The "explorers of *truth*" ("Erforscher der *Wahrheit*"), which, by virtue of their critical power, represent a threat to the "*law of agreement*" ("Gesetz der Übereinstimmung", FW 76) that men have slowly and laboriously established to give order to social life and to communication, are also a threat to the very order of relations and legitimacy. Modifying the image of things, as the man of knowledge does, giving them new colours and a new face, means above all breaking an interdict on discourse: questioning the confines of legitimacy, the frontiers of the exclusion and inclusion of authorized discourse (for example, on love as a moral dispositon), shifting attention to its conditions of possibility and so revoking its absolute moral, social and political authority.

If genealogy reveals processes and historical change, and performs what we might call a general critical function in this sense, Nietzsche nevertheless seems to be quite clear, as FW 14 shows perfectly in my view, that critical action must take place also and above all on another plane, that of an *individual* challenging by the subject who receives the philosophical communication, with which the subject must to a certain degree collaborate. This "therapeutic" equivalent of the history of judgments and moral valuations seems to me to emerge clearly in FW 335, where Nietzsche invites us to use it as a tool of the intellectual conscience *against* self-referentiality and the certainty of the moral conscience. The aim of this self-critical movement ("die Reinigung unserer Meinungen und Werthschätzungen") is, in this context too, the acquisition of the capacity to *create* ("die Schöpfung neuer eigener Gütertafeln"), in this case to *create oneself*:

> Let us, therefore *limit* ourselves to the purification of our opinions and value judgements and to the *creation of tables of what is good*

---

87   Brusotti (1997, 454ff).

that are new and all our own (...). We, however, want to *become
who we are* – human beings who are new, unique, incomparable,
who give themselves laws, who create themselves! To that end we
must become the best students and discoverers of everything lawful
and necessary in the world: we must become *physicists* in order to
be creators in this sense – while hitherto all valuations and ideals
have been built on *ignorance* of physics or in *contradiction* to it
(GS 335)[88].

There are three major claims behind FW 14: any definition of a
phenomenon reflects certain moral, social, cultural, historical context and the outcome of the competition between various pressures
to impose an interpretation on it; that pursuing such a knowledge,
through and in combination with the genealogical method, makes *self-
criticism* possible for the subject receiving the communication; and
this transformation of experience must take the form of an assumption of responsibiity, so to speak, of a self-creation (*Selbstgestaltung*)
and a complementary self-overcoming (*Selbstüberwindung*). This is
the therapeutic effect that, apart from its diagnostic effect and by virtue of it, knowledge and genealogical criticism can exercise, as space
for self-reflection, not just for an individual but for a whole civilization, the sedimentation of which can be found in each individual
reader.

In this sense I think there is a link with Derrida's wonderful description of deconstructive criticism as the assumption of responsibility towards the memory of history[89] seen as a succession of
interpretations, values and rules that remain *readable* by criticism.

---

88 FW 335, KSA 3.563: "*Beschränken* wir uns also auf die Reinigung unserer
    Meinungen und Werthschätzungen und auf die *Schöpfung neuer eigener
    Gütertafeln* (...). Wir aber *wollen Die werden, die wir sind*, - die Neuen, die
    Einmaligen, die Unvergleichbaren, die Sich-selber-Gesetzgebenden, die Sich-
    selber-Schaffenden! Und dazu müssen wir die besten Lerner und Entdecker
    alles Gesetzlichen und Nothwendigen in der Welt werden: wir müssen *Physiker*
    sein, um, in jenem Sinne, *Schöpfer* sein zu können, - während bisher alle
    Werthschätzungen und Ideale auf *Unkenntniss* der Physik oder im *Widerspruch*
    mit ihr aufgebaut waren".
89 Derrida (1994, 44) *déconstruction* shows "le sens de responsabilité sans limite,
    et donc nécessairement excessive, incalculable, devant la mémoire; et donc la
    tâche de rappeler l'histoire, l'origine et le sens, donc les limites des concepts de
    justice, de loi et de droit, des valeurs, normes, prescriptions qui s'y sont imposées
    et sédimentées, restant dès lors plus ou moins lisibles ou présupposées".

The responsibility and, in Derrida's sense, the *justice* of genealogical criticism consists in being able to read properly the traces these interpretations leave; but also, I would add, partly leaning on Derrida himself, in its consciously entering every circumstance, as *one of them*, in their succession and sedimentation: the *right* genealogical procedure is that which is capable of deconstruction, criticism, genealogy and *so* of self-deconstruction, self-criticism and self-genealogy. And this capacity is already provided for, as we can see for example in JGB 22, in Nietzsche's idea of perspectivism, in the Dionysian tragic philosophy, in the very theory of the will to power. This reflexive return of critical subjectivity that calls into question its own conditions of possibility, is a profoundly ethical stance: that is why I have spoken of the reader's assumption of responsibility in the framework of Nietzsche's genealogy, which is not given as a universal knowledge that can be transmitted, but as the *method* of the intellectual conscience – as an essentially self-critical position. Without this prospect of self-transformation, genealogy would to a certain extent betray the premises of its action[90].

Bibliography

Abel, Günter (1984), *Nietzsche. Die Dynamik der Willen zur Macht und die ewige Wiederkehr*, Berlin/New York (Walter de Gruyter).
Abel, Günter (2004), *Zeichen der Wirklichkeit*, Frankfurt am Main (Suhrkamp).
Barthes, Roland (1995), *Œuvres complètes*, édition établie et présentée par É. Marty, tome troisième, Paris (Seuil).

---

90   Butler (1997, particularly the *Introduction* and chapters. 2 and 3) has rightly drawn attention to the constitutive character of the subject's capacity to incorporate violence – as interdict, law, order etc. – and reiterate it autonomously towards oneself. As Foucault has already brought out, subjectivization is in this sense a productive, and even creative, subjection. Thus, for Butler it is this *active* connivance of the subject with the order of things and of language, with the schemas of subjection and so with the circumstances of his subjection, that is the condition of possibility for any (self)-criticism and any enterprise of liberation. Without this active participation, there would be no subjectivity and so not even any criticsm. It may be by virtue of this awareness that Nietzsche sees the possibility of a "new beginning" both as itself a disciplinary operation (ascetic, educational etc.) and above all as taking place to an extent thanks to those critical tools it calls into question (morality that criticizes itself thanks to its own moral values etc).

162 Chiara Piazzesi

Bourdieu, Pierre (1998), *La domination masculine*, Paris (Seuil).
Brusotti, Marco (1993), „Beiträge zur Quellenforschung", in: *Nietzsche-Studien* 22 (1993), 389–394.
Brusotti, Marco (2001), „Beiträge zur Quellenforschung", in: *Nietzsche-Studien* 30 (2001), 422–434.
Brusotti, Marco (1997), *Die Leidenschaft der Erkenntnis*, Berlin/New York (Walter de Gruyter).
Butler, Judith (1997), *The Psychic Life of Power. Theories in Subjection*, Stanford (Stanford University Press).
Campioni, Giuliano (2009a), "'Gaya scienza' e 'gai saber' nella filosofia di Nietzsche", in: Carmassi, C./Cermelli, G./Foschi Alberet, M./ Hepp, M. (ed.), *Wo Bleibt das 'Konzept'? – Dov'è il 'concetto'? Studi in onore di Enrico De Angelis*, München (Iudicium Verlag), 11–26.
Campioni, Giuliano (2009b), "Nachweis aus Claude Adrien Helvetius, Discurs über den Geist des Menschen (1760)", in: *Nietzsche-Studien* 38 (2009), 310–311.
Chaves, Ernani (2005), "L'amour, la passion: Nietzsche e Stendhal", in: Azeredo, V. D. (org.) (2005), *Falando de Nietzsche*, Ijuí (Editora da Universidade de Ijuí), 41–54.
Derrida, Jacques (1994), *Force de loi*, Paris (Galilée).
Elias, Norbert (2001), „Die Gesellschaft der Individuen", in: *Gesammelte Schriften*, Vol. 10, Frankfurt am Main (Suhrkamp).
Foucault, Michel (1976), *Histoire de la sexualité: La volonté de savoir*, vol. 1, Paris (Gallimard).
Foucault, Michel (1994), „Le sujet et le pouvoir", in: *Dits et écrits IV: 1980–1988*, Paris (Gallimard).
Foucault, Michel (1971), *L'ordre du discours*, Paris (Gallimard).
Freud, Sigmund (1921), *Massenpsychologie und Ich-Analyse*, Wien (Internationaler Psychoanalytischer Verlag).
Hahn, A. (1983), "Konsensfiktionen in Kleingruppen. Dargestellt am Beispiel von jungen Ehen", in: Neidhardt, F. (ed.), *Gruppensoziologie. Perspektiven und Materialien. Sonderheft 25 der Kölner Zeitschrift für Soziologie und Sozialpsychologie*, Köln (Westdeutscher Verlag), 210–232.
Helvetius, Claude Adrien (1760), *Discurs über den Geist des Menschen*, aus dem Französischen des Herrn Helvetius übers. v. J. G. Forkert, mit einer Vorrede Joh. Christoph Gottscheds, Leipzig und Liegnitz (D. Siegerts).
Illouz, Eva (1997), *Consuming the romantic utopia: love and the cultural contradictions of capitalism*, Berkeley (University of California Press).
Kaufmann, Jean-Claude (1992), *La trame conjugale. Analyse du couple par son linge*, Paris (Nathan).
Luhmann, Niklas (1982), *Liebe als Passion*, Frankfurt am Main (Suhrkamp).
Marton, Scarlett (2010), "De la réalité au rêve. Nietzsche et les images de la femme" in: Campioni, G./Piazzesi, C./ Wotling, P. (ed.) (2010), *Letture della Gaia scienza – Lectures du Gai savoir*, Pisa (ETS), 277–294.

Müller-Lauter, Wolfgang (1978), "Der Organismus als innerer Kampf. Der Einfluß von Wilhelm Roux auf Friedrich Nietzsche", in: *Nietzsche-Studien* 7, (1978), 189–223.

Piazzesi, Chiara (2010), "Die soziale Verinnerlichung von Machtverhältnissen: über die produktiven Aspekte der Selbstdisziplinierung und der Affektkontrolle bei Nietzsche und Elias", in: Günther, F./Holzer, A./ Müller, E. (eds.), *Zur Genealogie des Zivilisationsprozesses. Friedrich Nietzsche und Norbert Elias*, Berlin/New York (Walter de Gruyter).

Piazzesi, Chiara (forthcoming), "Pour une nouvelle conception du rapport entre théorie et pratique: la philologie comme éthique et méthodologie", in: *Actes du Colloque International 'L'art de bien lire'. Nietzsche et la philologie, Reims-Paris, 19–21 octobre 2006*, Paris (Vrin).

Saar, Martin (2007), *Genealogie als Kritik*, Frankfurt am Main (Campus Verlag).

Salaquarda, Jörg (1997), "'Fröhliche Wissenschaft' zwischen Freigeisterei und neue, Lehre"', in: *Nietzsche-Studien* 26 (1997), 165–183.

Sloterdijk, Peter (2009), *Du mußt dein Leben ändern*, Frankfurt am Main (Suhrkamp).

Stendhal (1965), *De l'amour*, Paris (Garnier-Flammarion).

Wittgenstein, Ludwig (1967), *Philosophical Investigations*, ed. Anscombe, G. E. M./Rhees, R. /von Wright, G. H., transl. by Anscombe, G. E. M., Oxford (Blackwell).

Wotling, Patrick (2007), "'*Comment pourrais-je écrire pour des lecteurs?*' La spécificité de l'écriture philosophique chez Nietzsche", in: Denat, C. (ed.) (2007), *Au-delà des textes. La question de l'écriture philosophique*, Reims (Presses de l'Université de Reims), 151–166.

Wotling, Patrick (1999), *La pensée du sous-sol*, Paris (Allia).

III. Instinct, Language, and Philosophy

Afternoon Thoughts

Nietzsche and the Dogmatism of Philosophical Writing

Scarlett Marton

Being an anti-dogmatic book *par excellence*, *Beyond Good and Evil* begins with its author manifesting his suspicion of dogmatic philosophy and ends with an expression of distrust concerning his own thoughts.

In the opening lines of his book, Nietzsche casts his bait:

> Suppose that truth is a woman – and why not? Aren't there reasons for suspecting that all philosophers, to the extent that they have been dogmatists, have not really understood women? That the grotesque seriousness of their approach to truth and the clumsy advances they have made so far are unsuitable ways of pressing their suit with a woman? What is certain is that she has spurned them – leaving dogmatism of all types standing sad and discouraged. *If* it is even standing! (KSA 5.11, BGE Preface).

When Nietzsche identifies truth with a woman, he allows us to guess that he means a charming woman employing all her astuteness and power of seduction; he induces us into thinking of a woman that will not allow herself to be conquered, and is thus a master at the art of manipulation. He seems to be suggesting that the beautiful, the coquettish, the graceful, the playful, the light, the gentle, the pleasant are her main characteristics. But if dogmatic philosophers have created a world inaccessible to her so as to protect themselves from her, it is our duty now to question this manner of proceeding. After all, they have understood nothing of women, and therefore, they have never grasped how to deal with truth.[1]

---

1   In KSA 5.155, BGE 220, Nietzsche again identifies truth with a woman: "in the end, [truth] is a woman: we should not do violence to her".

In desiring to conquer truth at any price, to possess her no matter what, dogmatic philosophers adopted "unsuitable ways of pressing their suit with a woman". They didn't realize that bashfulness is the feminine virtue *par excellence*; unwary, they wanted to see all.[2] Without constraints, they expected to undress a woman with their eyes; without embarrassment, they hoped to undress truth completely. But truth, being a woman, knows well that such truth doesn't exist, for she isn't the truth she is believed to be. In other words, truth, being a woman, takes the doctrinal truth they pursue as an affront. With her garments and adornments she moves out of their reach; bashful, she operates on a different record.[3]

We are led to affirm that by criticizing dogmatic philosophers in their behavior, Nietzsche praises, along the same lines, the woman that refuses to succumb to them. And, consequently, praises the truth. If Nietzsche identifies truth with a woman in order to attack the conception of truth that dogmatic philosophy works with, then we can suppose that he is also making use of this identification to introduce another concept of truth. Truth makes itself known as a woman dressed and adorned, and as a woman who can be seen, she unveils herself. However, this isn't the place to follow through with this interpretative hypothesis.

It is more important right now to emphasize that whoever makes a literal interpretation of what Nietzsche writes in *Ecce Homo*, is mistaken. In this book, while commenting on *Beyond Good and Evil*, he declares that, after *Thus Spoke Zarathustra*, "after the yea-saying part of my task had been solved it was time for the no-saying, *no-doing* half: the revaluation of values so far" (KSA 6.350, EH Beyond Good and Evil 1). This does not mean, however, that both parts of his task are disconnected. It would be a mistake to conceive the two sides of his thought, that is, the corrosive side of the criticism of values and the constructive side of a new world vision, as two

---

2   In the Preface to *The Gay Science*, he makes such a claim: "We no longer believe that truth remains truth when one pulls off the veil; we have lived too much to believe this. Today we consider it a matter of decency no to wish to see everything naked, to be present everywhere, to understand and 'know' everything'"(KSA 3.352, GS Preface to the Second Edition 4).

3   Cf. KSA 6.61, TI Maxims and Arrows 16: "*Between women. –* 'Truth? Oh, you don't know truth! Isn't it an attempt to assassinate all our *pudeurs*?"

unrelated compartments. It would be another mistake to grasp the two demands of his project of the revaluation of values, that is, to suppress the basis itself from which the values have proceeded and to engender new values, as two parallel determinations. It would be a mistake too to understand both of his needs, that is, the need of annihilating and the need of creating, as two independent attitudes. As Nietzsche writes in another passage of *Ecce Homo:* "I know the joy of destruction to a degree proportionate to my *strength* for destruction, – In both cases I obey my Dionysian nature, which does not know how to separate doing no from saying yes" (KSA 6.366, EH Why I am a Destiny 2). Destroying and constructing constitute moments of the same unfurling; annihilating and creating are movements that belong to the same process.

It is not by chance that in *Beyond Good and Evil*, passages in which Nietzsche performs his critical task are intertwined with others where he states his views. In the opening lines of the book, for instance, when he deals with the question of truth, while simultaneously contesting how dogmatic philosophers approach it, he makes clear that it is possible to conceive of it in a different manner that is in tune with his own philosophy.

Nietzsche resorts to a similar procedure when he tackles the dogmatists' conception of the philosophical activity. With seriousness and insistence, they are committed to erecting "sublime and unconditional philosophical edifices" (KSA 5.11, BGE Preface) that they suppose will reveal ultimate and definitive truths. Demonstrating a pure and disinterested knowledge they are dedicated to the building of philosophical constructions they believe to be universally valid. In opposition to this manner of conceiving philosophical activity, Nietzsche presents us with another, which is readily indicated in the book's subtitle. As a "Prelude to a Philosophy of the Future", *Beyond Good and Evil* introduces the philosophers of the future. And at the end of the Second Part, Nietzsche describes them.

It is indeed possible that they will be "new friends of 'truth'", but, Nietzsche adds, "they certainly will not be dogmatists" (KSA 5.60, BGE 43). This passage corroborates our interpretation, when we affirm that, in criticizing dogmatic philosophers in their behavior, Nietzsche introduces another conception of truth. And, in another passage, we read: "These philosophers of the future might have the right (and perhaps also the wrong) to be described as *those who attempt (Versucher)*. Ultimately, this name is itself only an attempt, and, if you will, a temptation" (KSA 5.59, BGE 42). As *Versucher*, they would both attempt and provoke; in sum, they would be men of experiments and temptations (*Versuchen* and *Versuchungen*)[4].

These are precisely the terms that Nietzsche uses in the Sixth Part of the book, entitled "We Scholars", when writing not on the philosophers of the future but on the true philosopher; he thinks it is he who feels the "weight and duty of a hundred experiments and temptations of life (*Versuchen und Versuchungen des Lebens*)" (KSA 5.133, BGE 205). We are therefore led to presume that when he picks the phrase "Prelude to a Philosophy of the Future" as a subtitle to his book, Nietzsche is not only presenting us with a different way of conceiving of philosophical activity but is already putting it into practice. He not only announces the emergence of philosophers of the future, but also includes himself among them.

The author of *Beyond Good and Evil*, an experimentalist in the first degree, never hesitates to invite his reader to experiment, be it due to understanding that we as humans are no more than mere experiences or due to believing that we should not avoid experimenting with ourselves. In his texts, the purpose of making experiments with thought equals chasing an idea in its multiple aspects, approaching a question from various angles, dealing with a particular theme by taking on various points of view, in a word: considering a problem from different perspectives. Adumbrated in his first writings, this purpose can be clearly traced back to *Human, all too Human* and it is finally claimed as his own purpose from *Thus Spoke Zarathustra* on. Embracing in an ever more decisive way what we would here hastily call "perspectivism", Nietzsche makes effective the experimental nature of his philosophizing[5].

Distrusting every kind of dogmatic attitude, our author assumes certain points of view in order to question them. Suspicious of all

---

4   In his translation of Nietzsche's book, Patrick Wotling explains the double meaning of the term *Versucher* in German. Cf. Nietzsche (2000, endnote 230).

5   Both Löwith and Kaufmann highlight the fundamentally experimental nature of Nietzschean thought and insist on how the philosopher applied the aphorismatic style to emphasize his experimentalism. The aphorisms are attempts at reconsidering the same questions, thus allowing for experimentation with one's thinking process. Cf. Kaufmann (1965) and Löwith (1978).

definitive certainty he anticipates ideas to try them out. For this precise reason, it is risky to consider his views to be true. We might say that *his* truths, being neither truths in the sense of dogmatic philosophy, nor opinions in the sense of what pre-exists reflexive thought, are of an experimental nature. Being neither doctrinal truths, nor mere opinions, they would be temporary; they would expire when others more in tune with the reflexive movement itself emerged.

* * *

Within the context of *Beyond Good and Evil* it is precisely against dogmatic philosophy that Nietzsche places his experimental philosophy. Already in the Preface, he justifies his suspicion of dogmatic philosophers:

> And perhaps the time is very near when we will realize again and again just *what* actually served as the cornerstone of those sublime and unconditional philosophical edifices that the dogmatists used to build – some piece of folk superstition from time immemorial (like the soul-superstition that still causes trouble as the superstition of the subject or I), some word-play perhaps, a seduction of grammar or even an over-eager generalization from facts that are really very local, very personal, very human-all-too-human (KSA 5.11f, BGE Preface).

In their presumptuousness, dogmatic philosophers have adopted commonplace starting points in order to construct their "sublime and unconditional" edifices, Nietzsche suggests. They departed from "a piece of folk superstition from time immemorial", as the superstition of the soul, for example. If in the field of physics there were those who sustained that reality consisted of tiny particles of matter, in the field of metaphysics Descartes – and not only him – thought the soul was "something indestructible, eternal, indivisible" (KSA 5.27, BGE 12). From there proceeded the idea of the "I" as fixed and stable, the subject as responsible for all his actions, including the action of thinking. The theory of materialistic atomism would find echoes in the doctrine of the "atomism of the soul". "Let this expression [sc. 'the atomism of the soul']", Nietzsche explains a little further in aphorism 12 of *Beyond Good and Evil*, "signify the belief that the soul is something indestructible, eternal, indivisible, that it is a monad, an *atomon*" (KSA 5.27, BGE 12). And he positively states: "*this* belief must be thrown out of science!" (KSA 5.27, BGE 12). Making strategic use of scientific knowledge, he wants to remove all metaphysical conception and, even more, all religious superstition. He proceeds, however, in a confidential tone: "Between you and me, there is absolutely no need to give up 'the soul' itself, and relinquish one of the oldest and most venerable hypotheses" (KSA 5.27, BGE 12).

For now, all is happening as if Nietzsche merely refused the idea of the soul as first introduced by Christianity and then taken up by metaphysics, without denying its existence. Proof of this is what he adds in the same aphorism of *Beyond Good and Evil*, when he states: "But the path lies open for new versions and sophistications of the soul hypothesis – and concepts like the 'mortal soul' and the 'soul as subject-multiplicity' and the 'soul as a society constructed out of drives and affects' want henceforth to have civil rights in the realm of science" (KSA 5.27, BGE 12). It is necessary first of all to abandon the idea of the soul as it has been imposed by Christianity and continued in metaphysics, to re-think it on a different basis. Borrowing the idea from Christianity, philosophers preserved this way of conceiving it and continued to consider the soul as eternal, unique and indivisible. By refusing the attributes that have been conferred upon it, at first glance what Nietzsche seems to be proposing is merely their inversion.

But, in view of Nietzsche's physiopsychology, this passage needs further interpretation. It is important to remind the reader that Nietzsche sustains that all organic forms take part in thinking, feeling, and willing, so that the brain is nothing else than a huge centralizing apparatus. It is for this reason that he introduces the concepts of "mortal soul", "soul as subject-multiplicity" and "soul as a society constructed out of drives and affects". Bringing to light the notion of instinctual configurations, he not only rethinks the notion of the soul on different bases, as he also radically criticizes dualisms and the oppositions of values that dogmatic philosophers work with, as we shall see below. And once more he carries out his critique while simultaneously advancing his own positions.

As an example of a "folk superstition from time immemorial", Nietzsche gives the superstition of the soul, and not by chance. We only need to go a step further in order to pass from this superstition to another starting point that dogmatic philosophers adopted while constructing their "sublime and unconditional" edifices. At last, the superstition of the soul continues to cause mischief as the superstition of the subject and the "I", that is, it continues to cause damage as a "seduction of grammar".

It is in religious superstition regarding the soul that the notion of the "I" originates. In conceiving of the soul as a "society constructed out of drives and affects", Nietzsche understands the "I" as nothing more than a "conceptual synthesis"[6], a synthesis that hides the relations of command and obedience among the drives. Seizing oneself as a fixed "I", one sees oneself as being exactly like the others to whom one relates socially. Nevertheless, it is not only within the social sphere that the notion of the "I" is used to conceal the distance between those who command and those who obey; it is above all on a physiopsychological level that the notion obscures the action of the instinctual configurations. Clearly opposed to the Cartesian conception of a *res cogitans*, it is to the instinctual configurations that Nietzsche resorts to reflect on the notion of the "I". When we say "I think", we believe to be in full possession of our thought. Considering thought as an act, one presumes that there must be a subject that goes through this act; conceiving this subject as stable and fixed, one makes it a unity. With this we lose sight of the dynamism of the instinctual processes that constitute the body itself. In this sense we can read the following statement: "a thought comes when 'it' wants to, and not when 'I' want. It is, therefore, a *falsification* of the facts to say that the subject 'I' is the condition of the predicate 'think'" (KSA 5.31, BGE 17). From this perspective, grammar, with its seductions, only leads philosophy astray.

Along with the starting points adopted by dogmatic philosophers to construct "sublime and unconditional" edifices that have already been mentioned, one more merits attention. Resorting to a far from rigorous logical procedure, they lay as the cornerstone of their edifices "an over-eager generalization from facts that are really very local, very personal, very human-all-too-human" (KSA 5.12, BGE Preface). In the First Part of the book, entitled "On the Prejudices of Philosophers", Nietzsche doesn't shy away from giving examples of this type of procedure, striving to disassemble it. Aphorism 5 is worthy of note, where by putting into effect his psychology of unmasking, he will try to prove

---

6   Cf. NL Herbst 1885 - Frühjahr 1886, 1[87] KSA 12.32 = WLN 61: "the 'I' (which is *not* the same thing as the unitary government of our being!) is, after all, only a conceptual synthesis".

that his philosophical peers "are all advocates who do not want to be seen as such; for the most part, in fact, they are sly spokesmen for prejudices that they christen as 'truths'" (KSA 5.19, BGE 5).

By trying to impose their vision as the only one that is valid, dogmatic philosophers do not tolerate being prohibited from transcending their actual situation, they cannot accept being limited to a certain perspective, and they do not admit being condemned to a particular visual angle. This way they deny "perspectivism, which is the fundamental condition of all life" (KSA 5.12, BGE Preface). Now, it is exactly the refusal of perspectivism that confers a dogmatic nature to their thought. Consequently, we will not hesitate to affirm that, from a Nietzschean perspective, not only are philosophers that aim at reaching ultimate and definite truths dogmatists, but also all of those that conceive of philosophy itself as the search for truth and understand this conception as the only one possible.

It is not by chance that immediately after having finished the Preface to *Beyond Good and Evil*, Nietzsche starts striking at the "will to truth". But it would be possible to interpret the unconditional will to truth either as the "will not to let oneself be deceived" or as the "will not to deceive"; and each interpretation would have its own presuppositions. As a "will not to let oneself be deceived", the will to truth would be a necessary precaution to avoid something which would be, at first glance, dangerous, nefarious and even fatal, i.e. the absence of truth. However, both truth and untruth can be harmful but also useful to life. Since this first interpretation must be rejected, there is no alternative: the will to truth must be understood as the "will not to deceive", not even oneself. On the Socratic trail, truth is related to virtue and whoever is "truthful" is virtuous. In sum, we are moving into the ground of morality[7]. This is why Nietzsche states:

> In fact, we paused for a long time before the question of the cause of this – until we finally came to a complete standstill in front of an even more fundamental question. We asked about the *value* of this will (KSA 5.15, BGE 1).

In order to demonstrate how such questioning is done, Nietzsche begins by investigating, in the second aphorism of the First Part,

---

7   We follow here the arguments presented by Nietzsche in KSA 3.575f, GS 344.

the valuations that are hidden behind the logical procedures of philosophers. He concludes that "the fundamental belief of meta-physicians is the *belief in opposition of values*" (KSA 5.16, BGE 2). Although in this aphorism the terms "philosophers" and "metaphysicians" are employed as interchangeable and, when he resorts to the noun "philosopher", he never qualifies it, Nietzsche actually keeps dogmatic philosophy as his primary target. In fact, it is precisely the dogmatic philosophers that, by refusing perspectivism, allow themselves to be taken over by an unconditional will to truth. And it is this will to truth that imposes certain valuations, in particular the valuation according to which truth has more value than appearance, deception and error. But besides the implication of moralization that is always present in the logical procedures of dogmatic philosophers, the will to truth demands, in order to legitimate itself, the complicity of metaphysics. Forgetting that deception is also a condition of life, they oppose knowledge to life; on the Platonic pathway, they create, in counterpart to this world, another to give shelter to truth[8].

But, as Nietzsche has made clear at the beginning of Part 1, his task is no longer about setting out in search of truth; it is rather about questioning the valuations that such a search obscures. This is why, in the third aphorism, he considers the instinctual configurations of dogmatic philosophers. He introduces the term "physiological" for the first time in his book, and demonstrates how in each form of life particular drives and particular values predominate. This is why he states: "behind all logic and its autocratic posturings stand valuations or, stated more clearly, physiological requirements for the preservation of a particular type of life" (KSA 5.17, BGE 3). Thus, in the aphorisms that follow this one, the fourth and the fifth, Nietzsche tries to show, from a new perspective, that the falsest judgements can be the most indispensable for a particular condition of life, which implies insisting once more on the lack of honesty on the part of philosophers. Finally, Nietzsche concludes this sub-movement by returning, in the sixth aphorism, to his physiopsychological observations, developing the idea that there is a close relationship between philosophical activity and instinctual configurations:

---

8   Among the texts where Nietzsche develops these ideas, see especially KSA 3.574–577, GS 344.

But anyone who looks at people's basic drives, to see how far they may have played their little game right here as *inspiring* geniuses (or daemons or spirits —), will find that they all practiced philosophy at some point, – and that every single one of them would be only too pleased to present *itself* as the ultimate purpose of existence and as rightful *master* of all the other drives. Because every drive craves mastery, and *this* leads it to try philosophizing (KSA 5.20, BGE 6).

By emphasizing the role played by the physiopsychological condition of the scholars, he shows how arrogant and unnecessary is all thought that despises its own starting point, how pretentious and useless is a philosophy that ignores its real motivations. At the end of the careful and meticulous examination that he makes of dogmatists, Nietzsche could well have reached this diagnosis: "'Will to truth' – that could be a hidden will to death" (KSA 3.576, GS 344).

* * *

The author of *Beyond Good and Evil*, being always so conscientious about his own intellectual honesty, has good reasons to cast suspicion over his own writings. Thus, in the last aphorism of the book, he exclaims: "Oh, what are you anyway, my written and painted thoughts! It was not long ago that you were still so colorful, young and malicious, so full of thorns and secret spices that you made me sneeze and laugh – and now? You have already lost your novelty, and I am afraid that some of you are ready to turn into truths: they already look so immortal, so pathetically decent and upright, so boring!" (KSA 5.239, BGE 296). Losing their temporary nature, they run the risk of becoming univocal, monolithic, inflexible truths. Being stripped of their experimental nature, they run the risk of becoming doctrine.

But let us not be mistaken! It is not only his book that runs this risk. Nietzsche is not referring exclusively to his own writings. "And was it ever any different?" (KSA 5.239, BGE 296) – he asks in the next period. Using his own thoughts as the basis for his examination, the author begins his reflection on the dogmatism of philosophical writing.

Now, Nietzsche himself asserts in Part 1, entitled "Prejudices of Philosophers", that most conscious thought, including philosophical thought, must be attributed to instinctive activity. But words are what make it possible for thought to become conscious. Intimately

connected, speech and consciousness belong to the gregarious existence of human beings. The weaker individual, believing to be the
most threatened, is compelled to ask his equals for help in order to
preserve his own life. In order to make his request understandable, he
needs language as much as consciousness. He needs to make use of
signs to communicate, but prior to this he must "know" how he feels
and what he thinks. This entails that consciousness is not a part of the
individual's life as such, but insofar as it emerges from his interaction
within his environment, it belongs to the "herd-aspects of his nature".
The same occurs with language; it also has its origins in social life.

Being mediated through consciousness and language, thought
belongs always already to a particular perspective: the gregarious
perspective. An individual's experiences, when they become conscious
and are expressed in words, may lose their personal, unique, singular
quality; being mediated through the herd-perspective, they run the
risk of becoming commonplace[9]. We can now understand what
Nietzsche says in the final aphorism of *Beyond Good and Evil*:
"So, what subjects do we copy out and paint, we mandarins with
Chinese brushes, we immortalizers of things that *let* themselves be
written – what are the only things we *can* paint? Oh, only ever things
that are about to wilt and lose their smell! Only ever storms that
have exhausted themselves and are moving off, and feelings that are
yellowed and late! Only ever birds that have flown and flown astray
until they tired and can be caught by hand, – by *our* hand!" (KSA 5.
239f, BGE 296).

Two ideas require our attention here. First of all, it is important
to note that if the greatest part of conscious thought is nothing more
than instinctive activity, it would be a mistake to assume that we could
have any kind of control over it. For this reason we can only write
what *can* be written, or in other words, what can be caught "with
our own hands". Secondly, one must note that it would be another

---

9   A passage in *Twilight of the Idols* can be read in the same light: "Our true ex-
     periences are completely taciturn. They could not be communicated even if they
     wanted to be. This is because the right words for them do not exist. The things
     we have words for are also the things we have already left behind" (KSA 6.128,
     TI Skirmishes of an Untimely Man 26). The standardization through language
     and language's deep connection with the gregarious side of man's existence are
     frequent themes in Nietzsche's work. In the essay *On Truth and Lying in a Non-
     Moral Sense*, language and gregariousness are already presented as inseparable.

mistake to suppose that, when experiences expressed in words become common, they can still keep their uniqueness. This is why we can only write those things that we have already left behind or, as Nietzsche says, "we only immortalize things that cannot live and fly for much longer, only tired and worn-out things!" (KSA 5.240, BGE 296). It is hard to deny that it is impossible to express the glow that thoughts had when they first appeared; it is impossible to communicate the livelihood they possessed when they emerged. At last, when thinking is translated into words, it loses its dynamism.

Nietzsche presents a similar idea in an unpublished poem. Written in July-August 1882, the same year Nietzsche published the first four books of *The Gay Science*, it has the same title of the book and the same sub-title of the forth part:

> '*The Gay Science*'. (Sanctus Januarius)
> This is not a book: what stands in books!
> In those sarcophagi and shrouds!
> The booty of books is in the past;
> But in this one there lives an eternal *today*[10].

If, on the one hand, Nietzsche puts forth the idea that only tired and worn-out things remain in books, on the other hand he reveals the desire to eternalize the present in his writings. To be in consonance with his own reflexive movement, to place himself in tune with the dynamics of thought – this was Nietzsche's aim in his writing. But how can the "eternal today" be alive in books?

Four years after writing the poem, Nietzsche seems to renounce his desire in *Beyond Good and Evil*. At the end of the book he leads us to believe that the morning thoughts, when written down, become "afternoon thoughts"; stripped of livelihood and of the glow they had when they first appeared, they are now pale traces of what they were for a little while. And so he concludes: "And I only have colors for your *afternoon*, my written and painted thoughts, perhaps many colors, many colorful affections and fifty yellows and browns and greens and reds: – but nobody will guess from this how you looked in

---

10   NL Juli - August 1882, 1[104] KSA 10.35: "'*Die fröhliche Wissenschaft*'. (Sanctus Januarius) Dies ist kein Buch: was liegt an Büchern! An diesen Särgen und Leichentüchern! Vergangnes ist der Bücher Beute: Doch hierin lebt ein ewig *Heute*".

your morning, you sudden sparks and wonders of my solitude, you, my old, beloved – *wicked* thoughts!" (KSA 5.240, BGE 296). One might say that the book ends in a circular movement, beginning with the author's suspicion of dogmatic philosophy and ending with the distrust of his own thoughts.

* * *

Nietzsche doubtlessly fears that his truths may also become doctrines. He is aware of the dogmatism that insidiously contaminates philosophical writing. Thus, a question imposes itself on us; we cannot avoid it. Why, then, write books?

Let us examine more closely the end of *Beyond Good and Evil*. In reality, it is not aphorism 296 that concludes the book, but the Aftersong "From High Mountains". In this Aftersong, Nietzsche expresses his waiting for friends, his disappointment when he sees them coming, his understanding that they are not akin to him, and finally, his desire for new friends.

At first glance, an examination of this Aftersong does not seem to supply us with any element concerning the question we have raised. The need for interlocutors is not enough to justify the writing of books.

The search for readers is definitely a recurring theme in Nietzsche's work. But equally recurrent in his work is the need to choose his readers. For, in order to communicate, one needs to start from a common ground. It is not enough to have the same ideas and to embrace the same conceptions. Giving words the same meaning or resorting to the same logical proceedings is not enough either. A lot more is needed; one must share experiences, experiences lived through. In the end, all communicating is making-common.

In aphorism 268 of *Beyond Good and Evil*, in dealing with language and communication, Nietzsche observes: "Now, assuming that needs have only ever brought people together when they could somehow indicate similar requirements and similar experiences by similar signs, then it follows, on the whole, that the easy communicability of needs (which ultimately means having only average and *base* experiences) must have been the most forceful of the forces that have controlled people so far" (KSA 5.222, BGE 268). It is mainly to guarantee their own survival that individuals relate with each other; it is to preserve their own lives that they communicate. The experiences they share are, therefore, the most basic and general; the experiences lived through by all are precisely the most common.

How can we understand that Nietzsche wanted to communicate if he criticizes so vehemently the "herd-perspective"? A little further on in aphorism 268, he warns: "Immense countervailing forces will have to be called upon in order to cross this natural, all-too-natural *progressus in simile*, people becoming increasingly similar, ordinary, average, herd-like, – increasingly *base!*" (KSA 5.222, BGE 268). The majority, when it feels threatened, will hold on to prejudices, beliefs and convictions; those who are the exception will succumb to their isolation, even if they are fearless. While gregarious individuals seek security and self-conservation, the rarest do not turn away from risk, but take a chance on life. In fact, they wouldn't know how to proceed in any other way.

This is why Nietzsche believes that the experiences he wants to share and to communicate are so unique. This is why he needs to find those who are akin to him. Both in his letters and books, he complains of the silence that burdens his work, of the loneliness in his life. Few are the friends, scarce are the readers. He believes to have been born posthumously[11]; his writings saw the light of day before the readers they address. He claims to be untimely[12]; his ideas are aimed at an audience that is yet to be. Aware that what he has to say is not gregarious in nature, in the course of his work, he never ceases to seek whoever could be akin to him. Thus, he does not address an apathetic listener who bows at whatever he hears, nor does he address a complacent reader who unconditionally accepts whatever is imposed on him. The relationship he hopes to establish with his interlocutors is different. He seeks those whose drives and affects are similar to his, or, in other words: those who have experiences that are analogous to his own.

---

11   Cf., for example, KSA 6.167, Preface to *The Anti-Christ*: "My day won't come until the day after tomorrow. Some people are born posthumously". Cf. also KSA 6.61, TI Maxims and Arrows 15 and KSA 6.298, EH Why I write such good books 1.

12   For example, in KSA 3.622–623, GS 371 ("We, incomprehensible ones"), we read: "Have we ever complained about being misunderstood, misjudged, misidentified, defamed, misheard, and ignored? This is precisely our lot – oh, for a long time yet! Let's say until 1901, to be modest – this is also our distinction; we wouldn't honor ourselves enough if we wanted otherwise".

Let us pursue the analysis of the Aftersong "From High Mountains". A close look allows us to note that the last two stanzas are somehow separate from the rest, as if the poem were divided in two parts. It was actually written as such. In Autumn 1884, Nietzsche wrote the poem, or to be more precise, what came later to be the first part, and gave it the name "The longing of the lonely"[13]. It was in the spring of 1886 that he wrote the following last two stanzas:

> *This* song is gone, – the longing cries are through,
> Their sweet sounds ended;
> The work of a magician I'd befriended,
> The friend of noon-time – but – no! don't ask who —;
> It was at noon, when one turned into two...
>
> Now we can feast, with triumph in the air,
> The fest of all fests:
> Friend Zarathustra came, the guest of all guests!
> The world can laugh, the gruesome curtain tear,
> The wedding day of light and dark was her...

(KSA 5.243, BGE Aftersong)

Contrary to what he had done in the first part of the Aftersong, Nietzsche now expresses the end of his longing for friends. Zarathustra put an end to it. It is from the study of this character that we shall try to find an answer to the question that has been raised: why, then, write books?

From the very beginning of *Thus Spoke Zarathustra*, the leading character lets himself be known through his interlocutors. Already in the Prologue, it is the saint of the woods who sees him as a dancer, as a child, as an awakened one (KSA 3.12, ZA Prologue 2). In the Third Part and back to the city, it is the teachers of resignation who say that he is "the godless one" (KSA 3.215, ZA III On Virtue that Makes Small 3). And, moving on, his animals call him "the teacher of the eternal return" (KSA 3.275, ZA III The Convalescent 2). In the Fourth and Final Part, in the dialogues with the soothsayer, the kings, the conscientious of spirit, the magician, the old pope, the

---

13   Towards the end of November 1884, Nietzsche sends Heinrich von Stein the poem and adds "in memory of Sils-Maria", referring to Stein's visit between the 26th and 28th of August of the same year. Cf. KSB 6.562–567.

ugliest human being, the voluntary beggar, and the shadow, all of
these seem to know him very well. Defining him in a positive way or
denying what he is, Zarathustra's interlocutors are masks of the mask
he already is.

If it is through his interlocutors that Zarathustra is revealed, it is
through Zarathustra that Nietzsche shows himself. In his early texts,
it was through those he then used to call masters that he spoke his own
ideas. He says in *Ecce Homo* that when he spoke of Schopenhauer or
of Wagner, he was in fact speaking of himself[14]. In *Human, All Too
human*, he is disguised as a free spirit; in *Beyond Good and Evil* he
places himself among the philosophers of the future.

A letter dated 20 July 1888 and addressed to Overbeck can perhaps
give us a clue to partly understand this procedure. In it Nietzsche
declares: "Besides, I'm artist enough to be able to cling to a state until
it becomes a form, until it takes shape. I created to myself those types
whose boldness gives me pleasure, 'the immoralist' for example, a
type never heard of before" (KSB 8.363, editors' translation). As a
philosopher of masks, he seems to prefer to hide rather than show
himself[15]. This is where prudence and caution step in.

Nietzsche deals with the mask in three passages of *Beyond Good
and Evil*. In the first one, he states: "Every profound spirit needs a
mask: what's more, a mask is constantly growing around every
profound spirit, thanks to the consistently false (which is to say
shallow) interpretation of every word, every step, every sign of life
he displays" (KSA 5.58, BGE 40). And in the second one he affirms:
"and sometimes even stupidity is the mask for an ill-fated, all-
too-certain knowing. – From which it follows that a more refined
humanity will have great respect for 'masks', and will not indulge in
psychology and curiosity in the wrong place" (KSA 5.226, BGE 270).
In both passages, Nietzsche seems to be referring to himself first of all
to express a warning and a request. He requests that people do not
try to interpret him and he warns that he may be misidentified. This
double demand comes up again, repeatedly, in his final texts and in
the letters he wrote at this time.

---

14   Cf. KSA 6.314, EH The Birth of Tragedy 4 and KSA 6.317 and 319, EH The
     Untimely Ones 1, 3.
15   Cf. along the same lines Heidegger (1961, 17) and Fink (1965, 15).

But Nietzsche also wants to highlight the difficulty of making himself understood, of sharing his thoughts[16]. Thus, in the third and final passage of *Beyond Good and Evil* in which he refers to the mask, he relates it with silence and solitude. So he asserts in aphorism 289: "In a hermit's writings, you can always hear something of the echo of the desert, something of the whisper and the timid sideways glance of solitude. A new and more dangerous type of silence, of concealment, rings out in his strongest words, even in his cries" (KSA 5.234, BGE 289). Supposing that a "philosopher was always a hermit first" and presenting himself as a hermit and a philosopher, Nietzsche suggests that there is something incommunicable in what he has to say. He speaks of experiences that were never shared. Born into solitude, his words are branded with silence. But there is another reason for their silence. Understanding that philosophy is always experimental and believing that a philosopher cannot have definitive opinions, Nietzsche puts forth the idea that his statements are to a certain extent provisional. What he says refers to just one moment of a process. "Every philosophy is a foreground philosophy – that is a hermit's judgement: 'There is something arbitrary in *his* stopping here, looking back, looking around, in his not digging any deeper *here*, and putting his spade away – there is also something suspicious about it.' Every philosophy *conceals* a philosophy too: every opinion is also a hiding place, every word is also a mask" (KSA 5.234, BGE 289).

It is, therefore, in order to avoid confusion and not to allow false interpretations that Nietzsche makes use of masks. It is also because he has exceptionally unique experiences and never withdraws from his search that he resorts to them. And it is finally as a means of protection – perhaps even of himself – that he masks himself. After all, as he says in this same aphorism: "don't people write books precisely to keep what they hide to themselves?" (KSA 5.234, BGE 289).

But the art of silence is, in fact, the art of speech. If, with his books, Nietzsche seeks concealment with them he is also expressing himself. And, once again, while he exercises his critical role, placing language under suspicion, he puts forth his positions, making way for the creation of a new language.

---

16   The three ideas can be found throughout the whole of *Thus Spoke Zaratusthra*, right from the very sub-title: "A Book for All and None".

Bibliography

Fink, Eugen (1965), *La philosophie de Nietzsche*, trad. Hans Hildenbrand et Alex Lindenberg, Paris (Minuit).

Heidegger, Martin (1961), *Nietzsche*, vol.1, Berlin (Günther Neske Verlag).

Kaufmann, Walter (1965), *Nietzsche, Philosopher, Psychologist, Antichrist*, New York (The World Publishing Company).

Löwith, Karl (1978), *Nietzsches Philosophie der ewigen Wiederkehr des Gleichen*, Hamburg (Felix Meiner Verlag).

Nietzsche, Friedrich (2000), *Par-delà bien et mal*, traduction, introduction et notes par Patrick Wotling, Paris (Flammarion).

Fearless Findings

Instinct and Language in Book V of The Gay Science

Werner Stegmaier

1. The Asymmetrical Opposition between Instinct and Language

Instinct and language have been opposed to one another for a long
time. Instincts were considered to be natural, involuntary, constraining
and unchangeable; language, on the other hand, was seen as being
spiritual, free, conscious, and adaptable. Language, emanating from
reason, was supposed to be as far apart as possible from the constraints of nature. Men, possessing both language and reason, were
supposed to free themselves from involuntary instincts. Drives,
affects and emotions were also considered involuntary conductors
of behavior, along with instincts. Drives were thought responsible
for the mere satisfaction of needs; feelings, for hasty decisions both
beneficial and harmful; emotions, for blind liaisons; and in contrast,
the instincts, for thoughtless orientations. Reason could be harmed
by all these, and was therefore meant to penetrate them, enlighten
them and hinder their harmfulness. The opposition between instinct and reason was therefore in itself evaluative, establishing a
valuation based on an opposition. Nietzsche attributes the powerful
implementation of this valuation mainly to Plato. As for Socrates,
who introduced it, Nietzsche believes him to have preserved an
ironic skepticism towards its usefulness (cf. BGE 191). A valuation
so strongly asymmetric as the one between instinct and reason must
have as a foundation strong instincts and needs, especially if it should
remain – as it did – almost unquestioned for thousands of years and
even through such difficult transformations as the transition from
Greek and Roman antiquity to the Christian middle ages and then to
the growing religious skepticism of Modernity. Nietzsche's hypothesis
is that this semantic opposition was needed to domesticate man. If

everybody was to be guided by reason, then all those who needed it (i.e. including the weakest and the most needy) would have to be able to establish their rights in every field and, thus, in the pleasure of living together, reach a peaceful agreement, whatever differences they may have had regarding other needs and instincts. Therefore, that very rationality was counter-factually supposed to be shared by everyone in equal measure. Rationality was supposed to lead to the insight of the necessity of universally valid laws, and thus to the voluntary submission to a morality equally compulsory for all and, therefore, common to all. From Socrates to Kant it was believed that a non-moral logic could ground a logical morality. Nietzsche saw through this construction, and attacked it, for he expected more of men than the submission to a common morality. The moral significance of freeing human language from human instincts in metaphysics, on the one hand, and the non-moral significance of the reconnection of human language to human instincts taking place during the 18th Century, on the other, became one of Nietzsche's common topics. In his early unpublished draft, *On Truth and Lie in a Non-Moral Sense*, Nietzsche (just as Herder had done before him) closely connects language and speech to involuntary conductors of human behavior[1]. Whereas, here, the question for Nietzsche was still how language and reason, as well as their concepts, originate in the drives and instincts[2], he would later come to focus on the limits of

---

1   Cf. Bertino (2011). [*Editors' note*: See also Andrea Bertino's paper in this volume.]

2   In a draft from 1869/70, *Vom Ursprung der Sprache*, Nietzsche surveyed the history of philosophy for views on the origin of language, and concluded: "Es bleibt also nur übrig, die Sprache als Erzeugniss des Instinktes zu betrachten, wie bei den Bienen - dem Ameisenhaufen u.s.w." (KGW II/2.188) [*Editors' translation*: "thus the only option that remains is to consider language as a production of instinct, as with bees and anthills, etc."]. This is how he understands "instinct" (in the language he used at that time): "Instinkt ist aber nicht Resultat bewusster Ueberlegung, nicht blosse Folge der körperlichen Organisation, nicht Resultat eines Mechanismus, der in das Gehirn gelegt ist, nicht Wirkung eines dem Geiste von aussen kommenden, seinem Wesen fremden Mechanismus, sondern eigenste Leistung des Individuums oder einer Masse, dem Charakter entspringend. Der Instinkt ist sogar eins mit dem innersten Kern eines Wesens. Dies ist das eigentliche Problem der Philosophie, die unendliche Zweckmässigkeit der Organismen und die Bewusstlosigkeit bei ihrem Entstehn" (KGW II/2.188) [*Editors' translation*: "However, instinct is *not* conscious deliberation, nor mere consequence of the bodily organization, nor the result of a mechanism that lies in the brain, nor the

philosophical knowledge itself. As Nietzsche's early concatenation of language and instinct has been widely discussed[3], I will focus on the later stage of his thought, in which this relation would be increasingly differentiated.

2. Nietzsche's Interweaving of Instinct and Language in Book V of *Gay Science*

In Book V of *The Gay Science*, which was added in 1887, Nietzsche once again discusses the relation between instinct and language in a new and surprising way. He deliberately dissolves the old asymmetrical oppositions or inverts their meaning[4]. On the one hand, he doesn't allow reason to remain in simple opposition to nature but connects it to nature in multiple forms, understanding both as having reciprocal

---

effect of a mechanism that comes to the spirit from the outside and is foreign to its essence, but rather the most distinctive accomplishment that springs from an individual's or a group's character. Instinct is even identical with the innermost kernel of a being. This is the actual problem of philosophy, the infinite purposiveness of organisms and the unconsciousness of their emergence"]. He invokes Herder and Kant. Later, in TL, he uses the concept of *"Trieb"*, "drive" ("Trieb zur Wahrheit", KSA 1.876 etc., "Trieb zur Metapherbildung", KSA 1.887), instead of *"Instinkt"*, "instinct"; as in Nietzsche's sources [cf. Meijers/Stingelin (1988)], the crucial concept is, however, that of *"Reiz"*, "stimulus" (KSA 1.876 etc.), as well as the equally preconscious and involuntary *"Nervenreiz"*, "nerve stimulus" (KSA 1.878 etc). But Nietzsche uses the concept of instinct in the preceding notes. Cf. NL 1869 – 1870, 3[15] KSA 7.63 = WEN 19–20: *"Language* came into being from the shout with the accompanying gesture: here the essence of the thing is expressed through the tone, the volume and the rythm, and the accompanying idea, the image of the essence, the appearance, through the oral gesture./An infinitely inadequate symbolism, grown in accordance with firm laws of nature: in the choice of the symbol it is not freedom but instinct that reveals itself./A symbol that has been *noticed* is always a concept: one conceives what one is able to name and distinguish" (see also NL 3[18] KSA 7.65). Afterwards, he develops the concatenation of language, image, and instinct in several of his notes from 1870 to 1873: NL 8[29] KSA 7. 232, NL 19[107] KSA 7.454. For the variety and change in Nietzsche's use of the concept of instinct, cf. Vinzens (1999). Unfortunately, this does not include a complete chronological analysis of Nietzsche's use of the concept. Such an analysis shall, however, be included in the respective article of the Nietzsche-Wörterbuch (NWB), edited by the Nietzsche Research Group (Nijmegen), Paul van Tongeren, Gerd Schank and Herman Siemens.

3   For the state of the art, see also Hödl (1997 and 2003), Emden (2005), Haaz (2006), Reuter (2009), Zavatta (2009), Andresen (2010), Bertino (2011).
4   Cf. Vinzens (1999, 110–128).

effects on each other[5]. He also creates a new semantics of reason, much closer to everyday language, for he no longer considers reason as completely transparent to itself, unitary and common to all, but rather as an unfathomable complexity (the body as a "great reason" (Z I On the Despisers of the Body), mutable and individual[6]. On the other hand, he does no longer consider natural instincts merely as a rigid *given*, but rather as something which naturally and involuntary *becomes*, and which, through a prolonged routine or discipline or even through rational insight, may gradually become so obvious, that it involuntarily conducts behaviour and then manifests itself as natural. Thus instinct surpasses reason: it creates a new kind of freedom, the lightness of action[7]. "Everything *good* is instinctive –", Nietzsche will write in *Twilight of the Idols* - "and consequently light, necessary, free" (TI The Four Great Errors 2); and in the *Antichrist* he observes at last that "to achieve a perfect automatism of the instinct, this is the presupposition of every type of mastery, of every type of perfection in the art of life" (A 57)[8].

In rejecting the asymmetrical valuation of reason and instinct, interweaving them instead, Nietzsche also gives speech and language a new sense. For Nietzsche, speech is voluntary (i.e. rational) and involuntary (i.e. instinctive) at the same time[9]. We have a limited view of what we say and what we want to say and, most of the time, we follow speech routines and well practiced language-games in which, without further ado, one word leads to the next. Speech routines, which become instinctive, unburden our orientation and set it free

---

5   Cf. BGE 3: "I kept a close eye on the philosophers and read between their lines for long enough to say to myself: the greatest part of conscious thought must still be attributed to instinctive activity, and this is even the case for philosophical thought. This issue needs re-examination. Just as the act of birth makes no difference to the overall course of heredity, neither is 'consciousness' *opposed* to instinct in any decisive sense – most of a philosopher's conscious thought is secretly directed and forced into determinate channels by the instincts".

6   Cf. Kodama (forthcoming).

7   Cf. Ponton (2007).

8   Cf. NL 1888, 15[25] KSA 13.421 = WP 440: "Genius resides in instinct; goodness likewise. One acts perfectly only when one acts instinctively" ("Das Genie sitzt im Instinkt; die Güte ebenfalls. Man handelt nur vollkommen, sofern man instinktiv handelt").

9   For the interweaving of language and body in Nietzsche's philosophy of language, cf. Kalb (2000).

for other things; whereas a fully reflexive speech would take up all of our attention[10]. Through such speech routines, however, philosophical knowledge also becomes limited; they make things seem obvious when in fact they are not. In order to perceive and break through such limitations, philosophical knowledge must expand its own linguistic leeway but without creating a private language, as has been done until now: philosophy's abstract terminology has always detached philosophical knowledge from the lived world creating a private fantasy world – which in turn seems to be the "real world"[11]. Accordingly, Nietzsche refused an abstract terminology, staying faithful to the language-games of natural language, which have themselves become instinctive; he thus had no need of recurring to the theory-healing therapy, which the later Wittgenstein recommends for philosophy and especially for the philosophy of language. Instead, Nietzsche further refined the use of natural language, elevating it, in philosophy, to unprecedented artistic levels. His philosophical language does not go beyond the limits of natural language, it just shifts them – and in this way, contrary to what used to happen to the language of old reason (which was supposed to be understood by everyone, but in fact never was), Nietzsche's language remains accessible to all, or to the majority at least, even though each one of us understands it within our own horizons and at different levels. Nietzsche's simple language – or, as we might now say, his instinctively understandable language – is intrinsic to the core of his philosophy, and it made it more popular than any other philosophy. To put it in terms of contemporary philosophy of language: Nietzsche's philosophy performs what it states; it shows what it says. Instinct and language are no longer connected in mutual opposition, as if they excluded each other; they are rather entangled or woven together, inasmuch as they intensify each other[12].

Nietzsche's interweaving of instinct and language, as it also occurs in his philosophical texts themselves, allows him to renounce to

---

10   Cf. Stegmaier (2008, 398–408).
11   Cf. GD Wie die 'wahre Welt' endlich zur Fabel wurde. [*Editors' note*: here as elsewhere, "leeway" translates *Spielraum*, a technical term in Werner Stegmaier's work, meaning "*eine geregelte Grenze unregelten Verhaltens*", i.e. a regulated perimeter within which unregulated behavior becomes possible: cf. Stegmaier (2008, 221 ff.).
12   And, thus, concepts become fluctuations (Fluktuanzen): cf. Stegmaier (1992 and 2008, 356–360).

argumentation and demonstration, for these appeal to a form of reason equally accessible to and valid for all. Instead of this, Nietzsche wants to surprise us – a fact that adds up to the everlasting attractiveness of his philosophy. He surprises us with the power of philosophical insights that greatly broaden the possibilities of philosophical knowledge in general, thus unsettling the traditional foundations of argumentation and demonstration. It is in this way that philosophy "creates" in Nietzsche's sense: it opens up new possibilities of understanding and shaping the world and oneself. But philosophy can only create from the available possibilities at a given moment – it must relate to them so as to broaden them, but always within specific leeways.

This broadening can, however, be painful and fearful. And it is pre-cisely because of this that most people (including renowned philoso-phers) retreat when confronted with them and decide to hang on to already familiar private worlds and "hinterworlds (*Hinterwelten*)" (ZA I On the Hinterworldly). The later Nietzsche increasingly sought philosophical insights capable of arousing fear; he believed their strength and rank to lie precisely in the fact that they incite fear[13]. Philosophical knowledge arouses fear in as much as it attacks and questions old instincts that have become self-evident, and it only overcomes this fear when it becomes equally obvious and instinctive, or (to use a Nietzschean word) when it gets incorporated (*einver-leibt*) (GS 110). Nietzsche's revaluations of values cannot be achieved through a single rational insight, but only gradually; in such a way that the refinement of his language may also refine his linguistic instincts and those of his most persistent readers, so that these refined

---

13   Cf. BGE 39: "Something could be true even if it is harmful and dangerous to the highest degree. It could even be part of the fundamental character of existence that people with complete knowledge get destroyed, – so that the strength of a spirit would be proportionate to how much of the 'truth' he could withstand – or, to put it more clearly, to what extent he *needs* it to be thinned out, veiled over, sweetened up, dumbed down, and lied about"; cf. also NL 1887, 10[3] KSA 12.455 = WLN 173: "*My new path to 'Yes'.*/My new version of *pessimism*: willingly to seek out the dreadful and questionable sides of existence: which made clear to me related phenomena of the past. 'How much 'truth' can a spirit endure and dare?' – a question of its strength. The *outcome* of a pessimism like this *could be* that form of a Dionysian *saying Yes* to the world as it is, to the point of wishing for its absolute recurrence and eternity: which would mean a new ideal of philosophy and understanding".

linguistic instincts become receptive to further subtleties in Nietzsche's language, as well as in their own language[14].

3. The Series of Aphorisms 354, 355, 371 and 381 in Book V of *The Gay Science*

Nietzsche does not only perform this: he also states it; he says what he shows. And he does so in four aphorisms of Book V of *The Gay Science*, aphorisms 354, 355, 371 and 381. Each one of them deserves an exhaustive contextual interpretation[15]. In this brief paper, however, I can only analyze their theses; and I will have to leave out the literary form of the aphorisms – which in Nietzsche is always extraordinarily important. Aphorism 354 is preceded, temporally and thematically, by aphorism 268 of *Beyond Good and Evil*, which will also be my starting point.

3.a. The Preparatory Aphorism 268 of *Beyond Good and Evil*. The Birth of Language's Violence from the Needs Intrinsic to Living in Society

In aphorism 268 of *Beyond Good and Evil*, Nietzsche resumes a theme from *On Truth and Lie in a Non-Moral Sense*, namely the conventionalization of experience and thought through language ("the obligation to lie in accordance with firmly established convention" (TL, 146), and he develops it, quite coherently, anchoring it in a heuristics of need. Already in the second *Untimely Meditation*, Nietzsche analyzed the action of men not only according to their "goals" but also according to their "powers and needs" (UM II 4, 77); and in the third *Meditation* his starting point was "needs, wants and wishes" (UM III 2, 133)[16]. He identified fundamental philosophical

---

14   In "Homer und die klassische Philosophie. Ein Vortrag", 1869 (KGW II/1.249), Nietzsche himself used the concept of "Sprachinstinkt" ("linguistic instinct"), but he later abandoned it.

15   Cf. Stegmaier, *Nietzsches Befreiung der Philosophie. Kontextuelle Interpretation des V. Buchs der Fröhlichen Wissenschaft* (forthcoming) and, programmatically, Stegmaier (2007). See also Stegmaier (2004 and 2008).

16   [*Editors' note*: Holingdale translates "*Kräften und Nöthen*" (KSA 1.271) with "energies and needs" (UM II 4, 77), and "*Nöthen, Bedürfnissen und Wünschen*" (UB II 4, 346) with "need, distress and desire" (UM III 2, 133). However, a more literal translation of *Kräften, Bedürfnissen* and *Wünschen* is crucial here.]

concepts through the needs that made them necessary; he placed, for instance, a "necessary truth" (*Nothwahrheit*) on the same level as a "necessary lie" (*Nothlüge*, UM II 10, 118), and searched methodically for the "real needs" behind the "hollowness of those tyrannical words and concepts" of conventional language (UM IV 5, 215). Through his heuristics of need and precisely because there is no moral merit in needs, Nietzsche achieved a non-moral perspective on language and reason, as well as on the morality that is inherent to them. In his books of aphorisms, his plan is to study "the needs of mankind" "to the last consequence"[17]. The first four books of *The Gay Science* are filled with forms of the term "need" (*Noth*), "needs" (*Nöthe*), "states of need" (*Nothstände*), "situations of need" (*Nothlagen*) and "to be necessary" ("*Noth-Tun*"). In aphorism 40, Nietzsche speaks directly of a "law of need" (*Gesetz der Noth*); in the new preface to *The Gay Science*, which he published together with Book V, he asks programmatically "whether it was not illness that inspired the philosopher" and "whether, on a grand scale, philosophy has been no more than an interpretation of the body and a *misunderstanding of the body*" (GS Preface 2); and in aphorism 370, in which he introduces his "*Dionysian* pessimism", he states as an introduction: "every art, every philosophy can be considered a cure and aid in the service of growing, struggling life; they always presuppose suffering and the sufferers" (GS 370).

In aphorism 268 of *Beyond Good and Evil*, Nietzsche traces the way in which experience and thought are conventionalized through speech back to the needs intrinsic to living in society. These needs compel us to find a quick understanding: "The greater the danger, the greater the need to agree quickly and easily about necessities" (BGE 268). Nevertheless, the language that develops from these needs only then becomes long-lasting if those that use it also use "the same words for the same species of inner experiences" (BGE 268). Within the evolution of a society, the commonly used means of speech are not selected according to the measure of individual experiences, but it is rather the other way round: individual experiences are selected according to the more commonly used means of speech. Those who,

---

17   NL 1880, 5[46] KSA 9.192, NL 1881, 15[9] KSA 9.636; see also: NL 1880, 6[302] KSA 9.276.

in a situation of need – which requires a quick understanding – do not follow commonly used language, are excluded, and thus, only those who experience the same with the same words remain. And only those who experience the same as others with the same words are then able to use words instinctively, without further thought. We "know", then, what others "want" with their words; and with words, values are also shared. However, the selection of individual experiences through common words is a form of violence; it is, according to Nietzsche, "the most violent violence that has controlled people so far" (BGE 268, translation modified). It is directed against those who are "more exceptional, refined, rare, and difficult to understand" (BGE 268). Precisely those who would be able to refine language and broaden their knowledge "will easily remain alone, prone to accidents in their isolation and rarely propagating" (BGE 268). The linguistic instinct of a community hardens and solidifies – and in this way it becomes immune to being challenged. "Immense countervailing forces", Nietzsche concludes at the end of the aphorism, "will have to be called upon in order to cross this natural, all-too-natural *progressus in simile*, people becoming increasingly similar, ordinary, average, herd-like —, increasingly *base*!" (BGE 268). He who, nonetheless, wishes to cross (*kreuzen*) and thwart (*durchkreuzen*) this process of vulgarization may easily be crucified (*gekreuzigt werden*).

3.b. Aphorism 354 of The *Gay Science*.
The Birth of Consciousness from the Language's Violence.

In aphorism 354 of The *Gay Science* —, whose title, "On 'the genius of the species'", evokes a parenthesis on Schopenhauer in aphorism 268 of *Beyond Good and Evil* —, Nietzsche, in a further surprising move of his heuristics of need, traces the development of consciousness (which in modernity had become the metaphysical presupposition of metaphysical reason) back to the conventionalization of experience and thought through the violence of language, a conventionalization that he understands as necessary for survival. He begins with "physiology and natural history" (GS 354). In most cases we think, feel, want, recall and "'act' in every sense of the term" without consciousness, i.e. purely instinctively, "insulting as it may sound to an older philosopher" (GS 354). The "alliance of the instincts", which Nietzsche had already introduced in aphorism 11 of Book I of

The Gay Science, guarantees in great part our orientation, whereas consciousness, "the latest development of the organic, and hence also its most unfinished and unrobust feature" (GS 11), is most often a danger to our orientation. Therefore, the question – which would never occur to an older philosopher – is how did consciousness become useful and why has it been preserved in evolution so far. Nietzsche's conjecture is as follows: it developed alongside language, it was incorporated as a linguistic instinct and, thus, it remained allied with other instincts which were also developing. With the "need to communicate", "need and distress" forced people "to communicate, to understand each other swiftly and subtly", and also "a person's (or animal's) *ability to communicate*" had to intensify and refine itself, especially from the moment this animal created "signs": "communication signs" which could be used independently of a specific situation, and hence, with certain generality (GS 354). But precisely because the meaning of these signs, of our linguistic signs, is no longer immediately clear in a given situation, they must be used with special care and they must be consciously chosen; they require consciousness[18]. They can easily be misunderstood and give rise to new and heavier needs. The use of linguistic signs independent of specific situations is linked to consciousness, but only to a certain degree: it would quickly overload consciousness if new speech and language routines were not formed simultaneously – i.e. if something similar to a linguistic instinct were not to transform once again the greatest part of speech into something easy, obvious and involuntary, and to lighten consciousness. Once again, Nietzsche's focus is the problem of vulgarization, or generalization. If consciousness develops in an individual speaker along with his ability to communicate in a general language, then what we understand as individual consciousness is always already general consciousness:

> "My idea is clearly that consciousness actually belongs not to man's existence as an individual but rather to the community- and herd-aspects of his nature; that accordingly, it is finely developed only in relation to its usefulness to community or herd; and that consequently each of us, even with the best will in the world to *understand* ourselves as individually as possible, 'to know ourselves', will always bring to

---

18   Cf. Stegmaier (2008, 333–346).

consciousness precisely that in ourselves which is 'non-individual', that which is 'average'; that due to the nature of consciousness – to the 'genius of the species' governing it – our thoughts themselves are continually as it were *outvoted* and translated back into the herd perspective" (GS 354).

3.c. Aphorism 355 of *The Gay Science*.
The Everyday Instinctual Fear of Facing the Unfamiliar and a New Philosophical Courage to Face the Unfamiliar

From what we have seen above, philosophical knowledge finds itself always already associated with the "herd perspective". According to aphorism 355, not only the "common people" but also philosophers so far have understood knowledge as the tracing back of something unfamiliar to something familiar (GS 355). It is obvious that the "instinct of fear" is dominant here – the fear of going beyond the usual, beyond what is fixed and regarded as safe. Logic is what most frequently helps philosophy and science to gain security, logic and the effort to structure knowledge logically. When something new, unfamiliar, and surprising obtains a logical order, it becomes no longer new, unfamiliar, and surprising. It has found a "reason", we can feel reassured by it, and the "feeling of security" is re-established. Natural mathematical sciences in particular proceed like this: they take "the *strange* as their object" and turn it into the object of objective knowledge (GS 355). But this knowledge is not only objective, but objectifying: nature as we commonly know it, with its sunrises and sunsets, landscapes of mountains and rivers, fields and woods, the colour play of flowers, variable weather conditions, the movements of the stars in the sky, etc., is reduced to abstract processes that conform to natural laws formulated by scientific knowledge itself, so that this knowledge transforms our familiar nature into an unfamiliar and constructed nature – i.e., into a strange object. For natural scientists, however, who have incorporated the language of mathematically formulated natural laws (so that these have become routine and finally instinct for them) such a strange object is no longer strange, but becomes, in a new way, familiar again. And when they reduce what is unusual and surprising in everyday, familiar nature to laws that are familiar *to them*, they are once again following the popular concept of knowledge: they are tracing something unfamiliar back to something familiar. After having turned nature into something strange, they recover it – as much as this may be possible – as a known, familiar, unsurprising nature. Here lies, according to Nietzsche, their "great security" (GS 355). Mathematical natural sciences represent the well succeeded historical experiment of a new estranging knowledge which, after having transformed the unfamiliar into the object of a new logical order, is still able of guiding itself by the old instinct of fear.

But Nietzsche further adds an enigmatic subordinate clause: "(…) while it is nearly contradictory and absurd even to *want* to take the non-strange as one's object…" (GS 355).

The mystery doesn't lie in the contradiction or absurdity of taking the non-strange as an object; for the non-strange, i.e. the known, the common, the familiar, obviously requires no knowledge. What is enigmatic here is rather the italicized word "*want*" ("*wollen*"). One *wants* something absurd when one transforms that which is well-known and usual into something strange, i.e. into an object of knowledge, – and this, even though it is already well-known and usual and provides our orientation with an unquestioned sense of security. Whoever wants this does no longer aim at obtaining tranquility through knowledge, but rather exposes his/herself consciously to unrest. In German, one says that one "wants", i.e. "wills" something when one is simply so resolute to obtain or achieve it, that one does not have any reasons or one does not intend to allege any reasons for it. "Reasons" are statements which we expect others to accept; their goal is an agreement and, therefore, they make the individual will superfluous. The sciences and philosophy, such as we know them, are based on reasons and exclude the personal will (indeed a "personal argument" is unacceptable in science). Therefore, whoever firmly *wills* something in philosophy, mistrusting its usual scientific nature, announces an unusual, unfamiliar, strange, wilfully personal way of philosophizing. This is (as the heading of Book V of *The Gay Science* indicates) the philosophizing of a "fearless" one. From the standpoint of knowledge born out of the "instinct of fear", that is something "nearly contradictory and absurd", but only "nearly": renouncing all reasons can in fact make sense in a narrower leeway, namely in the precise context of a philosophical knowledge that questions the traditional, instinctive meaning of knowledge, so as to open up new possibilities of thought and action – i.e., in the context of a "revolutionary" philosophizing that transgresses "normal" philosophizing, to use Thomas S. Kuhn's expression. We know what such a philosophy means for Nietzsche, a philosophy that does not trace the unfamiliar back to the familiar, but, on the contrary, tries to understand the known "as a problem", "as strange, as distant, as 'outside of us'" (GS 355). It means to expose oneself voluntarily to fear, to challenge one's sense of security, to jeopardize one's routine orientation, and in this way to transform oneself into an experiment for a new humanity,— a humanity that finally wants to admit that which has already taken place a long time ago, namely that the humankind (to use Nietzsche's favourite metaphor) drifts on the high, open sea, and from here must find totally new orientations out of its own inner strength. The meaning of philosophy, as Nietzsche understands it, could be just this: to harness one's fear of facing the unfamiliar and to have the courage to face the unfamiliar. In his heuristics of need, which he calls "genealogy" in the period after Book V of *The Gay Science*, Nietzsche provides many examples of this courage: he traced language, consciousness and knowledge back to needs that were yet to be discovered, and they remain, to most people, surprising, strange, and unacceptable.

3.d. Aphorisms 371 and 381 of Book V of *The Gay Science*. The Distinction of Being Misunderstood and the Selection of Readers through Subtler Laws of Style

Thus, Nietzsche consciously risks being either not understood, or misunderstood[19]. He *wants* to be misunderstood by the majority; as he later writes in aphorism 371, he sees that as his "lot", his "fate of height" and therefore a "distinction" (GS 371). He willingly accepts the consequence of such violence as is exerted in the process of generalization through language,— a process which is so easily welcomed by most people because it gives them a strong sense of security and orientation. The consequence of this is that those who are "more exceptional, refined, rare", those who question that violence and who were mentioned in aphorism 268 of *Beyond Good and Evil*,— they must also remain the "most difficult to understand" (BGE 268). In aphorism 381 of *The Gay Science* Nietzsche once again draws the consequence of this to *his* language, to *his* philosophical writing[20]. With

---

19   Cf. BGE 27 and Stegmaier (2000).
20   For the interpretation of this aphorism, see Stegmaier (2007).

his language, he consciously wants to choose his "listeners", those with whom he "wants to communicate", and "simultaneously" to erect "barriers against 'the others'" (GS 381). Nietzsche wants to take charge of the selection undertaken by any language, he wants to take advantage of the violence brought about by this selection, in order to use it for his own purpose, namely to gain the courage to face surprising and unfamiliar knowledge about that very selection and violence. He sees his opportunity in using "subtler laws of style" (GS 381), in *his own* style, which is a style not merely for readers but also for "listeners" who have not only eyes for the type of reasons that beget objectivity – thus excluding all that is "other", deviant, nuanced, or briefly, all that is individual —, but who also have "ears" for tone and rhythm, for the "music" of what is being said[21], i.e. for what expresses the writer's individuality. The subtler laws of his style, as he describes them, demand a more refined ear: surprising truths emerge without any long arguments but rather in sudden and surprising ways; their effect is cold and disturbing, so frightful that one can only bear them for a very short time. And this is exactly why they select: they are apt to be misunderstood by those who cannot bear to hear them, "asses and old maids of both sexes to whom life offers nothing but their innocence" (GS 381). Nietzsche's writings are not meant to disrupt these people's sense of security, but to "inspire" them to be what they are and to do what they are able to do (GS 381). In this group we also find, most importantly, the "scholars", to whom Nietzsche dedicates a whole series of aphorisms in Book V of *The Gay Science*[22]. Those, however, who are capable of hearing his language have, according to Nietzsche, "different needs, grow differently, digest differently" (GS 381), briefly: they have different instincts. And yet, Nietzsche here no longer speaks of "instinct", but rather of "taste", and he refers to "a taste for independence, for quick coming and going, for wandering, perhaps for adventures"— and, finally, for something *simultaneously* voluntary and involuntary, conscious and unconscious, free and coercive, reasonable and instinctive: "dance" (GS 381). Although one can never fully be sure of understanding another person, especially someone like Nietzsche, one can dance another person's dance,

---

21 Cf. Stegmaier (2004).
22 Cf. GS 344, 348, 349, 366.

including Nietzsche's dance – though only with our own legs and our own swing. And while instincts guide our behavior unreflectively and involuntarily (that is still their function), taste also has a feeling for nuances, for those subtleties of understanding which can no longer be captured conceptually and for those subtleties of language which can no longer be captured linguistically[23]. In the end, as is well known, Nietzsche has said of himself: "I am a nuance"(EH The Case of Wagner 4).

Bibliography

Andresen, Joshua (2010), "Truth and Illusion Beyond Falsification: Re-reading 'Truth and Lie'", in: *Nietzsche-Studien* 39 (2010), 255–281.

Bertino, Andrea Christian (2011), *"Vernatürlichung". Ursprünge von Friedrich Nietzsches Entidealisierung des Menschen, seiner Sprache und seiner Geschichte bei Johann Gottfried Herder*, Berlin/New York (Walter de Gruyter).

Emden, Christian J. (2005), *Nietzsche on Language, Consciousness, and the Body*, Illinois (University of Illinois Press).

Hazz, Ignace (2006), *Nietzsche et la métaphore cognitive*, Paris (Harmattan).

Hödl, Hans Gerald (1997), *Nietzsches frühe Sprachkritik. Lektüren zu Ueber Wahrheit und Lüge im aussermoralischen Sinne*, Wien (WUV).

Hödl, Hans Gerald (2003), "Metaphern ohne Referenten. Anmerkungen zur neueren Diskussion um Nietzsches Sprachphilosophie", in: *Allgemeine Zeitschrift für Philosophie* 28, 183–199.

Kalb, Christof (2000), *Desintegration. Studien zu Friedrich Nietzsches Leib- und Sprachphilosophie*, Frankfurt am Main (Suhrkamp).

Kodama, Hakaru (forthcoming), *Nietzsches Begriff der Vernunft*.

Meijers, Antonie/Stingelin, Martin (1988), "Konkordanz zu den wörtlichen Abschriften und Übernahmen von Beispielen und Zitaten aus Gustav Gerber: Die Sprache als Kunst (Bromberg 1871) in Nietzsches Rhetorik-Vorlesung und in 'Ueber Wahrheit und Lüge im aussermoralischen Sinne'", in: *Nietzsche-Studien* 17 (1988), 350–368.

Ponton, Olivier (2007), *Nietzsche - Philosophie de la légèreté*, Berlin/New York (Walter de Gruyter).

Reuter, Sören (2009), *An der 'Begräbnisstätte der Anschauung'. Nietzsches Bild- und Wahrnehmungstheorie in Ueber Wahrheit und Lüge im aussermoralischen Sinne*, Basel (Schwabe Verlag).

Stegmaier, Werner (2007), "Nach Montinari. Zur Nietzsche-Philologie", in: *Nietzsche-Studien* 36 (2007), 80–94 (English translation by Lisa Anderson: "After Montinari. On Nietzsche Philology", in: *The Journal*

---

23 Cf. Stegmaier (1992, 348 ff).

of Nietzsche Studies 38 (Fall 2009), 5–19; Portuguese and French translations are forthcoming).

Stegmaier, Werner (forthcoming), *Nietzsches Befreiung der Philosophie. Kontextuelle Interpretation des V. Buchs der Fröhlichen Wissenschaft.*

Stegmaier, Werner (2000), "Nietzsches Zeichen", in: *Nietzsche-Studien* 29 (2000), 41–69.

Stegmaier, Werner (1992), *Philosophie der Fluktuanz. Dilthey und Nietzsche*, Göttingen (Vandenhoeck & Ruprecht).

Stegmaier, Werner (2008), *Philosophie der Orientierung*, Berlin/New York (Walter de Gruyter).

Stegmaier, Werner (2004), "'Philosophischer Idealismus' und die 'Musik des Lebens'. Zu Nietzsches Umgang mit Paradoxien. Eine kontextuelle Interpretation des Aphorismus Nr. 372 der Fröhlichen Wissenschaft", in: *Nietzsche-Studien* 33 (2004), 90–128.

Stegmaier, Werner (2008), "Schicksal Nietzsche? Zu Nietzsches Selbsteinschätzung als Schicksal der Philosophie und der Menschheit (Ecce homo, Warum ich ein Schicksal bin 1)", in: *Nietzsche-Studien* 37 (2008), 62–114.

Stegmaier, Werner (2007), "Zur Frage der Verständlichkeit. Nietzsches Beitrag zum interkulturellen Kommunizieren und Philosophieren", in: *Allgemeine Zeitschrift für Philosophie* 32.2 (2007), 107–119.

Van Tongeren, Paul/Schank, Gerd/Siemens, Herman (forthcoming), *Nietzsche-Wörterbuch*, vol. III, Berlin/New York (Walter de Gruyter).

Vinzens, Albert (1999), *Friedrich Nietzsches Instinktverwandlung*, Basel (Schwabe Verlag).

Zavatta, Benedetta (2009), "Die in der Sprache versteckte Mythologie und ihre Folgen fürs Denken. Einige Quellen von Nietzsche: Max Müller, Gustav Gerber und Ludwig Noiré", in: *Nietzsche-Studien* 38 (2009), 269–298.

IV. The Critique of Morality and the Affirmation of Life

Philosophy as a 'Misunderstanding of the Body' and the 'Great Health' of the New Philosophers[1]

Marta Faustino

In the second aphorism of *Beyond Good and Evil* Nietzsche famously writes that "the fundamental belief of metaphysicians is the *belief in oppositions of values*" (BGE 2). Being and nothing, truth and lie, good and evil, thing-in-itself and appearance, body and soul, reason and passion are only a few of the examples of the oppositions Nietzsche refers to, that is, of the asymmetrical values that metaphysics always postulated as if they were radically separated, opposed and contradicting entities. As is well known, Nietzsche's philosophy is characterized by an "attempt" to invert this deeply ingrained tendency – an attempt that must in fact be carried out further by a whole "new breed of philosophers", the "philosophers of the dangerous 'Perhaps'" (BGE 2). This attempt aims at dissolving all the ancient metaphysical asymmetries and oppositions by putting forward the hypothesis that perhaps there are no opposites at all and what constitutes the value of all good and respected things is precisely the fact that they have "an incriminating link, bond, or tie to the very things that look like their evil opposites" (BGE 2).

The opposition between the body, the instincts, drives and affects, on the one hand, and the soul, reason, consciousness, thought and language, on the other, is not an exception to this. In Zarathustra's famous expression, the "soul" is "just a word for something on the body", and "reason", as traditionally understood, is no more than a "small reason", totally subordinated to and governed by the "great reason" of the body (ZA I On the Despisers of the Body). It follows from this that all activities like thinking, reasoning, or reflecting do

---

1 This paper wouldn't have been possible without the financial support of a PhD Scholarship from FCT (Fundação para a Ciência e Tecnologia). I would like to dedicate this article to Prof. João Constâncio, who introduced me to the study of Nietzsche.

not occur in an independent domain, whose nature might be radically
different from the body: on the contrary, they are highly dependent,
conditioned and determined by it. It is not possible to dissociate them
from the collective activity of the instincts, drives and affects at work
in every organism, and hence it is not possible to dissociate them from
the whole state of the body or organism that produces them.

However, I shall not focus on the nature of the interconnection
or interlacement that Nietzsche establishes between body and soul,
passion and reason, instincts and language (or consciousness) – a topic
which is extensively discussed elsewhere in this volume.[2] Instead, I
would like to explore some of the most important consequences of
such an interlacement in Nietzsche's philosophizing. I shall try to show
that the thesis here implied is not just one among others – a secondary
or marginal thesis that could be added or subtracted to the remaining
corpus of Nietzsche's philosophy. It is rather an insight that we find at
its core: it determines its roots, its method, and its orientation towards
its intended goals. It justifies, in particular, Nietzsche's task of assessing
modernity from the viewpoint of a physician of culture, as well as his
redefinition of philosophy's goal in terms of the promotion of health
rather than in terms of (absolute) truth. Accordingly, it inaugurates a
radically new form of philosophizing.

Thus, in the preface to *The Gay Science*, which Nietzsche added in
1886 together with the fifth book of the same work, he asks himself
whether, "on a grand scale, philosophy has been no more than an
interpretation of the body and a *misunderstanding of the body*" (GS
Preface 2). According to Nietzsche, there have always been certain
vital needs and physiological conditions hidden behind the disguise
of supposedly objective, rational, ideal, spiritual doctrines, and
such needs and conditions have not only influenced all thought and
philosophy so far, but actually conditioned and determined it through
and through. Nietzsche recognized, as probably no other philosopher
did, the deep dependence of all knowledge, including philosophical
knowledge, on life and on the demands that it imposes to all beings.
On the one hand, this means that everything that has been called
knowledge so far is nothing but a collection of fictions, falsifications,
human constructions, that were gradually incorporated and whose

---

2   Cf. João Constâncio's , Werner Stegmaier's and Patrick Wotling's papers in this
    volume.

existence can only be justified by their utility to the preservation of the species and their necessary character as a condition of life (cf. GS 110). In order to survive and make the world understandable, habitable and comfortable, human beings had to create a permanent, identical and stable world via the creation of the concepts of thing, substance, cause and effect, even though what truly exists is, according to Nietzsche's conception, nothing but a permanent and endless flux of change, transformation and becoming. In his own words, in aphorism 121 of *The Gay Science*,

> We have arranged for ourselves a world in which we are able to live – by positing bodies, lines, planes, causes and effects, motion and rest, form and content; without these articles of faith no one could endure living! But that does not prove them. Life is not an argument; the conditions of life might include error (GS 121).

In claiming to capture being and imagining to know things through these concepts and "articles of faith", philosophy has always shown itself blind to its own genesis. It never realized that its activity doesn't serve the spirit at a purely abstract level, but only and exclusively the body. Given that it is derived from laws inherent to life itself, it only gives expression to the oldest organic imperatives and vital demands, which are necessary to the preservation of the species.

On the other hand, however, it follows from Nietzsche's insight into the deep interconnection between knowledge or thought and organic life that, on a second level, the philosophical activity of any philosopher cannot be separated at all from the specific life and idiosyncrasies of the author that produces it, that is, from the general condition of his organism and the type of instincts that govern or have become dominant in it. As Nietzsche writes in *Beyond Good and Evil*, conscious thought does not essentially distinguish itself from instinctive activity, even in the case of philosophical thought. In his words,

> (...) most of a philosopher's conscious thought is secretly directed and forced into determinate channels by the instincts. Even behind all logic and its autocratic posturings stand valuations or, stated more clearly, physiological requirements for the preservation of a certain type of life (BGE 3).

Thus, all thought belongs, ultimately, to a body and, therefore, it is only and exclusively through this same body that all thought should be analysed, interpreted, evaluated; behind the language of a philosopher one shall always find precisely the instincts that such a language expresses. And here lies perhaps the biggest innovation of Nietzsche's philosophizing: if philosophy has always been nothing but a misunderstanding of the body, Nietzsche tried to develop, with his philosophy, the art of interpreting it well.

Accordingly, he examines and evaluates not only all philosophical thought before him, but also all other cultural manifestations (works of art, ideologies, political systems or moralities) in a radically new and unprecedented way: instead of reflexively looking at their logical perfection, adequacy to reality, veracity or originality, he asks which instincts or organic conditions are thereby expressed. Each and every form of cultural manifestation is thus seen as a symptom of the type of life, the type of instincts, the type of body that produced it. In his words, referring to philosophy in particular,

> All those bold lunacies of metaphysics, especially answers to the question about the *value* of existence, may always be considered first of all as symptoms of certain *bodies*; and if such world affirmations or world negations lack altogether any grain of significance when measured scientifically, they give the historian and psychologist all the more valuable hints as symptoms of the body, of its success or failure, its fullness, power, and high-handedness in history, or of its frustrations, fatigues, impoverishments, its premonitions of the end, its will to an end (GS Preface 2).

In this way, Nietzsche develops what we could call a psycho-physiology of culture, that is, a psychological and physiological treatment, analysis and evaluation of all cultural manifestations. As a symptomatology, this allows him to determine the general condition of that same culture – and in particular, as we should say in Nietzschean terms, its condition of health or sickness.[3]

To classify a certain culture and all its manifestations, be it at the level of art, philosophy or literature, politics, science or moral, as healthy or ill, would sound at least strange to the ears of any preceding philosopher. Nevertheless, Nietzsche seems to see himself

---

3 For a comprehensive and detailed study of Nietzsche's psycho-physiological treatment of culture cf. Wotling (1995).

as a "physician of culture" (*Arzt der Cultur*),[4] and he wishes, for the future of philosophy, the emergence of a "philosophical *physician* (*philosophischer Arzt*) in the exceptional sense of the term", that is, in his words, "someone who has set himself the task of pursuing the problem of the total health of a people, time, race or of humanity", and who, for the first time, would "summon the courage" to push his suspicion to its limits and to "risk the proposition" that "what was at stake in all philosophizing hitherto was not at all 'truth' but rather something else – let us say, health, future, growth, power, life..." (GS Preface 2). Therefore, his use of the notions of health and sickness and his presumable self-understanding as "physician of culture" are neither strange, nor peripheral to his own philosophizing. Instead, they determine the core of his philosophical project, thereby reflecting a radical change in the orientation and goals of his thinking relative to all previous philosophy. More concretely, the "truth", as traditionally understood, is no longer the main focus, the guiding thread or the ultimate goal, but rather health, i.e. the promotion of life and the enhancement of the organism.[5]

In fact, Nietzsche seems to be doing nothing besides making conscious the unconscious instinct which, according to him, has been hidden behind the mask of "truth" and always guided and fostered philosophy, namely the fundamental instinct that struggles for "health, future, growth, power, life". In other words, Nietzsche's idea is that philosophy has always answered to the specific needs

---

4   Even though Nietzsche never expressly called himself a "physician of culture", we can assume that he saw himself as such. In 1873 he projected an essay with the title "Der Philosoph als Arzt der Cultur" ("The philosopher as physician of culture", KSA 7. 545, 23[15]) and throughout his posthumous fragments it is possible to ascertain that he wanted to write a true "life's doctrine of health" ("Gesundheitslehre des Lebens"), that should then be published as one of the *Untimely Meditations* with the title "Gesundheit und Krankheit" ("Health and Sickness") (KSA 8. 188, 10[20], p.188). Even though Nietzsche never systematized this doctrine, it is reflected in every aspect of his philosophy, and it functions as a guideline throughout the whole of his work. About this theme, cf. Ahern (1995); Cherlonneix (2002 a and b).

5   E.g. BGE 4: "We do not consider the falsity of a judgement as itself an objection to a judgement; this is perhaps where our new language will sound most foreign. The question is how far the judgement promotes and preserves life, how well it preserves, and perhaps even cultivates, the type".

of its author, and therefore, it has always reflected what seemed to favour his "health, future, growth, power, life". However, given that philosophy can be understood as a misunderstanding of the body, Nietzsche seems to believe that, even though these goals have always been pursued, its pursuit has almost always led to the opposite. Once again, the problem lies in the depths of the organism and should be understood through an assessment of the organism's condition. As Nietzsche writes, once again in the Preface to *The Gay Science*,

> For assuming that one is a person, one necessarily also has the philosophy of that person; but here there is a considerable difference. In some, it is their weaknesses that philosophize; in others, their riches and strengths. The former *need* their philosophy, be it as a prop, a sedative, medicine, redemption, elevation, or self-alienation; for the latter, it is only a beautiful luxury, in the best case the voluptuousness of a triumphant gratitude that eventually has to inscribe itself in cosmic capital letters on the heaven of concepts (GS Preface 2).

In the majority of cases, though, it is distress that philosophizes, as in all sick thinkers – and perhaps sick thinkers are in the majority in the history of philosophy (GS Preface 2).

What does it mean, however, to state that sick philosophers have prevailed in the history of philosophy?[6]

What does Nietzsche understand here by "sickness"? And what would its opposite be, the health of the philosopher, or, more precisely, the "great health" that in aphorism 382 of *The Gay Science* Nietzsche seems to ascribe to his "new philosophers", the "philosophers of future"?

Although in an unsystematic way, Nietzsche develops throughout his work a very complex theory of health and sickness, which is

---

6   Nietzsche's suggestion that sickness prevailed hitherto in the history of philosophy, should evidently be read in line with the ambiguity that characterizes his relation to the majority of previous philosophers. The fact that Nietzsche finds sickness as the general characteristic trait of the history of western philosophy does not mean that he completely rejects it, nor does it prevent him from expressing some admiration for the great philosophers, like Plato, Spinoza or Kant. The transition from sickness unto health in philosophy is meant as a *development* — as an overcoming, and not as simple rejection.

obviously impossible to present in all its depth and detail in such a short paper as this.[7]

Some points should, nevertheless, be emphasized. Nietzsche often uses the terms metaphorically, that is, as general categories of evaluation that substitute for the ancient moral formulae and enable him to evaluate, "beyond good and evil", a multiplicity of phenomena, be it an individual or a culture, an age, a morality, a philosophy or an ideology. On a first level, though, they preserve the literal meaning they have, for example, in medicine: health and sickness designate a certain physiological condition of the organism in its relation to itself and to the external world.

That doesn't mean, however, that Nietzsche preserves the meaning of the notions of health and sickness as understood by medicine or even the meaning that we intuitively tend to ascribe them. On the contrary: his conception of these notions goes against each and every usual understanding of them. To begin with, Nietzsche denies that health can be brought into a general and universal definition, i.e. that health (or sickness) could mean the same to all human beings. "For there is no health as such", writes Nietzsche in book III of *The Gay Science*, "and all attempts to define such a thing have failed miserably" (GS 120). According to Nietzsche – and in accordance with the attempts that are being made today, more than 100 years after his death, to change the official definition given by the World Health Organization (WHO)[8] – health is something absolutely personal and individual, depending on "your goal, your horizon, your powers, your impulses, your mistakes and above all on the ideals and phantasms of your soul" (GS 120), briefly: on the individuality of each person. In this sense, "there are innumerable healths of the body" (GS 120), and consequently, what is healthy in a person "could (...) look like the opposite of health in another" (GS 120). In general terms, and disregarding the singularities of each individual, health is a completely indefinable and indeterminable concept.

On the other hand, according to Nietzsche's conception, a human being is an organism, that is, a unity in which a multiplicity of forces

---

7   See footnote 3 for references. For a detailed study on the meaning of health and sickness in Nietzsche's thought, cf. Cherlonneix (2002).

8   Cf. for example, Bircher/Wehkamp (2006, 44-77).

(instincts, drives and affects) coexist in a permanent struggle for their own enhancement and supremacy over all others. Each force struggles for itself and serves its own interests and goals, but each force is also of the utmost importance for every other force, because it is resistance, or more precisely, the overcoming of resistances, that allows each force to grow and expand its power. Struggle and fight are, thus, necessary conditions in any organism: a complete immobility would bring about its destruction. This being so, it is not hard to understand that for Nietzsche health is not a permanent or stable state of equilibrium. In a healthy organism that is in complete harmony with its own nature, the coordinated activity of the instincts, drives and affects is directed towards growth, expansion, enhancement and constant self-overcoming, even when this means, under certain circumstances, putting self-preservation at risk. A will to peace, equilibrium and stability or, in other words, the supremacy of the instinct of self-preservation, is, for Nietzsche, a sign or a symptom of weariness, exhaustion and, precisely, of sickness, since it contradicts the natural process of the organism.[9]

Now, it is exactly this instinct of self-preservation along with the *"instinct of fear"* that Nietzsche finds behind most philosophies produced so far. As we saw at the beginning, he believes that philosophy until now has done little besides conserving the errors that are necessary for the preservation of the species. According to the formula presented in aphorism 355 of *The Gay Science*, philosophy, like every-day knowledge, converts something strange, unusual or unfamiliar into something familiar, that is, trivial, every-day, well-known, so that one "feels at home", one is neither surprised nor disturbed by the course of events and therefore enjoys a "sense of security" (GS 355). The need for certainties and the demand for something firm and solid to which one may cling are typical of religions, but also, according

---

9 Cf. GS 349: "To wish to preserve oneself is a sign of distress, of a limitation of the truly basic life-instinct, which aims at *the expansion of power* and in so doing often enough risks and sacrifices self-preservation. (...) and in nature it is not distress which *rules*, but rather abundance, squandering — even to the point of absurdity. The struggle for survival is only an *exception*, a temporary restriction of the will to life; the great and small struggle revolves everywhere around preponderance, around growth and expansion, around power and in accordance with the will to power, which is simply the will to life".

to Nietzsche, of all scientific and philosophical thought. It is always the sign of a huge *"instinct of weakness"* in the face of reality (cf. GS 347). In this sense, all thinkers have been essentially cowards, they haven't had the courage to break with what was already established, to make new experiences and risk new, dangerous and unknown paths that could really enlarge the possibilities of knowledge and enable the expansion of life itself.

On the other hand, this conservation of the errors that are necessary to the preservation of the species has the perverse effect of leading to the construction and affirmation of another world, beyond and apart from the real one, different from the world of "life, nature and history" (GS 344). Although this other world is a fiction, it is opposed to "this world, *our* world" (GS 344) as if it were the "true world", so that life, nature, history, and individuality may then be devaluated, negated or calumniated in relation to it (cf. GS 344). Such moralized views of the world, of the subject and of life, which after all, according to Nietzsche, always prevailed in the history of philosophy, prevent the organism's growth, expansion and self-overcoming. They are, once again, signs of sickness. In Nietzsche's words,

> Every philosophy that ranks peace above war, every ethic with a negative definition of happiness, every metaphysics and physics that knows some *finale*, a final state of some sort, every predominantly aesthetic or religious craving for some Apart, Beyond, Outside, Above [*Abseits, Jenseits, Ausserhalb, Oberhalb*], permits the question whether it was not illness that inspired the philosopher (GS Preface 2).

What, then, distinguishes Nietzsche's philosophy from the previous ones? And what does he aspire to with his "new philosophers" or "philosophers of the future" – those who are still to come and in whom Nietzsche lays his higher hopes, those to whom he ascribes "the most comprehensive responsibility" for the future "development of humanity" (BGE 61)? According to Nietzsche's description in *Beyond Good and Evil*, such philosophers will probably still be "friends of 'truth'" (BGE 43), but they won't be dogmatists: "It would offend their pride, as well as their taste, if their truth were a truth for everyone" (BGE 43). They won't be skeptics either, at least

not in the traditional sense of the term (BGE 208, 210), nor mere
critics (BGE 210), even though all critical work in philosophy will
be an important "tool" for their own philosophy (BGE 210, 211). In
extreme contradiction to the old philosophers, the new philosophers
shall essentially be experimenters (*Versucher*, BGE 42) and men of
experiments (*Menschen der Experimente*, BGE 210). They will feel,
in Nietzsche's words, "the weight and duty of a hundred experiments
and temptations (*Versuchen und Versuchungen*) of life" (BGE 205),
they will constantly put themselves at risk, and in their "passion for
knowledge", they will go further with "bold and painful experiments",
they will love to experiment "in a new, perhaps broader, perhaps more
dangerous sense" (BGE 210). Thus, once again in deep contrast with
the earlier philosophers, these philosophers of the future won't serve,
nor propagate the ancestral tables of values; on the contrary, they will
necessarily be "the bad conscience of their age" (BGE 212) and fight
against the long established ideals in accordance to which philosophy
has always been practised (BGE 212). They will therefore cruelly
vivisect the virtues of their time and expose how much hypocrisy,
lying, and comfortableness is intrinsic to the followers of present-
day morality. In opposition to the typical cowardice and laziness of
the old philosophers, these new philosophers will want to elevate
philosophy precisely to the heights where one feels least at home (cf.
BGE 212). They are thus characterized by a new courage in the face
of the new, the strange, the dangerous, in the face of the adventures
and challenges of the still unexplored seas of knowledge. Above all,
though, these new philosophers will have, Nietzsche writes, "more
to do than just to know something – they have to *be* something new,
mean something new, and *present* new values!" (BGE 253, cf. BGE
211). The great task of these new philosophers, which gives them
such a prominent role in Nietzsche's thought and transforms them
into men of the most comprehensive responsibility, consists, then,
in the fearless and courageous exploration of undiscovered fields of
knowledge, through which it should be possible to destroy the ideal
of the present and create new values.

Like the old philosophers, these new philosophers will certainly be
physiologically conditioned. But as one could already expect, it won't
be sickness which will determine them. On the contrary: in a way that
shall sound strange to those who are used to the language of previous
philosophers, Nietzsche presents as a pre-condition to the new phi-

losopher's task a fundamental physiological condition: the attainment of "great health" (*grosse Gesundheit*).[10]

As Nietzsche explains in aphorism 382 of *The Gay Science*, which is dedicated, precisely, to the "great health",

> We who are new, nameless, hard to understand; we premature births of an as yet unproved future – for a need for a new end, we also need new means, namely, a new health that is stronger, craftier, tougher, bolder, and more cheerful than any previous health. Anyone whose soul thirsts to experience the whole range of previous values and aspirations, to sail around all the coasts of this 'inland sea' (*Mittelmeer*) of ideals, anyone who wants to know from the adventures of his own experience how it feels to be the discoverer and conqueror of an ideal, or to be an artist, a saint, a lawmaker, a sage, a pious man, a soothsayer, an old-style divine loner – any such person needs one thing above all – *the great health* (GS 382).

What characterizes this "great health"? And what distinguishes it from the other, "normal", forms of health? In his texts, Nietzsche uses the adjective "great" (*gross*) quite frequently – sometimes in its usual sense, but in particular cases (generally highlighted in italics) he uses it in a very particular, almost "technical" sense. In these cases, he seems to want, first, to free the concept from its common, traditional meaning and to build his *own* concept. Secondly, in accordance with the purpose of dissolving the ancient oppositions of metaphysics, the "great" concepts of Nietzsche have generally another particularity: the fact of being elevated, reinforced, and enhanced precisely by their apparent opposites.[11]

---

10 It is debatable whether the "great health" Nietzsche refers to is or is not the health of the new philosophers. Directly and expressly Nietzsche ascribes it only to the "free spirits" (HH I Preface 4), to the "redeeming man" (GM, II. 24) and to Zarathustra (EH Zarathustra 2). However, Nietzsche clearly presents the new philosophers as free spirits and redeemers of present reality. This interpretation is further supported by the fact that, at least in aphorism 382 of *The Gay Science*, Nietzsche seems to treat as identical the new possibilities that "great health" opens up and the task that he ascribes to the "philosophers of the future" in *Beyond Good and Evil*.

11 This clue to the interpretation of Nietzsche's use of "great" (*gross*) was given for the first time by Werner Stegmaier (2008, 110-111): "*Nietzsche nennt 'gross' nicht so sehr das, was anderes überragt, sondern das, was von seinem Gegensatz nicht negiert wird, an ihm nicht zugrundegeht, sondern ihn für sich noch fruchtbar machen, an ihm wachsen kann.*" I am, however, not completely sure that this rule

So it is, for example, with the "great reason" (the reason of the body, which transforms the "little reason", the traditional reason, into its tool and instrument)[12], the "great tolerance" (which tolerates intolerance itself and even grows through it)[13], the "great love" (for example, Zarathustra's love for mankind, which is reinforced by a great contempt for present-day mankind)[14]

, the "great seriousness" (which is achieved through a sense of parody regarding all the things that have been considered serious until now)[15] – and also with the "great health".

In this sense, great health is the one that, instead of being weakened or ruined by its apparent opposite – sickness —, is even enhanced and reinforced by it. This actually reflects the structure of the organism as I described it above: just as every force in the organism needs adversaries, resistances and obstacles to manifest and reinforce itself, health also needs to overcome its opposite in order to become bigger, stronger, richer and deeper. In this sense, not only should one not fear and avoid sickness at any cost, but one should welcome it instead: in fact, one should even seek for sickness as the most powerful device for the enhancement of health.[16]

Thus, the great health is not a permanent state that one could acquire once and for all, but a dynamic and always unfinished process, which "one doesn't only have, but also acquires continually, and must acquire because one gives it up again and again, and must give it up!…" (GS 382).

The core of Nietzsche's concept of the "great health" is precisely this dynamic relation between health and sickness, getting sick and

---

applies to all the occurrences of the term "great" in Nietzsche. In a significant number of cases, though, as in the ones mentioned above, the rule seems to be perfectly applicable. In the case of the "great health", the rule is confirmed in all occurrences (Cf. HH I, Preface, 4; GC, 382; GM, II, 24 and Nachlass 1885-1887, KSA 12. 108, 2[97]).

12 Cf. Z I On the Despisers of the Body; BGE 201.
13 Cf. A 38.
14 Cf., for example, Z II On the Pitying, On The Tarantulas; Z III On Virtue that Makes Small 3.
15 Cf. GS 382.
16 Cf. TI Arrows 8: "What doesn't kill me makes me stronger"; and NW Epilogue, 1: "And as far as my long infirmity is concerned, isn't it the case that I am unspeakably more indebted to it than I am to my health? I owe a higher health to it, a health that becomes stronger from everything that does not kill it off!"

recovering. The greater the disease, and the harder the recovery, the greater will be the health achieved after the process of overcoming the disease. The one who seeks to attain this great health shall therefore expose himself to danger and confront the worse diseases and difficulties, in order to surpass them and transform them to his or her own advantage. To discover the amount of sickness one can bear and overcome is, precisely, the dangerous experiment of the great health. As Nietzsche writes in a posthumous fragment:

> Health and sickliness: be careful! The yardstick remains the body's efflorescence, the mind's elasticity, courage and cheerfulness – but also, of course, *how much sickliness it can take upon itself* and *overcome* – can *make* healthy. What would destroy more tender men is one of the stimulants of *great* health (WLN 78).[17]

Those who are capable of great health are therefore, in Nietzsche's words, "braver, perhaps, than is prudent and often suffering shipwreck and damage" (GS 382), but they are also, and above all, "healthier than one would like to admit, dangerously healthy; ever again healthy" (GS 382). With this kind of health, one returns from every convalescence "*newborn*, having shed one's skin, more ticklish and malicious, with a more delicate taste for joy, with a more tender tongue for all good things, with merrier senses, joyful with a more dangerous second innocence, more childlike, and at the same time a hundred times subtler than one had ever been before" (GS Preface 4).

The great health can thus be described as a particular kind of force, robustness and plasticity of the organism, a singular will to life, growth and expansion, which predisposes to danger, risk, adventure and challenge of one's own limits. This sort of experimentation and constant challenging of oneself opens up, in turn, a huge amount of new possibilities and perspectives, which is why it is so important for knowledge and for the new philosophers of the future. It is in this sense that Nietzsche claims that life itself could be a means to knowledge and an experiment for the seeker for knowledge (cf. GS 324). This is how Nietzsche himself understood and lived his own life. If, for many, knowledge can be "a bed to rest on, or the way to one, or a diversion or a form of idleness", as it certainly was for many

---

17 KSA 12. 108, 2[97] (Nachlass 1885-1887)= WLN, 78.

previous thinkers, Nietzsche believed that it should be "a world of dangers and victories in which heroic feelings also have their dance-and playgrounds" (GS 324). After all, the seeker of knowledge lives and must live "in the thundercloud of the highest problems and the weightiest responsibilities" (GS 351), and he must take leave "of all faith and every wish for certainty", thereby maintaining himself "on light ropes and possibilities and dancing even beside abysses" (GS 347).

Among the multiple dangers and victories, to which the seeker for knowledge is subject to, Nietzsche stresses precisely the importance of the temporary submission to sickness and victorious recovery, as the most efficient means to knowledge and self-knowledge.[18]

In fact, an episode of sickness gives the sick person the opportunity of experiencing something about herself and the world, which would never be possible in a state of health – and if it is the case that a philosopher gets sick, Nietzsche believes, then he should bring all of his scientific curiosity into his sickness.[19]

Moreover, if philosophy has always been practised by sick thinkers, to submit oneself to sickness seems to be the best way to find out and understand the paths into which thought has been forced so far. Through the temporary surrender to sickness, Nietzsche writes,

> one acquires a subtler eye for all philosophizing to date; one is better than before at guessing the involuntary detours, alleyways, resting places, and *sunning* places of thought to which suffering thinkers are led and misled on account of their suffering; one now knows where the sick *body* and its needs unconsciously urge, push, and lure the spirit – towards sun, stillness, mildness, patience, medicine, balm in some sense (GS Preface 2).

---

18 Cf., for example, GS 120: "the great question (...) whether we can *do without* illness, even for the development of our virtue; and whether especially our thirst for knowledge and self-knowledge do not need the sick soul as much as the healthy". In the Preface to *Human All To Human I*, he speaks of "a health which may not dispense even with illness, as a means and fish-hook of knowledge" (HH I Preface 4, translation modified). For the relation of sickness and its overcoming to the particular problem of knowledge cf. Montebello (2001). For an analysis of sickness as "philosophical criterion" in Nietzsche's thought, cf. Bilheran (2005).

19 Cf. GS Preface 2: "A psychologist knows few questions as attractive as that concerning the relation between health and philosophy; and should he himself become ill, he will bring all of his scientific curiosity into the illness".

In order to overcome the current paradigms of thought and tables of values one has, first of all, to live them through, in one's own skin, to submit oneself to them and suffer them in one's own flesh, so that later, in a movement of recovery or convalescence,[20] one can destroy, overcome and recreate them. This "art of transfiguration", Nietzsche writes, "just *is* philosophy" (GS Preface 2). Having used the experience of his own body and the multiple episodes of sickness and recovery he went through as his most important tool for knowledge, Nietzsche gave himself as an example. As he writes retrospectively in *Ecce Homo*,

> To be able to look out from the optic of sickness towards *healthier* concepts and values, and again the other way around, to look down from the fullness and self-assurance of the *rich* life into the secret work of the instinct of decadence – that was my longest training, my genuine experience, if I became a master of anything, it was this. "I have a hand for switching *perspectives*: the first reason why a 'revaluation of values' is even possible, perhaps for me alone (EH Why I Am So Wise 1).

As a precondition to the singularity of his philosophizing and its prominent place in the history of Western thought, Nietzsche presents, once again, the fact of having been "healthy to the core" (*im Grunde gesund*, EH Why I Am So Wise 2, my translation). He himself seems to have attained the kind of health that he aspires for his new philosophers of the future, the health which is a "superfluity of formative, curative, moulding and restorative forces" – the "great health" (HH I Preface 4). In his view, this "great health" would allow those new philosophers to pursue a new ideal, "a peculiar, seductive, dangerous ideal" (GS 382) – the ideal of a spirit that, like Nietzsche, "plays naively, i.e. not deliberately but from overflowing abundance and power, with everything that was hitherto called holy, good, untouchable, divine" (GS 382). This ideal, Nietzsche continues, is "the ideal of a human, superhuman well-being and benevolence that will often enough appear *inhuman* – for example, when it places itself

---

20 For this stress on the importance of the movement of recovery or convalescence, cf. Sílvio Pfeuffer (forthcoming), "'Fröhlichkeit' im Spannungsfeld zwischen Krankheit und Gesundheit — 'diese Kunst der Transfiguration *ist* eben Philosophie'".

next to all earthly seriousness heretofore" (GS 382). Even though such an ideal may seem a "parody" when compared to everything that has ever been called serious, and even though it seems to challenge Nietzsche's own philosophical seriousness, "it is perhaps only with it", Nietzsche writes at the end of the aphorism dedicated to the great health, "that *the great seriousness* really emerges; that the real question mark is posed for the first time; that the destiny of the soul changes; the hand of the clock moves forward; the tragedy *begins*" (GS 382).

Bibliography

Ahern, Daniel R. (1995), *Nietzsche as Cultural Physician*, Pennsylvania (The Pennsylvania State University Press).

Bilheran, Ariane (2005), *La Maladie, Critère des Valeurs chez Nietzsche. Prémices d'une Psychanalyse des Affects*, Paris (L'Harmattan).

Bircher, Johannes/Wehkamp, Karl-Heinz (2006), *Das ungenutzte Potential der Medizin – Analyse von Gesundheit und Krankheit zu Beginn des 21. Jahrhunderts*, Zürich (rüffer & rub).

Cherlonneix, Laurent (2002), *Nietzsche: Santé et Maladie: l'Art*, Paris (L'Harmattan).

Cherlonneix, Laurent (2002), *Philosophie Medicale de Nietzsche: la Connaissance, la Natur*, Paris (L'Harmattan).

Montebello, Pierre (2001), *Vie et Maladie chez Nietzsche*, Paris (Ellipses).

Pfeuffer, Sílvio (forthcoming), "'Fröhlichkeit' im Spannungsfeld zwischen Krankheit und Gesundheit – 'diese Kunst der Transfiguration *ist* eben Philosophie'".

Stegmaier, Werner (2008), „Schicksal Nietzsche? Zu Nietzsches Selbsteinschätzung als Schicksal der Philosophie und der Menschheit (Ecce Homo, Warum ich ein Schicksal bin 1)", in: *Nietzsche-Studien* 37 (2008), 62–114.

Wotling, Patrick (1995), *Nietzsche et le problème de la civilization*, Paris (PUF).

From the Nietzschean Interpretation of Philosophical Language to the Semiotics of Moral Phenomena: Thoughts on *Beyond Good and Evil*

André Muniz Garcia

The Relation between Language and Life in Nietzsche's Early Writings

Throughout the past one-hundred years of research into Friedrich Nietzsche's thought, one of the themes that is constantly discussed by scholars is the meaning of his radical critique of the fundamental concepts and principles of the philosophical tradition. According to Nietzsche, these are, in the final analysis, structurally conditioned by the logico-grammatical form of Indo-European languages. Without directly entering into the merit of the premises that sustain this argument, it can be said that in the most important 19th century German philosophical circles such concepts and principles were still interpreted as originating from the faculties of the spirit, as products of a purely formal activity (in the Kantian sense), or as products of the logic of reason (in the Hegelian sense); but Nietzsche tried to destroy this idea of a purely spiritual origin of such concepts and principles. As the vast research made by the *Nietzsche–Forschung* has demonstrated, the logico-grammatical arrangement of languages that are based on predicative structures of the type "S is P" (subject, copula, and predicate) is already the object of Nietzsche's attention in the early and intermediary periods of his work, but in his maturity, it became the focus of his analysis of the origin, scope, and limits of the fundamental categories of reason.

Inspired by an ample bibliography that he read while still a young man[1], Nietzsche takes effort in pointing out, as can already be seen in the annotations and study projects of the so-called *Militärzeit*,

---

1   Cf. Bönning (1987), Crawford (1988), Emden (2005), Stack (1983), Behler (1994), Fietz (1992).

that with the collapse of the supremacy of reason and the emergence of other disciplines of knowledge, such as history, the natural sciences, the science of language (*Sprachwissenschaft*) and physiology[2], the principle foundation of philosophical thought was in need of a profound revision, that inevitably would dispense with any concern regarding the formal capacities of the spirit. Nietzsche belongs to a period that rejects the promise of a universal and necessary knowledge by means of reason: in this period, the attempt, especially present in German idealism, of giving *systematic unity* to particular visions of the world is lost. This is the context where one should fit Nietzsche's project of reinterpreting, via a meticulous examination of language, the conceptual clothing created by philosophers, especially in Germany, for justifying their systems.

In BGE, Nietzsche diagnoses "the prejudices of philosophers" and identifies the linguistic webs[4] of the predicative structure of language. The procedure of putting an inherent state of things (attribute) in relation (verb) to a permanent state (subject) has long been the basis for the "eternal" concepts and principles of the traditional philosophical discourse. Following the logic of *our* language, philosophers have believed that for all variable things captured by our senses there is a universal form that comprehends them and gives them substantiality. Besides being the basis for the formalization of reality by means of categories of thought, language has been the means through which contingent experiences have achieved a stable meaning for man.

This conversion of contingent states of affairs into permanent states – which guided European thought – had called the attention, as stated earlier, of young Nietzsche. It was already in this light that he first tried to understand Schopenhauer's and Lange's arguments against Kant, especially regarding the relation of the thing in itself to the I of transcendental appercetion in the empirical perception of objects.[3] The thing in itself, insofar as it is thought of as something that abides, as the ground of all phenomena, is conditioned by the logico-lingustic relation between subject and predicate. Kant's well-known statement in the 2nd edition's Preface to the *Critique of Pure Reason* is a distinct sign of this: it would be absurd to assert that

---

2   On this topic, see Schnädelbach (1999).
3   A more detailed interpretation of this is presented in Garcia (2008). Cf. Alisson (1983, 24 ff).

there can be phenomena "without anything that appears" (KrV BXXVI/XXVII). Some of Nietzsche's early drafts, such as the draft "On Schopenhauer"[4], dated 1867/8, and the lecture, "On the Origin of Language" written in 1869/70, aimed at clarifying the "natural origin" of language and its function in relating concepts to objects – a process that is indispensable for rational reflection. However, it is worth stressing, Nietzsche's thoughts on language in these writings were not incorporated in his first work, whose backbone, paradoxically, is Schopenhauer's metaphysics of the will. Nietzsche intentionally prepared a break with the position he held from 1866 to 1870 and then returned to it later. Interpreters have not yet sufficiently studied why he abandoned his conception of language as a natural phenomenon in *The Birth of Tragedy* and opted for a conception that is strictly metaphysical.

Few Nietzsche scholars have tried to explain systematically why *On Truth and Lying in a Non-Moral Sense* was an essay Nietzsche "kept secret"[5]. This work is of central importance for understanding Nietzsche's idea that language is essentially figurative, a transposition (metaphoricalization) of perceptions and stimuli into images (representations) and sounds (words, concepts). This, according to Nietzsche, is what allows for those stimuli to obtain a semantic unity. The importance of this text for the aims of this article is this: it presents, for the first time and in a clear way, Nietzsche's (non-metaphysical)

---

4   The starting point of this text is the critique of the fundamental proposition of the Schopenhauerian system, as stated in the first volume of *The World as Will and Representation*: the world is will. The concept of will, correlated with "thing in itself", is refuted in *On Shopenhauer* following, at least, four fundamental steps: (i) that the will, as a thing in itself, is a "hidden category"; (ii) that the opposition between the world as will and as representation reveals itself to be false; (iii) consequently, the predicates attributed to the will are only comprehensible when compared to the predicates created in the domain of the will as representation and (iv) that the justification of the concept of thing in itself is only possible "with the help of a poetic instinct *(mit Hülfe einer poethischen Intuition)*". Cf. BAW III, 354.

5   In the Preface, written in 1886, to the second volume of *Human, All too Human*, Nietzsche makes clear that already in 1873, upon writing TL, he found himself "deep in the midst of moral skepticism" (HH II Preface 209), or put in another way, "the intensifying of pessimism as understood hitherto" had led him to "believe in nothing anymore, not even in Schopenhauer" (HH II Preface 209). On TL, cf. Hödl (1997), Bönning (1987), Crawford (1988), Emden (2005), Behler (1994), Borsche (1994), Otto (1994), Reuter (2004), Žunjic (1987).

thesis about the motivation that leads man to crystallize stimuli and consequently to appeal to the categories of reason in order to immunize himself against the domain of the instincts and sensations. I shall now focus a little longer on this argument, since it is from it that I shall try to extract some of the fundamental elements of Nietzsche's mature interpretation of language, especially as presented in BGE.

The renowned phrase which Nietzsche uses for the first time to designate man's motivation to regulate perceptions and stimuli according to an absolute criterion is: *Trieb zur Wahrheit* ("drive for truth"). We pause here to consider this phrase as such. First, it is worth saying that it is unusual in German, and that, with it, Nietzsche expects to distance himself from the tradition (French and German) that assumes that the longings and desires of human reason are our motivation for understanding contingent relations and for giving meaning to our lives and to the world as such.

If one thinks along the lines of the theoretical assumptions of ancient Greek philosophy, or even of rationalism or idealism, the connection between drives and truth presents itself as entirely contradictory. According to the Platonic tradition, empirical motives cannot, or at least, as Kantianism would put it, are not sufficient to place our understanding of the world on the right track towards truth. According to this tradition, truth is attained only when the certain, apparent or indeterminate is subsumed under a universal norm, i.e. under a rule given by reason; the means to this end vary according to the philosophical school. Nonetheless, and Nietzsche seems to be uncompromising here, the *purposes* of such a regulation of reality are not "rational", as tradition would have it, but "vital." In TL, the transfer of the debate regarding the conditions of the possibility of human knowledge from the formal capacities of reason (or the spirit) to *conditions of life* is highly emphasized: it is need (*Not*),[6] Nietzsche argues in this unpublished text, that leads man to organize reality according to concepts.

In TL, Nietzsche's language is not habitual in philosophy, yet is illuminating for the attentive reader: man is forced to search for a "peace

---

6   "To the extent that the individual wants to maintain himself against other individuals, in the natural state of things he has used the intellect mostly for dissimulation alone; but since man, out of necessity as well as boredom, wants to live in a society or herd, he needs a peace settlement and he tries to make at least the most brutal *bellum omnium contra omnes* vanish from this world." (TL 1, 254f).

treaty", or for a convention, in which given categories of thought can be effectively accepted and shared, in order to preserve a particular type of life, that is, the life of that "clever animal" (*kluges Thier*) mentioned at the very beginning of TL: the animal that invented knowledge. It is this convention that guarantees the unambiguous validity of certain concepts as organizers of contingent states, and so such a convention "looks like the first step towards the acquisition of that mysterious drive for truth" (TL 1,143), for "that which is to count as 'truth' from this point onwards now becomes fixed, i.e. a way of designating things is invented which has the same validity and force everywhere, and the legislation of language also produces the first laws of truth (...)" (TL 1,143).

From the various perspectives that emerge in TL, we point out that which presents the search for truth as a *condition* for a certain living being to survive. Nietzsche's splendid metaphors, as well as his eschewal of articulating his hypothesis systematically, could deceive some readers to affirm hastily that here is an attempt to reconstruct a historic moment in which truth had its point of origin, as a sort of follow up to the emergence of linguistic conventions. Our interpretation makes the idea of this historical point meaningless.

It is clear that Nietzsche supports a historico-evolutionary perspective, according to which truth developed from a convention made possible by language, and that this might have been motivated by a vital need of survival. This argument is illustrated by the idea of the "clever animal": constrained by a strong need and a strong drive, and also aided by language, man developed a regulatory conceptual framework, which he strived to use as a means to the end of bringing durability and peace to the eddy of volitions and needs of life. The "force of cognition" (*die Kraft des Erkennens*) is no more than "an aid supplied to the most unfortunate, most delicate and most transient of beings" (TL, 141). Knowledge is intrinsically connected to the "conditions of life" (*Lebensbedingungen*).

The Concept of "Need" and the Relation between Language and Life: a possible Guideline for Interpreting Part 1 of *Beyond Good and Evil*

Beyond Good and Evil plays a central role in Nietzsche's mature thought on need and the relation between language and the conditions

of life. With rich rhetorical resources, BGE deals with the analysis of
the relation between the logico-grammatical structure of language and
philosophical thought as part of a much wider subject matter, which
is the problem of the moral valuation of life. In the Preface, Nietzsche
tries to make clear that, on the one hand, Plato's invention of "pure
spirit" and "the Good in itself" – "the worst, most prolonged, and
most dangerous of all errors" (BGE Preface)— derives fundamentally
from the "seduction of grammar" (BGE Preface), i.e. from the belief
in the absolute validity of the category of the grammatical subject;
but, on the other hand, he also presents this diagnostic, not as local,
but rather as bearing on the effects of Platonism in the wider context
of European thought. In Nietzsche's words, this error has created
"a magnificent tension of spirit in Europe, the likes of which the
earth has never known" (BGE Preface), and so far, he stresses, the
attempts to cool this tension have been tenuous and ineffective[7]. "The
European", he affirms, "experiences this tension as a crisis or state
of need (*Nothstand*)" (BGE Preface). The term *Nothstand* denotes a
vital state of man, but, complementarily, it is also understood in this
context as the state of a suffering life, a negative state of the European
spirit, i.e. of philosophy itself. This could be a symptom, Nietzsche
affirms right afterwards, "that spirit does not experience itself
so readily as 'need' (*Noth*)" (BGE Preface); the tension of spirit is
such – or, to use Hegel's phrase, "despair" is such – that "the European"
is unable to experiment with his spiritual tension. The *Nothstand* is
the motivation for modern philosophical thought, but it also becomes
an obstacle. It was by not finding resistance in the realm of the spirit
that Platonism was able to spread, constructing that which would
become European philosophy. Thus, the task Nietzsche marvelously
put forward to philosophy arises, as is presented in the last lines of
the Preface of BGE: it should be possible to experience this tension
in accordance with a new need, it should be possible for philosophy
to take for itself, Nietzsche affirms, "the whole need of spirit" (BGE
Preface), in such a way that the tension may then grow out of a new
vital and "free" motivation, thereby being freed from that state of
privation and numbness that has prevailed in European philosophy

---

7   Nietzsche cites two attempts in this passage: the Jesuit movement and the
     democratic enlightenment, the ideal of reason as a moral source of politico-social
     emancipation.

so far. "Free spirit" is, in fact, the denomination given by Nietzsche to this new "philosophizing" that arises from a thought experiment inspired on *a new need*, or, from a direction in thought whose driving force is, fundamentally, life itself as abundance.

In accordance with our interpretation, Part 1 of BGE is structured precisely on the hypothesis mentioned previously, which was that the principal pillars of European thought were built on the unexplored land of the spirit's *need*. It is in examining this land that Nietzsche tries to show that there is a close bond between the innermost desires of philosophical thought in Europe and what he calls, in BGE 1, "the will to truth" (a phrase which recalls TL's "drive for truth").

With an already firm philosophical vocabulary in the later writings and a non-metaphysical concept of the will (*der Wille*), Nietzsche introduces an hypothesis, not exactly on the "origin" of the search for truth, such as was suggested in TL, but rather on what kind of motivation has oriented philosophy so far. "*What* in us really wills the truth?" (BGE 1), is the main question, from which he extracts at least two guidelines for his main argument in Part 1 of BGE: (i) truth is not the rational end for which thinking longs for and, from this, (ii) there is some need which directs the spirit towards truth. First, Nietzsche attempts to refute the prejudice that truth is factual, something given and unquestionable for the philosopher, "*transcendentalment claire*", as Descartes has put it in a famous letter to Mersenne in 1639.[8] Truth is not contained as *evident* in human reason, and cannot it be simply derived from it. Thus an unsolved question remains: if truth is not factual, not an unquestioned "given" of the spirit – so that philosophical thought could instead have been directed toward non-truth, uncertainty –, then why is there a motivation that orients philosophy in the direction of truth?

Aphorism 1 of BGE is one of Nietzsche's aphorisms most rich with questions. The amount of questions it contains does not, however, point to a Nietzschean relativism. As emphasized in BGE 3, it is rather a matter of relearning to question – of putting the question in a different way, thereby expanding the horizons of thought. In my view, this is precisely Nietzsche's way of questioning the value of truth. Truth is something that helped philosophical thought to measure

---

8   Descartes, René (1973/1978), 597.

itself, qualify itself, quantify itself, in short: truth, as a value, has had a "regulative importance" (BGE 3) for philosophizing. In BGE 3, Nietzsche uses logic as a paradigmatic example. Since the most general forms of thought have been formulated with the aim of determining the truth or falseness of judgments, logic, in its most basic function of preserving types of life, is nothing more than an instrument that simplifies phenomena, thereby making the world understandable. Its "regulative importance" means that while it creates rules that give order to thought, it is driven by an aim, namely that of making understandable what is contingent and undetermined. Therefore, logic posits a value: in providing *schemes* for what is contingent, it makes an *evaluation* in favour of the non-contingent. As a valuation, logic presupposes the value of truth and makes an assumption about how truth *should* be verified[9].

Accordingly, Nietzsche defends that truth, as a value, should be examined in a broader context than that of logic, or, put differently, truth should not be analyzed merely in relation to judgment, reasoning, and objective knowledge, but directly in relation to life (cf. BGE 1, 3, 4). This is not only a new question, but moreover a new method of questioning in philosophy. Life is to be conceived of as the center towards which the fundamental questions of thought gravitate. This is what Nietzsche is driving at in BGE 3, where his pronouncements may perhaps sound imprecise, unfounded, or just plain irritating to some readers: "the greatest part of conscious thought must still be attributed to instinctive activity, and this is even the case for philosophical thought" (BGE 3), he writes. The value of truth hides "physiological requirements for the preservation of a particular type of life (*Art von Leben*)" (BGE 3). Yet assertions of this kind hide a great difficulty that, more often than not, is not noticed by the readers. What specifically is, so to speak, the homogenous element that connects life and truth, the physiological demand for the preservation of life and logic? What authorizes Nietzsche to establish such relationships? Is he not imprecise and incoherent if he doesn't present sufficient elements to clarify his assertions?

---

9   E.g. NL 9[97] KSA 12.389 = WP 516: "Logic is the attempt to comprehend the actual world by means of a scheme of being posited by ourselves; more correctly, to make it formulatable and calculable for us —".

Already in the first aphorisms of BGE, the problem of the value of truth leads to the problem of the evaluation of life. As normative criterion, the search for truth is a need of a particular type of life; truth is supposed to give thought an absolute guarantee that contingency and the senses are determinable, i.e. what Nietzsche calls "appearence" (*Schein*) in BGE 3 is determinable. In short: it is in this context that expressions like "physiological requirement" for preservation, "instincts" that force (*zwingen*) a philosopher's thought "into determinate channels (*in bestimmte Bahnen*)" (BGE 3), gain philosophical vigor and meaning. The will to truth is an expression of a need of preservation, a spiritual need of "the European" himself, – a need to abide in a permanent state, free of mutations, where thought could maintain its abstract motion of regulating reality without any unfortunate surprises. By the end of aphorism 3, the universal value that philosophy attributes to the concept of truth is removed from the mere domain of reasoning and logic, i.e. of knowledge in general, and moved to the domain of the need of the spirit. Truth, Nietzsche affirms, could be "precisely what is needed for the preservation of beings like us" (BGE 3)[10]. The yearning of "the European" for a universal measure is interpreted here as a type of person's physiological requirement to control the contingent relations of life. In the final analysis, this describes the type of life that yearns to standardize life itself[11]. Nietzsche takes this decisive step in aphorism 4:

> We do not consider the falsity of a judgment as itself an objection to a judgment: this is perhaps where our new language will sound most foreign. The question is how far the judgment promotes and preserves life, how well it preserves, and perhaps even cultivates, the type. And we are fundamentally inclined to claim that the falsest judgments (which include synthetic judgments *a priori*) are the most indispensable to us, and that without accepting the fictions of logic, without measuring reality against the wholly invented world of the

---

10 In a posthumous note from April – June 1885, he affirms: "*Truth is the kind of error* without which a particular kind of living creature could not live." NL 34[253] KSA 11.506 = WLN 16.

11 This hypothesis is treated in detail by Nietzsche in Aphorism 5 of the section "Morality as Anti-Nature" of *Twilight of the Idols*. Here he affirms: "A condemnation of life on the part of the living is, in the end, only the symptom of a certain type of life (...)".

unconditional and self-identical, without a constant falsification
of the world through numbers, people could not live – that a
renunciation of false judgments would be a renunciation of life, a
negation of life (BGE 4).

The heart of this thesis is the strict bond between modalities of human
knowledge and the preservation of types, between life and the values
that philosophy has produced so far – the greatest example of this
being the Kantian synthetic judgments *a priori*. The nourishment
of European thought in all its forms has always depended on this
relation between knowledge and the preservation of types of life.
Thus, the attentive reader of Nietzsche's "new language" should
find the guideline of his thought in Part 1 of BGE, which carries
out a programmatic and rigorous investigation into the tradition of
European philosophy, as well as on other related areas of knowledge –
such as is the case with his attack on the *Naturwissenschaft*. The
central thesis thus appears to be this: philosophical thought developed
and strengthened itself following a need for the regulation of life,
having thus allowed for the preservation of certain types. Moreover,
Nietzsche further believes that from this need of preservation there
emerged a positivistic spirit which was made possible by means of
concepts, principles, and norms not really derived from reason – as
is suggested by tradition —, but by the logico-grammatical structure
of language that conditions the way of thinking of those "types" that
share in it. The themes Nietzsche repeatedly focuses on throughout
Part 1 of BGE – the seduction of grammar, the critique of the subject,
the false universality of philosophical discourse etc. – cannot be
analyzed, we believe, separately from his more general hypothesis
on the "prejudices of philosophers"; and at the heart of such an
hypothesis we find, as stated previously, the theme of life, of need, of
states of need, of the yearning to give meaning to life.

Nietzsche dedicates a great amount of attention not only to the
function of Kant's synthetic judgments *a priori* (BGE 4, 11), or to
the value of Kant's concept of a "thing in itself" (BGE 2, 16), or to the
value of his "categorical imperative" for life (BGE 5), but also to the
presuppositions of universal, philosophical discourses, such as that of
the Stoics – "living according to nature" (BGE 9) –, or of the Atomists,
for whom the atom is a "fact" (*Tatbestand*) and a substance that
remains unalterable and indecomposable in any natural occurrence

(BGE 12, 22). In this same perspective, he revisits Schopenhauer's interpretation of the concept of the will as an immediately intelligible unity of that which, for Nietzsche, is precisely "the most complicated", sc. the tensions between affects, instincts, volitions, and thoughts (BGE 16, 19). He makes a concealed reference to that "inconsistency" which is Spinoza's principle of *conatus* (BGE 13), a principle that reduces all life to forces of preservation. His scrutiny of the Cartesian proposition "I think", landmark of modern philosophy, is also rigorous (BGE 16, 17). I do not intend here to exhaust the list of names and trends in European thought mentioned, or purposely implied, in the 23 aphorisms that constitute Part 1 of BGE. My intention is to emphasize the rigor and reach of Nietzsche's interpretation, his problematizing of the conceptual and linguistic apparatus, as it is within it that he finds material for investigating the tensions of the spirit. The diagnostic he promotes in Part 1, his diagnostic of European culture and its ideals, is not based on mere empirical observation of facts and daily events of his time, nor does it consist of generic theses on this culture's history, but rather on a detailed and, so to speak, hermeneutic reading of that which was effectively inherited by 19th century German philosophy, namely the prejudices, convictions and beliefs that remain in the discourse and thought of European man. Nietzsche offers a list of the certainties and beliefs that, by sheer "atavism" (BGE 20), remain untouched in European culture. In this sense, Nietzsche's examination of such concepts and principles as "I", "cause and effect", "soul", "substance", "matter", "thing in itself", "free will", "*causa sui*", etc., is not merely a general critique of the assumptions that structure the logic of philosophical thought. Above all, it is rather a profound reflection on those needs and interests of the spirit which produced and fostered the tradition's philosophical discourse. From this follows Nietzsche's objection to the way philosophers have so far reflected upon this conceptual apparatus. Not having understood the logic that regulates thought in general, the tradition has interpreted the fundamental concepts of philosophical language as though they were obvious, undeniable axiomatic formulations. Hence, Nietzsche's effort to revisit the language of philosophy and how this language is written and affirmed.

In fact, Nietzsche conceives his way of making philosophy as suspicion (*Misstrauen*, BGE 10, 12), as "disbelief in everything built

230 André Muniz Garcia

yesterday and today" (BGE 10)[12]. His suspicion regarding Europe's ideals results from his questioning of tradition, from his enlarged understanding of the dynamics and of the assumptions of European philosophy, and especially, from his rejection of any and all self-evidence: of a concept, a principle, or of any belief bequeathed by philosophical discourse. The beginning of BGE 19 is a good example of this rejection of any and all self-evidence:

> Philosophers tend to talk about the will as if it were the most familiar (*bekannteste*) thing in the world. In fact, Schopenhauer would have us believe that the will is the only thing that is really familiar (*bekannt*), familiar (*bekannt*) through and through, without pluses or minuses (BGE 19).

The adjective *bekannt* in German – repeatedly used in this passage – indicates something that one has a prior knowledge of, something that is essentially familiar. In the particular case of Schopenhauer, he found this familiarity in the expression "I want", and thought it denoted the clear and immediate presence of acts of will (BGE 16). In BGE 20, Nietzsche deals precisely with atavism, i.e. with the concepts that are shared and disseminated, without being questioned, by those who think in accordance with a "familiar" grammatical logic. Hence the prejudices of philosophers: constrained by the form of language, they constructed their theories and tried to ground their theses as though these were self-evident. This is why Nietzsche proposes the creation of a "new language" that will sound "most foreign" (BGE 4) to the Western tradition of thought, which lacks "the sharpest of ears" (BGE 10).

Language, Evidence and Symptoms: Nietzsche's Treatment of Moral Phenomena in BGE 186 and 187

The hypotheses Nietzsche developed in Part 1 of BGE are of great value to understand the ground upon which European philosophical thought built a rigorous *system* for the valuation and interpretation of reality, a vision of the world that became victorious, according to

---

12 Cf. GS 346: "The more mistrust, the more philosophy." ("*So viel Misstrauen, so viel Philosophie*", KSA 3.580). This way of understanding philosophy already appears in HH I, especially in Aphorisms 614 and 635.

Nietzsche, exactly because it gave the European man the possibility to schematize different areas of life in accordance with a rigorous conceptual apparatus. While investigating this conceptual apparatus, Nietzsche realized not only what were the conditions of its emergence, but, moreover, showed how philosophy in the West, throughout two millennia, never accomplished a definitive break from the value projected by each word, each affirmation, each conclusion of the several philosophical perspectives it gave rise to.

As one can read in the Platonic dialogues, philosophy aims at wisdom and wants to become universal knowledge. Thus, it has disregarded the fact that it is itself a particular form of understanding the world. Philosophy has its own limited horizons, which Nietzsche thinks he has analysed with great care in Part 1 of BGE; these limits are the very limits of all languages of Indo-European descent (BGE 20). In this way, what allows Nietzsche to connect thoughts and philosophical theories separated by centuries of tradition is his problematization of the presuppositions of all philosophical discourse, i.e. an examination of what it means to "understand" philosophical words, propositions, statements – and why they can be taken to be self-evident. Thus, he affirms in GS 346 that the principal task of the so-called philosophers of the future is to be suspicious of everything that was created by the ideas of the "the European". To be suspicious or problematize what it means "to understand" in philosophy, the alleged self-evident nature of philosophical discourse and its "familiarity", is the intention behind Nietzsche's principle interventions in all of the domains of the spirit (theory of knowledge, ethics, aesthetics, and logic): it is, above all, a rigorous and dynamic method of interpretation, not only of a particular way of thinking in philosophy, but of the most general elements of philosophical discourse (writing, speaking, affirming, concluding, etc.). In order to clarify the importance Nietzsche gives to this subject matter, we propose here an analysis of the first two aphorisms of Part 5 of BGE. These two aphorisms problematize the way philosophers attempt to ground morality.

First, the very title of Part 5 should be emphasized: "On the Natural History of Morals". *Naturgeschichte* is a word with a clear meaning, and pertains to the 19th century debate regarding the new perspectives opened up by the natural sciences on the historical evolution of the cosmos, flora and fauna systems, of geological formations, and especially regarding the historical evolution of man: in short,

Nietzsche abandons both the creationist model (in theology) and the foundational method (in Classical moral philosophy), and embraces the scientifico-evolutionary perspective[13]. Thus, the title of Part 5 refers to this 19th century context, in which the belief in reason, as a source from where cognition and morality were supposed to stem, fell apart. It is precisely to this context that Nietzsche refers to in the first lines of BGE 186, where he refers to the recent attempt in Europe to "scientifically" analyse morality – which indirectly indicates an important distancing from his positions taken in the second section of *Human, All Too Human* (volume I), regarding the promising reach of scientific investigation into the deciphering of moral sentiments, a perspective inherited from the Darwinist Paul Rée.[14]

---

13   Cf. *Naturgeschichte* in Ritter, J./Gründer, K. (1984). In a posthumous note from the autumn of 1884 – the autumn of 1885, the word *Naturgeschichte* appears to be connected to the name of the Darwinist Friedrich von Hellwald (NL 39[21] KSA 9.627), who between 1883 and 1885 published two volumes of his work *"Die Naturgeschichte des Menschen"*. From what Nietzsche affirms in another note, spring of 1881 – summer of 1882, his feelings regarding the intellectual production of von Hellwald was not positive: "Hellwald, Häckel und Consorten – sie haben die Stimmung der Spezialisten, und eine Froschnasen-Weisheit. (...) Diese Spezialisten haben sie [sc. eine Empfindung für das Dasein] nicht und sind deshalb so „kalt"; Bildungskamele, auf deren Höckern viel gute Einsichten und Kenntnisse sitzen, ohne zu hindern, daß das Ganze doch eben nur ein Kamel ist" (NL 11[299] KSA 9.556). Ernst Häckel, renowned Darwinist, was a personal friend of Paul Rée. The title of BGE Part 5 may have been inspired in W. E. H. Lecky's *History of European Morals*. Cf. Van Tongeren (1989). However, it is clear that Nietzsche rejects the English type of evolutionary "natural history of morals".

14   Regarding the scientific rigor of the psychology of Paul Rée, Nietzsche writes effusively: "However credit and debit balance may stand: at its present state as a specific individual science the awakening of moral observation has become necessary, and mankind can no longer be spared the cruel sight of the moral dissecting table and it's knives and forceps. For here there rules that science which asks after the origin and history of the so-called moral sensations and which as it progresses has to pose and solve the sociological problems entangled with them: – the older philosophy knows nothing of the latter and has, with paltry evasions, always avoided investigation of the origin and history of the moral sensations." On Rée as a Darwinist, Ruckenbauer (2002, 90) argues: „Paul Rées Selbsteinschätzung weist jedenfalls in eine eindeutige Richtung: Er stand ganz im Banne des neuen Paradigmas und rehte sich selbst unter die „Darwinianer" ein. Das geht nicht zuletzt aus einem Brief an Ernst Haeckel vom 27.2.1876 unzweifelhaft hervor. Darin beklagt Rée die noch immer geringe Zahl an Gelehrten, die in ihren Ideen Darwin anhingen. Das Schreiben schließt mit seinem eigentlichen Anlaß: „Beifolgend nehme ich

Nietzsche takes note of this perspective. The science of morality (*Wissenschaft der Moral*), according to Nietzsche, is a "young, neophyte, clumsy, and crude" (BGE 186) movement in European thought that is directed toward the positivism of the so-called *moralis philosophia*. Nietzsche examines the prejudice that supports this positivism, namely the claim that the origin of moral phenomena can be scientifically demonstrated with reference to the laws of nature. Now, this was exactly Paul Rée's aim, who in the Preface of *The Origin of the Moral Sensations*, made use of an analogy between the aim of his investigation and that of geology.[15] Due to the inaccuracies of philosophical method, affirms Rée, only natural science in its most recent configuration, sc. the theory of evolution, is able to examine and map out, with rigor and scientific objectivity, the origin of the most ordinary moral sentiments, such as: good, evil, conscience, responsibility, justice, etc.[16]

However, it should be noted that a few lines below, still in BGE 186, Nietzsche generalizes and assembles all the philosophical schools and trends into one group: the philosophers, all who in Europe until now have tried to treat morality scientifically. He writes:

Philosophers have all demanded (with ridiculously stubborn seriousness) something much more exalted, ambitious, and solemn

---

mir die Freiheit Ihren, dem großen Fortbildner der Darwinischen Lehre eine kurze Zusammenfassung der moralischen Probleme, im Anschluß an Darwin, vorzulegen". Dabei handelte e sich um einen ersten Entwurf von „Der Ursprung der moralischen Empfindungen" – damals noch unter dem Arbeitstitel „Abriß einer Moralphilosophie" –, den Rée zusammen mit seinen „Psychologischen Beobachtungen" an Haeckel sandte".

15   "Gleichwie der Geologe zunächst die verschiedenen Funktionen aufsucht und beschreibt und dann nach den Ursachen forscht, durch welche sie entstanden sind, so auch hat der Verfasser [implicit in this text] die moralischen Phänomene zunächst aus der Erfahrung aufgenommen und ist dann der Geschichte ihrer Entstehung, soweit es in seinen Kräften stand, nachgegangen". Rée (2005, 23).

16   Regarding this context, Ruckenbauer (2002, 95–96) comments: "Die Philosophie [as understood by *Paul Rée*] existiere als Wissenschaft eigentlich gar nicht, da sie vorwiegend „übernatürliche Bedeutung" zum Erklärung ihrer Probleme mache (*Entstehung des Gewissens*, 5). (...) In Rées Sicht tragen näherhin zwei Gründe Schuld am zurückgebliebenen Zustand der Moralphilosophie: „1) die Naturwissenschaftliche Methode des Vergleichs und der genetischen Entwicklung, welche allen zum Verständnis des Moralischen führen kann, ist erst in neueren Zeit zur Anwendung gekommen. 2) Natürliche Erklärungen der moralischen Phänomene erscheinen besonders gotteslästerlich und staatsgefährlich." (Entstehung des Gewissens, 6).

as soon as they took up morality as a science: they wanted morality
to be *grounded*, – and every philosopher so far has thought he
has provided a ground for morality. Morality itself, however, was
thought to be 'given' (BGE 186).

It would, again, be too vague to say that this grouping of philosophers is justified by the simple fact that all philosophers make a foundational claim concerning morality. Nietzsche does not use, and this
seems clear in his argument, the term "ground" in the metaphysical sense of tracing back the conditioned to an unconditional first
cause. Nietzsche was aware that the new methods and techniques of
analysis derived from the natural sciences shaped other goals, which
are distinct from those of the metaphysical tradition. The common
element of all scientific discourses on moral phenomena – and this
is what Nietzsche appears to want to emphasize – is what he calls
the "ridiculously stubborn seriousness", or the philosophers' demand
for "something much more exalted, ambitious, and solemn" (BGE
186). However, it is not enough to connect, without further clarification, seriousness and science: Nietzsche needs to explain how the
basis of this relationship is constructed. Such a relationship comes
to be when philosophy refuses to adopt a "more modest" stance, as
Nietzsche would say, and instead examines morality from the standpoint of objectivity, systemization and universality. This is essentially
what Nietzsche understands here to be the search for a "ground". On
the other hand, what every moralist's thought reveals of itself is that
it takes morality as a "given", as self-evident, as a *factum* – and this
is what interests Nietzsche the most. The pathos of seriousness, as
Nietzsche points out in GS 88, betrays "how shallow and undemand-
ing [one's] mind has been in playing the field of knowledge so far"
(GS 88). The demand for objectivity and truth hides the weakness of
scientific seriousness.

Thus Nietzsche's philosophical effort will have to focus, again, on
the problem of self-evidence: what philosophy has so far taken to
be "given" and immediately intelligible is, in truth, questionable and
doubtful; its origin is historically obscure, hidden by relationships
that do not necessarily follow each other in a causal order[17]. In fact,

---

17 Cf. GM II 12: „(...) und die ganze Geschichte eines „Dings", eines Organs,
    eines Brauchs kann dergestalt eine fortgesetzte Zeichen-Kette von immer neuen
    Interpretationen und Zurechtmachungen sein, deren Ursachen selbst unter sich

the result of this new philosophical approach is simply this: one must seek new ways of examining moral phenomena beyond a *science* of morality. Morality itself must be problematized. In other words: what Nietzsche intends is to raise radical suspicion against the way traditional moral philosophy has tried to make its interpretations scientific-like. In this direction he claims:

> (...) moral philosophers had only a crude knowledge of moral *facta*, selected arbitrarily and abbreviated at random – for instance, as the morality of their surroundings, their class, their church, their *Zeitgeist*, their climate and region, – precisely because they were poorly informed (and not particularly eager to learn more) about people, ages, and histories, they completely missed out on the genuine problems involved in morality, problems that only emerge from a comparison of many *different* moralities. Strange as it may sound, the problem of morality itself has been *missing* from every 'science of morals' so far (...) (BGE 186).

This passage presents a concrete hypothesis regarding the fetters that have so far prevented philosophers from clarifying, not the ground or origin of morality, but its facticity. Nietzsche's idea is that their common culture shapes their morality, i.e. their basic values. Moral philosophers are fettered to cultural processes from which their ideas and beliefs emerge, so that the words, signs, representations, values, rules and principles they create are, in fact, essentially the same as those of "their surroundings, their class, their church, their *Zeitgeist*". Their very identity is dependent on the identity of the group they belong to, and this identity is a particular morality, a bundle of values and customs that are taken for granted and function as if they were valid for all.

Thus, Nietzsche focuses his investigation on how people understand their identity, i.e. on the values that regulate the relations among

---

nicht im Zusammenhange zu sein brauchen, vielmehr unter Umständen sich bloss zufällig hinter einander folgen und ablösen. „Entwicklung" eines Dings, eines Brauchs, eines Organs ist demgemäss nichts weniger als sein Progressus auf ein Ziel hin, noch weniger ein logischer und kürzester, mit dem kleinsten Aufwand von Kraft und Kosten erreichter progressus, – sondern die Aufeinanderfolge von mehr oder minder tiefgehenden, mehr oder minder von einander unabhängigen, an ihm sich abspielenden Überwältigungsprozessen, hinzugerechnet die dagegen jedes Mal aufgewendeten Widerstände, die versuchten Form-Verwandlungen zum Zweck der Vertheidigung und Reaktion, auch die Resultate gelungener Gegenaktionen". KSA 5,314f.

persons who share in the same culture, values that they understand immediately in the same way. An age is defined by what is familiar, unquestionable, and easily accepted by those who share in the same culture. Thus, the spirit of an age (*Zeitgeist*) is not defined, as Hegel suggests[18], by the actuality and destiny of a people's *rational* principles, values, thoughts, and customs, but rather, Nietzsche proposes, by the concrete history of how a group, a community, or a people have constituted themselves as a group, a community, or a people through the *conventional* institution of their signs, values, thoughts, and customs (as shown by Josef Simon)[19].

In this way, instead of considering morality to be a rational ordering of insights, interests, and behaviours, Nietzsche believes morality to be brought about by a complex, yet vigorous process of moralization and this process to be already a symptom showing certain values being taken for granted in a shared "understanding", or "herd-perspective". This seems to be Nietzsche's idea in a posthumous note written after BGE, in which he denies that the European might be a "superior type of man". He writes:

> 'Understanding' is not a sign of highest force, but of *throughout fatigue*; *moralization* itself is a '*décadence*' (NL 5[89] KSA 12.223 = WLN 122).

But what is the real importance of this statement for the more general thesis presented by the first aphorism of BGE Part 5? And how does Nietzsche articulate this relationship between understanding and morality – between taking a basic set of valuations for granted and the development of culture? And how does he articulate this relationship– and this seems to be the most decisive – between the spirit of an age and what he calls "moralization", which is here understood as a process inherent to European history? First, it is necessary to point out that such a hypothesis does not differ from the general goal of Part 5: Nietzsche's "natural history of morality" is not a "scientific" investigation. In BGE 186, Nietzsche does set the task of "collecting material, formulating concepts, and putting into order the tremendous realm of tender value feelings and value distinctions that live, grow, reproduce, and are destroyed" (BGE 186). But he intends

---

18 This idea is elaborated, for instance, in Hegel (2007).
19 Simon (1989), especially section 24: *Zeichenkonvention*.

this "collecting of material" – which is more similar to the ancient historians' collecting of material than to an evolutionary "science" of morals – as a means to the end of philosophical reflection. The "typology" envisioned by Nietzsche is propedeutical in relation to a new type of philosophical reflection, which dispenses with "scientific proof". Moreover, the focal point of his interest is not *variety*, but rather the most elevated manifestations of the spirit in philosophy, literature, poetry, music, and science. This is my main hypothesis in this paper. To borrow a well-known phrase from BGE 285, Nietzsche's principal concern is with "the greatest thoughts" that gave origin to the "greatest event": European culture. These thoughts are the ones he really intends to collect and describe, and the philosophical conclusions he draws from his collecting and describing do not claim to be definitive "truths"[20].

It is against this backdrop that we interpret the long quotation in BGE 186 from the "scientific" work of Arthur Schopenhauer, *On the Basis of Morality*. Nietzsche writes:

> For example, let us listen to the almost admirable innocence with which even Schopenhauer describes his own project, and then we can draw our conclusions as to how scientific a 'science' could be when its ultimate masters are still talking like children or old women. 'The principle', he says (p. 136 of the *Grundprobleme der Moral*), 'the fundamental claim, on whose content all ethicists *actually* agree: *neminem laede, immo omnes, quantum potes, juva* [harm no one, but rather help everyone as much as you can] – this is *actually* the claim that all moralists attempt to ground... the *actual* foundation of ethics that people sought for millennia, just as they have looked for the philosopher's stone' (BGE 186).

Schopenhauer's language reveals his innocence. Whereas, in the end, Schopenhauer wants to *say* that compassion is "actually" the ground of morality, Nietzsche aims to point out that Schopenhauer's "compassion" is just one aspect of the dominant morality in European culture. Nietzsche purposefully highlights the German adverb *eigentlich* ("actually"), recurrent in Schopenhauer's discourse. This adverb is a kind of "sign", or "symptom" that something is being taken for

---

20   On this topic see Stegmaier (1992, especially the chapter "Aphorismus versus System", 279 ff).

granted by a given group or community. And in fact, Schopenhauer, in his "innocence", does not hesitate in presenting the principle, "harm no one, but rather help everyone as much as you can", as self-evident; only the "ground" of this principle is, of course, supposed to have been missing for centuries. The principle of harming no one and helping everyone as much as one can is agreed upon by all simply because it is the result of a process of moralization. Abolishing such a principle would imperil the reciprocal understanding, the sense of stability, security, and confidence among the individuals that constitute the group. Moralization is the most elementary and immediate process through which values are created and the most diverse ways of thinking, feeling, wanting, and acting get schematized and become self-evident in a culture; they vary from one culture to another, but their schematization is always what gives sustenance and stability to a culture. In Nietzsche's language, they become "dominant". Morality is, as Nietzsche says in a posthumous note from the autumn of 1887, "the only *scheme of interpretation* (*Interpretationsschema*) by which man can endure himself"[21]. Schopenhauer, also, was not free of the need to take for granted the "scheme of interpretation" that enabled his culture to endure itself. Even Schopenhauer, even "a pessimist who negates both God and world" (BGE 186) – even he "*stops* before morality" (BGE 186).

As a "scheme of interpretation", morality dynamically configures itself in different ways within different cultures – according to the different *needs* of each culture and of each individual within a culture. There are as many different moralities as there are different needs. This does not exclude that all European moralities have something in common, i.e. that there is one dominant morality. One of the aims of BGE 187 is precisely to clarify this point.

This aphorism focuses on one of the "greatest thoughts" of European culture: Kant's categorical imperative. Nietzsche seems to paraphrase a well-known passage from the second *Critique* – the deduction of the moral law as *Faktum der Vernunft*[22]. Kant believes that there is a

---

21   NL 10[121] KSA 12.527 = WP 270
22   See, for example, Kant KpV, § 7, A 56: „Doch muß man, um dieses Gesetz ohne Mißdeutung als *gegeben* anzusehen, wohl bemerken: daß es kein empirisches, sondern das einzige Faktum der reinen Vernunft sei, die sich dadurch als ursprünglich gesetzgebend (*sic volo, sic iubeo*) ankündigt".

categorical imperative "in us", but what is actually meant by this "in us"? According to Kant, all men, without exception, recognize the content of the imperative as a self-evident law, and the imperative is itself a "fact of reason", because there is a rational identity common to all men. But for an age when this very idea of reason has fallen apart, what remains from Kant's claim? For Nietzsche, the question actually becomes, "what do claims like this tell us about the people who make them?" (BGE 187). Nietzsche questions the evidence for the Kantian claim by searching for the *purposes* hidden behind the very creation of the claim, as he had done with Schopenhauer. He is not concerned with the man Kant as such, but rather with the motivations, dispositions and implicit purposes of Kant's philosophical statement[23]. In BGE 6 Nietzsche had already declared that in order "to explain how the strangest metaphysical claims of a philosopher really come about, it is always good (and wise) to begin by asking: what morality is it (is *he* —) getting at?" (BGE 6). Any philosophical morality bears witness to "*who*" the philosopher is that created it – "which means, in what order of rank the innermost drives of his nature stand with respect to each other" (BGE 6). Philosophers, as individuals or as "particular types of life", create philosophical propositions because they are compelled to overcome this or that *need*. Now, in BGE 187 he takes precisely the further step of describing some of the needs that philosophical theses, and especially philosophical moralities, are meant to satisfy:

> There are moralities that are supposed to justify their creator in the eyes of others, and other moralities that are supposed to calm him down and allow him to be content with himself; still other moralities allow him to crucify and humiliate himself. He can use some moralities to take revenge, others to hide, and still others to transfigure himself and place himself far and away (BGE 187).

The plurality of moralities results from the particular needs of a plurality of particular types of life, and this allows us to see how complex the "problem of morality" is for Nietzsche. It includes the great task of classifying the different types of morality, but also the

---

23   On psychology as a form of "philosophyzing about persons" and the status of the "types" that emerge from this kind of psychology, cf. Stegmaier (1994, 94–96) and also Van Tongeren (1989, 49 ff).

task of understanding it as a manifestation (or "symptom") of life, or of different "types of life" – or even, according to BGE 188, of "nature"[24]. It is in naturalizing morality that Nietzsche distances himself from the traditional perspectives on moral phenomena in philosophy. In the language of BGE 187, moral phenomena are, for Nietzsche, "just a *sign language of the affects*" (BGE 187). That is to say, the historico-evolutionary process we call morality is now analysed as a semiotics or "sign language" of physiological needs of particular types of life. Insofar as this calls for a philosophy of *signs*, nothing is more natural than to begin by questioning the philosophical discourse as such – its signs, its valuations, its prejudices, affirmations and denials. Philosophical discourse is, thus, the fertile land where Nietzsche finds the signposts that enable him to discover the most subtle and refined changes and processes in the domain of organic, affective, instinctive life. In short: language is the source from which Nietzsche draws, with the greatest precision, his diagnostics of the physiological needs that have created all forms of morality so far. Such forms have helped man to "endure himself", they have preserved and even cultivated particular types of life – and they still do.

Bibliography

Alisson, Henry (1983), *Kant's Transcendental Idealism*, New Haven and London (Yale University Press).

Behler, Ernst (1994), "Die Sprachtheorie des frühen Nietzsche", in: Borsche, T./ Gerratana, F./Venturelli, A. (ed.), *„Centauren-Geburten". Wissenschaft, Kunst und Philosophie beim jungen Nietzsche*, Berlin/New York (Walter de Gruyter), 99–111.

Böning, Thomas (1987), *Metaphysik, Kunst und Sprache beim frühen Nietzsche*, Berlin/New York (Walter de Gruyter).

---

24 Cf. for example Stegmaier (1994, 20): „*Moral* in der Perspektive des Lebens läßt sich demnach bestimmen als das *Ensemble von Wertvorstellungen eines Einzelnen, nach denen alle leben sollen, damit er selbst leben kann*; die Moral ist, in Nietzsche eigenen Begriffen, Funktion der Erhaltungs- und Steigerungsbedingungen Einzelner. (…) Soweit Individuen, Familien, Gruppen, Gesellschaften, Kulturen ihre Erhaltungs- und Steigerungsbedingungen mitein-ander teilen, wird dieses lebensbedingte Unbedingte ihrer Moral sie miteinander verbinden. Auf andere dagegen, die diesen sozialen Gruppen nicht angehören, wirkt ihre Moral unvermeidlich diskriminierend; eben dadurch, daß eine Moral einige zu einer Gemeinschaft zusammenschließt, schließt sie andere aus".

Borsche, Tilman (1994), "*Natur-Sprache. Herder – Humboldt – Nietzsche*", in: Borsche, T./Gerratana, F./Venturelli, A. (ed.), „*Centauren-Geburten*". *Wissenschaft, Kunst und Philosophie beim jungen Nietzsche*, Berlin/ New York (Walter de Gruyter), 112–130.

Crawford, Claudia (1988), *The beginnings of Nietzsche's theory of language*, Berlin/New York (Walter de Gruyter).

Descartes, René (1973/1978), *Oeuvres*, vol. II, Adam/Tannery (ed.), Paris (Vrin).

Emden, Christian J. (2005), *Nietzsche on Language, Consciousness, and the Body*, Illinois (University of Illinois Press).

Fietz, Rudolf (1992), *Medienphilosophie. Musik, Sprache und Schrift bei Friedrich Nietzsche*, Würzburg (Königshausen & Neumann).

Garcia, André L. Muniz (2008), *Metáforas do corpo: reflexões sobre o estatuto da linguagem na filosofia do jovem Nietzsche*. Disserta,ão de Mestrado. Universidade Estadual de Campinas, Instituto de Filosofia e Ciências Humanas: Campinas, 2008. The dissertation can be downloaded from this link: http://libdigi.unicamp.br/document/?code=vtls 000439120.

Hegel, G. F. W. (2007), *Vorlesungen über die Geschichte der Philosophie*, Frankfurt am Main (Suhrkamp).

Hödl, Hans Gerald (1997), *Nietzches frühe Sprachkritik. Lektüren zu „Ueber Wahrheit und Lüge im aussermoralischen Sinne"*, Wien (WUV).

Otto, Detlef, (1994), „Die Version der Metapher zwischen Musik und Begriff", in: Borsche, T./Gerratana, F./Venturelli, A. (ed.), „*Centauren-Geburten*". *Wissenschaft, Kunst und Philosophie beim jungen Nietzsche*, Berlin/New York (Walter de Gruyter), 167–192.

Rée, Paul (2005), *Der Ursprung der moralischen Empfindung*, Bonn (DenkMal Verlag).

Reuter, Sören (2004), "Reiz – Bild – Unbewusste Anschauung: Nietzsches Auseinandersetzung mit Hermann Helmholtz' Theorie der Unbewussten Schlüsse in ‚Über Wahrheit und Lüge im Aussermoralischen Sinne'", in: *Nietzsche-Studien* 33 (2004), 351–372.

Ritter, Joachim/Gründner, Karlfried (1984), *Historisches Wörterbuch der Philosophie*, Band 6, Basel/Stuttgart (Schwabe Verlag).

Ruckenbauer, Hans-Walter (2002), *Moralität zwischen Evolution und Normen*, Würzburg (Königshausen und Neumann).

Schnädelbach, Herbert (1999), *Philosophie in Deutschland: 1831 – 1933*, Frankfurt am Main (Suhrkamp).

Simon, Josef (1989), *Philosophie des Zeichens*, Berlin/New York (Walter de Gruyter).

Stack, George J. (1983), *Lange and Nietzsche*, Berlin/New York (Walter de Gruyter).

Stegmaier, Werner (1994), *Nietzsches Genealogie der Moral*, Darmstadt (Wissenschaftliche Buchgesellschaft).

Stegmaier, Werner (1992), *Philosophie der Fluktuanz. Dilthey und Nietzsche*, Göttigen (Vandenhoeck & Ruprecht).

Van Tongeren, Paul (1989), *Die Moral von Nietzsches Moralkritik: Studien zu 'Jenseits von Gut und Böse'*, Bonn (Bouvier Verlag).

Žunjic, Slobodan (1987), „Begrifflichkeit und Metapher", in: *Nietzsche-Studien* 16 (1987), 149–163.

Zarathustra's Laughter or the *Birth of Tragedy* from the Experience of the Comic

Katia Hay

> *Und „wo Lachen und Fröhlichkeit ist,*
> *da taugt das Denken Nichts":*
> *— so lautet das Vorurteil dieser ernsten*
> *Bestie gegen alle „fröhliche Wissenschaft"*
> FW 327

The aim of the following paper is, firstly, to provide an interpretation of Nietzsche's reference to *Zarathustra* (and most particularly, to Zarathustra's *laughter*) in his preface to *The Birth of Tragedy*. It is my intention to analyze its structural significance in order to show that Nietzsche's analysis of tragedy cannot be understood as a *tragic* or a pessimistic interpretation, but as one that emerges from the experience of the *comic*, which, in its turn, must be understood as a form or a result of overcoming the utter absurdness of human life. This will lead us to a further analysis concerning the function of laughter (both as a concept and as a rhetorical method) in Nietzsche's philosophy as a whole. In effect, the fundamental question underlying my study is the question about the possibility of articulating a philosophy that constantly tries to incorporate moments of self-awareness or self-criticism.

The particular difficulty of determining the beginning of things (the beginning of life, the beginning of time, the beginning of con-sciousness, in fact, the beginning of anything at all) is that it always takes place *after* the events have occurred. We cannot determine the beginning of meaningful events - the meaning a person or a book will have in our lives - until this meaning has taken place, i.e. until *we* have given them the meaning and have searched for the origin and the sense of the present in the past, that is: until we conceive a narration of the beginning. As Sartre would say, it is in our recollec-tion, in our personal stories that occurrences acquire a beginning, a sense and a meaning.[1] Or, to put it in other words, the beginning is always retrospectively discovered and retroactively posited. And this problematic not only affects the relation between our experiences and our personal narratives; it is also constitutive for the construction of philosophical and scientific theories (such as we can see in Fichte, Schelling, Hegel or Heidegger), and, moreover, it is intrinsic to philosophy itself, i.e. to the process of producing and writing philosophical texts.[2] The real meaning of a text, the sense of a book always takes place once it is already finished. This definitely would explain why it seems almost natural and certainly necessary to compose the prologues, prefaces and introductions *after* the text has been finished. There is so to say a fundamental gap – a temporal but not necessarily logical gap – between the introduction and the rest: indeed the beginning always takes place après-coup.

In Nietzsche's case, the *gap* separating the preface (which he explicitly conceived as *An Attempt of Self-Criticism*) from the original manuscript is quite significant (15 years!). Moreover, if we bear in mind that *The Birth of Tragedy* is Nietzsche's first philosophical text, we could assume that the preface should be seen, not only as an introduction to this particular essay, but also to his philosophical work as a whole. For at the same time he indicates to us how to understand his texts, he is also showing us how he understands himself and his beginning as a philosopher. In fact, it seems that 1886 was, for Nietzsche, a moment for reconsidering and re-determining the meaning of his philosophy all together; he did not only write a new preface to the *Birth of Tragedy*, but also to *Menschliches, Allzumenschliches, Morgenröte* and *Die fröhliche Wissenschaft*.

On the other hand, if the discovery or rediscovery of the beginning of his philosophy only takes place after having found his own style and after having developed his own philosophical approach, one could

---

1   See Sartre (1964, 59–63): "Nothing happens while you live [...] there are no beginnings. Days are tacked on to days without rhyme or reason [...] But everything changes when you tell about life [i.e. when you narrate life]; things happen one way and we tell them in the opposite sense [...] In reality it's by the end that one begins. The end is there, invisible and present, and that is what gives words the pomp and ceremony of a beginning".

2   Cf. NL 6[4] KSA 12.232, my translation: "I always needed some years distance, in order to feel that imperious pleasure and energy, which is required to present (*darstellen*) such an experience, and the survival of such a condition".

object that, in this particular case, Nietzsche is actually reinventing the meaning of his book. And yet, one must also acknowledge the fact that the meaning and the sense we discover in the preface are by no means alien to the book itself. Quite to the contrary, and as Nietzsche himself notes, they remain hidden under and veiled by "all the errors of youth" and by what he calls his "youthful courage and youthful melancholy" (*voller Jugendmuth und Jugend-Schwermuth*, (BT/AS 2)[3].

It may not be difficult to grasp what Nietzsche means when he says that his book was too "courageous" and "too arrogant to prove its assertions" (KSA 1.14, BT/AS 3); that he wanted to explain too many things and that this form of arrogance, this certain metaphysical arrogance, was doomed to failure (especially if we consider his later works). For sure, these statements can be ascribed to Nietzsche's general critique of Metaphysics, to his negative attitude towards the widespread effort amongst philosophers to elaborate a perfectly comprehensible logical system, and to his (hidden) desire – as he describes in the 1886 preface to *Daybreak* – "to be incomprehensible, concealed, enigmatic" (KSA 3.11, D Preface 1)[4]. More intriguing, however, and more important to understand this special form of self-criticism is to comprehend what Nietzsche means when he reflects about his "youthful melancholy" as something which had impeded him from attaining his goal and also from saying *what he wanted to say*. In fact, it seems Nietzsche consciously decided to address this issue in the very last paragraph of his preface, leaving only a hint about the proper way to interpret it.

In what could be regarded as an internal discussion between the mature and the young philosopher, Nietzsche encourages the *young* pessimists - his young melancholy friends, the "young Romantics"- to:

> learn the art of comfort in this life – you should learn *to laugh*, my young friends, even if you really are determined to remain pessimists. [...] Or, to speak the language of that Dionysian friend called

---

3   KSA 1.13. [*Editors' note*: Speirs' translation of *The Birth of Tragedy and Other Writings* is used throughout this paper; cf. References and Citations].

4   See also KSA 2.164, HH I 190: "when an author denies his talent, merely to make himself the equal of his reader, he commits the only deadly sin that the reader will never forgive him for (if he should notice it)" [*Editors' note*: Faber and Lehmann's translation].

> *Zarathustra*: [and now quoting from his *Zarathustra*] Zarathustra
> the truth-teller, Zarathustra the true laugher, not an impatient man,
> not a man of absolutes, someone who loves jumps and leaps to the
> side [...] I throw this crown! I have sanctified laughter; you higher
> men, *learn* to laugh, I beseech you (KSA 1.21, BT/AS 7).

With these last sentences from his *Zarathustra*, Nietzsche presents the
latter as a decisive clue to (re-)interpret both his essay on ancient Greek
tragedy and his philosophy. It is, therefore, certainly not a coincidence
that youth and melancholy (*Schwermut*) are also important topics in
his *Zarathustra*.

   In the chapter "The Stillest Hour", Zarathustra hears from an
inaudible voice that there is something which he has not learnt yet,
namely to lead his own path without fear and without shame: "That is
what is most unpardonable in you: you have the power, and you do not
want to rule [...] You must yet become a child, and without shame"[5].
But, in order to become a child (which has a very specific meaning
for Zarathustra) he must first "overcome his youth" (KSA 4.189).
In his stillest hour Zarathustra's burden is provoked by his lack of
self-consciousness, which in its turn is a result of his overconfidence:
"You are not yet humble enough for me. Humility has the toughest
hide" (KSA 4.188). The adolescent Zarathustra is overwhelmed by
the world, overwhelmed also by his own identity,[6] and, like Hamlet,
overwhelmed by the tragic knowledge that nothing can change the
eternal nature of things.[7] So, in a certain sense, Zarathustra's pain,
at this point, is very similar to what Nietzsche considered to be the
real subject of Greek tragedy, namely the pain of Dionysus: the pain
of the god who experiences the anguish of individuation in himself.[8]

---

5   KSA 4.189. [*Editors' note*: Parkes' translation of *Thus spoke Zarathustra* is used
     throughout this paper; cf. References and Citations]
6   "Ah, is it my word? Who am *I*? I wait for one more worthy; I am not even worth
     being broken by it" (KSA 4.188).
7   BT 7: "Dionysiac man is similar to Hamlet: both have gazed into the true essence
     of things, they have acquired knowledge and they find action repulsive, for their
     actions can do nothing to change the eternal essence of things; they regard it as
     laughable or shameful that they should be expected to set to rights a world so out
     of joint." (KSA 1.57, BT).
8   BT 10: "But one may also say with equal certainty that, right down to Euripides,
     Dionysos never ceased to be the tragic hero [...] In truth, however, this hero is
     the suffering Dionysos of the Mysteries, the god who experiences the sufferings
     of individuation " (KSA 1.71, BT).

A suffering which - in his *Birth of Tragedy* - Nietzsche considers to be "the source and ground for all suffering, as something in itself reprehensible" (*Quell und Urgrund alles Leidens, als etwas an sich Verwerfliches*, KSA 1.71, BT 10).

Conversely, in *Zarathustra* this form of apathy or melancholy (which certainly results from a *misconception* of the boundaries between life and art),[9] is regarded as a *symptom* of youth; and 'youth', as we have seen above, is something which must be overcome. The seemingly insurmountable troubles and gloomy spirit pervading and haunting young thoughts must be surmounted and replaced with the lightness and vividness of a child; an idea, which also provides a possible reading of the image of the bridge: "What is great in the human is that it is a bridge and not a goal" (KSA 4.16, ZA Preface 4). Thus, when Nietzsche says that his first book is full of youthful melancholy, he means that his book was, in a sense, too pessimistic and grievous, and that this solemn romanticism is not a sign for some kind of deep, mature wisdom, but of unripeness.[10] Quoting the laughing-truth-sayer Zarathustra, what Nietzsche claims in his preface to the *Birth of Tragedy* is the necessity to overcome pessimism, to overcome Romanticism, to overcome melancholy, and also, to overcome Christianity: for Jesus, says Zarathustra, was also too pessimistic and too young to overcome himself:

> Verily, too early did that Hebrew die whom the preachers of slow death honour [...] He still knew only the tears and the heavy heart (*Schwehrmut*)[11] of the Hebrew, together with hatred on the part of the good and the righteous – The Hebrew Jesus: then he was overcome by a yearning for death. If only he had remained in the wilderness and far from the good and the righteous! Perhaps he would have learned to live and learned to love the earth – and to laugh as well! (KSA 4.95, ZA I On Free Death).

---

9   Cf. NL Ende 1870 - April 1871, 7[29] KSA 7.145: „Die Tragödie ist schön, insofern der Trieb, der das Schreckliche im Leben schafft, hier als Kunsttrieb, mit seinem Lächeln, als spielendes Kind erscheint. Darin liegt das Rührende und Ergreifende der Tragödie an sich, daß wir den entsetzlichen Trieb zum Kunst- und Spieltrieb vor uns sehn". See also ZA II On the Poets.
10   Cf. ZA I The Stillest Hour: "Oh Zarathustra, your fruits are ripe, but you are not ripe for your fruits!" (KSA 4.189).
11   The German word here is *Schwermut* which other authors rightly translate with "melancholy".

From these passages we can assume that when Zarathustra encourages us to *learn to laugh*, he is encouraging us to learn to overcome ourselves, to overcome our romantic, melancholic, pessimistic, nihilistic (but still adolescent) "truths". Laughter somehow symbolizes the act of overcoming, of surpassing and is therefore a characteristic feature of the *Übermensch* and Zarathustra himself.[12] Moreover, one could also say that laughter becomes a symbol of Nietzsche's philosophy as such, or at least of an important aspect or moment of his philosophy.[13] And yet, when Zarathustra says, as Nietzsche recalls in his preface, that we must learn to laugh, he also means that we must learn to laugh *properly*. For sure, it is not a question of laughing any kind of laughter.[14] Zarathustra's laughter is not an ignorant laughter; it is not even an evil and despising laughter, except for when contempt is also a sign for respect.[15] Laughter must be a symbol, as he says in the *Gay Science*, of height and lightness, even of gloat, but "with good conscience" (KSA 3.506, GS 200)[16]. It is as if there were a difference between an unconscious, almost immediate, animal, dumb laughter, and an active and conscious laughter: a divine, gay laughter that can only be attained after having learnt to take life with a certain distance or as he would say in his *Gay Science* as a "means to knowledge" (GS 324)[17].

---

12 In his *Nachgelassene Fragmente* (NL Herbst1881, 13[4] KSA 9.618f), Nietzsche also uses laughter as a way of expressing his profound criticism and consequent overcoming of certain (pessimistic) philosophers such as Schopenhauer: "Ich lache über die Aufzählungen des Schmerzes und Elends, wodurch sich der Pessimismus zurecht beweisen will – Hamlet und Schopenhauer und Voltaire und Leopardi und Byron. »Das Leben ist etwas, das nicht sein sollte, wenn es sich nur so erhalten kann!« – sagt ihr. Ich lache über dies »Sollte« und stelle mich zum Leben hin, um zu helfen, daß aus dem Schmerze so reich wie möglich Leben wachse".

13 See the motto (added in 1887) of Nietzsche's *Gay Science*: "This house is my own and here I dwell,/I've never aped nothing from no one/and – laugh at each master, mark me well,/who at himself has not poked fun" (KSA 3.343, GS).

14 Cf. Z Preface 5: "When Zarathustra had spoken these words, he looked at the people again and was silent. 'There they stand.' He said to his heart, 'there they laugh: they do not understand me, I am not the mouth for these ears." (KSA 4.18)

15 Z Preface 3: "I love great despisers, for they are the great reverers and arrows of yearning for the other shore" (KSA 4.14).

16 Cf. NL 11[183] KSA 9.512: "lachen, spotten, ohne Verbitterung vernichten!"

17 "*Life as a means to knowledge* – with this principle in one's heart one can not only live bravely but also *live gaily and laugh gaily!*" (KSA 3.553).

Indeed, the comprehension of what it means to *laugh properly* evokes important questions concerning Nietzsche's criticism of morality and his existential and philosophical standpoints. But, in a sense - and this is what I believe to be one of Nietzsche's central points in his preface to *The Birth of Tragedy* – this same preoccupation was also underlying his analysis of the so called "Greek cheerfulness" or Greek *Heiterkeit* in his early writings. As we can read in *The Dionysiac World View*:

> Measured against the gravity, the sanctity and severity of other religions, Greek religion is in danger of being underestimated as a playful fantasy – unless one includes in one's representation of it an often overlooked trait of most profound wisdom, so that the Epicurean life of the gods suddenly appears to be a creation of that incomparable artist-people, indeed almost as its supreme creation (KSA 1.560, my translation).

In other words, the insight we get after understanding the meaning of Zarathustra's laughter is by no means opposed to Nietzsche's thoughts in his essays on Greek tragedy and Greek religion. Quite on the contrary, Nietzsche's reference to Zarathustra and to laughter is rather an invitation to pay special attention to certain elements of his essay, which otherwise might pass unnoticed. It is as if Nietzsche were giving us a special key to reread *The Birth of Tragedy* in order to understand its 'real' meaning – a meaning that, as Nietzsche stresses, was latently present at the moment of its first conception. It is as if Nietzsche were reminding us that it would be false to believe that the truth or the essence of tragedy and the Dionysian should lead to a melancholic and pessimistic view of life, to a negation of life.

Indeed, with those lines in mind, where Zarathustra-Nietzsche encourages us to learn to laugh, the passage from the *Birth of Tragedy* (also depicted in other early writings),[18] where king Midas chases the wise *Silenus*, may acquire a new tone; we gain a new interpretative perspective. In fact, this whole scene, where the reader is supposed to understand "popular Greek wisdom" can be read as a comical scene, rather than a tragic one.

> Yet we must call out to this spectator who has already turned away: 'Do not go away, but listen first to what popular Greek wisdom has

---

18   Cf. *Die Geburt des tragishen Gedankens* (KSA 1.588).

to say about this inexplicable serene existence you see spread out
before you here.' An ancient legend recounts how King Midas for
a long time hunted the wise *Silenus*, the companion of Dionysos,
without catching him. When Silenus finally fell into the king's hands,
the King asked what was the best and most excellent thing for human
beings. The daemon remained silent, stiff and unmoving, until,
forced by the King to speak, he finally broke out into shrill laughter
and said: "Wretched creature, born for a day, child of accident and
toil, what is the most unpleasant thing for you to hear? The very
best thing is utterly beyond your reach not to have been born, *to be
nothing*. However the second best thing for you is: to die soon (KSA
1.35, BT 3).

Apart from the funny image of King Midas desperately chasing a satyr,
not truly understanding the meaning of his hunting, searching for a
truth he is not really prepared to hear; what is interesting here is that
the terrible and cruel truth, a truth that only Silenus and Dionysus can
bear, is accompanied by a "shrill laughter". Silenus laughs, because
he knows more about men than men do. He laughs because he knows
the secret about life's senselessness, and he knows that this knowledge
is necessary for overcoming oneself. But this does not mean that he
is immune to life's futility; on the contrary, like the Dionysiac man
he is "painfully broken" (BT 7)[19]. His laughter is thus indispensable,
because it provides him with the necessary distance which enables
him to cope with this truth, to overcome it. He laughs and in that
very instance he detaches himself from himself – which by no means
implies a loss of sense; it rather implies a form of acceptance of the
absolute absurdity ("a release from the disgust at absurdity", KSA
1.57, BT 7, my translation), and a special form of dealing with the
total lack of sense and permanent contradiction of the world. The
alleged cheerfulness of the ancient Greeks was not the result of a lack
of profundity, lack of pain and lack of severity, as many had thought,
but a result of this very insight; the acceptance and the overcoming
of it.[20]

---

19   KSA 1.57. See also "Die dionysische Weltanschauung" 3 (KSA 1. 568), where
     Nietzsche refers to Dionysus as that „zwiespältige[s] Wesen".
20   See also GS Preface 4: "Those Greeks were superficial – *out of profundity!*" (KSA
     3.351).

Furthermore, for Nietzsche, this unbearable truth expressed by the satyr also sets the basis for understanding (Greek) art. In fact Nietzsche's approach to art is almost phenomenological; it's not so much a question of what art represents, but about its function or meaning for life.[21] Art is not to be understood as a representation of something (of the "Absolute" for instance, like it had been for Hegel or Schelling) or the fulfillment (through a heroic character) of a superhuman integrity, which would awake the desire to imitate art – to imitate Goethe's Werther, for instance! Art is seen as the eternal force of creating new meanings and reinventing new forms. And this is only possible after having realized that the true ground of reality is a formless, dionysiac whirl of chaotic, senseless energies. For Nietzsche, this realization is only fully manifested in Greek tragedy and Greek comedy. This is why he says that "the sublime and the comical are a step beyond the world of beautiful semblance"(KSA 1.567, The Dionysiac World View 3).

In a certain sense, one could say that the satyr's laughter also expresses this very insight and hints towards this possible overcoming and this possible joyfulness (which is decidedly not frivolous or naïve).[22] Silenus' laughter reflects the hidden secret about an eternal source of creativity. And this is precisely Nietzsche's standpoint. In other words, Nietzsche's perspective is not itself tragic,[23] his approach is not pessimistic, romantic, resigned, that is, Schopenhauerian;[24] it rather emerges from the perspective or the experience of the absurd and the comic, i.e. from the experience of overcoming one's own *tragic* or fatal fate.[25] Therefore, although "tragedy" or the "tragic" have traditionally been perceived as major themes in Nietzsche's *Birth*

---

21 BT/AS 2: "[...] the task this reckless book first dared to approach: *to look at science through the prism of the artist, but also to look at art through the prism of life.*" (KSA 1.14).

22 Cf. NL 19[7] KSA 9.676: "Eine ernste Kunst ist Lachen".

23 One should also be careful about mistaking tragedy and the dionysiac with the tragic. When Nietzsche refers to the "tragic" he describes it as an "irresolvable conflict" (KSA 1.75, BT 11).

24 Indeed Zarathustra's affirmativeness and joyfulness goes hand in hand with Nietzsche's revaluation of Schopenhauer's conception of Greek tragedy as a representation of resignation: "how differently Dionysus spoke to me! How alien to me at the time was precisely this whole philosophy of resignation!" (BT/AS 6, KSA 1.20).

25 Cf. "*Amor fati*" (GS 276, KSA 3.521).

of Tragedy, it is important to see the extent to which Nietzsche's analysis is different from other (romantic and/or metaphysical) comprehensions of the tragic. It is important to see the extent to which Nietzsche's interpretation of tragedy, Nietzsche's perspective is much more *detached*. As he would say a year later in his *Genealogy of Morality*, the great tragedian "like every artist, [...] only reaches the final summit of his achievement when he knows how to see himself and his art *beneath* him, - and knows how to *laugh* at himself." (GM III 3, KSA 5. 342. Diete's translation).

In his *Birth of Tragedy* Nietzsche refers to life as the "Divine Comedy of life" (KSA 1.27, BT 1) and we find a similar idea in his *Gay Science*. But in the latter Nietzsche notes that "at present, the comedy of existence has not yet 'become conscious' of itself; at present we still live in the age of tragedy, in the age of moralities and religions" (KSA 3. 370, GS 1). And some lines above he had said: "To laugh at oneself as one would have to laugh in order to laugh *from the whole truth* – for that, not even the best have had enough sense of truth, and the most gifted have had far too little genius!" (KSA 3.370, GS 1). That is to say: in Nietzsche's texts we find a direct link between the notion of laughter and the notions of overcoming and self-awareness, so that it does not seem at all erroneous to consider that Nietzsche's standing point in his analysis of tragedy is given through the experience of the comic: "to see tragic natures succumb and still be able to laugh [...] this is divine" (KSA 10.63, 3[1] 80, my translation).

According to Hegel, ancient Comedy announces the destruction of the Greek world: it is the sign of the overcoming of a certain worldview, namely of the "tragic" worldview. But in the worldview of the Greeks, as Nietzsche rightly notes, tragedy and comedy are essentially intertwined, coexistent and interdependent. As Plato pointed out in his *Symposium* – tragedy and comedy need to be thought together. Comedies, we could argue, were not accidentally intended to be played during the same religious festivities as tragedies, but were necessary to create a distance, a background, a perspective out of which the tragic could be readily understood.[26] And this is precisely the perspective out of which Nietzsche is seeking to understand the essence of Greek tragedy.

---

26   Cf. Ley (2006).

However, if, as we have argued until now, Nietzsche believes that what he is disclosing in his preface is already present in his essay on Greek tragedy, then there must be another reason for him to consider his book a relative failure. Likewise, Nietzsche's exclamation "learn *to laugh*, my young friends" (KSA 1.21, GT/VS 7) must bear another meaning and function. Indeed, we must not forget that Nietzsche not only uses the term *laughter*; he also uses laughter as a certain rhetorical method. Nietzsche very often makes the reader laugh; so much so that, as Deleuze said, to read Nietzsche without laughing would almost be like not reading Nietzsche at all.[27] Therefore, our task must also be to consider these moments of laughter (and complicity) between the reader and the text in order to comprehend their significance for understanding Nietzsche and the experience of reading his texts. In a sense, it is a question about the ways in which Nietzsche's particular use of language helps him to communicate thoughts without having to make them explicit, without having to say them, i.e. forcing the reader's intuition to bring other non linguistic, more basic or instinctive elements in play in order to grasp the hidden meaning of the texts.

At a second glance, the main purpose of Nietzsche's preface seems to be to explain what he was actually saying in his *Birth of Tragedy*, but had failed to convey properly, due to what we might call his *stylistic immaturity*. That is, what Nietzsche criticizes from his essay is its *formal* aspect; as if he had not found the right style to express his thoughts in order to be truly understood:

> I wonder if the reader understands which task I was already daring to undertake with this book? I now regret very much that I did not yet have the courage (or immodesty?) at that time to permit myself a *language of my very own* for such personal views and acts of daring, laboring instead to express strange and new evaluations in Schopehauerian and Kantian formulations, things which fundamentally ran counter to both the spirit and the taste of Kant and Schopenhauer (KSA 1.19, BT/AS 6).

In a similar vein he says that he "ought to have sung [...] and not talked! What a pity it is that I did not dare to say what I had to say at the same time as a poet" (KSA 1.15, BT/AS 3). In brief, Nietzsche

---

27   Deleuze (2003, 257).

believes he should have been less explicit: he should have "sung", he should have spoken "as a poet", he should have been less "convinced", less "arrogant"; but all of this only *in order to* be more expressive, more eloquent, in order to say more than can be said through words and logical arguments taken from other thinkers, imitating their style and conceptual frameworks.

It is indeed quite significant that, for Nietzsche, all these "errors" do not involve the content of his thoughts, but rather the *way* in which they were presented and defended. One could almost say that, from a Nietzschean point of view, in order to criticize Kant or Schopenhauer, one needs to create a new language, a new style, lest one remains Kantian or Schopenhauerian by using their same expressions. To conceive, for instance, the principle of individuation as the source of all suffering (see above), even if one uses this concept in an entirely different context and meaning, is to depend too much on Schopenhauer: on *his* philosophy and on *his* language. So, when Nietzsche says that his first book is full of youthful melancholy, he means to say that his book was too pessimistic, grievous and immature *both* in its form and in its content. Or, to put it in other words, to learn to laugh means, for Nietzsche, also to learn to write:

> I repeat: I find it an impossible book today. I declare that it is badly written, clumsy, embarrassing, with a rage for imagery and confused in its imagery, emotional, here and there sugary to the point of effeminacy, uneven in pace, lacking the will of logical cleanliness, very convinced and therefore *too arrogant to prove its assertions* (KSA 1.14, BT/AS 3).

Certainly, Nietzsche's sarcastic witty and hyperbolic self-criticism makes it difficult to grasp with clarity his sharp precisions. And yet, this may be the true characteristic of his "new" style; namely the new style that he has developed throughout his texts and openly uses for his preface. It is a style full of contradictions and paradoxes that constantly shows how language can say more than it says, and how by being or seeming less "convinced", less *scientific*, the text can actually "prove" its assertions. It is a style that constantly tries to incorporate moments of self-awareness and self-criticism, and it does so by breaking what seems to have become the natural or logical discourse in philosophical texts. It is a style that forces the reader to read more intuitively, showing him that, in the end, all interpretation is always already an act of creation. It is a style that is aware of its own paradoxes and is constantly questioning itself. Indeed this form of self-criticism (which cannot be made explicit, for it is somehow beyond the text, in the sense that it is within the text and at the same time refers to the text as if it were a new – a second – text) still needs to be somehow transmitted to the reader.

I believe that this hidden or implicit form of communication with the reader (where the text reflects upon itself and its own impossibility or futility) is given through laughter. Or, to be more precise, Nietzsche's *obvious* use of paradoxical settings and contradictory sentences forces the reader to engage in a very special relation with the text, in which humor and laughter are essential. In this sense, laughter may be the original gesture of a form of true comprehension: the comprehension namely of the necessity or unavoidability of contradiction. As a result, the contradictions in Nietzsche's writings, far from rendering our comprehension of Nietzsche more difficult, far from being a mere result of the representation of a contradictory world, are essential in our understanding of his texts; which also implies an understanding of the difficulty – almost impossibility – of writing, i.e. of fixating meanings without falling into paradoxes. Moreover, if we didn't perceive these contradictions *qua contradictions*, we would lose a lot of the meaning lying *behind* or *underneath* the text. As F. Schlegel argued in his "On Unintelligibility",[28] I argue that "incomprehensibility" – in this case *contradiction* – does not manifest a lack on the part of the author, nor a deficiency on the part of the reader, but is due to "the movement of discursive communication proper to the text".[29]

In Nietzsche's preface to the *Birth of Tragedy* there are many passages where Nietzsche's rhetorical use of contradictions and paradoxes can be seen as a hint or even a conspiratorial wink to the reader, who will at least smile to himself as a sign of having solved some kind of riddle, that is of course, if he should notice it:

> Whatever underlies this questionable book, it must have been a most stimulating and supremely important question and, furthermore, a profoundly personal one— as it is attested by the times in which

---

28   Cf. Leventhal (1994, 305).
29   Leventhal (1994, 305).

it was written, and *in spite of* which it was written, the turbulent
period of the Franco-Prussian War of 1870–71. While the thunder
of the Battle of Wörth rolled across Europe, the brooder and
lover of riddles who fathered this book was sitting somewhere in
a corner of the Alps, utterly preoccupied with his ponderings and
riddles and consequently very troubled and untroubled at once,
writing down his thoughts about the Greeks. (KSA 1.10, BT 1)

Here, Nietzsche describes the way in which the creation or process
of writing is similar to a battle, a struggle. In the end, the author
has to make peace with himself, in order to "reach […] a settled
and definitive view". However, the whole setting and the whole
comparison is rather comical and, in a sense, full of contradictions.
Nietzsche says he was "troubled and untroubled at once". There are
different ways in which one could understand this, but if we think
about our immediate reaction to this sentence, there is a good chance
of it being a smile; a smile that reflects a form of comprehension which
is beyond contradiction. The realization of this utterly contradictory
sentence, and the fact that it actually *makes sense*, provides us with a
totally new understanding of the whole. And the truth is that, what
Nietzsche might be saying in this particular beginning, is that there are
no "great events"[30], because whatever may take place within history,
one is always worried and preoccupied with him/herself. Even in the
most important moments of history: we are fighting *our* own battle.
It is thus not at all surprising when Nietzsche suggests that Dionysus,
the Antichrist, Nietzsche and Zarathustra are in fact the same.[31] Or,
when he stresses that when he was talking about Greek tragedy, he
was really talking about the problem of morality, Christianity and
science, that is: *his* own issues.[32]

Once again, the question is not so much whether or not we can
understand contradictions, but to see the extent to which the identification of contradictions may contribute to a deeper comprehension
of the text; a comprehension, which goes beyond the mere logical

---

30 Cf. Z II On Great Events.
31 Cf. KSA 1.18–21, BT/AS 5–7.
32 Cf. KSA 1.18, BT/AS 5: "Perhaps the best indication of the depths of the
    anti-moral tendency in the book is its consistentely cautious and hostil silence
    about Christianity."

congruence of discursive articulation. It is not about resolving contradiction, it is not even about accepting contradiction as something constitutive to life;[33] it rather amounts to an attempt of showing *the necessity of contradiction* (Nietzsche talks about a struggle) *in the process of understanding and writing* philosophical texts. The acknowledgment of the fact that Nietzsche constantly seems to negate what he has just affirmed a line, a page or a book earlier; this sort of *deconstructive* force underlying his writings is the only means we have to fully understand his texts, i.e. to understand the different levels of meaning as well as the instances of self-reference, which somehow manifests itself as a form of "dramatic irony" between the text and the reader: a hint to the fact that there is always so much more we can say without saying it, without making it explicit.

Nietzsche's contradictory and controversial texts, with their sheer impossibility show us the limits of language, and hence, the everlasting and unattainable process of saying the unsayable: "we despise all that can be explained"(NL 13[1] KSA 10.420, my translation), he writes. Nietzsche uses contradictions and paradoxes to force us to see the multiple meanings which lie beyond or behind the text, meanings which would lose their entire magic if they were made explicit – in the same way that when you make a joke explicit it somehow stops being as funny. Furthermore, this is also Nietzsche's particular way of recalling and making us aware of the fact that the origin of language is not linguistic: language is a slow process of translation and creation. In other words: what allows us to comprehend a text, to grasp a thought or a theory, the whole process of comprehension is not merely linguistic, but always relies and is driven by other more hidden elements, such as desires, needs, wants and instincts.

Bibliography

Deleuze, Gilles (2003), *Desert Islands and Other Texts, 1953–1974*, transl. by Michael Taormina, Cambridge (MIT Press).
Hegel, G.W.F. (1969 [1816]), *Science of Logic*, transl. A.V. Miller, New York (New York Humanities Press).

---

33 Cf. Hegel (1969 [1816]), 439: "[...] contradiction is the root of all movement and vitality. It is only in so far as something has a contradiction within it that it moves, has an urge and activity".

Leventhal, Robert S. (1994), *The Disciplines of Interpretation: Lessing, Herder, Schlegel and Hermeneutics in Germany, 1750–1800*, Berlin/ New York (Walter de Gruyter).

Ley, Graham (2006), *The Theatricality of Greek Tragedy: Playing Space and Chorus*, Chicago/London (University of Chicago Press).

Sartre, Jean Paul (1964), *Nausea*, transl. by Lloyd Alexander, New York (New Directions Pub. Corp.).

Stammering in a Strange Tongue: The Limits of Language in *The Birth of Tragedy* in the Light of Nietzsche's "Attempt at a Self-Criticism".

Maria Filomena Molder

> *You need to forget about a couple of things*
> *if you are going to be fair to* The Birth of Tragedy
> (EH BT 1)

> *A tremendous hope is speaking out of this essay.*
> *Ultimately, I have no reason to take back my hope*
> *that music will have a Dionysian future (...).*
> *I promise a* tragic *age: tragedy, the highest art*
> *of saying yes to life, will be reborn when humanity*
> *has moved consciousness of the harshest though most*
> *necessary wars* without suffering from it...
> (EH BT 4)

1. An Eye a Hundred Times More Demanding

Having read with great dedication *The Birth of Tragedy*, *Thus Spoke Zarathustra* and *The Gay Science* as a young woman, it meant for me a very strong experience which gave rise to the intuition – which can never be absolutely proven – that Nietzsche is not a thinker for the young but rather a thinker that never stopped being a young man himself, which is visible in the severe consequences of his oeuvre's reception but mostly in the rigours to which he submitted himself as an author. That is, in the constitution of his work, there are profits that he did not reap in life, due to the suffering (beyond the acknowledgement that pain is something inextricable from life) that stemmed from being misunderstood and was brought about, on the one hand, by the actual reception of his writings and, on the other hand, by that eternal youth (youth throws away what it receives, it loses faith on the loved ones, and opens a secret in order to protect itself from those who love it) that was Nietzsche's own inadaptation. As he himself writes in the "Attempt at a Self-Criticism": "before a much older [he writes fifteen years after BT], a hundred times more demanding, but by no means colder eye". Such an inadaptation is the watermark of his thought, whose touchstones are to be found in the constantly self-evaluating attempts (including prefaces and prologues) that would culminate in *Ecce Homo*.

2. You Need to Forget about a Couple of Things

The dazzling encounter with the initiation to Nietzsche that reading *The Birth of Tragedy* represents does not prevent a sense of puzzlement before the scarcity of quotations from Greek sources. Right at its beginning, in order to expose the physiological manifestation of the Apollinian impulse, Wagner is mentioned. When Aeschylus' *Prometheus* is discussed, the major source is Goethe's fragment. *Faust* is quoted several times. Greek authors, mainly Heraclitus, Socrates and Euripides, are superseded, in number and intensity, by Goethe but also by Kant and Schiller. However, there is no comparison to Schopenhauer's presence, especially in the long quote in Section 16 (*The World as Will and Representation* §52), which is part of the heart of an eternally youthful expectation, as much unsustainable as invincible, that would never leave Nietzsche: the expectation to live tragedy once again, to experience the rebirth of Dionysian music (which at that time he believes to be hearing in Wagner's *Tristan und Isolde*[1]), by inverting the order of time[2]. This expectation is expressed in Section 20 as an injunction, something akin to a scream: "Let no one try to blight our faith in a yet-impending rebirth of Hellenic antiquity" (BT 20).

---

1   "To these genuine musicians I direct the question whether they can imagine a human being who would be able to perceive the third act of *Tristan and Isolde*, without any aid of word and image, purely as a tremendous symphonic movement, without expiring in a spasmodic unharnessing of all the wings of the soul?" (BT 21).

2   "[...] except that we, as it were, pass trough the chief epochs of the Hellenic genius, analogically in *reverse* order, and seem now, for instance, to be passing backward from the Alexandrian age to the period of tragedy" (BT 19). Perhaps that is the reason why Goethe, Schiller e Winckelmann "could not succeed in breaking open the enchanted gate which leads into the Hellenic magic mountain" (BT 20). We should also be reminded of the end of GS 382, which mentions the "great health" and announces that "the *tragedy* begins…".

In *Ecce homo*, at the end of the chapter on *The Birth of Tragedy* (in the passage we have used as epigraph), that expectation's last version is presented and deepened, becoming more precise. He affirms that he has no reasons to renounce his hope on a Dionysian rebirth: "I promise a *tragic* age: tragedy, the highest art of saying yes to life, will be reborn when humanity has moved beyond consciousness of the harshest though most necessary wars without suffering from it..." (EH BT 4). It is rather extraordinary that, in this last work of his last year of lucid creativity, Nietzsche returns to that same expectation through the intensification of his understanding, his unshakable belief in the reemergence of tragedy, the purest of signs of the problem that Nietzsche had become to himself.

3. What Must We Forget?

If we follow the demands of the "Attempt at a Self-Criticism" (he shoots his arrow from his bow unflinchingly) and the ever so suggestive formula from *Ecce homo*, we must forget Kant and Schopenhauer, Hegel (to our surprise, Nietzsche admits his influence) and, above all, Wagner. Are we wrong in doing it?

Perhaps we shouldn't forget about any of them, for in the way they become observable within *The Birth of Tragedy* the most precious thing also becomes visible, among the many precious things about Nietzsche, which is his ability to face the day, evaluating it while also evaluating his forces in relation to it. And his day is Kant's and Schopenhauer's, the two great "dragon-slayers"[3], that is, the heroes of pessimism, those who have not been overwhelmed by the theoretical optimism which completely mortifies the energy of modern man. Nevertheless Schopenhauer is special, he is the "peerless" one, the Dürer knight, demanding, fearful, brave, free of illusions. With Schopenhauer, Nietzsche confirmed, in all of the pages of *The World as Will and Representation*, a precocious anticipation that pervades *The Birth of Tragedy* in all directions: life is pain.

---

3   Cf. BT 18, where Nietzsche presents the idea of a "new art" as "the art of metaphysical consolation", also mentioned at the end of the "Attempt" when he asks his friends to learn "the art of *this-worldly* comfort", which implies learning to laugh (as his own Zarathustra) and to "dispatch all metaphysical consolation to the devil – metaphysics in front" (BT/AS 7, translation modified).

Wagner, however, is more than his own day, for he has changed his pain into an experience of exaltation, making audible the dissonance of the world's heart through the splendor of *Tristan und Isolde*'s third act. In this case, as it had happened with Schopenhauer, there is no reverence whatsoever. It is rather an almost mystical enthusiasm. In succumbing to the power of Wagnerian music, the young Nietzsche is able to redeem a view of the world that would otherwise destroy him – Wagner, the modern artist *par excellence* (whose influence has corrupted "the grandiose Greek problem", as Nietzsche writes in the "Attempt", Section 6), bestows him with the intimacy of his own heart. That is the reason why we should not forget any of those names, even when it may seem to us – sometimes uncannily – that Nietzsche is decanting new wine in old wineskins, and these wineskins will burst with the new wine. For instance, when Nietzsche appropriates the opposition between the phenomenon and the thing in itself, we feel an insurmountable disproportion between such opposition and the pair Apollo/Dionysus, and the same happens when he refers (time and again) to the strident concepts of the "One" and "Being", tarnishing the fertility of the double principle that he had found.

4. Almost Perfect Mottos

A questionable book, a strange and almost inaccessible book, an *impossible* book, a book perhaps for artists who have also an analytical and retrospective penchant, a first book, a *proven* book, an audacious book, an impossible book, a book for initiates, an arrogant and rhapsodic book. This is the complete listing of the most outstanding attributes of *The Birth of Tragedy*, loosely distributed by the author himself throughout the "Attempt" (the italics are his as well). From the impossible nature of the book stems also a series of formal and stylistic criticisms – badly written, ponderous, embarrassing, image-mad and image-confused, sentimental, effeminate, uneven in tempo[4], without the will to logical cleanliness, very convinced, disdainful of proof – to end up in an almost jesting seriousness: "a book for

---

4   The reader cannot fail to notice this. Actually, the last sections of *The Birth of Tragedy* do not have the same rhythm as the first ones. One reason may be found in the uncontinuous nature of the writing, or maybe because Wagner's presence becomes evermore strident.

initiates", shaped upon "a lot of immature evergreen personal experiences, all of them close to the limits of communication" (BT 2).

5. A Problem with Horns

One must emphasize that, if Greek quotations are quite rare in *The Birth of Tragedy*, the marks of their fingers are abundant. Nietzsche speaks of the enigma, the labyrinth, the soothsayers and the interpretations of dreams[5]. In the "Attempt" he begins precisely by introducing himself as "a riddle-friend" (BT/AS 1). And in the magnificent beginning of Section 2, he immediately enters the Hellenic waters: "What I then got hold of, something frightful and dangerous with horns but not necessarily a bull, in any case a *new* problem".

Something frightful and dangerous with horns is the definition a Greek might give of an enigma.[6] To have horns means that there are two ways out; one may be the solution, but both can lead us to our end. If we find the solution, we shall be stricken by our own arrogance (Oedipus); if we do not find it, we're lost in our own fragility (Homer). It is a problem with horns, but Nietzsche adds one further clause: "not necessarily a bull". What does this mean? The

---

5   Among other examples: "The labyrinth, as we must call it, of the origin of tragedy" (BT 7). It is very interesting that the bond between the word (*logos*) and Apollo and the oracle's *mania* are never mentioned explicitly in the book, although they constitute, along with the bow and the arrow, the most decisive constellation of both philosophy and tragedy. However, Nietzsche allows us to find it precisely in the interpretation of dreams: "Let us imagine the dreamer: in the midst of the illusion of the dream world, he calls out to himself: 'It's a dream, I will dream on'. What must we infer? That he experiences a deep inner joy in dream contemplation, he must have completely lost sigh of the waking reality and its ominous obtrusiveness. Guided by the dream-reader Apollo, we may interpret all these phenomena in roughly this way" (BT 4). The relationship between Apollo and the Muses is also omitted. Dionysus is the intoxication, and the Muses are related to a specific sort of intoxication that makes one dance, sing, celebrate; but the articulation of the voice, the word, can never be separated from that very same intoxication (moreover, in *Twilight of the Idols* an Apollinian intoxication is mentioned, whereby Nietzsche draws near to Plato's thesis of the four forms of *mania*). However, this omission is not exactly a case of blindness, nor of unconscious partiality, but rather the resonance of the effects of seeing something that engulfs and enchants, that veils and dissolves other things, namely the Dyonisiac.

6   Cf. Colli (1974, 1975 and 1977).

bull is, among the Greeks, one of Dionysus' animal manifestations (and also of Zeus'). If we remind ourselves of the Minotaur as a profound Dionysian figure, precisely due to the raw relationship to animality (Pasiphae's passion for the sacred bull), we realize that "not necessarily a bull" is a sort of warning, a challenge, something translatable as "let's not overreact, let's face the image as an image". In other words, in presenting the Greek matrix, which is itself an enigma for the reader, he points out with one hand to the dangers that await those who are expecting to glimpse the birth of tragedy and, with the other hand, makes the humorous gesture (we can see here the creation of the mask) of inviting one to jump out of such a matrix. Something frightful and dangerous with horns, the *new* problem, science "considered for the first time as problematic, as questionable", for "the problem of science cannot be recognized in the context of science" (BT/AS 2). We shall return to this.

6. Points of View. Questions of Fertility

In Section 7 of *The Birth of Tragedy*, we read:

> With this chorus the profound Hellene, uniquely susceptible to the tenderest and deepest suffering, comforts himself, having looked boldly right into the terrible destructiveness of so-called universal history as well as the cruelty of nature, and being in danger of longing for a Buddhistic negation of the will. Art saves him, and trough art – life. (BT 7, translation modified)

We should consider this passage as a touchstone for the filling of the old wineskins with new wine, a passage in which we witness, if we may describe it thus, the wineskins succumb to the effects of a new and powerful harvest: after looking into the destructive impulse of the so-called universal history and the cruelty of nature, art saves the Greeks from the Buddhistic negation of the will. This is not, however, enough. If art saves the Greeks from drowning in pessimist resignation, life still needs to save art. What does this mean? There is no ultimate solution to such a question. Perhaps not even a temporary answer. However, some traces of an answer were left by the Greeks, from Homer to the tragic writers, namely in their recounting of what has happened, what one has gone through, one's life. When we recount our life, no matter how awful it may be, that life becomes separated from us and it becomes an object of contemplation, – it then gives us pleasure to gaze upon evil, upon the pain that is ours, so that we accept life in its entirety. This is what Odysseus and his swineherd discuss. This is what Io does (in *Prometheus Bound*), when she recounts the terrible things of her life in order to give pleasure to the Oceanids and Prometheus, who, in turn, tells her of the terrible things that are yet to come, both to her and the Oceanids' delight[7]. This is not at all an aesthetization of life, but rather an example of what art does to life and, on the other hand, of how we recognize life in art. Not a single Greek poetic text – and especially the tragedies, where the pain of living has imprinted its indelible marks – shows any desire for another life: there is never a condemnation of life, and one can even sense a sort of implicit laughter, an irresistible lightness among the verses secreted by human misfortune. This becomes quite clear in the lyrical delirium of the choruses (as, for instance, in the fifth stasimon of the chorus in *Antigone*). It is not exactly consolation what comes to the fore, but a trace of levity, something freeing, which Nietzsche translated as "saying yes to life".

Nietzsche recognizes the young man that he had been, and he never became strange to the task that that book was bold enough to attempt for the first time: to gaze upon science through the perspective of art and upon art through the perspective of life. Despite it all, however, he was not able to keep that kind of innocence.

---

7   Allow us to quote a brief, yet telling portion of the text: "**Io:** Do not hide from me what is my doom to suffer. **Prometheus:** It is not that I do not grudge you what you ask of me. **Io:** Why then do you hesitate to tell me the whole truth? **Prometheus:** Not from ill will. I shrink from shattering your heart. **Io:** Come, do not take more thought for me than I would wish. **Prometheus:** Since you're determined, I must tell you. Listen then. **Chorus:** Not yet. Let us too share this pleasure. Let us ask first the story of her affliction, and hear the ruin of her life from her own lips. Then let her learn from you what she must yet endure." (*Prometheus Bound*, vv. 625–634). Here lies an element that became awkward for the moderns and that brings art closer to something that is not human, something that goes well beyond the understanding set on the human and to which we only have access through that which art does to life. Aristotle is very perspicacious and attempts a theoretical resolution in the plane of mimetic representation when he asks why is a painted corpse less repugnant than a real corpse. Cf. *Poetics* 4, 1448b9.

7. The Disciple of a Still "Unknown God"

"As a philologist and man of words, I baptized it, not without taking some liberty – for who could claim to know the correct name of the Antichrist?) – in the name of a Greek god: I called it the Dionysian" (BT/AS 5). What has been baptized? A counter-doctrine, a counter-evaluation of life, purely Anti-Christian, that will judge morality from the point of view of appearance, art, illusion, of the very need of perspective and error (BT/AS 4, 5). Although, as Nietzsche himself points out, there is no explicit criticism of Christianity in *The Birth of Tragedy*, the very fact that he passes it over in silence is already a declaration of hostility; instinctively, he has declared war to that "*hostility to life*, a furious, vengeful antipathy to life itself", which reverberates with an "eternal No" (BT/AS 5). The "artist's metaphysics" – no matter how arbitrary, pointless, fantastic it may sound – is its best touchstone, for, *in nuce*, "what matters is that it betrays a spirit who will one day fight at any risk whatever the *moral* interpretation and significance of existence" (BT/AS 5).

It will never be too much to underline not only his self-presentation – "a philologist and a man of words" –, but also the invaluable reservation, which is a sort of compass for all attempts at understanding the Dionysian: "not without taking some liberty". He who speaks is someone "who knows", an "initiate". In that measure, singing and dancing are still a desire, a vocation, an injunction in a fiery composite of words. This means neither contempt for the low value of words, nor an accusation of being enclosed in words. Philosophy is a discursive activity, and the most authentic effort on the part of the philosopher is to seek and find the best words to describe that which he or she sees and experiences. In its supreme, ultimate version, such an effort becomes a baptism. Such is the case of Nietzsche's Dionysian. And this baptism does not invalidate the fact that one is dealing here with a still unknown god. In truth, this "still" is a deep mine, the treasure of Nietzsche's own thought, the proof of its depth and credit.

A strange, a foreign voice speaks through Nietzsche's mouth, he is the apostle of an unknown god, yet to be found, an apostle who "concealed himself for the time being under the scholar's hood, under the gravity and dialectical ill humor of the German, even under the bad manners of the Wagnerian" (BT/AS 3). He, the young Nietzsche, is "a spirit with strange, still nameless needs, a memory bursting with questions, experiences, concealed things after which the name of Dionysus was added" (BT/AS 3). We should never, at any moment, forget to keep the name of Dionysus close to these "strange, still nameless needs", to a crammed memory (of questions, experiences of secret things to which the name of Dionysus is associated). Even when named, these "strange, still nameless needs" will remain strange, that is to say, the name of Dionysus acts as a goldsmith's mark that reveals the genuine character of the instinctive experience, of strange needs, but these still demand from words a monstrous effort, which includes the effort to answer the question, "What is the Dionysian?"

Everything that Nietzsche has said, stammering, all of the visions that have been forced to exit their silent intimacy through alien words, everything Kantian and Schopenhaurian, is priceless: to renounce the violence with which morality threatens life, to warn against that same violence. His instinct is this refusal to condemn life, an instinct that he baptized with the name of a Greek god (this point can never be too much emphasized and stressed) in the presupposition of forwarding a counter-doctrine and a counter-evaluation of life, one such that allows victory over the moralist optimism of modernity.

In these passages we observe one of the most fertile versions of the relationship between instinct and language, associated to Dionysian intoxication (*Rausch*). Even when named with the name of a god, those strange and nameless needs, to wit, the very amalgam of Nietzsche's life itself, must be mortified through words and through a search for words, until "the tragedy *begins*" (GS 382) and the still unknown god becomes a peer. Neither the content of an utopia, nor a fulfilled desire, but "*a tremendous hope*" (EH BT 4).

8. To Stammer in a Strange Tongue

My idea is that Nietzsche only stammered in a strange tongue (BT/AS 3) because he faced his day. That is to say, we cannot forget the way he was affected by his day: his enthusiastic submission to Wagner and the deep affinity he had with Schopenhauer. These affections, having become so glowing with the heat of his visions, could not but make him stammer. That is the very sign of *The Birth of Tragedy*'s originality, a sign that finds no peer in any other future text. We notice in this "beginner's book" a kind of innocence that relates to

the ability of seeing something that stands just before him as if it had
never been seen before, even if it had actually been seen before. And
this innocence is revealed precisely by this overspilling of his vision,
immeasurable in terms of a previously known measure. Clearly we find
here the question of the limits of language. Stammering has to do with
the strange voice, the foreign voice that acts as the Dionysian in him,
which means that Nietzsche is not controlling that which he sees and
hears, he has no power over the object (if we can call the Dionysian an
object), and this powerlessness does not silence him completely only
because he found a language conferred to him by Schopenhauer, and
at least in part also by Kant[8], whom he knew and admired, a language
in which he spilt the mixture of perplexed memories, experiences and
occult things to which his spirit converged, "a spirit with strange,
still nameless needs". In effect, an abyss separates stammering from
shutting up. Stammering is a sign that even when one is unable to
use words in order to dominate what one hears, it is still through
words that a path is broken open[9]. Those who hear us stammer are
disturbed by this because since we are not able to say the complete
sentences and instead utter them in fits and starts, in impulses,
the composition is not clear in its conceptual understanding. That
"stammering in a strange tongue" asks us not to forget a word of
The Birth of Tragedy, although we cannot in any way save Wagner's
"bad manners" and Schopenhauer's pessimistic resignation, which

---

8   And this has nothing to do with a Kantianization or an (even easier)
     Shopenhauerization of Nietzsche. More often than not there is the temptation of
     reading *The Birth of Tragedy* from, for instance, the perspective of the Kantian
     opposition between beauty and the sublime. In my view, that can be actually
     interesting but also useless, for this is the kind of research that, having found
     analogies or points in common between certain themes/theses in the authors read
     by Nietzsche and those that Nietzsche's stammering awoke for the first time and
     forever in *The Birth of Tragedy*, avoids facing the difficulties that are inherent to
     the originality of Nietzsche's intuitions, especially the one on the Dionysian.
9   Similarly to Delphi's Pythia, who stammered crazy words (the divine possession
     spilt in human language) that had to be submitted to an interpretative system, a
     translation, as it were, in order to be transformed into a communicable oracle.
     Cf. Colli (1975). One should also remember here Wittgenstein's note in which he
     presents his way of philosophizing as a philosophizing "with toothless gums &
     as though I took speaking without teeth for the right way, the more worthwhile
     way". Cf. Wittgenstein (1998).

are precisely what did not survive Nietzsche's visionary energy[10]. The lament of not having been brave or humble enough "to permit myself in every way an individual language of my own for such individual views and hazards" (BT/AS 6) sounds always very surprising. But how could he allow himself a language of his own, if it had not been molded yet, if he did not yet obey the disciplinary rigours of style, if his fate was not yet ciphered in his masks?

9. An Invitation to the Mask

What perils await the deeper man, the man with unknown resources? He goes down paths that others, perhaps everyone, are fearful to tread, lonely, immaculate paths, that family members and trusted friends do not even glimpse in their dreams, and that they must keep on ignoring for their own good and for that one man's safety. The mask is the mediator of one's safety, it is the guarantor of one's demure, of the trust in life and its freedom, and at the same time it quietens the heart and the head of the others:

> Somebody hidden in this way – who instinctively needs speech in order to be silent and concealed, and is tireless in evading communication – *wants* and encourages a mask of himself to wander around, in his place, through the hearts and the heads of his friends. And even if this is not what he wants, he will eventually realize that a mask of him has been there all the same, – and that this is for the best. Every profound spirit needs a mask: what's more, a mask is constantly growing around every profound spirit, thanks to the consistently false (which is to say *shallow*) interpretation of every word, every step, every sign of life he displays. – (BGE 40).

The problem of the mask (the problem Nietzsche became to himself) is something that he is not yet aware of in *The Birth of Tragedy*. The opposition between "esoteric" and "exoteric", inseparable from the mask, is not visible either (Cf. BGE 30). In that text there is a great, unreserved generosity, a trusting enthusiasm that would never

---

10   This obeys Nietzsche's own admonition, avoiding conciliatory and legitimizing interpretations of the reification of his veneration and enthusiasm: "(…) I tried laboriously to express by means of Schopenhauerian and Kantian formulas strange and new valuations which were basically at odds with Kant's and Schopenhauer's spirit and taste!" (BT/AS 6).

return again. And so *The Birth of Tragedy* provides us with the best conditions to confirm that the errors of the interpreters – "the consistently false (which is to say *shallow*) interpretation of every word, every step, every sign of life he displays" (BGE 40) – protect the author, forging a mask, even if in the end he did not wish for it.

For that reason, for the fact that Nietzsche is more exposed here, *The Birth of Tragedy*, more than any other future work, is "a book for initiates" (music is an experience for initiates), "an audacious book", "an inaccessible book", a secret jewel-case that will not allow itself to be open just by anyone. In the "Attempt", even though the gaze is a hundred times less indulgent, he cannot by any means understand this lack of self-awareness, this failure to be on guard against the reader, precisely due to his love for the reader (or, maybe better, to the love the reader has for him), because from the moment on when Nietzsche realized that he had to deceive the reader, even his most intimate ones, he became someone "who instinctively needs speech in order to be silent and concealed, and is tireless in evading communication" (BGE 40), and, therefore, he can no longer understand the experience of being in a situation in which one unguardedly communicates a perplexity. This is a book for the initiate where music is concerned, and that is why it is a book closed within itself. It is a book of exaltation and dance, but at the same time, as Nietzsche confesses, he "should have sung and danced" instead of speaking (BT/AS 3). On the one hand, this is his very mode of speaking, that of "a philologist and a man of words". But on the other hand, it cannot be only a rhetorical instrument. He should have sung and danced, in other words, he shouldn't have stammered, he shouldn't have risked so much, he shouldn't have made it easy, for he had promised a common intoxication at least for some, in the best of cases. Like the filling of the old wineskins with the new visions, this common intoxication finds many obstacles[11].

Despite the fact that Nietzsche was not familiar, in *The Birth of Tragedy*, with the discipline of the disguise – he is not wearing the mask (the masks) yet, he is not Dionysus yet (as he will utter in *Ecce Homo*) —, we find him out of himself, ecstatic with Wagner's

---

11 A very different risk but, nonetheless, akin to those he refers to in the passage we quoted from *Beyond Good and Evil*.

music and with his eyes set on Schopenhauer, lucidly inebriated by the discoveries he had made about the Greeks, and we hear him stammering, dedicated to "a task so uncongenial to youth!" (BT/AS 2). What task is this? To consider that there is a problem with science, to consider that science is immature[12], a deceiver, a liar, the product of despondency and decadence, – which makes *The Birth of Tragedy* a "fearless book". A book whose aim is to change the prism (*Optik*) from which one looks at science – which should be art—, and the prism from which one looks at art – which should be life[13].

10. The Remains of a Still „Unknown God"

Let us focus on the stammering – this time, however, through the description of one who sees himself as "a mystic and an almost maenad-like soul" (BT/AS 3). A soul "almost undecided whether it should communicate or conceal itself" (BT/AS 3) stammers as if talking in a foreign tongue. These are the dangers in which Nietzsche lives (and about which he speaks in *Beyond Good and Evil*).

As it is known, the Dionysian cult is a feminine cult *par excellence*. The Maenads are the delirious followers of their god. Dionysus drags the women away from the economy and organization of the home, he snatches them from their family lives. They forsake their looms, they undo their braids and let their hair fall down, they run away, they recognize neither father nor husband nor brother nor son (the best source being Euripides' *The Bacchantes*). Let us be reminded of Pentheus not being recognized by Agave. Nietzsche is an almost maenad-like soul[14], or in other words, almost a woman that has

---

12 That a young man recognizes science's immaturity as a grave problem is a beautiful evidence of Nietzsche's eternal youth, which relates to his demand of not deceiving himself.

13 I find here traces of the following dictum of Goethe's: "Kehren wir nun zur Vergleichung der Kunst und Wissenschaft zurück; so begegnen wir folgender Betrachtung: da im Wissen sowohl als in der Reflexion kein Ganzes zusammengebracht werden kann, weil jenem das Innre, dieser das Äußere fehlt, so müssen wir uns die Wissenschaft notwendig als Kunst denken, wenn wir von ihr irgendeine Art von Ganzheit erwarten." Cf. Goethe (1982), *Materialen zur Geschichte der Farbenlehre*, vol. 14, 41.

14 This "almost" seems to have the same rhetorical and conceptual value as "not necessarily a bull", which is to say that it avoids the reification of the image and provides us with the conditions to establish a genealogical bond with Dionysus,

abandoned all the (anthropological, social and psychological) traces of her own individuation.

Dionysus' identity cannot be fixated either. He is the dismembered child, the hunter, Zagreus ("the third Dionysus"), but he is also the benevolent, soft lord, the terrifying, cruel force: "[Dionysus], as a boy, he was thorn by the Titans and now is worshiped in this state as Zagreus [...] In this existence as a dismembered god, Dionysus possesses the dual nature of a cruel, barbarized demon and a mild, gentle ruler" (BT 10). He is the only god that has a relationship with childhood, who has a childhood epiphany, in an alchemical amalgam of dismemberment and resurrection, which Nietzsche uses in order to discuss the redemption brought about by tragedy. A maenad-like soul, a tormented, arbitrary, indecisive soul, he says. But why is this? Precisely because he is not cautious and for that reason he does not know if he is communicating or hiding himself (which is something that he will know later on, even if we will not).

It is a pity that he hasn't been bold enough to speak as a poet (perhaps he could have, Nietzsche sighs and suggests, but what would the poet say: Zarathustra?) – or as a philologist (although he does sees himself as a philologist, perhaps he should have made much more use of this gift): everything is yet to be found, yet to be unburied: especially "the problem that there *is* a problem here" (BT/AS 3), that the Ancients are not an antiquarian's object and that the Greeks will remain inaccessible as long as we do not answer the question: "What is the Dionysian?"

11. Pain, Pessimism, Abundance

In the first section of the "Attempt", Nietzsche traces the contours of *The Birth of Tragedy*: to write a huge question mark (a recurrent image

---

as an "initiate and disciple". Moreover, one should be reminded that the male followers of Dionysus behave and adorn themselves as Maenads, as Tiresias and Cadmus (Pentheus' grandfather) do. Pentheus himself is dressed up and made up as a woman (so that he can observe without peril the women of his house, who fled in Dionysian delirium) with Dionysus' own help. Here we recognize the concurrence of theatrical metaphor and tragic irony (the character acts in good will towards his own destruction, that is, his transformation into an actor, aided by Dionysus).

throughout the essay) before the "'cheerfulness' of the Greeks and of Greek art" (BT/AS 1), developing the opposition (or false opposition) between pessimism (is it really a sign of collapse?) and abundance. Where pessimism is concerned, sometimes it engenders an excessive love for life, other times the opposite. Whatever the case may be, the bond between pessimism and the attraction towards the fullness of life is for Nietzsche as disturbing as it is co-natural, which is why he speaks of a "pessimism of strength", a boldness that originates in a demand to clash swords with the most difficult, terrifying and also the most worthy of enemies (and these are "the paths whose existence must be concealed from his closest and most trusted friends", BGE 40).

Was not the yearning for beauty developed from want, need, melancholia, and deprivation? Where did tragedy come from? It came from an immense fullness. Still, it seems to be precisely the opposite, it seems that tragedy emerged at the exact moment when the fracture between god and humans become more and more problematic and epic health became anemic. But this problematic fracture that deepens human pain against a background of something yet to come never engenders a No to life. This is what Nietzsche means when he mentions, in *The Birth of Tragedy*, "the metaphysical consolation – with which, I am suggesting even now, every true tragedy leaves us" (BT 7, translation modified). Physiologically speaking, what Nietzsche calls a "metaphysical consolation" derives from the "Dionysian madness", the orgiastic *mania*.

12. The Greek Forms of Madness

The relationship with pain, a very persistent and resilient relationship among the Greeks, according to Nietzsche, but also within Nietzsche himself, resurfaces in section 4 of the "Attempt". And associated to that relationship, madness appears. Could we consider madness the opposite of a symptom of degeneration or decadence? The theme of madness is crucial in Greek culture, and one finds one of its most precious and compulsory sources in Plato's *Phaedrus*, in which the whole cast of the *maniai* is established: the oracular or mantic *mania* (Apollinian) and the orgiastic one (Dionysian). And two additional ones, which stem from the former two: poetic *mania*, which has Apollo as its aegis[15] and erotic *mania*, whose origin is Dionysus.

That the fourth kind of *mania*, the erotic, originates in the orgiastic, is disturbing, for that means that Plato, even though he never phrases it as such (the presentation of Eros helps us, however, to notice this), realizes that philosophy has a Dionysian matrix, detectable at the point when speech ceases. For instance, at the end of the erotic path, as described by Diotima through Socrates, the lover, after over passing through the bodies, the souls, all sensible figures and epistemic devices, including the logos, falls into the great sea of beauty. This "falling into" means that *theôria*, contemplation, has a limit, after which one reaches an energy that we can call beauty, or life, or perhaps something that is still looking for a name, but that is surely related with the orgiastic delirium, which implies to sever, to abandon all bonds.

"Should it have been madness, to use one of Plato's phrases, that brought the greatest blessings upon Greece?" (BT/AS 4). In effect, the Greeks do not see the *maniai* negatively. Socrates is so monstrous and so mysterious because he does not seem to be Greek; he is (as Nietzsche presents him in BT 12) a "newly born daemon". Also because, with two exceptions, madness does not touch Socrates: first, Phaedrus' love speech, in which, completely drunk, he is delirious, and second, in Diotima's speech (in *The Symposium*), in which Socrates is very close to those who are possessed by someone else, which turns him, as it were, into a medium: the words he speaks do not belong to him. In both of these cases, the Socratic armour, all of his defense system, has been destroyed, cracked open, shattered, gone to pieces. In that, he is undoubtedly Greek. Not that irony is unknown amongst the Greeks, but the way Socrates has distributed his irony turns him into a "typical *non-mystic*" (BT 13). To have no access to intuition, to be averse to the intuitive, is not considered a good thing for a Greek, but it may be attractive (as proven by Alcibiades), although it may also prove

---

15   There are no muses of painting, sculpture or architecture. There are only muses of the direct expression of the voice and the body. There are muses for all poetic and musical genres: epic, lyric, dramatic; there is a muse of history (the voice that celebrates); there is a muse of the stars (the voice of admiration for the musical order of the universe). No matter how close they are to the body, painting, sculpture and architecture always imply mediations. But a muse cannot stand mediations; she is the intimacy of our voices and our bodies.

fatal. As Nietzsche understood very well, Socrates, who is responsible for the end of tragedy, is monstrous and incomprehensible. This view is expressed in the invective "O Socrates, Socrates, was that perhaps your secret? O enigmatic ironist, was that perhaps your – irony?" (BT/AS 1), where irony reveals itself to be a ruse, "a delicate self-defense against the truth" (BT/AS 1).

13. What is Dionysian?

"(…) the Greeks, as long as we lack an answer to the question "what is Dionysian? remain totally uncomprehended and unimaginable as ever." (BT/AS 3).

Although we should not entirely neglect common intoxication – a state in which boundaries are lost, a letting go and falling into an oblivion that makes one sing and dance —, it is not coincident with Dionysian intoxication, for the latter allows us to see something that otherwise could not be seen. Dionysian intoxication is, for Nietzsche, very clearly, a condition of lucidity, which is to say, only the intoxicated can be lucid. What is Dionysian? The name for an instinct still looking for a name, a name for strange needs, a name of a yet unknown god, a name of a "thousand-named" god. What is Dionysian? The crystal clear, terrifying, inebriating intoxication: the sweet, violent, supremely creative life, forgetful of all conventions and bonds, the abyssal animality. Therefore, in order to understand the origin of tragedy, Nietzsche had to follow the footsteps of animality, and he came face to face with the satyr. Through the satyr, we do not only have an access to animality, hidden and swerved within the human being, but we also perceive the intimate bond between the god and animality: "Where does that synthesis of god and billy goat in the satyr point?" (BT/AS 4). This is the crucial question.

14. Blue and Yellow

Among the Greeks, people have access to their own animality through the gods. There is, however, one god that appears as the enemy of animality: Apollo. Apollo, the monster-slayer, Apollo the killer of all that implies occultation (but we would have to speak about Apollo's own occultation, which has to do with the very conditions of the "ars venatoria"), all that is before the word, all that is darkness, the night of secret and irruptive forces. Animality is the verso to Apollo. Apollo fears animality, but he cannot live without it, without Dionysus (thus revealing the magical bond between the monster-slayer and the monsters themselves), as one can read in section 4 of *The Birth of Tragedy*.

Dionysus: he unfastens, drags, snatches and calls from afar, like the blue colour, which is for Goethe the first clarity of obscurity. Apollo: the one who comes and appears to us like the yellow colour, which, also according to Goethe, is the first shadow of clarity[16]. In the play between the first shadow of clarity and the first clarity of obscurity, we can comprehend the inseparability of the monster and its slayer.

Although Apollo is the source of all other gods (as correctly understood by Nietzsche), he is not the origin of Dionysus (but he did contribute to the metamorphosis of the barbarian, wild Dionysian element). The point is, Dionysus is animality in its wholesomeness, its completeness, incomprehensible and untamable, life's full energy, which makes us move and has no fixed figure, rather originates and dissolves all figures.

To be exact, Dionysus is not an Olympian god. We are forced to put (like Nietzsche asks us to) a question mark in relation to his identity. The most fertile of Dionysus' origins, tragically speaking, is Theban: born of Semele (sister of Agave, daughter of Cadmus, the founder of Thebes) – the woman who was struck down by her lust to see Zeus in all his supreme splendor, the lightning bolt, – and then of his father's thigh, who salvaged the baby from the dying mother's womb. This is the very motto of *The Bacchantes*, which enacts the conflict between Pentheus and Dionysus.

Apollo did not engender Dionysus. Dionysus was not born out of a dream, out of the dramatic scene, but he is the source of all dramatic scenes. Apollo is the construction of the scene, as it were, but Dionysus is the source itself, it is the heart of all construction, from which the keystone has been removed. Suffice it to read the fifth stasimon of *Antigone*'s chorus, in the moment when she has been already condemned and Creon is already vacillating. The chorus invoke in all verses the god of the thousand names, dyeing all the city of Thebes: from the fountains to the mountains, the rivers, the

---

16   Cf. Goethe (1982, *Die Farbenlehre*, vol. 13, §§69–70, 150–151).

high walls, and its inhabitants. The chorus is delirious, and it is with this intoxication, which is precisely poetic intoxication, that Dionysus becomes inseparable from the pain in which all of them are immersed, a pain that shall not meet any other redemption than this orgiastic delirium.

15. Antigone-Cassandra

Let us focus on the final steps of section 4 of *The Birth of Tragedy*:

> And here the sublime and celebrated art of *Attic tragedy* and the dramatic dithyramb presents itself as the common goal of both these tendencies whose mysterious union, after many and long precursory struggles, found glorius consummation in this child – at once Antigone and Cassandra. (BT 4).

Why them and not Oedipus or Prometheus, to whom Nietzsche dedicates so much attention while developing decisive theses on the relationship between Dionysus, philosophy, sacrilege and the excess particular to the Titans (BT 9)? We must decipher this surprising choice. Both are women. Antigone, who lends her name to one of Sophocles' tragedies, is condemned for obeying the voice of the blood, she is the one who walks towards death terrified by her fate and not wishing to confront it by imagining herself as a goddess (as the chorus grotesquely tempted her to do). She walks towards Hades (according to Heraclitus, yet another of Dionysus' names), neither as a living person, nor as a dead one. Cassandra, on the other hand, is a secondary character, the only secondary character of all tragedies that became a protagonist to Nietzsche. In truth, Cassandra is the secret of Aeschylus' *Agamemnon*, the most enigmatic figure of the tragic myths.

Who is Cassandra? She is a princess of Troy, priestess of Apollo, whose mission is prophetic: she cannot but speak, for she has seen. And what has happened? Apollo placed a curse on Cassandra, for at first she seemed to yield to his lusty intentions, but then she fled from him. As a result, Apollo let her keep her gifts as a soothsayer, but condemned her to discredit: she says all that she sees and she sees all that she says, but no one will believe her. In *Agamemnon*, she speaks of Agamemnon's and her own death, but no one believes her. Aeschylus shows a chorus stricken by her words but unable to understand them, unable to share her vision – everything that she says sounds like an incomprehensible stammering, and therefore the chorus cannot act as her interpreter, and wastes all possibilities of decipherment one after the other.

Although Cassandra affirms that she does not wish to sing her mourning song, this is exactly what she does. Here the Dionysian element appears in its most brutal form, for the mask no longer protects the character: Cassandra beseeches not to be forgotten, but as soon as she enters the palace, the chorus forgets her. Her name will never be mentioned again. This moment, when Cassandra moves out of the scene and is immediately forgotten by the chorus, is a terrible moment (with no comparison to other moments of any other tragedy). But that is only natural, for that which is not seen is forgotten, unless the word preserves it; no one will remember her, she is the nameless one now, she is very close to a unique experience of dissipation, which is supremely tragic (the complete fall of individuation): the innermost interweavement between Apollo and Dionysus could not be clearer.

We cannot but find connections and affinities with the Nietzsche who wrote *The Birth of Tragedy*, an apostle of an unknown god, a prophet who could not but speak because he had seen, unguarded, unprepared, and he could not but communicate his vision through words already in use.

16. A Proven Book

Inclement towards the writer of the *The Birth of Tragedy* – "in spite of the problem which seems congenial to old age, the book is marked by every defect of youth" (BT/AS 2)–, the "Attempt at a Self-Criticism" reveals itself as a document of the Nietzschean form of life. This time, with a gaze "a hundred times more demanding", he recognizes his book as a "proven book" (BT/AS 2) – for Nietzsche does not know what false modesty is, and in that attitude, he couldn't be more Greek –, a book in which we can observe a young man in his effort to decipher and communicate "how Dionysus spoke to me" (BT/AS 6).

Bibliography

Aeschylus (1961), *Prometheus Bound and Other Plays*, transl. Vellacott, P., Penguin (London).

Aristotle (1995), *Poetics*, transl. Halliwell, S., Harvard (Harvard University Press).

Colli, Giorgio (1974), *Dopo Nietzsche*, Milano (Adelphi).

Colli, Giorgio (1975), *La Nascita della Filosofia*, Milano (Adelphi).

Colli, Giorgio (1977), *La Sapienza Greca*, vol. I, Milano (Adelphi).

Goethe, J. W. (1982), *Werke. Hamburger Ausgabe in 14 Bänden*, vol. 13 and 14, Trunz, E. (ed.), München (DTV/ C. H. Beck).

Wittgenstein, Ludwig (1998), *Vermischte Bemerkungen/Culture and Value. A Selection from the Posthumous Remains*, ed. von Wright, G.H, revised by Pichler, A., transl. Winch, P. Oxford (Blackwell).

Contributors

Andrea Christian Bertino, Ernst-Moritz-Arndt-Universität in Greifswald (Germany)

Maria João Mayer Branco, Universidade Nova de Lisboa/FCSH/IFL (Portugal)

João Constâncio, Universidade Nova de Lisboa/FCSH/IFL (Portugal)

Marta Faustino, Universidade Nova de Lisboa/FCSH/IFL (Portugal)/ Ernst-Moritz-Arndt-Universität in Greifswald (Germany)

André Garcia, Universidade Estadual de Campinas (Brazil)

Katia Hay, Universidade de Lisboa (Portugal)

Scarlett Marton, Universidade de São Paulo (Brazil)

Maria Filomena Molder, Universidade Nova de Lisboa/FCSH/IFL (Portugal)

Chiara Piazzesi, Ernst-Moritz-Arndt-Universität in Greifswald (Germany)

Werner Stegmaier, Ernst-Moritz-Arndt-Universität in Greifswald (Germany)

Patrick Wotling, Université de Reims/ Cirlep EA 4299 (France)

Complete Bibliography

Abel, Günter (2001), „Bewusstsein – Sprache – Natur. Nietzsches Philosophie des Geistes", in: *Nietzsche-Studien* 30 (2001), 1–43.

Abel, Günter (1984), *Nietzsche. Die Dynamik der Willen zur Macht und die ewige Wiederkehr*, Berlin/New York (Walter de Gruyter).

Abel, Günter (1998), *Nietzsche. Die Dynamik der Willen Zur Macht und die ewige Wiederkehr*, Berlin/New York (Walter de Gruyter).

Abel, Günter (1985), „Nominalismus und Interpretation. Die Überwindung der Metaphysik im Denken Nietzsches", in: Simon, J. (ed.) (1985) *Nietzsche und die philosophische Tradition*, Vol. 2., Würzburg (Königshausen & Neumann), 35–90.

Abel, Günter (2004), *Zeichen der Wirklichkeit*, Frankfurt am Main (Suhrkamp).

Aeschylus (1961), *Prometheus Bound and Other Plays*, transl. Vellacott, P., Penguin (London).

Ahern, Daniel R. (1995), *Nietzsche as Cultural Physician*, Pennsylvania (The Pennsylvania State University Press).

Albus, Vanessa (2001), *Weltbild und Metapher. Untersuchungen zur Philosophie im 18. Jahrhundert*, Würzburg (Königshausen & Neumann).

Alisson, Henry (1983), *Kant's Transcendental Idealism*, New Haven and London (Yale University Press).

Andresen, Joshua (2010), "Truth and Illusion Beyond Falsification: Re-reading 'Truth and Lie'", in: *Nietzsche-Studien* 39 (2010), 255–281.

Aristotle (1995), *Poetics*, transl. Halliwell, S., Harvard (Harvard University Press).

Babich, Babette (2006), *Words in blood, like flowers. Philosophy and Poetry, Music and Eros in Hölderlin, Nietzsche and Heidegger*, Albany (State University of New York Press).

Barbera, Sandro (1994), "Ein Sinn und unzählige Hieroglyphen. Einige Motive von Nietzsches Auseinandersetzung mit Schopenhauer in der Basler Zeit", in: Borsche, T./Gerratana, F./Venturelli, A. (ed.), *"Centauren-Geburten". Wissenschaft, Kunst und Philosophie beim jungen Nietzsche*, Berlin/New York (Walter de Gruyter), 217–233.

Barthes, Roland (1995), *œuvres complètes*, édition établie et présentée par É. Marty, tome troisième, Paris (Seuil).

Behler, Ernst (1994), "Die Sprachtheorie des frühen Nietzsche", in: Borsche, T./Gerratana, F./Venturelli, A. (ed.), *"Centauren-Geburten". Wissenschaft, Kunst und Philosophie beim jungen Nietzsche*, Berlin/New York (Walter de Gruyter), 99–111.

Behler, Ernst (1996), "Nietzsches Sprachtheorie und der Aussagecharakter seiner Schriften", in: *Nietzsche-Studien* 25 (1996), 64–86.

Bertino, Andrea (2011), *"Vernatürlichung". Ursprünge von Friedrich Nietzsches Entidealisierung des Menschen, seiner Sprache und seiner Geschichte bei Johann Gottfried Herder*, Berlin/New York (Walter de Gruyter).

Bilheran, Ariane (2005), *La Maladie, Critère des Valeurs chez Nietzsche. Prémices d'une Psychanalyse des Affects*, Paris (L'Harmattan).

Bircher, Johannes/Wehkamp, Karl-Heinz (2006), *Das ungenutzte Potential der Medizin – Analyse von Gesundheit und Krankheit zu Beginn des 21. Jahrhunderts*, Zürich (rüffer & rub).

Blondel, Éric (2006), *Nietzsche, le corps et la culture. La philosophie comme généalogie philologique*, Paris (L'Harmattan).

Blumenberg, Hans (1998), *Paradigmen zu einer Metaphorologie*, Frankfurt am Main (Suhrkamp).

Blumenberg, Hans (1979), *Schiffbruch mit Zuschauer*, Frankfurt am Main (Suhrkamp).

Blumenberg, Hans (2007), *Theorie der Unbegrifflichkeit*, Frankfurt am Main (Suhrkamp).

Böning, Thomas (1987), *Metaphysik, Kunst und Sprache beim frühen Nietzsche*, Berlin/New York (Walter de Gruyter).

Borsche, T./Gerratana, F./Venturelli, A. (ed.) (1994), *„Centauren-Geburten". Wissenschaft, Kunst und Philosophie beim jungen Nietzsche*, Berlin/New York (Walter de Gruyter).

Borsche, Tilman (1994), "Natur-Sprache. Herder – Humboldt – Nietzsche", in: Borsche, T./Gerratana, F./Venturelli, A. (ed.), *„Centauren-Geburten". Wissenschaft, Kunst und Philosophie beim jungen Nietzsche*, Berlin/New York (Walter de Gruyter), 112–130.

Bourdieu, Pierre (1998), *La domination masculine*, Paris (Seuil).

Brodersen, Arvid/Jablonsky, Walter (1935), *Herder und Nietzsche oder die philosophische Einheit des Goethejahrhunderts*, Trondheim (Det Kongelige Norske Videwnskabers Sleskabs Skrifter 10).

Brusotti, Marco (1993), „Beiträge zur Quellenforschung", in: *Nietzsche-Studien* 22 (1993), 389–394.

Brusotti, Marco (2001), „Beiträge zur Quellenforschung", in: *Nietzsche-Studien* 30 (2001), 422–434.

Brusotti, Marco (1997), *Die Leidenschaft der Erkenntnis*, Berlin/New York (Walter de Gruyter).

Buddensieg, Tilmann (2006), *L'Italia di Nietzsche*, traduzione di Laura Novati, Milano (Libri Scheiwiller).

Butler, Judith (1997), *The Psychic Life of Power. Theories in Subjection*, Stanford (Stanford University Press).

Campioni, Giuliano (2009a), "'Gaya scienza' e 'gai saber' nella filosofia di Nietzsche", in: Carmassi, C./Cermelli, G./Foschi Alberet, M./ Hepp, M. (ed.), *Wo Bleibt das 'Konzept'? – Dov'è il 'concetto'? Studi in onore di Enrico De Angelis*, München (Iudicium Verlag), 11–26.

Campioni, Giuliano (2009b), "Nachweis aus Claude Adrien Helvetius, Discurs über den Geist des Menschen (1760)", in: *Nietzsche-Studien* 38 (2009), 310–311.

Chaves, Ernani (2005), "L'amour, la passion: Nietzsche e Stendhal", in: Azeredo, V. D. (org.) (2005), *Falando de Nietzsche*, Ijuí (Editora da Universidade de Ijuí), 41–54.

Cherlonneix, Laurent (2002), *Nietzsche: Santé et Maladie: l'Art*, Paris (L'Harmattan).

Cherlonneix, Laurent (2002), *Philosophie Medicale de Nietzsche: la Connaissance, la Natur*, Paris (L'Harmattan).

Clark, Maudemarie (1990), *Nietzsche On Truth and Philosophy*, Cambridge/New York/Port Chester/Melbourne/Sydney (Cambridge University Press).

Colli, Giorgio (1974), *Dopo Nietzsche*, Milano (Adelphi).

Colli, Giorgio (1975), *La Nascita della Filosofia*, Milano (Adelphi).

Colli, Giorgio (1977), *La Sapienza Greca*, vol. I, Milano (Adelphi).

Constâncio, João (2011), *On Consciousness: Nietzsche's Departure From Schopenhauer* forthcoming in Nietzsche-Studien 40.

Cox, Christoph (1999), *Nietzsche: Naturalism and Interpretation*, Berkeley/Los Angeles (University of California Press).

Crawford, Claudia (1988), *The beginnings of Nietzsche's theory of language*, Berlin/New York (Walter de Gruyter).

Dahlhaus, Carl (1994), *Die Idee der Absoluten Musik*, Kassel (Bärenreiter Verlag).

David, Pascal (2002), "Hören und lieben lernen – Nietzsche und das Wesen der Musik", in: Seubert, H. (ed.), *Natur und Kunst in Nietzsches Denken*, Köln (Böhlau Verlag), 137–151.

Derrida, Jacques (1994), *Force de loi*, Paris (Galilée).

Descartes, René (1973/1978), *Oeuvres*, vol. II, Adam/Tannery (ed.), Paris (Vrin).

Deleuze, Gilles (2003), *Desert Islands and Other Texts, 1953–1974*, transl. by Michael Taormina, Cambridge (MIT Press).

Dufour, Éric (2005), *L'esthétique musicale de Nietzsche*, Villeneuve d'Ascq (Presses Universitaires du Septentrion).

Elias, Norbert (2001), „Die Gesellschaft der Individuen", in: *Gesammelte Schriften*, vol. 10, Frankfurt am Main (Suhrkamp).

Emden, Christian J. (2005), *Nietzsche on Language, Consciousness and the Body*, Illinois (University of Illinois Press).

Figal, Günter (2001), *Nietzsche. Eine philosophische Einführung*, Stuttgart (Reclam).

Fietz, Rudolf (1992), *Medienphilosophie. Musik, Sprache und Schrift bei Friedrich Nietzsche*, Würzburg (Königshausen & Neumann).

Fink, Eugen (1965), *La philosophie de Nietzsche*, trad. Hans Hildenbrand et Alex Lindenberg, Paris (Minuit).

Foucault, Michel (1976), *Histoire de la sexualité: La volonté de savoir*, vol. 1, Paris (Gallimard).

Foucault, Michel (1994), „Le sujet et le pouvoir", in: *Dits et écrits IV: 1980–1988*, Paris (Gallimard).

Foucault, Michel (1971), *L'ordre du discours*, Paris (Gallimard).

Freud, Sigmund (1921), *Massenpsychologie und Ich-Analyse*, Wien (Internationaler Psychoanalytischer Verlag).

Fürst, Gebhard (1988), *Sprache als metaphorischer Prozess. Johann Gottfried Herders hermeneutische Theorie der Sprache*, Mainz (Matthias-Grünewald-Verlag).

Gaier, Ulrich (1990), "Herders Abhandlung über den Ursprung der Sprache als ‚Schrift eines Witztölpels'", in: Gabriel, G./Schildknecht, C. (ed.) *Literarische Formen der Philosophie*, Stuttgart (Metzler), 155–165.

Garcia, André L. Muniz (2008), *Metáforas do corpo: reflexões sobre o estatuto da linguagem na filosofia do jovem Nietzsche*. Dissertação de Mestrado. Universidade Estadual de Campinas, Instituto de Filosofia e Ciências Humanas (Campinas), 2008. The dissertation can be downloaded from this link: http://libdigi.unicamp.br/document/?code=vtls000439120.

Gerber, Gustav (1871), *Die Sprache als Kunst*, vol. 1, Bromberg (Mittler).

Goethe, J. W. (1982), *Werke. Hamburger Ausgabe in 14 Bänden*, vol. 13 and 14, Trunz, E. (ed.), München (DTV/C. H. Beck).

Hahn, A. (1983), "Konsensfiktionen in Kleingruppen. Dargestellt am Beispiel von jungen Ehen", in: Neidhardt, F. (ed.), *Gruppensoziologie. Perspektiven und Materialien. Sonderheft 25 der Kölner Zeitschrift für Soziologie und Sozialpsychologie*, Köln (Westdeutscher Verlag), 210–232.

Hamann, Johann G. (1957), *Briefwechsel*, ed. W. Ziesemer /A. Henkel, vol. III, Wiesbaden (Insel Verlag).

Harth, Dietrich (1986), "Kritik der Geschichte im Namen des Lebens. Zur Aktualität von Herders und Nietzsches geschichtstheoretischen Schriften", in: *Archiv für Kulturgeschichte* (68), 407–456.

Haym, Rudolph (1954 [1880]), *Herder nach seinem Leben und seinen Werken*, vol. 2, Berlin (Rudolf Gaertner).

Hazz, Ignace (2006), *Nietzsche et la métaphore cognitive*, Paris (Harmattan).

Hegel, G.W.F. (1969 [1816]), *Science of Logic*, transl. A.V. Miller, New York (New York Humanities Press).

Hegel, G. F. W. (2007), *Vorlesungen über die Geschichte der Philosophie*, Frankfurt am Main (Suhrkamp).

Heidegger, Martin (1961), *Nietzsche*, vol. 1, Berlin (Günther Neske Verlag).

Heidegger, Martin (1991), *Nietzsche I and II, The Will to Power as Art. The Eternal Recurrence of the Same*, transl. David Farrell Krell, New York (Harper Collins).

Helvetius, Claude Adrien (1760), *Discurs über den Geist des Menschen*, aus dem Französischen des Herrn Helvetius übers. v. J. G. Forkert, mit einer Vorrede Joh. Christoph Gottscheds, Leipzig und Liegnitz (D. Siegerts).

Herder, Johann Gottfried (1985–2000), *"Ideen zur Philosophie der Geschichte der Menschheit"*, in: Bollacher, M. (ed.), *Johann Gottfried*

Herder. Werke. 10 in 11 Bänden, vol. 6, Frankfurt am Main (Deutscher Klassiker Verlag).

Herder, Johann Gottfried (2002), "Treatise on the Origin of Language", in: *Herder's Philosophical Writings*, transl. Michael N. Forster, Cambridge (Cambridge University Press).

Herder, Johann Gottfried (2002), *Fragments on Recent German Literature*, in: Herder (2002), *Philosophical Writings*, transl. Michael N. Forster (Cambridge: Cambridge University Press).

Hödl, Hans Gerald (1997), *Nietzsches frühe Sprachkritik. Lektüren zu Ueber Wahrheit und Lüge im aussermoralischen Sinne*, Wien (WUV).

Hödl, Hans Gerald (2003), "Metaphern ohne Referenten. Anmerkungen zur neueren Diskussion um Nietzsches Sprachphilosophie", in: *Allgemeine Zeitschrift für Philosophie* 28, 183–199.

Illouz, Eva (1997), *Consuming the romantic utopia: love and the cultural contradictions of capitalism*, Berkeley (University of California Press).

Janaway, Christopher (2007), *Beyond Selflessness, Reading Nietzsche's Genealogy*, Oxford/New York (Oxford University Press).

Kant, Immanuel (2004 [1781]), "Kritik der reinen Vernunft", in: *Werke in sechs Bänden und Wörterbuch*, Weischedel, W. (ed.), Berlin (Wissenschaftliche Buchgesellschaft).

Kaiser, Stefan (1994), "Über Wahrheit und Klarheit. Aspekte des Rhetorischen in ‚Ueber Wahrheit und Lüge im außermoralischen Sinne'", in: *Nietzsche-Studien* 23 (1994), 65–78.

Kalb, Christof (2000), *Desintegration. Studien zu Friedrich Nietzsches Leib und Sprachphilosophie*, Frankfurt am Main (Suhrkamp).

Katsafanas, Paul (2005), "Nietzsche's Theory of Mind: Consciousness and Conceptualization", in: *European Journal of Philosophy* 13, 1–31.

Kaufmann, Jean-Claude (1992), *La trame conjugale. Analyse du couple par son linge*, Paris (Nathan).

Kaufmann, Walter (1965), *Nietzsche. Philosopher, Psychologist, Antichrist*, New York (The World Publishing Company).

Kaufmann, Walter (1974), *Nietzsche. Philosopher, Psychologist, Antichrist*, Princeton (Princeton University Press).

Kaulbach, Friedrich (1981/1982), "Nietzsches Interpretation der Natur", in: *Nietzsche-Studien* 10/11 (1981/1982), 462–464.

Kodama, Hakaru (forthcoming), *Nietzsches Begriff der Vernunft*.

Kofman, Sarah (1972), *Nietzsche et la métaphore*, Payot (Paris).

Lacoue-Labarthe, Philippe (1979), *Le sujet de la philosophie. Typographies I*, Paris (Aubier-Flammarion).

Leiter, Brian (2002), *Nietzsche on Morality*, London (Routledge).

Levanthal, Robert S. (1990), "Herder's Foundation of the Human Sciences", in: Mueller-Vollmer (ed.) *Herder Today*, Berlin/New York (Walter de Gruyter), 173–189.

Leventhal, Robert S. (1994), *The Disciplines of Interpretation: Lessing, Herder, Schlegel and Hermeneutics in Germany, 1750–1800*, Berlin/New York (Walter de Gruyter).

Ley, Graham (2006), *The Theatricality of Greek Tragedy. Playing Space and Chorus*, Chicago/London (University of Chicago Press).

Löwith, Karl (1978), *Nietzsches Philosophie der ewigen Wiederkehr des Gleichen*, Hamburg (Felix Meiner Verlag).

Luhmann, Niklas (1982), *Liebe als Passion*, Frankfurt am Main (Suhrkamp).

Lupo, Luca (2006), *Le colombe dello scettico. Riflessioni sulla coscienza negli anni 1880–1888*, Pisa (Edizioni ETS).

Man, Paul de (1987), *Allegorien des Lesens*, transl. Werner Hamacher and Peter Krumme, Frankfurt am Main (Suhrkamp).

Marton, Scarlett (2010), "De la réalité au rêve. Nietzsche et les images de la femme", in: Campioni, G./Piazzesi, C./Wotling, P. (eds.) (2010), *Letture della Gaia scienza – Lectures du Gai savoir*, Pisa (ETS), 277–294.

Meijers, Antonie/Stingelin, Martin (1988), "Konkordanz zu den wörtlichen Abschriften und Übernahmen von Beispielen und Zitaten aus Gustav Gerber 'Die Sprache als Kunst' (Bromberg 1871) in Nietzsches Rhetorik-Vorlesung und in 'Ueber Wahrheit und Lüge im aussermoralischen Sinne'", in: *Nietzsche-Studien* 17 (1988), 350–368.

Montebello, Pierre (2001), *Vie et Maladie chez Nietzsche*, Paris (Ellipses).

Müller-Lauter, Wolfgang (1978), "Der Organismus als innerer Kampf. Der Einfluß von Wilhelm Roux auf Friedrich Nietzsche", in: *Nietzsche-Studien* 7, (1978), 189–223.

Müller-Lauter, Wolfgang (1999a), *Nietzsche. His Philosophy of Contradictions and the Contradictions of His Philosophy*, Urbana and Chicago (University of Illinois Press).

Müller-Lauter, Wolfgang (1999b), *Über Werden und Wille zur Macht, Nietzsche- Interpretationen I*, Berlin/New York (Walter de Gruyter).

Nehamas, Alexander (1985), *Nietzsche. Life as Literature*, Cambridge MA/ London England (Harvard University Press).

Neis, Cordula (2003), *Anthropologie im Sprachdenken des 18. Jahrhunderts. Die Berliner Preisfrage nach dem Ursprung der Sprache*, Berlin/New York (Walter de Gruyter).

Otto, Detlef (1994), "Die Version der Metapher zwischen Musik und Begriff", in: Borsche, T./Gerratana, F./Venturelli, A. (ed.), *"Centauren-Geburten". Wissenschaft, Kunst und Philosophie beim jungen Nietzsche*, Berlin/ New York (Walter de Gruyter), 169–190.

Otto, Detlef (1998), "(Kon-)Figurationen der Philosophie. Eine metaphorologische Lektüre von Nietzsches Darstellungen der vorplatonischen Philosophen", in: *Nietzsche-Studien* 27 (1998), 119–152.

Pfeuffer, Sílvio (forthcoming), "'Fröhlichkeit' im Spannungsfeld zwischen Krankheit und Gesundheit – 'diese Kunst der Transfiguration *ist* eben Philosophie'".

Piazzesi, Chiara (2010), "Die soziale Verinnerlichung von Machtverhältnissen: über die produktiven Aspekte der Selbstdisziplinierung und der Affektkontrolle bei Nietzsche und Elias", in: Günther, F./Holzer, A./ Müller, E. (eds.), *Zur Genealogie des Zivilisationsprozesses. Friedrich Nietzsche und Norbert Elias*, Berlin/New York (Walter de Gruyter).

Piazzesi, Chiara (forthcoming), "Pour une nouvelle conception du rapport entre théorie et pratique: la philologie comme éthique et méthodologie", in: *Actes du Colloque International 'L'art de bien lire'. Nietzsche et la philologie, Reims-Paris, 19–21 octobre 2006*, Paris (Vrin).

Plato (1900, repr. 1991), "Phaedo", in: *Platonis Opera Tomus*, ed. I. Burnet, Oxford (Clarendon Press).

Ponton, Olivier (2007), *Nietzsche - Philosophie de la légèreté*, Berlin/New York (Walter de Gruyter).

Poellner, Peter (2000), *Nietzsche and Metaphysics*, Oxford (Oxford University Press).

Rahden, Wolfert von (2004), "'Nie wirklich satt und froh...' Nietzsches Herder", in: Groß, S./Sauder, G. (ed.), *Der frühe und der späte Herder: Kontinuität und/oder Korrektur*, Saarbrücken (Synchron Wissenschaftsverlag der Autoren), 459–477.

Rée, Paul (2005), *Der Ursprung der moralischen Empfindung*, Bonn (DenkMal Verlag).

Renzi, Luca (1997), "Das Ohr-Motiv als Metapher des Stils und der «Zugänglichkeit». Eine Lektüre der Aphorismen 246 und 247 von Nietzsches «Jenseits von Gut und Böse»", in: *Nietzsche-Studien* 26 (1997), 331–349.

Reuter, Sören (2009), *An der "Begräbnisstätte der Anschauung". Nietzsches Bild- und Wahrnehmungstheorie in ,Ueber Wahrheit und Lüge im aussermoralischen Sinne'*, Basel (Schwabe Verlag).

Reuter, Sören (2004), "Reiz – Bild – Unbewusste Anschauung: Nietzsches Auseinandersetzung mit Hermann Helmholtz' Theorie der Unbewussten Schlüsse in ,Über Wahrheit und Lüge im Aussermoralischen Sinne'", in: *Nietzsche-Studien* 33 (2004), 351–372.

Richardson, John (1996), *Nietzsche's System*, Oxford/New York (Oxford University Press).

Ridley, Aaron (2004), *The philosophy of music. Theme and Variations*, Edinburgh (Edinburgh University Press).

Ritter, Joachim/Gründner, Karlfried (1984), *Historisches Wörterbuch der Philosophie*, vol. 6, Basel/Stuttgart (Schwabe).

Ruckenbauer, Hans-Walter (2002), *Moralität zwischen Evolution und Normen*, Würzburg (Königshausen und Neumann).

Saar, Martin (2007), *Genealogie als Kritik*, Frankfurt am Main (Campus Verlag).

Salaquarda, Jörg (1997), "'Fröhliche Wissenschaft' zwischen Freigeisterei und neue ,Lehre'", in: *Nietzsche-Studien* 26 (1997), 165–183.

Sartre, Jean Paul (1964), *Nausea*, transl. by Lloyd Alexander, New York (New Directions Pub. Corp.).

Schacht, Richard (1985), *Nietzsche*, London/Boston/Melbourne/Henley (Routledge & Kegan Paul).

Schacht, Richard (1996), "Nietzsche's kind of philosophy", in: Magnus, B./Higgins, K. M. (ed.), *The Cambridge Companion to Nietzsche*, Cambridge/New York (Cambridge University Press), 151–179.

Schnädelbach, Herbert (1999), *Philosophie in Deutschland: 1831–1933*, Frankfurt am Main (Suhrkamp).

Simon, Josef (1984), "Das Problem des Bewusstseins bei Nietzsche und der traditionelle Bewusstseinsbegriff", in: Djuric, M./ Simon, J., *Nietzsche in der Diskussion, Zur Aktualität Nietzsches*, vol. II, Würzburg (Königshausen und Neumann), 17–33.

Simon, Josef (1999), „Der Name ‚Wahrheit'. Zu Nietzsches früher Schrift ‚Über Wahrheit und Lüge im außermoralischen Sinne'", in: Riedel, M. (ed.) *"Jedes Wort ist ein Vorurteil", Philologie und Philosophie in Nietzsches Denken* Köln/Weimar/Wien (Böhlau), 77–93.

Simon, Josef (1987), "Herder und Kant. Sprache und 'historischer Sinn'" in: Sauder, G. (ed.) *Johann Gottfried Herder 1744–1803*, Hamburg (Felix Meiner), 1–13.

Simon, Josef (1989), *Philosophie des Zeichens*, Berlin/New York (Walter de Gruyter).

Sloterdijk, Peter (2009), *Du mußt dein Leben ändern*, Frankfurt am Main (Suhrkamp).

Spiekermann, Klaus (1992), *Naturwissenschaft als subjektlose Macht? Nietzsches Kritik physikalischer Grundkonzepte*, Berlin/New York (Walter de Gruyter).

Stack, George J. (1983), *Lange and Nietzsche*, Berlin/New York (Walter de Gruyter).

Stegmaier, Werner (2001), „Die Substanz muss Fluktuanz werden. Nietzsches Aufhebung der Hegelschen Dialektik", in: *Berliner Debatte Initial* 12.4 (2001), Themenheft "Unaufhörliche Dialektik", 3–12.

Stegmaier, Werner (2007), "Nach Montinari. Zur Nietzsche-Philologie", in: *Nietzsche-Studien* 36 (2007), 80–94 (English translation by Lisa Anderson: "After Montinari. On Nietzsche Philology", in: *The Journal of Nietzsche Studies* 38 (Fall 2009), 5–19; Portuguese and French translations are forthcoming).

Stegmaier, Werner (forthcoming), *Nietzsches Befreiung der Philosophie. Kontextuelle Interpretation des V. Buchs der Fröhlichen Wissenschaft.*

Stegmaier, Werner (2006), "Nietzsche's doctrines, Nietzsche's signs", in: *Journal of Nietzsche Studies* 31, 20–41.

Stegmaier, Werner (1994), *Nietzsches Genealogie der Moral*, Darmstadt (Wissenschaftliche Buchgesellschaft).

Stegmaier, Werner (1985), "Nietzsches Neubestimmung der Wahrheit", in: *Nietsche-Studien* 14 (1985), 69–95.

Stegmaier, Werner (2005), "Nietzsches Philosophie der Kunst und seine Kunst der Philosophie. Zur aktuellen Forschung und Forschungsmethodik", in: *Nietzsche-Studien* 34 (2005), 348–374.

Stegmaier, Werner (2000), "Nietzsches Zeichen", in: *Nietzsche-Studien* 29 (2000), 41–69.

Stegmaier, Werner (1992), *Philosophie der Fluktuanz. Dilthey und Nietzsche*, Göttingen (Vandenhoeck & Ruprecht).

Stegmaier, Werner (2008), *Philosophie der Orientierung*, Berlin/New York (Walter de Gruyter).

Stegmaier, Werner (2004), "'Philosophischer Idealismus' und die 'Musik des Lebens'. Zu Nietzsches Umgang mit Paradoxien. Eine kontextuelle Interpretation des Aphorismus Nr. 372 der Fröhlichen Wissenschaft", in: *Nietzsche-Studien* 33 (2004), 90–128.

Stegmaier, Werner (2008), "Schicksal Nietzsche? Zu Nietzsches Selbsteinschätzung als Schicksal der Philosophie und der Menschheit (Ecce Homo, Warum Ich Ein Schicksal Bin 1)", in: *Nietzsche-Studien* 37 (2008), 1–53.

Stegmaier, Werner (1994), "Weltabkürzungskunst. Orientierung durch Zeichen", in: Simon, J. (ed.) (1994), *Zeichen und Interpretation*, Frankfurt am Main (Suhrkamp), 119–141.

Stegmaier, Werner (2007), "Zur Frage der Verständlichkeit. Nietzsches Beitrag zum interkulturellen Kommunizieren und Philosophieren", in: *Allgemeine Zeitschrift für Philosophie* 32.2 (2007), 107–119.

Tietz, Udo (2000), "Phänomenologie des Scheins. Nietzsches sprachkritischer Perspektivismus", in: *Nietzscheforschung* 7, 215–241.

Van Tongeren, Paul (1989), *Die Moral von Nietzsches Moralkritik: Studien zu 'Jenseits von Gut und Böse'*, Bonn (Bouvier Verlag).

Van Tongeren, Paul/Schank, Gerd/Siemens, Herman (forthcoming), *Nietzsche-Wörterbuch*, vol. III, Berlin/New York (Walter de Gruyter).

Venturelli, Aldo (2003), *Kunst, Wissenschaft und Geschichte bei Nietzsche. Quellenkritishe Untersuchungen*, transl. from Italian by Leonie Schröder, editorial collaboration of Silke Richter, Berlin/New York (Walter de Gruyter).

Vinzens, Albert (1999), *Friedrich Nietzsches Instinktverwandlung*, Basel (Schwabe).

Wittgenstein, Ludwig (1998), *Vermischte Bemerkungen/Culture and Value. A Selection from the Posthumous Remains*, ed. von Wright, G.H., revised by Pichler, A., transl. Peter Winch, Oxford (Blackwell).

Wittgenstein, Ludwig (1967), *Philosophical Investigations*, ed. Anscombe, G. E. M./Rhees, R./von Wright, G. H., transl. by Anscombe, G. E. M., Oxford (Blackwell).

Wotling, Patrick (2007), "«*Comment pourrais-je écrire pour des lecteurs?*». La spécificité de l'écriture philosophique chez Nietzsche", in: Denat, C. (ed.) (2007), *Au-delà des textes. La question de l'écriture philosophique*, Reims (Presses de l'Université de Reims), 151–166.

Wotling, Patrick (2008a), "La culture comme problème. La redetermination nietzschéenne du questionement philosophique", in: *Nietzsche-Studien* 37 (2008), 1–50.

Wotling, Patrick (1999), *La pensée du sous-sol*, Paris (Allia).

Wotling, Patrick (2008b), *La philosophie de l'esprit libre. Introduction à Nietzsche*, Paris (Flammarion).

Wotling, Patrick (1995), *Nietzsche et le problème de la civilisation*, Paris (PUF).

Wotling, Patrick (2000), traduction, introduction et notes de Nietzsche, *Par-delà bien et mal*, Flammarion (Paris).

Zavatta, Benedetta (2009), "Die in der Sprache versteckte Mythologie und ihre Folgen fürs Denken. Einige Quellen von Nietzsche: Max Müller, Gustav Gerber und Ludwig Noire", in: *Nietzsche-Studien* 38 (2009), 269–298.

Žunjic, Slobodan (1987), „Begrifflichkeit und Metapher", in: *Nietzsche-Studien* 16 (1987), 149–163.

Zusi, Peter (2006), "Toward a Genealogy of Modernism, Herder, Nietzsche, History", in: *Modern Language Quarterly* 67.4, 505–525.

Name Index

Subject Index

www.ingramcontent.com/pod-product-compliance
Lightning Source LLC
Chambersburg PA
CBHW070019100426
42740CB00013B/2556